The Genetic Connection:
The Lightning Bloodline

Dr. Julio Antonio del Marmol
"The Cuban Lightning"

Based on a True Master Spy Story

© Copyright 2025 Dr. Julio Antonio del Marmol.

All rights reserved. No part of this publication may be reproduced, stored in a retrieval system, or transmitted, in any form or by any means, electronic, mechanical, photocopying, recording, or otherwise, without the written prior permission of the author.

ISBN: (sc) 978-1-68588-046-0
ISBN: (hc) 978-1-68588-038-5
ISBN: (e) 978-1-68588-046-0

Because of the dynamic nature of the Internet, any web addresses or links contained in this book may have changed since publication and may no longer be valid.

Any people depicted in stock imagery provided by Thinkstock are models, and such images are being used for illustrative purposes only.
Certain stock imagery © Thinkstock.

Cuban Lightning Publications, Int rev. 10/31/2023
www.cuban-lightning.com

Forward

Dr. Julio Antonio Del Marmol

The Character of
Dr. Julio Antonio del Marmol

My Open Declaration of the Exemplary Qualities of Dr. Julio Antonio del Marmol on the Day of My Centennial

I am Dr. Hector Zayas-Bazan y Perdomo of the University of Havana, also known as "the Professor." For me it has been a great honor and a source of pride to be the political, intellectual, and ideological guides of Julio Antonio del Marmol from a very early age. From the moment we met, this young man cultivated my sympathy and trust through his extraordinary qualities. Over the years, I grew to love him as the son I never had and wished to have. His patriotism, courage, and high sense of honor are the most important of his qualities, as are his moral and religious values. While still extremely young, he proved to us his friends his extreme loyalty and his natural talent for leadership that without doubt he inherited from his great-grandfather, Major General Donato del Marmol y Tomayo, who fought to free Cuba during the Ten Years War against Spain. A hundred years later, almost to the day, Julio Antonio del Marmol repeated history through his brave example to follow in the footsteps of his great ancestor. His path was slightly different and more complicated, taking him inside the strange machinery of espionage. He risked his life thousands of times in his noble effort to free Cuba. Over time, his task grew to become something perhaps a little more difficult and a more Gordian task: protecting the Americas and the world at large from the corruption and infiltration of the Marxist ideology.

Over the years, our relationship grew to be cordial and loving like a family, united working daily shoulder to shoulder towards the same goals and ideals of restoring freedom to Cuba. Dr. Julio Antonio del Marmol never stopped or had any hesitation or fear to put at risk his personal freedom or his life in defense of our cause and our fight to protect democracy, liberty, and religious freedom that the totalitarian regimes around the world indiscriminately attempt to rip out of our hands. That is why, in his great generosity, love of his fellow man, and extreme dedication to our cause and our fellow fighters, this man has gambled his life repeatedly while defending the equilibrium to our democracies and freedom around the world.

I want to say very clearly on this my centennial in a very loud voice, yelling if necessary so that the world can hear me, that Dr. Julio Antonio del Marmol is not only a brave warrior and patriot like his great-grandfather, but also an extremely intelligent man. Julio Antonio is a true gentleman with a high standard of discipline and respect of the principles of our society, as well as being a humble follower of the only true king of the world and in the universe, the Lord Jesus Christ. That is why I, Dr. Hector Zayas-Bazan, live without any doubt in my mind that Dr. Julio Antonio del Marmol is the authentic new man, not the one the Communists have tried to sell to us. He is the original, not the imitation. That is why we should show him to future generations as the flag for our principles of democracy and freedom. All these many qualities I mentioned before prove to us through his life's trajectory an example for all of us, and fighting for God and liberty for all of mankind, all the while demonstrating a genuine respect for our brothers and sisters in the human race. His beautiful altruism, courage, and optimism are only possessed by the titans of mankind.

I write this letter as a corroboration of my deepest, profoundest thoughts that I sincerely profess for Dr. Julio Antonio del Marmol.

Letter of Reference from Dr. Hector Zayas-Bazan y Perdomo

Professor at the University of Havana
Mentor of Dr. Julio Antonio del Marmol

This book, in my opinion, could easily be titled The Naked Truth. Dr. del Marmol told me once, way back before the terrorist attack on 9/11, something in his usual poetic fashion when he tried to convince me of his concerns that I have remembered ever since: "When a healthy tree loses its leaves outside the ordinary routine of the change in seasons, we have to look at the root of that tree to find the disease in order to cure the dying tree and at the same time prevent it from infecting all the other trees around it."

This is exactly what Dr. del Marmol presents us in his new book, The Genetic Connection—The Lightning Bloodline. It is very difficult for us, growing up in this free society, to understand that so much of the vindictive evil related in this book is not the product of fiction from a novelist. Starting with my primary order from Dr. del Marmol, I can assure you as an active participant in many of the actions related in this story that he has a vast responsibility and the ability to maintain modesty by not exaggerating a single hair in this story. Of course, it's not necessary in this particular case, as he narrates the facts exactly as they occurred. I am an eyewitness on many occasions to the truth of this account. He has also meticulously subtracted from these narrations the precise methodology used by our intelligence agencies, and so has secured their present and future efficiency.

Now I move on to my secondary order. I have known Dr. del Marmol for over five decades, and I can assure you with confidence and conviction that this man is alive only by extraordinary miracles, and there is no doubt in my mind that he still lives because our Lord has been behind him all this time. It is the only way I can explain the failure of multiple attempts our enemies have made against his life. It is with joy that I can say today that we have him still around us in 2025, with the same optimism, persistence, and hope that I have known from him all this time, from the day he stepped off one of our planes after being flown out of the Navy base in Guantanamo.

As I read these pages of this extraordinary story, I often grew frustrated by our sense of impotence, thinking what a pity it was that Dr. del Marmol had not been able to be more specific in some details. He would then convince the reader that his story is more accurately a depiction of real life than any other story written until now.

As a member of the intelligence community for most of my life, I can assure you that the way Dr. del Marmol describes in this book is exactly how the events unfolded. I, O'Brien, strongly recommend that you not only read this book and recommend it to your family and friends, but also that you read all of the books that this extraordinary man writes and releases in the future. I assure you without any holding back, that we all, without exception—carpenters, mechanics, doctors, even the presidents of this country as well as other world leaders—have a lot to learn from the experiences of this amazing man.

"O'Brien," Newport Beach, CA.

Introduction

Codenamed by His Own Enemies as "the Cuban Lightning", over the Past 60 Years He Has Become a Legend to the Cuban People and Freedom Fighters Around the World. Who Is Dr. Julio Antonio del Marmol?

1. At the age of 7, he wrote a protest song because of a confrontation with a Marxist leader, the father of his best friend.
2. Appointed the youngest military commander in the Cuban revolution at the age of 11½, becoming a close confidant of both Castro brothers and Che Guevara to such an extent that Fidel and Che competed to be able to claim to be his mentor.
3. Recognizing that the leaders were not planning to deliver what they had promised the Cuban people during the revolution, he turned against them and confronted his father, who was still loyal. His father, enraged at the change of heart in the son he was so proud of, called him a traitor, and threw him out of the house, He then became the youngest spy in history before he had turned 12, taking secrets out of Fidel Castro's office over the next ten years undetected. He passed the information he collected to Guantanamo naval base using the codename JUBATE. The information he transmitted included photos of the

nuclear missiles when they first arrived from the Soviet Union, still in their packing crates, and the evolving plans he witnessed regarding the Kennedy assassination, meeting all of the key players in the plot, such as Lee Harvey Oswald, Jack Ruby, and the small squad of the actual assassins who executed the master plan developed by Che Guevara. It was Che Guevara who privately told Dr. del Marmol that it would be a hundred years before any light shone on it, and even then, the truth would be lost to history because of all the competing conspiracy theories that would cause people to disbelieve it. He even transmitted the details revealed by the assassins about how the operation transpired at a celebratory event held in an elite mansion in Havana. To avoid being too deeply involved with the revolution, he took educational opportunities to give him an excuse to get away from them: attending music school, studying law, and eventually becoming a Doctor of Veterinary Medicine and attaining a PhD in Genetics.

4. His cover blown by American politicians in 1971, he had to escape Cuba, leaving behind his wife and young son. He took with him the small team of friends who had helped him in his espionage work and, following maps given to him by the global intelligence community, managed to navigate the mine fields surrounding Guantanamo Bay laid by the communist government to seal off both that escape route as well as a path for infiltrators sent by the West into the country. One of his friends failed to follow his instructions and died in the mine field; but the rest of them swam for over 12 hours to get inside the naval reservation.

5. He arrived in Florida and refused the money sitting in an account which had been accumulating for the previous decade and more as compensation for his work, stating that accepting it would make him, in his eyes, a mere mercenary; what he did was done out of principle. He then struck a unique deal in the annals of the history of intelligence: that he would work with US intelligence (and other allied intel agencies), but never for them.
6. He survived the first of what would eventually amass to 56 attempts on his life by assassins sent by Castro and other communist regimes around the world.
7. Upon relocation from Florida to California, his handler introduced him to then-governor of California Ronald Reagan, at the historic Culver Hotel.
8. Fascinated by the young man, Reagan embraced the youth and offered him the greatest confidence by bringing the 23-year-old man under his wing.
9. His contact arranged a cover as a dealer in newspaper vending machines in five cities throughout Orange County, California for the Herald Examiner newspaper. This dealership gave him the financial freedom to pursue his missions, during which he would cross the Mexican border and from there disappear to go wherever he needed to go in the world.
10. With the facilitation of the intelligence community, he has multiple passports, giving him freedom to travel internationally under various aliases.
11. He remains a non-citizen in the U.S., a permanent resident; the benefit of the U.S. being that nothing comes back on the country if he gets into trouble during one of his missions.

12. In 1976, he decides to publish an account of his life inside Cuba in Spanish. This book is such a success in the Spanish-speaking market that it goes through several editions, selling millions of copies worldwide. He was eventually awarded a prestigious international journalism award for this book and received shortly after publication several letters from heads of state from several nations in the Free World, praising him for his courage and relentless opposition to totalitarianism around the world. Pope Saint John Paul II even commissioned a crucifix made of Venetian glass and cherry wood as a gift in recognition of his fight for political and religious freedom. In 2010, the textbook version of this work is translated into English as Cuba: Russian Roulette of America.
13. Unable to touch him directly, his enemies assassinated his only son as well as a few other family members in retaliation for what he was exposing about them. This was a dagger thrust into his soul, a wound which will never fully heal; but he has continued his fight against these totalitarian Marxist dictators around the world.
14. In the 80's, during the Reagan Presidency, Dr. del Marmol had the honor of serving Reagan by running the most daring and effective secret operation, codenamed The Zipper. This operation caused the uprising of the university students in East Germany to tear down the Berlin Wall as well as the economic collapse of the Soviet empire. The mechanism was to clone U.S. currency using the paper, plates, and magnetic ink from the Treasury Department.
15. Near the end of the operation, a setback occurred when the United States Secret Service got wind of what was

going on. They arrested him for counterfeiting and indicted him for 75 years and 6 months. He was more than publicly exposed; he was embarrassed as the news was carried internationally by newspapers, even interrupting the 1988 Summer Olympics in Seoul with the news of his arrest. He even made the Guiness Book of World Records for the Biggest Counterfeit Arrest.

16. He held onto his integrity, keeping silence and not revealing the names of anyone else involved in the operation, including the President, even in the face of extreme pressure and outright torture (at one point, in addition to beating him, one agent poured boiling hot water on his groin, scalding his testicles badly). The President intervened and worked a deal with the federal judge on the case to release Dr. del Marmol, serve a few months in a federal camp, and be given permission to leave the country to Baja California, Mexico for an indefinite period to one of the safe houses he maintained there.

17. Following a short period of time, he returned to the US to resume his undercover fight, bringing to the FBI the critical information which led them to arrest Cuba's most valuable asset to penetrate the State Department, Ana Belen Montes, and causing her recruiter to become a fugitive in Sweden.

18. He also brought information to the U.S. government warning of an imminent attack on New York City by terrorists, which became 9/11. He later was present at the actual death of the real Osama bin Laden.

Principles for Them and Us
"The abuse of other people's freedom is the beginning of the extermination of our own freedom and the abuse of freedom itself."

Dr. Julio Antonio del Marmol

Speaker

Dr. del Marmol is an engaging speaker. He was invited to be a panelist at LosCon 41, when the theme was "Cloak and Dagger". Not only did he sit in on some panels as a professional spy, but also had the unique honor of being given a solo panel to discuss his life experiences and handle questions from attendees. He was also given his own table to display his books and sign autographs and provide photo opportunities.

Dr. del Marmol at LosCon41

Videos Which Will Tell You More

Go to YouTube and our channel, Cuba Events Today. Once there, search for the titles of the following videos:
Who Is the Cuban Lightning?
The Ghost Trailer
Appearance on Newsmax
Black Tears: the Havana Syndrome
My Cuba Stolen from Me
Born in the Wrong Place
Evil Minds Interceptor
Surviving Loco
Insanity, I Love It!
Cuba: Paradise or Hell
The Devil by the Horns, Hallelujah
I Believe in My Dreams
Wonders of Our Memories
Karma Book Trailer
Dios el Universo y Nuestro Amor
The Cuban Lightning: The Zipper
Jamba #1: Spy Hide and Seek
The Broken Rainbow: Mysterious Dark Karma
Jamba Rhapsody #9: Mi Habana Vieja
Mujer Aprende a Vivir (certified by TuneCore at 500 streams)
You can also go to the Fox News website and search for the op-ed they invited him to write in rebuttal to an article they had posted by a professor at UCLA which likened Che Guevara to a Christ-like figure: "Likening Che Guevara to Jesus Christ is despicable. I saw him execute his best friend."

International Journalism Award for Dr. del Marmol's first book

Crucifix of Venetian glass and cherry wood commissioned by Pope Saint John Paul II the Great

Pope John Paul II gift to me

Acknowledgements

I am a very lucky man because I have a great group of people by my side that I not only consider my friends but also who are the most capable, sacrificing professionals equal to the ones I've risked my life with over the past 50 years in their dedication and values. This group has made possible the publication of this book. To them, with all my heart today, I give the best of my love, gratitude, and sincerest thanks to every one of these fantastic warriors. In order of seniority, I would especially like to thank O'Brien: a great friend, a great individual with extraordinary values, thank you for your contributions you have made in many different ways to this project, as well being loyally by my side and watching my back for almost all of my career. I know for a fact you have never done that before for anyone. To my right arm and great friend, Tad Atkinson: for your dedication to every detail in research and many hours of hard work with me, never hesitating to sacrifice even your personal and private family time in order to make this happen. To Steve Weese: thank you for the many pieces of computer and graphic work as well professional enhancement of photos to improve the quality of the book. To Carlos Mota: my thanks for your dedication and multiple contributions and sacrifices you have made in order to make this happen. To Gervasin Neto: for your constant loyalty and many hours standing on your feet or hiding between cars in order to maintain our security with your group of people you've coordinated to watch our backs, continually keeping informed of any suspicious activity that occurs in our surroundings. To Mimi: for your great companionship, loyalty, and support for the many hours by my side helping the development and sacrifice of your own time to make sure that my good security is in place. To our editor, Nathan Jospeh Sitton Marchand: who managed to make this book as easy to read, using his magic touch to polish this piece of coal and bring to you, the readers, what I consider to be a very rare diamond. It makes all of us very proud to be involved in this project. Your professionalism, vast knowledge, and dedication have made this book a great piece for future generations. To all of you, my friends who remain in the shadows, who contributed in one way or another to making this book and helping me to bring the truth to the public, you have given the best of yourselves, putting forth your best effort to educate future generations. God bless you all. I embrace you as the Christian warriors that you all are and thank you all from the bottom of my heart.

Dr. Julio Antonio del Marmol

Forgiving, But Never Forgetting

Innocent, naïve, and ignorant, I put my hand on the hot plate once. I might forgive my innocence, naivety, and ignorance, but I cannot forget my pain, or I will get burned again and again. Man is the only animal that puts his feet in a hole on the road and falls miserably, hurting himself and the next day at the same time in the same place, steps once more in the same hole, falling miserably and this time breaking his leg. This is what you get when you forget. Yes, just forgive, but never forget.

Dr. Julio Antonio del Marmol

Chapter 1: One More Close Shave

    I had just arrived at LAX from Mexico still in disguise. The first thing I did when I got off the plane was walk to a public telephone booth. I called O'Brien, my contact in the intelligence community. He answered, "Thank God you're OK. I was starting to worry about you."

    I replied, "Thank you very much for your concern, old man, but you shouldn't worry. Worry gives you extra wrinkles. Remember always that I'm protected by a Supreme Being, a lot more powerful than anything we can imagine. "

    "I know, I know. You got it?"

    "Yes, all the details from the horse's mouth, the principal financier of the royal leader of the terrorist group we've been circling around. I hope the big guys behind you give this the urgency this requires. Don't let me down like they did before with the normal bureaucracy, or we will have a real massacre on our hands."

    "Is it that serious?" he asked in concern.

    "More than I can even tell you over the phone. I need to see you immediately. Let's meet at my house in Corona del Mar. How much time do you need?"

Figure 1 Corona del Mar

"I'm not in town, but I'm going to jump on a plane right now and be there as soon as possible. I'll call you at your house as soon as I land, probably in a few hours."

"Every minute wasted could be lives lost. You have no time to waste here. The lives of thousands of innocent civilians are in play."

"Jesus Christ! Don't say anything more. I'll be there as soon as possible."

"I'll see you at my house. I'll make a lobster thermidor to make my news easier to digest." We said goodbye and hung up. I walked to the airport parking structure with my ticket in hand, looking for my Jaguar XJSC. It was a beautiful convertible, white exterior with a dark blue removable hard top. I clicked the button to unlock the car and got behind the wheel, beginning to remove my facial disguise once I was inside the car. I started up the car and left the airport, driving to Orange County along the 405 Southbound freeway. As I left the freeway, I noticed a Ford sedan was tailing me. I then spotted a second one join in the pursuit of me. I have always been fascinated with cars, and loved to customize every car I own, frequently inventing or adding some unusual features to make each car unique. Because of my life experiences, these unique features frequently are defensive or weapons, and this car was no different, equipped with several tricks for just such a situation.

    I saw almost immediately that both cars were not driven by professionals as I was aware of them both at once. As I exited the freeway onto the Pacific Coast Highway, I changed my route to avoid going directly to my house. I observed that they were closing the distance aggressively. I saw a hand emerge from the front passenger window holding a gun. He started to fire at my tires; clearly, they didn't know that I had airless tires which could not under any circumstance go flat.

    I accelerated. They were very close now, and I made a sudden turn to the right and allowed a piece of the roof to fly off. The roof had two panels, each of which was attached to the central bar of the convertible's hard top structure. Near the center panel were two handles one twisted to unlock the panel from the bar. It was easy to do with my right hand while continuing to steer the car with my left, which I did as I made the sharp turn. It hit the windshield of the first car, which veered into oncoming traffic. The second car continued; this time three men began to shoot at me. I sped up even more to 65 or 70 miles per hour, blowing through red lights, but my persistent assailants continued their pursuit. I slammed on my brakes at a signal light which turned red and released the second panel, which flew into the windshield of the other car.

Figure 2 Dr. del Marmol's Jaguar

    I had now lost both panels of the convertible roof, but I was at least rid of both cars. I watched in satisfaction as the other car lost control, taking out several parking meters and scattering pedestrians. The car flew into the window of a Wells Fargo branch office, right across from my favorite bakery, C'est Si Bon. In confusion, several cars pulled off to the side while I blew the powerful airhorn of my Jaguar, clearing the way before me. I heard police sirens in the distance through the open roof of my car.

I kept driving along the Pacific Coast Highway, taking the exit which took me to the Balboa Peninsula, turned around, and saw that no one was behind me now. I slowed down, continued down the Peninsula at a very slow speed, continually checking my mirrors to see that the coast was clear before I got onto the Ferry which would take me to my house. I had no more tails. Once I was absolutely sure no one was following me, I drove onto the empty ferry and drove my Jaguar all the way to the front. I didn't turn off the engine as a precaution, continually checking the right and left mirrors as well as the inside mirror. For a few minutes I felt like I had nothing more to worry about.

Figure 3 The Jaguar with the top completely down

Assuming that I was in the clear, I didn't pay attention to a Ford Bronco with a massive deer killer bumper as it drove onto the ferry. To my surprise, the driver of the Bronco suddenly accelerated, hitting my car in the rear and pushing it towards the rail. I thought he wanted to shove me into the ocean. I looked in the rearview mirror and saw that he was making no move. Very slowly and not taking my eyes off of his reflection in the rearview, I reached over and casually opened the glove compartment and pulled out the gun I kept there. He still made no move. I pulled my hand back so that my movements were shielded by my body, and carefully cocked the gun and concealed it in my waistband, covering it with my jacket. Still keeping my eyes on the man, I slowly opened my car door and got out. I took a couple of steps, keeping him in my line of sight at all times and walked toward the bumper of my car.

I caught his eye and spread my hands out in amazement as I smirked at him as I shook my head in disgust. I pointed at the bumper of my car wordlessly and exaggeratedly shrugged my shoulders as if mocking his complete inattention. I could tell by now that he was actually harmless, and that this was an accident. What he did next confirmed my deduction.

He got out and apologetically said, "I'm really sorry, sir. It's a new car, and I'm not used to how much that bumper sticks out in front of my car." He handed me a card. "If there's any damage to your car, please let me know and I will pay for it."

I felt a little better as I got back into my car. The ferry docked and I drove my car off, heading to my house. I went inside, finished removing my disguise and took a quick shower to finish cleaning any makeup residue off. Then I changed to my classic yellow Land Cruiser, another of my beautiful creations which looked more like a Defender Land Rover than the Toyota it really was and drove to the nearby Gelson's Market to buy the lobsters I had promised to greet O'Brien with when he came to visit me. I called my lady friend, Zuyen, to alert her to my plans and to expect company.

Figure 4 The "Defender"

It was around 5:30 in the afternoon when I pulled into the Gelson's parking lot. As I did, I noticed two sedans, one olive green and the other black, with two men in each car. What attracted my attention was that they all wore earpieces, much like Secret Service, and that they were talking into them. They were also wearing sunglasses, and at that hour, with the sun setting over the Pacific Ocean, it was simply too late in the day for such eyewear. I drove to the other side of the parking lot to make it more difficult for them to observe me from their current position. I got out of the Defender and locked the doors. As I walked into the market, I did not see the two vehicles park next to mine on either side of the Defender, each sedan facing a different direction. Two of the men got out and followed me inside.

I grabbed a shopping cart and began to put items from the produce isle into it: asparagus, carrots, tomatoes, etc. Passing by the canned vegetables isle, I added some cans of tomato sauce before heading to the seafood department. On my way in, I grabbed some caviar before stopping before the glass display of beautifully arranged seafood. My cell phone rang. It was O'Brien.

I said, "Yes, everything is OK. When do you think you'll be able to meet me tonight?"

"I've gotten everything arranged and should be there by 8 pm. Will that work?"

"Perfect. Dinner should be ready by then, so come hungry."

"OK but be very careful. More than usual. What you have is too valuable and we can't afford to lose it."

"I know. Don't worry about it. No one even knows that I'm in the country; I just came in through Mexico."

"OK, that's fine. Just be extremely careful, all right?"

I smiled. "OK, Papa. We'll see each other later."

Unobserved by anyone else, the two men had entered the market, each taking a shopping cart, and then heading off in different directions as they followed me. I approached the service counter and saw my friend John, a grey-haired man who was the seafood department manager.

He saw me and said cordially, "Hello, Dr. del Marmol! It's been a long time since we've seen each other."

I returned his smile with one of my own. "Ola, John. How are you doing? It's a great pleasure to see you again—you look good! How's your family?"

"Everyone's fine, thank you. My little girl, Jenny, is going to be sweet sixteen in a little while."

"My God! Jenny—sixteen? What happened to the time? It went by so fast!"

"Yes." John was wrapping up some shrimp, as he knew what I was about to order. "Two pounds?" he asked by way of confirmation.

"A little more. Add a couple of pounds, as I have some guests coming over tonight. It's better to have more than not enough."

John smiled. "How many lobsters?"

"Four, please."

John went over to the lobster tank and pulled out the four I pointed out to him and began to wrap them. "When are you going to invite me to one of your great scuba fishing trips on your yacht? Do you still have that yacht?"

"Yes. Possibly next month, for my birthday."

John smiled and winked as he made the OK hand gesture. "Don't forget me, OK? We'll have a lot of fun. Every time you take me with you when you go fishing, I bring you luck, and we catch a lot of fish and other seafood."

I smiled. "Yes, it's true. And when you don't come with us, we return empty and half drunk."

"You see?" He smiled in satisfaction.

We said goodbye and I headed towards the front of the store to check out. A line was already formed before several of the cashiers, so I picked one. One of the men who had been following me was in the line next to me. The other man came and run into him.

The man who was in line said angrily, "What the hell is wrong with you? Are you blind or something, or not looking where you're going? Look at what you did to my shoe!" He licked his finger and rubbed the barely visible scratch on his shoe.

The second man said apologetically, "I'm sorry. It was unintentional. I was thinking of something, I don't even know what it was now, and I didn't even see you. I'm very sorry." The first man glared at him angrily and continued to work on his shoe. "Hey man, I'm sorry—I really didn't mean to."

The first man didn't even look up at him. It was clear everyone that saw the exchange thought that first man was a complete imbecile, shaking their heads as they wondered what was wrong with him. I looked at him in surprise as I took my wallet out in preparation to pay.

The second man asked me, "How is it possible somebody could react so out of line and crazy over something so little?"

I replied, "Don't worry about it. Those people are the ones who try to torture other people for small mistakes like that. They will find somebody down the road one day that will make them feel just the same, and then they will feel how you do right now."

The cashier was a young, thin innocent blonde girl. She was giving me my change and said, "Oh my God! I've never heard such beautiful words in my life. What you just said is so very, very nice."

I smiled pleasantly as I looked at her. "Thank you." I looked at her name badge on her blouse. "Have a good day, Janet."

"You, too, sir. Thank you."

The man followed me into the parking lot, trying to catch up to me. "Can you believe that guy? I didn't do anything to his shoe, and you saw how he reacted. My God, some people don't have any class at all! Or they're stressed out—I don't know what's wrong with people these days."

It was all too strange. My senses were so taut that I had to force myself to listen to the man. I nodded in agreement. "Don't worry about it. It's not a big deal, just go home and forget about it." I was getting worried because this man was getting closer to me. In an attempt to get away from him, I maneuvered my cart between cars. He matched me in another row. I reached the Defender and realized that he was parked next to me. I began to load the groceries into my car when out of nowhere the first man appeared with his cart. The other man turned in behind me, so I was trapped between the two of them and the two vehicles.

The first man said, "You idiot! How would you like it if I did the same to you and drove my cart against your car?" He shoved the cart with all his strength as if towards the other man's car, but instead—much to my concern—he hit the Defender, scratching the paint.

I said, "My friend, what on Earth is wrong with you? Look what you did to my car."

He looked at me and started towards me as if getting ready to fight me. As I took a step back to assume a defensive posture, a hand grabbed my right shoulder. As I turned to look, I caught a flash of metal in someone's hand just before I was struck a vicious, hard blow to my forehead by someone wearing a pair of brass knuckles. Stunned and semiconscious, I dropped to the ground. The other two men moved fast and began a systemic, professional beating with batons, making sure that I didn't get back up.

Dimly aware of my surroundings, I heard rather than saw two men ransacking the Defender, clearly searching it for something. What focus I could manage was on the man who had acted as a decoy for this ambush, who was screwing a suppressor onto his gun.

A new voice yelled, "I can't find anything in here."

The first man replied, "What? It has to be here."

"No, there's nothing here," was the response.

The first man had continued to hit me while his friend was getting ready to kill me. He stopped now and went to join the search of my car. The second man put the muzzle of his pistol to my right ear as he prepared to fire. Seeing that, the third man said, "Wait, we can't find anything. We might need him. Fuck!"

The second man pulled his pistol away. "We can't waste any more time. We've already created too much of a commotion here." I heard him get inside my car as he joined the search.

Unfortunately, at that moment an elderly couple saw what was happening as they were heading to their own car. I heard a old woman's voice exclaim, "What are you doing?" This was followed by a duel popping noise and a pair of thuds on the asphalt as the two people were shot dead. I opened my eyes as I began to recover and saw the two men I had seen in the driver's seat of the sedans collect the two bodies and put them in the trunk of one of their vehicles calmly, as if they did this every day.

I was dizzy and faint. I looked around carefully and saw the four men searching my Land Rover. Slowly, I reached into my jacket pocket to pull out my 9MM pistol. Keeping my hands over the gun, I waited for my vision to clear. I could feel the blood on my cheeks from the wound on my forehead. So no one would notice, I covered my weapon under my jacket and waited to recuperate more.

Meanwhile, one of the men in the car started to remove the vinyl cover from the spare tire to find some diskettes and microfilms in a magnetic box attached to the wheel. He smiled in satisfaction and turned towards me, pistol in hand. As he put the pistol against my forehead, I sprang into action, grabbing the gun, forcing it away from my body. A shot rang out, the metallic clang of a nearby car telling us where it went. I pulled out my own gun and fired three times at point blank range, hitting the man standing over me in the jaw each time.

The power of the impact at such close range threw his body back. The other men turned in confusion, pulling their weapons as they looked around to see where the attack was coming from. I fired four more shots at the largest man who held the silver box with the microfilm in it. He fell, hit twice in the head and twice in the chest. The box clattered to the ground and rolled beneath the Land Rover. One of the other men dove to the ground to retrieve it while hoping at the same time to take cover.

From my position on the ground, I fired twice more, but both shots missed, hitting instead the tires. The man rolled out from under the Land Rover and beneath another car. I couldn't get a clear shot at him, nor could I stand. From the pain when I attempted to, I guessed I had a broken leg, so I started to roll on the ground towards the Range Rover near my side. I had to get away since I had lost visual contact with the other two men. I also knew I was low on bullets—I had twelve in the magazine plus another in the chamber when I began, so after my nine shots I only had four left in my gun, or two rounds for each of my enemies.

I began to crawl, firing twice more to distract my assailants. By now, a crowd had gathered, yelling for the police, running out of various stores to see what all the shooting was about and to see what was going on. I was covered in blood and filth, with no knowledge of the current status of my enemies. I had no way of knowing that by now they had given up on trying to kill me but had instead focused their attention on recovering the bodies of their teammates and exiting the area through different entrances. I could hear sirens in the distance, getting closer and closer. As I rolled along the ground I ran into a man and saw dark pants, shiny shoes, and a black suit. It was still difficult for me to see anything, and so I trained my pistol on the figure.

John's voice said, "No, no, Dr. del Marmol. It's me, John. What happened?"

"Someone attacked me and beat me up." I could barely make him out, but now that I had his voice some details became clearer for me. I handed him my gun. "Please save this pistol and don't let anyone see it."

As I began to lose consciousness, I saw John put the pistol beneath his apron and heard him say, as if in a tunnel, "Don't worry, my friend. No one is going to see anything."

Chapter 2: The Penetration and Castration

Naturally, I was later told everything that happened to me while I was unconscious. I was transported to Hoag Hospital, where I was stabilized and put in the ICU in a medically induced coma. My sweetheart, Zuyen, was met at the hospital by O'Brien and Elizabeth, where they were told about my condition: the medically induced coma was due to severe head trauma and a double fracture to my cranium. I had a severe concussion, and they even had found a blood clot that they had to treat. I needed to remain in a coma not only to heal but also so I could be closely monitored in the event of another clot forming over the next twenty-four hours. In addition to my head injuries, my right leg was broken in two places, near the ankle and close to the knee. While not bad, my jaw likewise was fractured, along with a fracture in the ulna of my right arm. That I was still alive was attributed to a miracle, but because of my extensive injuries I was not to be moved.

  O'Brien solemnly promised Zuyen that I would be protected round the clock, which reminded her that I had told her only that afternoon about a diskette I wanted O'Brien to have in the advent of something like this happening. Readers of my other books will recall that my psychic capabilities had been enhanced and expanded as a result of my training at the Montauk Project. A consequence of this is that, even when my physical body and mind are heavily sedated or incapacitated, I have the ability to shift my awareness in time, projecting it into the past.

Mexico City International Airport
11:45 PM
Earlier in the year 2000

Figure 5 Mexico City International Airport

    Elisabeth drove the white Lincoln Navigator, O'Brien sat up front with her, while Zuyen sat in back with me. I was about to embark on another dangerous mission into Cuba. Very much in love, she was practically sitting in my lap while I gazed into her eyes as I stroked her beautiful hair. She looked away at the rain drops pattering against the window. She looked back at me and slid her hand through my beard while I caressed her lips and chin with my hand. We smiled, and she leaned in to kiss me passionately on the lips.

O'Brien turned slightly to see into the back and smiled. He said to Elizabeth, "I think our friend is lucky. For the second time in his life, he has found a great love."

Elizabeth glanced up into the rear-view mirror and smiled. She nodded and shared a smile with O'Brien. We ignored them as the horizons of our world narrowed to include only Zuyen and me. Elizabeth drove into the airport parking lot and O'Brien coughed politely to attract our attention.

"Well," he said, "we're at the airport."

Zuyen and I hugged, and I asked O'Brien, "Do you have the tickets?"

With a completely straight face, O'Brien answered, "No." Then he held an envelope out to me.

I took the envelope with a smile. "OK, thank you."

"Don't mention it."

I looked at Zuyen. "We'll see each other next week on St. Martin's Island."

"OK, take care of yourself for me."

I smiled. "OK. And *you* take care of yourself for me."

O'Brien gave Zuyen a strong hug. He said, "Thank you for everything. It's a great pleasure to have met you."

Elizabeth also gave Zuyen a hug and whispered, "Don't worry. I'll take care of him."

Zuyen said, "Thank you. God bless you." She got into the driver's seat and rolled down the window. I leaned in and kissed her through the window. "Take care of yourself, my love", she said as she drew back.

I stepped back and released her hand as she drove off. O'Brien said, "OK, lover, we have to get on the plane."

I blew a kiss at the departing car and watched until it disappeared in the airport traffic while Elizabeth and O'Brien waited anxiously.

Sept 11, 2000
International Waters

It was very cold shortly after midnight that morning. A deep-sea fishing boat lay hove-to twelve miles off the Cuban coast. At that distance, she was just outside of Cuba's territorial waters and so free to fish without any permissions or permits. On the seaward side of the boat, however, fishing was not on anyone's mind. I was getting ready for a long swim and another insertion inside the communist security network of Cuba.

The captain Marrero spoke to me as he helped me lower the net bag with the equipment I was going to need over the side. "I know I don't have to say this to you, but for my peace of mind I have to. Be very careful, and once you get close enough that you can start using that snorkel, conceal your scuba tank someplace safe so you can get it on your way back out. If they catch you with even so much as the respirator to that scuba tank, they'll shoot you on sight for being a CIA agent."

I nodded. "Yes, I know. Don't worry. I know the protocol very well. I will send you a signal when I'm ready for you to pick me up—it's already a long swim, and I don't want to have to keep swimming all the way to Miami. I'm not leaving until I have the information about what these terrorists are planning, so wait for my signal through our usual channels."

We shook hands, and I slipped into the cold waters for my long swim.

Figure 6 Dr. del Marmol penetrating Cuba

Port of Caibarien
Province of Santa Clara, Cuba
North Coast, Fishing Village

Several hours later, I emerged from the ocean, dragging behind me a yellow net bag with the things I needed for my mission. I made my way to the location where I was to meet my contact and settled in to wait. I checked the luminous face of my watch, a Seiko Marine Master, to see if I was on time, early, or too late. It was four am, which meant I was nearly an hour early for that meeting.

A beautiful woman with European features but olive skin and very long, black hair ran along the boardwalk. She was semi-naked, clad only in a thin white gauze dress which looked like it had been violently torn. Part of the top was ripped; as she ran she tried to cover her beautiful breasts and peach colored nipples escaped her control and popped out into view before being hastily tucked back with her left hand.

The communist government's new ambition was to desperately bring tourists to different towns throughout the island in order to spread the money around instead of simply concentrating it all in Havana. The small port town for Caibarien was no an exception; they built in the center of the town a humongous monument representing a huge crab to symbolize the crab fishing industry there. The woman looked like she was running from someone, glancing behind her frequently as she ran. She stopped by the enormous rocks around the sculpture of the crab, seeking a place to hide in the gardens and bushes, or at least among the broken rocks. The monument had been designed by the artist Florencio Giabert Perez in 1983 and had become one of the revolution's great monuments around the island.

Figure 7 The Crab Statue in Caibarien

I was able to identify with great concern that the running woman was my contact. I had no idea what was happening or was waiting for me there. It was going to be better for me to wait and observe until I could find out what was really happening. Another thing that had not been factored in was the large storm which was about to hit the island. I wondered a great deal not only about the situation she was in but also why she didn't stop at the foot of the crab where we were supposed to meet and hide there.

I was to receive specific information and be transported to the capital of Havana, where I was to meet my second contact, who would then link me in the chain of command of a particular terrorist camp. It was clear highly specialized training was being conducted, and we wanted to determine what their mission was. This individual in Havana that I was to meet in the old Hilton (now called the Havana Libre) had direct contact with the principal financier for the al-Qaeda group and was willing, for a certain amount of money, to give me the details and schematics of what the plan was all about. The training had been going on for several months already, but our intelligence had failed so far to penetrate the terrorists and find a reliable contact to provide what we needed. Finally, I had the opportunity through these people in Caibarien. This cell of freedom fighters against the communist government of the Castro brothers had a safehouse here.

I tried to follow the woman at a safe distance so that I could determine what was going on before I approached her. Even though it wasn't time for our meeting yet, I wanted to be certain that, when I made my move, it would be secure. Moving from building to building and in between cars, I followed the woman closely as she made her way around the crab statue. She didn't even know what angle she was going to be safe in, and so continually changed her position.

Suddenly, soldiers from the communist government appeared even as I blinked, stopped very close to the sculpture where the woman was hiding. They had arrived in a Soviet version of the Jeep, a GAZ 64. Four soldiers and what appeared to be an officer jumped out of the vehicle and began to coordinate their next moves. I closed behind some vehicles and buildings on the other side of the street, hiding behind a semi truck loaded with lumber for building. I looked inside the truck. Normally the driver would be sleeping inside the cabin to make sure the load would not get stolen, but I saw no one.

As I looked at the soldiers talking, the officer pointed in my direction. Apparently they were looking for someone specific, whether my contact or someone else. From his gestures, it was clear he was setting up a search pattern for his squad. To my surprise, only two soldiers were left behind. The other two followed the officer and got back into the GAZ 64. The two who were supposed to check my area gave military salutes and began walking in my direction.

I knew that if I didn't get out of there they would find me. There was no place to go where I could not be seen if I left. If I ran, they would not hesitate to shoot me. I had no other alternative than to confront them and leave my hiding place. I hated to improvise, but there was no choice. I put my improvised plan into motion at once. I took a deep breath and realized that I had to thank God that I was facing two men instead of five. I laid my net bag with my gear behind the rear tire of the truck on the opposite side of the soldiers. Trying not to make any noise, I pulled out a carbon dioxide gun, normally used by us to drive sharks into a frenzy by shooting one shark so that they would attack the injured one and leave us alone.

It was the only weapon I was supposed to bring with me, along with my Commando knife, which was tied to my leg. On more than one occasion on my trips in and out of Cuba, I had confrontation with sharks, and it was almost a routine thing to shoot one. Once the cylinder entered the shark, the air it released would cause the animal to explode. It wasn't a small gun, about twice the size of a normal pistol, and I hid it as best I could on my back, held up by my belt. I grabbed the net bag, slung it over my left shoulder, and put my plan in motion.

I got out in plain view, walking towards the soldiers. I whistled one of my favorite melodies from my musical repertoire, "My Cuba Stolen from Me," as if I had no worries, having just returned from a diving trip and now on my way home. The soldiers were surprised when they saw me. As I walked towards them, they started to get agitated, commanding me to stop. I kept my eyes not only on them but also behind them as I watched the silhouette of the half-naked woman leave her hiding place. I saw as she crossed beneath one of the streetlights that she was holding an object in her right hand, very close to her leg. I also saw she had no shoes and walked very silently as she crept up behind the soldiers as they focused on me. With her left finger held to her lips for silence, she rushed up behind them swiftly.

I understood the danger she had put herself in. With my right hand behind my back to hold the gun, I ignored what they said to me, instead saying, "Good evening, comrades. You have nothing to worry about, I'm a local. I have nothing against you."

They didn't believe me and trained their Soviet PPSh-41 submachine guns on me, removing the leather straps from their shoulders as they loudly commanded me to stop walking and lie on the ground, pointing at the dirty asphalt street.

I replied, "I'm a fisherman. I live here."

They didn't listen or didn't care. They continued to issue their threats and commands, unwrapping their guns from their shoulders, pointing them at me. "Get your hands up if you don't want to be shot."

I raised my hands high, releasing my grip on the gun as I did, putting my life in the hands of God and the woman. I could see that she was planning to put them down. I unslung my net bag from my shoulder. "Don't shoot—I can't lie on the ground with this bag on my shoulder. I'm putting it on the ground. I'm your friend, I don't have any weapons." I put my bag on the ground.

They got more agitated, and one yelled loudly, "Don't make any false moves if you don't want us to turn you into Swiss cheese from head to toe with these machine guns."

The other soldier had never heard that before and laughed in a more relaxed fashion. He asked, "If you're a fisherman, where are your fish? Have you already sold your fish as contraband to the people in town?"

"No, I didn't catch anything. The water is still too turbulent because of the storm."

Both soldiers shook their heads. Knowing this weather, they had to ask themselves who would go fishing in it. The other one yelled, "Don't make any more excuses and put your belly on the asphalt, OK?"

"OK, no problem. I'm getting on the ground right now. Calm down. I live close by, over here."

They were by now around twenty feet from me. I could see the shadowy form of my contact, Atacia. In the reflection of the streetlamp behind them, I saw her raise the object she held. She hit the first soldier to my right. He immediately collapsed onto his belly on the asphalt like they had wanted me to do. Unfortunately, as he fell, he turned the gun towards himself, shooting himself into two pieces, riddling himself like the Swiss cheese he had mentioned.

As I watched him flop around on the ground, Atacia moved behind the other soldier, who had turned to see what was going on. She hit him in the head right above the ear, and he dropped to the ground on his knees. As he dropped, she snatched the machine gun away from him in a rapid disarm move before the trigger could get pulled. After she secured the weapon, she gave him a strong kick in the jaw, knocking him down, hitting his head against the pavement.

I had by now pulled the CO_2 pistol from my back. I noticed that Atacia was now pointing the machine gun at me. I raised my arms above my head and said calmly, "Atacia, is that you? It's a really dark night with no moon."

She replied, "Yes, it's me. And who are you? Where are you coming from?"

"I come from Heaven," giving her the recognition phrase. "I'm in the light of the Lightning on God's side."

She lowered the machine gun. "I had to make sure. I'm sorry."

"Nothing to be sorry about. I had to make sure myself, as well, at the very least that you weren't on the side of these guys."

I leaned down and picked up my net bag. She continued to kick the semi-conscious soldier with her feet. I tried to stop her, saying gently and compassionately and soothingly as I grabbed her by the right arm, "Leave him alone. He's not a threat to us anymore."

She looked at me with tear-filled eyes. "It's easy for you to say. These two pigs raped me a little while ago." She showed me the bruising by her left breast and the large bruise over her abdomen. She took the machine gun and put it against the head of the soldier who was beginning to regain consciousness. He opened his eyes in terror, as if he were seeing the Devil before him. Looking into her hate-filled eyes, he knew she was fully ready to blow his brains out.

I said, "Atacia, calm down. Remember, you're not like them. If you kill him, that will stay with you for the rest of your life. He doesn't deserve that you pull yourself down to his level. He is down in evil, another disciple of Satan. You are a higher being, by the Supreme Architect, a place he will never be able to enter for his filthy, perverted mind." I pointed at the other soldier. "He already has his trip to his mentor in Hell. Look at how he killed himself. That blood is not on your hands. Maybe God protected you. This one is still alive. Not only could this complicate our mission, it is up to us to save if not hundreds but thousands of innocent lives."

She looked at me unconvinced. "What do you mean? We leave another disciple of the Devil alive, so he can continue to rape and kill our friends, families, and innocent people, with no consequences or punishment with impugnity? Is that what you're telling me? That I have to let go?"

I bent over slowly. "There are many ways ot redeem your honor and still give punishment to your assailants." I drew my knife, cut the belt on the soldier's pants. I pulled his panted down to the knees at he watched in puzzlement.

She put the muzzle beneath his jaw. "You want to see your brain fly from the top of your head like popcorn?"

He froze. I then cut the elastic band on his underwear, leaving him completely naked. I took the machine gun from Atacia and handed her the knife. I saw the soldier's terror as he looked at me in disbelief that his imagination was right. I said, "Eye for an eye, tooth for a tooth. These two soldiers are the ones who raped you?"

Tears ran down her cheeks as she nodded. She held the knife in a tight grip, the knuckles white as she bit her lower lip. "Yes. These degenerates." She looked at me in confusion. "What do you mean? I don't know to castrate this pig. I never even liked to watch when my father did it."

I shook my head. "There's an old saying here in Cuba—by starting to learn to cut balls you learn how to castrate."

"How do I do it?"

"All you have to do is make a little incision in the skin in the center of both testicles. You don't cut it; you just saw it back and forth like cutting a rope. It gives time for the blood to coagulate so that the animal, or man in this case, doesn't bleed to death. Eventually you sever the tissue, and it breaks. From that same incision is stick your fingers in, get its brother like a little elastic band, pull it out, and saw away again. One thing I'll tell you know, you have to tie him up and gag him, because the screaming of this pig will be heard all the way to Havana, and we don't want to attract the attention of the other soldiers in town." I pulled a rope out of my bag and handed it to her.

She then started to remove her panties. "We need a gag, and I think I'll give him a taste of his own medicine."

She tied and gagged him with the rope and panties, and I said, "When you're finished, put a piece of that rope around his neck with his testicles tied to it with a little note for his comrades explaining why you did what you did. Not only will this give you the gratification of not killing the man, but it will give you satisfaction for the rest of your life. You'll also be doing a good deed for this town and a lesson for the other communist pigs who try to do to a young girl what they did to you. You have treated him like an beast, and this will be a lesson, I assure you, which will cause a communist rapist to think twice before doing this."

The soldier saw the determination in her face and tried to get up to escape. She kicked him back on the ground. Atacia followed my instruction to the teeth with great success and finished castrating the man after a little while. The man, mercifully, passed out from the pain.

I said, "We'd better get out of here as soon as possible. We've wasted a lot of time, and the one thing we don't want to happen is for the rest of those soldiers to return and find this guy with the sign around his neck as well as the dead man."

The night was nearly ended and the door to morning was opening at a fast pace, even though this morning didn't start with sunshine like most due to the storm closing in on the town. The new day was as dark as the night, which was perfect for our plans to leave our hiding place by the crab sculpture and head toward the safe house to which she was to deliver me.

As we put distance between ourselves and the scene of conflict, I felt cold light sprinkles on my face. At this early hour, there were few people on the street and even fewer cars left in that town to create any traffic. I knew that this incident would delay my exit from that town, and I had to prepare myself physically and mentally. It was typical for the communist regime to put a price on someone's head for bounty hunters, because someone would have to pay for what was done to the one man. Such resistance could spread across the island like a 150-mph hurricane force wind; they could not admit how the freedom fighters brought justice for the abuses of the communist Cuban government.

I walked a short distance behind Atacia with my eyes glued on her. She knew the area like the palm of her hand, and she took me to the least trafficked places in this ghost time, avoiding the principal streets while using the alleys and other short cuts to avoid any encounters with soldiers or the communist police. As we came out of an alley, she stopped and signaled with both hands for me to drop down. I did that at once, because even though no one knew who I was and I had a French passport, I knew that though they didn't even have toilet paper, the government of the repressive regime had sophisticated computers for their intelligence network. All they would have to do is get my fingerprints and they would know exactly who I was. Normally, as part of my preparations I would bring a little box containing elastic fingerprints that I put over my fingers as a disguise. But I had not expected any confrontation on this mission; now the unanticipated rape turned all of my plans upside down. I wasn't supposed to get involved in these kinds of things, but I had no alternative since she was a woman, a human being, and my contact.

I had been walking behind her at a prudent distance; if anyone saw her, they wouldn't notice both of us. She suddenly stopped, her attention caught by approaching lights as she held her hands high and sharply dropped them to indicate that I should drop to the ground at once, which I was already doing due to the sudden halt.

Two Soviet GAZs appeared at the mouth of the alley where we were going to exit. The soldiers jumped out of the jeeps and used the searchlights on their doors to scan the entire area. Even though the lights were very powerful, lying on the dirty ground as we were the beams went over us without illuminating us. After a few tense minutes, it appeared the soldiers saw nothing unusual and returned to their vehicles. I thanked God for Atacia's opportune signal and her being so on the ball. We were covered not only by the total darkness in that alley but also the storm God had sent blackened the sky like night. That alley had so many boxes and bags of trash that had accumulated over the past several weeks. The poor sanitary service the government had on the island did not allow for regular trash pickup; the darkness and the trash proved to be our best allies in getting out of that bad situation.

    I followed my guide closely and we finally left the downtown area and entered the suburbs, approaching a huge colonial hacienda. It was in such bad shape that the metal gates hung loosely from the hinges. The rusted metal had nearly corroded all the way through. After making our way through the wild vegetation, we entered what was once a beautiful garden kept by the owners of the mansion. The gardens were so abandoned that the whole place had an air of desolation about it, reminding me more than a little of Dr. Frankenstein's castle. The salt from the sea water had taken a significant toll over the many decades of poor maintenance of this luxurious mansion, like everywhere else on the island. These beautiful residences, once serving wealthy families, were now rendered uninhabitable by anyone.

    We entered by the double front doors. In the past it must have been a beautiful entry hall, but now heavy two by four boards were nailed to both doors to keep them together. I thought to myself, "My God. We should film a movie here and show the people around the world what's really going on in Cuba." Of course, any film maker that came there to do this, the MQ-1 would be sent to kill the filmmaker and his entire family. That's what their platoons were trained to do. It was like a boarded-up house when a hurricane was approaching to protect houses and minimize the damage the winds would do, but in Cuba this kind of ramshackle repairwork was everywhere.

Apparently this showed on my face. I noticed a smile on Atacia's face. Perhaps she was amused by my surprise at seeing something which was a daily thing for everyone in Cuba. I looked at her and smiled. "What's up? What is it? What are you smiling for?"

"Oh, nothing. Don't worry about it."

"What are you thinking?"

She smiled again as she opened a heavy wooden door leading into the back of the mansion. "You don't have to see the rest, which has been vandalized and burglarized by the government. This is just the leftovers. Thank God this has never been discovered, and we keep it close to our hearts to keep it that way. Please don't reveal this location to anyone. This is for our survival."

"Hm." Evidently the resistance on the island that had not given up and let the government intimidate them, even though they had firing squads continually executing young kids on charges they never committed save for rebelling against and protesting against the government. It was just like the Nazi Gestapo. I said, "Let me tell you one thing. Whatever you don't want to tell me you don't have to. I don't know why you brought me here today, but I'm going to ask you again. You smile mischievously like you have a joke I don't know about. Truthfully, though, this brings a very sour taste to my mouth because I don't like to be walking in the dark like this. I feel like you don't have enough confidence or trust to tell me whatever is in your head. You keep looking at me with all that mystery, and it makes me feel very uncomfortable. I feel I have the right to tell you how I feel, especially after saving your life. Communication in our work is of extreme importance, especially when we're dealing with such an evil adversary. He has multiple faces, multiple sexes, and multiple hearts. You are a witness to this—how many betrayals have we dealt with in the previous years and survived by the grace of God?"

Atacia shook her head, embarrassed, but determined not to spill what was in her mind. She then nodded as she smiled. "I understand. Please be patient. I know there's nothing worse than not knowing what you want to know, and I realize you have a vivid imagination and extraordinary reflexes."

I didn't reply but just nodded unhappily. She opened the door and we passed into the kitchen of the mansion. It looked like it hadn't been used in years. All the implements for the culinary arts which hung on the walls were filled with cobwebs. It appeared to me as if no one hadn't even fried an egg here since the beginning of the communist revolution. She stopped before a small, extremely filthy 1960's Frigidaire with its door half hanging from its hinges. Though it was obviously not working, it was still connected to the electrical outlet. She got down on both knees and unplugged the unit. I wondered why it was still plugged in if it wasn't working. She put both hands beneath it without difficulty and moved it away from the kitchen counters on its wheels, leaving an opening in the dirty wall behind it. She stood up and moved behind to remove two large marble tiles from the floor which were not cemented in place. She put both hands in the hole which revealed a crank which looked like the old crank starters on a car. As she began to turn the crank the wall began to move to the right, revealing a small alcove with door which led either deeper into the mansion or a secret passage.

She beckoned me with her left hand to come in. We both went to the door, and she bent down again to replace the tiles and grabbed a wire connected to the bottom of the refrigerator on both sides. She used this wire to pull the unit back into place. She turned to kneel towards the door, removing another two tiles, revealing another crank apparatus. As she turned this second crank, the hidden door closed. I smiled mischievously this time. I pointed at her jokingly and said, "After so many times I've come in and out of this location, you never brought me to this place before. Why are you doing it now?"

"Remember, in our line of work, information that does not need to be revealed which could be detrimental to ourselves and the lives of others should be kept quiet, even to the most trusted people close to you. Need to know. Now you need to know after what happened tonight because I know what the communists will put in motion. I've been here all these years. You've been in and out. This will start a very bloody hunt for whoever they decide to portray as the perpetrator of this counter-revolutionary act. They sometimes create an imaginary spy from the CIA or somewhere else in the world, even characters which don't exist like the Lightning, who only live in the imaginations of these repressive and destructive G-2 agents. They'll need some ghost to prove that they haven't been sleeping at their posts. That's why they create these crazy characters. This will probably be more than one—one to have killed the one soldier and one to have done the castration. I won't be surprised if they create a new television series on Sector 40 on Sundays. The plot will be about how the famous master spy, the Lightning, after he commits these crimes against the people gets trapped by the G-2 or MQ-1 and executed before a firing squad." She smiled in satisfaction. She ran her fingers through her hair as she scratched her head. "Of course, after executing this particular spy all these times, he always miraculously returns to life in the next episode." She raised both arms high. "Only the imbeciles with mosquito brains which have been brainwashed in chlorine watch this program on Sector 40 on Sundays."

  I was the one to smile this time mysteriously. I shook my head and asked, "You know what? I need you to tell me a little more about that non-existent master spy, the Lightning. I had no notion they were using this as propaganda for the communist government. Why don't you give me a few more details, please?"

Chapter 3: Jimbo the Limbo

Atacia replied, "It will be a great pleasure to debrief you in full detail about all that has transpired during your absence from the island. But please, before we start anything at all, I want you to give me the luxury of taking these filthy, stinking clothes off of my body and having a deep shower." She turned slightly and sniffed her right armpit. She raised her head back up as she pinched her nose shut with her fingers. "Yuck! My God, a human being can smell so bad when there's no proper time to clean yourself and the lack of deodorants." She was clearly not happy with the smell check under her arm.

We continued walking along a long corridor between boxes of what looked like wine, champaign, and cylinders of propane gas—it looked more like a survival store's storage area. There were even kerosene lamps, rows of rope, boxes with all kinds of preserved food like sardines and sausages. I figured that this was how the resistance survived their noncompliance of the regulations and restrictions on food and other necessities imposed on the island to subjugate and force the people to rely on the government. I wondered where they had gotten all these supplies.

We came to another large door, aluminum with iron frame, and if I was surprised before by the stores we had just walked past, a bigger surprise waited for me. Atacia pulled out a key tied to a piece of string around her neck. She unlocked the door and with a gesture of her head invited me inside. She smiled in great satisfaction as she looked at me and my awed face and startled look in my eyes. Once I recovered from my surprise I said, "Where did all of this come from? What you have stored here is more precious than gold in this country."

She smiled. "The thief who steals from another thief has one hundred years of pardon in Paradise. I'll give you the details later."

I figured they had taken them from the cargo of ships that had entered into the port through contacts which worked on the piers. This room, the largest one we had entered, I could see stacked along the walls very expensive colognes and women's perfume like Monsieur Givenchy, Cartier, and several other French brands, clothing, canned hams from Spain, and boxes of chocolate bonbons filled with different liqueurs. She grabbed one of these and ripped the plastic off as we walked. She put it in front of my face and said, "Try these, they're my favorites. They're filled with Grand Marnier."

"You rang my bell. That's my favorite liqueur." I popped one in my mouth and rolled my eyes as if I was in Heaven as I savored the delicate flavors.

She popped two into her mouth. "I'm sorry," she said around the chocolate, "but I'm hungry."

She put the box before me again, indicating I should take more, saying, "We have a lot in common. This is my favorite as well. It might surprise you how much alike we are."

We sat down at a long, fancy Nicoletti leather sofa from Italy, which looked like a Picasso to me. She put the box of bonbons between us and opened two tiny travel bottles of champagne, offering one to me and downed the other virtually in one gulp. "I don't know what it is about chocolate and champagne, but the French people know how to enjoy life. Between you and I, do you know that chocolate and champagne minimize nervous stress?"

"No, I didn't know that. I've learned something new from you today."

"For me, the Grand Marnier isn't just a liqueur; it's my medicine. Just a few sips when I'm extremely stressed out and it tranquilizes my nervous system so that I don't need any medication."

We looked at each other and smiled as we continued eating those delicious bonbons. She opened a few more of those travel bottles of champagne. As we did, my eyes looked over the ragged tatters of a dress she still wore. She had managed to tie a couple of pieces together to partially cover her beautiful, firm breasts. Not even thinking twice myself, I was perhaps a little indiscrete as I looked at her exposed thighs. I said, "It must be horrible for any woman, especially for you, to have a forced sexual penetration. It must be very painful because it's unwanted and so therefore you're not relaxed, especially in a violent manner as these pigs did to you."

She shook her head. With a mouth full of chocolate she said, "No, no, no, no. They didn't manage to penetrate me." She raised the side of the ragged dress and showed me the bruising under her breasts and over her stomach. "Why do you think they left these bruises on my body? I didn't allow those miserable pigs to penetrate me. While the other held me, every single one that tried I managed to kick in the testicles with whatever part of my legs I could move. One of them I completely nailed with my fingernails on his penis. When one of them hit me in the back of my head with his rifle, he almost knocked me out. The others tried to take advantage of my sudden lack of resistance but thank God I didn't completely lose consciousness; I was only stunned for a few seconds.

"As I recovered, they assumed that I wasn't going to offer anymore resistance, and the ones holding my arms released me. They started to take their pants down while I felt another near the edge of my vagina with his genitals, which I grabbed with both hands, dug my nails into the skin of his penis, and with the last of my strength I pulled up sharply. I never heard in my life such a distressed scream of pain come out of a wannabe rapist's throat. He jumped in the air like a circus clown or a jack in the box with a spring in his ass. That's when I jumped up and ran as fast as I could, using their confusion to my benefit. Thinking clearly, I didn't run towards our meeting place. I didn't want to bring you any heat, which is why I kept going instead of stopping. I didn't know how far behind me they were in that darkness. When I saw you leave that lumber truck and understood your intentions to confront them, I realized this was the perfect opportunity since only two of them were left. The odds were equal, so I took my chance. I knew I had to do something to help you put them down. If we couldn't put those two down, this unfortunate rape incident would be created into the counter-revolutionary act which would put both of us in front of a firing squad with no remedy at all, since in this country there's no laws or constitution—it's whatever they say while what we say has no value at all."

I smiled ironically. "That will never happen."

She looked at me in confusion. "What do you mean?"

I said with very strong conviction, "Something I can assure you, and you can be sure of this, I might lose my life in what we're doing, but I will never allow these communist pigs to catch me alive and put me before the firing squad to use me as propaganda to intimidate the rest of the population. I am always prepared for that moment, and tonight, when I least expected it, I came very close. But I've been even closer than this many times, and my guardian angel and Savior has gotten me out of it every time."

Atacia took my hand and squeezed it strongly with a small smile on her face. She said in a deeply moved voice with a tender expression and moist eyes, "Let's hope that that never happens." She leaned across the sofa and gave me a small kiss on my cheek.

"Thank you, but you don't have to worry at all. I've been a hunter of these master deceivers and will continue to be until the last day of my life."

"OK, my hero and savior. Forgive me for my weakness. I will try to not show that level of emotion again."

"No, no—that is wonderful. Please—every time that comes out of your heart it is like a cool glass of champaign and one of those delicious bonbons in the summertime to mine."

"OK, I want to ask you to please excuse me for a few minutes. It won't take me too long, but I've been distracted by your delightful conversation and have delayed my shower. Each minute I'm more uncomfortable."

"You look fine, and maybe I'm a wild animal, but your smell turns me on." She slapped me playfully on my arm. "It's OK. Take your time. I will follow your example when you come back and take one myself. Between the salt water on my body and the perspiration from our early morning exercise, I feel the same way now as you do. With a clean body we have fresh minds which think much better and function at optimum condition. We need to have very clear minds, because after what we did just now to those soldiers, we will need very, very cool minds to be able to play the game to our benefit and leave these particular local enemies behind. We have a lot of big fish to fry."

Atacia smiled slightly. She stood up, turned, and walked towards the area where the bathroom must be. As she walked, she said, "Don't worry—I won't make you wait too long."

"You don't have to rush yourself at all. Enjoy your shower because the only thing we can do now is wait for our enemies' next move. Here we can rest our bodies and minds, maybe get a few hours of sleep to be better prepared for whatever is coming."

She turned back to me with a mischievous smile. "Are you sure that is all you think we can do after we take a good, deep shower?" She said nothing more but kept walking towards the back. As she walked, she let her tattered dress slide to the floor, showing her form and beautiful buttocks, the gauze fluttering slightly before settling onto the black and white marble tiles, before she disappeared into the shadows created by the dim light at the back of the room.

She reappeared a little while later from the room she had vanished into, her still damp hair tied up on top of her head. She was wrapped in a beautiful satin bathrobe with Chinese symbols; but clearly wasn't from China as it had Versace labels everywhere. Before she even got close to me, I perceived a profound, delicious fragrance in my nose. Like an electric shock in my brain, I was certain I recognized that fragrance but to be sure, I asked, "What is the name of the perfume you have on? It grabbed my attention and awakened my sexuality."

She raised her eyebrows with a small smile, "Do you like it?"

"Yes, very much."

"Well, that is the purpose."

"I not only like it, I love it. But I'm dying to know what the name is because it brings back a distant memory of long ago."

"Oh. Hm. I hope it's not a bad memory, but the name is Paloma Picasso."

I nodded without saying a word, just remembering that was fragrance I had smelled all the time on Lauren. It wasn't precisely the best of my relationships; many years back I was the one who bought that perfume to that beautiful woman who broke my heart. Even though I hold no grudges in my heart for anyone, and I have no complaints about our intimate relationship, the way it ended was not on the friendliest of terms. All those memories flashed back to me for a few seconds, and my face changed from a smiling one to a more serious, as I was transported back into the past. Her feminine instincts caught this, and Atacia asked, "If this perfume brings you any bad memories, I can make it disappear like Houdini in a few seconds. I have others that are more to my preference."

"No, no, no—please," I replied immediately, making a little effort to push my smile back onto my face. To reassure her, I added, "You should not get rid of this perfume. It's always been my favorite and it's clearly suited to the pH in your skin. It makes an extraordinary compliment to you. Under no circumstance should you change it." I added with conviction, "I believe, always, that we should make bad memories disappear, as one nail gets another out, with a good one. That is the only way we can get it out of our minds and maintain our sanity. Memories should always be refreshed, recycling bad memories into new, pleasant ones. The best remedy, as I always say, is to take the devil by the horns. We wipe away those bad feelings and memories and replace them with beautiful, fresh, and most recent ones that will act as a very warm summer breeze, taking away once and for all the leftovers of the ashes of an old, bad memory."

Atacia flopped down on the sofa. She looked at me in mild surprise with a small smile. She placed a hand on one of my knees. "Wow! That sounds so beautiful. I don't know that you were a poet and philosopher, too."

I smiled and put my hand on top the hand which rested on my knee. I stood up, releasing her hand as I did. "I don't intend to be either one. I just say what is in my heart and speak out from the pain of my past experiences."

She said seriously, "Yes, yes. That is why it is so beautiful, and I'm absolutely certain you have had too many of those as you've navigated so many oceans in both the New and Old Worlds." I started to walk towards the bathroom. She called after me, "I left everything necessary for your perfect comfort in the bathroom, adding a royal blue jogging suit. It's only been used by captains of ships—navy blue with golden strips on the sleeves and pants."

I shook my head. "I swear, if I weren't here what I've heard from you, you are either a magician or a mind reader, because those are actually my favorite colors, and I love any clothing related to the sea. But you didn't have to go to that trouble. Any clothes will be better than this wetsuit that I'm wearing. But it's appreciated that you try to please me, and you do it so well with such certainty. Thank you very much."

"You're welcome."

I walked into the bathroom, guided by the light at the end of the corridor. I saw more that made this place look like the backstage of a movie studio set. Fake beards and mustaches, hats of all styles and times, clothing for men and women of different eras, weapons, smoke grenades—everything one could find on a movie set these people had stored here. I could not contain my curiosity and spent more time than I ought to have exploring all these things. Finally, I realized that I would need weeks to carefully go through everything stored there and left them behind to get my shower.

To my surprise, there was hot water. I didn't expect that—but with the propane gas tanks I had seen earlier, they very likely had their water heater connected to one of them. I enjoyed it tremendously as I always like to relax my nervous system of taking a deep bath or hot shower, and I needed relaxation this day.

After I finished my shower, I noticed something which gave me an even greater surprise. Over the vanity, on top of the enormous, long mirror, I saw a bottle of my favorite cologne, Monsieur Givenchy. Ever since sale of it had been discontinued in the States, I had to go through the hassle of crossing the Mexican border into Mexicali or Tijuana to get my favorite cologne. I saw a box at the end of the vanity and opened it. There were twelve more bottles inside. I shook my head with a small smile. I did not recall ever mentioning to this woman that this was my favorite fragrance, and I knew there was no hint of that scent on me after my long swim in the ocean. I shook my head again. Perhaps I had mentioned it on one of previous my trips during an encounter with her. This verged on the border of strange and spooky.

I put on the jogging suit, which fitted perfectly. I sprayed myself with that cologne and looked at myself in the mirror. "Not bad for an old man," I said aloud. "Definitely overdressed for this country and this particular town."

I turned and started to walk back to the room where Atacia waited for me. As I got close, I heard a beautiful modern music song, and instrumental piece, playing on a cassette player. I went into the room and saw she had set up one next to where she sat on the sofa; there was also a small rattan mobile bar by her. The song was "Summer of Love". There was an open bottle of champagne in a silver bucket on top of a transparent plastic tray. Two filled flutes were on the tray next to the bucket, golden bubbles ascending from the bottom of each glass to the surface. Atacia grinned at me joyfully and handed me one of the flutes. "My God, that jogging suit was tailored right for you. You look like a movie star."

"Yes, but not for this country or town, unless I want to be arrested; I just have to show up and they'll put me in jail for being a capitalist. But thank you very much for your compliment."

"Oh, no! Turn around. You look so good; you turn me on."

"Girl, please don't embarrass me."

"No, no—really! You look great in that suit! It defines your upper body so well and shows off the muscles in your torso. It's very attractive; you've told me before on a couple of occasions, and I don't know if you were joking or not, that I woke up your sexual instinct. You do the same—you stimulated my sexual instincts when I saw you come in the room, something I didn't think would be possible after what happened today with those pigs. But as you told me a little while ago, the bad memories we should pull like a bad tooth out of our thoughts and replace them rapidly with ones that are beautiful and fresh to cleanse our minds. I believe I will follow your remedy to the tooth. Afterwards, I will know if you're right or wrong." She said that last with a joking smile on her lips. She put her flute close to mine. "Cheers. Will you please help me to forget those horrible moments I went through today?"

"Of course." I took another sip of my glass before putting it on top of the bar. I took her face in both of my hands. "Love, I will always be at your disposition for anything at any time. Whenever your intentions are noble and good, I will put my life on the line to make you happy and replace those bad memories, so you can forgive. Never forget; but purify your body and spirit with forgiveness. I will be honored for you to have me as a good and great new memory to heal those bad ones."

She put her glass down next to mine and opened her arms. She gave me a strong bearhug. She murmured in my ear very tenderly, "Thank you very much. You are a real gentleman."

"And you are a precious and brave princess, not only for your beauty but also for your courage, which will remain in my memory for the rest of my life. I can never forget that you, in your worst moment, ran in a different direction to avoid jeopardizing my security. When we think of others before ourselves, that is pure love."

She gave me a kiss on the lips which grew more and more passionate as our excitement grew. She unzipped my jacket, leaving my chest open. I removed it and let it drop to the floor. She opened her bathrobe, allowing my chest to caress her breasts very gently. I slowly slipped her bathrobe over her shoulders, allowing it to slide to the floor and unite with my jacket.

As we continued to kiss, she caressed my naked chest with her nails. I very tenderly circled her breasts with my fingers. We slowly let ourselves lie down on the sofa and made love for a long time, until we were both completely satisfied and exhausted.

A little while later, we gazed into each other's eyes, and she caressed her long nails along my face. "Thank you. I don't know if you know this, but this was the first time I have ever been with a man in my brief life."

"Did I hurt you?"

"No. You've been so gentle that I hardly felt any pain at all."

Thunder shook the entire place at that moment. We looked at each other in surprise, not expecting such a loud noise. We heard the metal door open right after the crash of thunder. She put her right hand to her mouth in fear. She reached down to the floor to grab her bathrobe and half-covered her naked body.

As the door opened, a tall, powerfully built man with a long beard appeared, pistol in his right hand. He burst into the room and demanded loudly, "Who is here? Is anybody here?"

Atacia looked at me. I was completely surprised, but she recognized the voice and put her finger to her lips. She called out in reassurance, "Jimbo the Limbo!"

"Yes," came the reply.

"It's me, Atacia!" The man put the gun down, taken by surprise. She turned to me. "Don't worry—it's my paternal half-brother."

I smiled and whispered close to her ear, "Let's hope your brother is not jealous. I don't like that large pistol he has in his right hand at all. It would be ironic to die after all we've been through at the hands of a jealous brother." I made a circle around my temple with my index finger. "Especially if he's in Limbo."

She smiled and hit me on the shoulder. "No, it's not like that at all. I'll explain it to you later. He's an artistic soul but very smart. That's how he earned that nickname in the family. He was born with Down's

Syndrome and so has a great heart that is too big for his chest. His nobility and honor are immense." As she spoke, the tremendous admiration for her brother reflected in her eyes and voice.

I could see the great love and affection she had for her half-brother. I said, "You are very fond of your brother, aren't you?"

She gave me a small smile. "Without limit. I assure you that after he gets to know you a little, you can put your life in his hands. That's something we can't say about many people. He'll put his life on the line to defend you if necessary. It's part of his personality."

I smiled and nodded. "I see now why you are so fond of him. These attributes are not easy to find in anyone, especially these days. I believe that your brother will be my brother as well, and I will appreciate his friendship and trust very much. We need more people like him in this corrupted world."

Atacia smiled. "I hope so. If you get to love him, that will make me very happy." She took the bathrobe and wrapped herself in it before Jimbo got close to us. She raised her voice to call out. "Jimbo, we're back here, sitting on the sofa!"

Jimbo came over to us and saw her still tying her bathrobe on and I was shirtless, dressed only in my jogging suit pants. He realized that he might have interrupted some kind of intimate moment between us. He immediately apologized, showing his embarrassment. With a cracked voice filled with hesitation, he said, "Oh, God! I'm sorry, I apologize for interrupting you guys. But as you didn't show up in the place where you were to bring our contact, I thought something bad had happened. And if you couldn't get to me, it was logical to bring him to this place, the last source of security we have. That's why I decided to look for you here."

Atacia smiled again, trying to reassure him. "No, no—Jimbo, you didn't interrupt anything other than a conversation that we can continue anytime later." We exchanged mischievous glances; since we were already done, it was true that he hadn't interrupted anything. She had never introduced me to any member of her family on any of my previous trips to Caibarien. It hadn't been necessary before; now it was, so she made the introductions.

I held out my hand to Jimbo. "It's a great pleasure to meet you, Jimbo. Your sister is a great woman, and it's a pleasure to meet her brother. My name is Dr. Valentine."

He took my hand and shook it in a very strong grip. He said, "The pleasure and honor are mine. I finally get to meet you, Dr. Valentine. My sister has proudly said many times that you are one of the greatest freedom fighters. You are well-known as a master of disguise and a shadowy ghost that the communists hate and fear. You normally come during the lightning and thunder of a storm and leave in the sunshine. They can never figure out how to get their hands on you for many decades now. You've earned the admiration of all the people of Cuba. You are on the same level as the greatest warriors for the freedom of Cuba, like the Cuban Lightning, the Alpha 66 organization, or the group that former Commander Matos founded, the CID, just to mention a few. All these people have risked their lives for years, several dying in the process, to restore to the Cuban people the freedom we've been expecting for over four decades that the Castro brothers and the Marxist-Leninist system has ripped away out of the hearts of everyone."

As I heard those beautiful words, I could not help but smile mischievously when he mentioned the Cuban Lightning. I said to Jimbo, "Thank you very much, Jimbo. The reality is all Cubans who raise their voices in protest against the abuses and oppression of this Marxist totalitarian regime have my great respect, and I'm very proud to call them not only Cuban warriors and patriots but heroes for our cause, not only here in Cuba but all over the world. The Marxist-Leninists, like the Nazis and all other totalitarian regimes, are like a cancer spread by Satan to destroy our beautiful world. If we don't eradicate this by the roots, they will spread until they destroy without compassion all of humanity at large."

Jimbo stood up from the chair he had pulled up in front of the sofa. Emotionally, he opened his arms. "Will you allow me to give you a hug, brother?"

I smiled, stood up, and took the few small steps over to him. With a big smile on my face, I opened my arms and said, "Of course, Jimbo. I embrace you not only as my brother connected through your sister, but also as a brother in the cause. I will die to defend you and any member of your family."

I felt his emotion as he embraced me in a vast bear hug. As he embraced me, he said in my ear, "Let's hope that whatever emotions you share with my sister bear fruit, and I hope it's a boy, another major patriot for our great fight against the evil of the Marxist-Leninist ideology. Welcome to our family. It gives me great happiness to see my sister Atacia being so savvy to pick you as a good genetic connection to bring to our blood more Cuban patriots."

I smiled. "You don't even know the complete bloodline."

He separated from me, confused. "What do you mean?"

"Those are things we shouldn't discuss yet. I promise I'll give you more details in the future."

He held my arm. "OK, one day at a time. As you say, we're not only looking for the freedom of the Cuban people, but we're looking towards the freedom of every person with good principles and morals around the world united by the values and golden rules of God.

Atacia looked at us with immense joy in her face as she saw that Jimbo and I were bonding together and how he held me in a friendly manner with both of his hands on top of my shoulders. His smile changed and he said in a worried voice with legitimate concern, "You guys don't even know how close you came to being used by the propaganda machine of this regime and the tremendous embarrassment you gave to the entire system. According to what I've heard in town, don't even dare to leave here until everything calms down. Don't let anyone see the two of you together even then. The communists have brought everyone in uniform from the different provinces and are combing the entire area in a search for you.

He looked at Atacia. "You know our father is the assistant to the Prime Secretary to the Communist Party here in Caibarien and all the surrounding towns. He told me a little while ago that news of the soldier that was castrated before the crab statue last night spread all over the island in a few hours. The number of the enemies continues to grow, starting with six, and twelve was the last number I've heard: men dressed in scuba gear, coming out of the ocean, and with an evidently local woman with long, wavy black hair serving as their contact and guide, which he testified as the one who castrated him. He saw her very close." Jimbo looked at Atacia intensely and raised both of his thick eyebrows, as if waiting for confirmation about our involvement in this.

    Atacia nodded. "Yes, I did it. And I'm very proud of it. He's very lucky to be alive. All I did was enact justice. This is not the first time these savage pigs raped young girls in the middle of the night. People are too scared to denounce them, and those that aren't wind up suffering worse than the rape itself as the government retaliates. That soldier should be thankful to him," she added, pointing a finger at me, "my hero. I was going to cut his throat, but he told me that I didn't want to have that on my conscience and suggested instead the castration, which would not only be a psychological lesson to these assassins and evil, Satanic individuals about raping young girls right on the boardwalk, but that it would be more memorable to all of them for many years as a learned lesson to be more decent and better men, treating women with the respect their own mothers deserve. The castration this morning will make them think twice before the next one. Most young girls are under twelve through seventeen or eighteen, minors, little young girls; for God's sake, it's becoming an epidemic in this country, and the authorities, savage, criminals that they are look away because they are either part of it or enjoy hearing the tales. This morning marked an end of terror for the victims. Maybe more people will speak up and force the government to do something about it. The corrupt army and police of this regime have created Hell on this island."

Jimbo said, "OK, guys, I got it. I understand. Did you suffer?" he asked Atacia.

"You must be kidding! I defended myself like a cat on the ground, with the claws out."

"Good. At least they didn't get away with it, at least not with you. But unfortunately, every action creates a reaction, and this one is not good for you guys. You'll have to stay here for a while. You cannot go anywhere. I'll leave now so I don't attract attention at the port. I'll stop by a couple of times a week to check on you. But please follow my instructions. All the roads will be blocked." He pointed to me. "We'll have to postpone your transfer to the capital until everything goes back to normal and they give up. I'm pretty sure someone will be found that they can blame and put in front of the firing squad to alleviate the embarrassment you just created for them. Please," he repeated, "not only for your sakes but for all associated with you guys—including our family—don't move from here. Look at it as a small vacation."

"How little?" I asked.

"I don't know. It all depends on what the government does. But you can be sure it's not just your lives but those of anyone associated with you. Stay here until I let you know it's safe to transfer you to the capital."

"Don't worry about it. Leave in peace; we won't move from here until you give us the green light that everything has settled down."

Atacia gave her brother a big hug. He extended his hand to me, and we shook hands before he drew me into another hug. He said in my ear, "Please—my sister is stubborn. Don't let her leave here. Her life is in every bit as much danger as yours."

"Don't worry. Go in peace. We won't do anything until you return and tell us everything is fine."

He left. After he closed the door, Atacia came over to me with a huge grin. "I'm sorry that you're stuck with me for Heaven knows how long, however long it lasts."

I smiled back. "I cannot think of any better companion with whom to spend a small or long vacation than you."

"Thank you. The same here." She looked into my eyes as she held my chin with her right hand. "Remember, God works in mysterious ways. He knows better why He does what He does. "Maybe, after all, you needed a small vacation, and for me," she added with sparkling mischievous eyes, "it will be the perfect honeymoon. Though we're not married, it will give us a trial period and time that neither of us normally has to get to know each other better. Maybe when everything normalizes in Cuba and freedom and happiness return, maybe we will be the pioneers to start the first family with no shame on our lips from the Marxist-Leninist system." She took both my hands, one at a time, in hers as we slowly sat down, gazing into each other's eyes. She gave me a tender kiss on the lips. As we got more comfortable and the kiss became more passionate, my mind flew back many years to my childhood, when we still lived in harmony before the pestilent boots of Satan and his disciples took over our beautiful island of Cuba.

Chapter 4: The Connection's Link

Guane, Pinar del Rio, Cuba
1953

    I was only six when I began to be plagued by nightmares. Those were bad enough, but I would awaken with scratches all over my body. I feigned forgetfulness of the details of the nightmares, partly because I didn't want to worry them more than they already were, and partly because I didn't understand and was a little frightened of them in consequence. The scratches I had no answers for, anyway, so there was mystery enough surrounding the nightmares. Even my father's brother, an OB/GYN, was perplexed. All he could do was give me a tranquilizer to sedate me sufficiently to sleep the rest of the night. On this latest occasion he took my father to one side to discuss something with him that he knew would be rejected outright, but it had to be tried.

    Uncle Emilio said, "We've already tried everything and performed every test we can do. Physiologically, there is nothing wrong with him. My colleagues at the University of Havana have concluded this is something new. The scratches themselves and loss of memory are entirely inexplicable. You might not believe what I'm going to say."

    "What?" my father demanded.

"Science calls it the genetic connection. Those who believe in the paranormal and spiritual believe it is a spiritual connection."

"For God's sake, don't tell me you believe in that witchcraft!" Papi stood up. "Do you know what you're saying, Emilio?" He gestured to Mima and Majito, our maid who was like a second mother to me. They were standing there in shocked surprise. "They will take what you're saying seriously."

"Science has limitations," my uncle replied. "Sometimes we have to have an open mind and look for answers in a different way when the scientific method isn't enough when looking for answers. We have no answers to what is afflicting your son; we simply do not know. Normally, in any average kid, nightmares and fevers disappear in the first few years of life. We have no answers or any way to respond to the symptoms. In my medical opinion, you should take him to a spiritual doctor to explore what science cannot explain.

He was clearly unhappy and continued distastefully, "You know better than anyone that I'm a doctor and don't believe in these kinds of things. But he's my nephew. Every time I see him like this and have to sedate him, it breaks my heart. I don't know what else to do for him. Let these people try. My colleagues agree and think you might as well try."

"Thank you very much, my brother," Papi said as he hugged Uncle Emilio and kissed him on the cheek.

When I woke the next morning, on a beautiful September day, I saw both Mima and Papi were by my bedside. Majito was in a chair by the corner, either sleeping or dozing. I said, "Good morning, Mima."

She got up and came over to me to hug me. "Good morning. Do you remember what happened last night?"

As I had before, I answered, "No. What happened?"

"Don't worry about it. It's nothing. Let's go have breakfast, and then we have to go somewhere."

Papi said, "My boy is smiling this morning. He looks like he's better."

Mima said, "Yes, he doesn't have a fever. After we have breakfast, we're going to take him over to Gollita."

At that Majito opened her eyes. "Gollita?" She glanced at Papi, knowing his views on the subject quite well. "Are you sure?"

Mima said reassuringly, "Don't worry about it. We had a long conversation about it last night."

I smiled. "OK, Mima. Maybe I can finally go to sleep and not have any nightmares anymore."

"You don't have to fear, even though some people say she's a witch."

"No, Mima," I protested, "that can't be true. My friend Alfredo said she cured his father from headaches he'd been having for years. Doctors tried everything to cure him, and nothing worked. If she cured Alfredo's father, she must be a good person. She can't be a witch."

She smiled at me. "Who do you take after to be so smart?"

"I take after my Mima and Papi."

Mima gave me a kiss. "OK, let's get ready. I'm going to go get dressed."

Majito stayed in the room to get my clothes ready. I looked at her and said, "I don't understand why men hurt other men. I don't understand why there is so much violence."

Majito saw the tears on my cheeks as I looked at the birds flying around outside my window. She began to cry herself, sensitive to my pain as she had literally been taking care of me since the day I was born. I also could never fool her. She said, "I know that you remember these nightmares. You don't want to tell your mother, father, or me because you don't want to scare us." She dried her tears. "You can tell me the truth."

I burst into tears at that. "Yes, Majito—the nightmares are horrible."

"Don't worry, my prince. We're going to put an end to these nightmares. But you have to promise me that you'll tell Gollita everything. You have to tell her everything, no matter how horrible the nightmares are. Do you promise me?" I nodded, but that wasn't enough. "Do you promise me?" she repeated.

"Yes, I promise."

"Let me tell you about a world with a black prince. He wears black clothes, rides a black horse, and has a black heart. He's mean; he's the one that makes people cry. Those born in connection with this black prince represent the bad, the dark, and the ugly. There's another prince, too, a white prince. He wears white and rides a white horse. He shines like the sun. He represents love and beauty, the good and the fair. Everyone born in connection with him is destined to be extraordinary people who would give their lives for the rest of us. Remember that there are people that will make good all their lives. Do you want to be like the white prince or the black prince?"

Without hesitation I replied, "The white prince."

"Even if you have nightmares?"

"I don't care. I don't want anything to do with the bad prince. I want to be good, noble, and full of love."

She smiled and hugged me. "You are a good prince, good, noble, and full of love."

"I love you, too, Majito."

Mima, Majito, and I were driving through town, pulling up to a wooden house. Chickens, ducks, and goats roamed freely around the yard, and strange-looking clothes were hung out to dry on the clothesline anchored to two of the many poinciana trees on the property. Majito gave me a kiss on the cheek and crossed me in blessing. We got out and waited on the patio. Gollita came out and took my left hand. Her eyes registered shock, and then I suddenly was assailed by a man wearing 19th century clothing assaulting a girl in a barn. I covered my eyes with my right arm for a moment and then looked into her eyes.

She let go of my hand and smiled. Majito took my other hand. As we went inside the house, Gollita said, "We have a lot to talk about."

I nodded my head. "Yes."

Once inside, she gestured to Mima and Majito to be seated in some quaint wood and leather chairs. Mima said, "I would like to be present when you talk to him."

Gollita shook her head. "No, my angel—it is between the two of us. You can work with us in whatever comes afterwards."

Majito said to Mima in a soothing tone, "Let her do her work."

We went into another room that was decorated with images of different virgins and saints: Santa Barbara, San Lazaros, the Virgen de la Caridad del Cobre, and more. Different fruits were set out in front of each saint.

"Close your eyes," she said. I felt liquid sprinkled onto my face. "What did you see on the patio when I held your hand? Did you see what I did?" I nodded and opened my eyes. She smiled, closed her eyes, and sprinkled herself with what I now saw was water. "I want you to tell me exactly what you see. We're not going to tell anyone what we see.

    I swallowed hard but did not answer. After waiting for a moment, she smiled. "You don't have to tell me if you don't see anything. I don't want you to make anything up. But if you do see something, tell me so that I can help you."

    I replied, "Of course I see it, of course. I see a grumpy, dirty old man with a beard, drunk and doing bad things to a little girl. He keeps pushing it and pushing it, and it hurts her. He's a bad guy, a bad guy."

    Gollita held me to her. "You see exactly what I see, now tell me what you see in your nightmares."

    "I see people getting their heads cut off. I see what seems to be my grandfather, but who isn't either of my grandfathers, getting burned alive. I see people throwing me into the fire and burning, too. I see men throwing me into the ocean with chains on and then sharks eating me."

    I began to cry, and she held my hand. "Calm down, prince. You are a medium."

    "What's that?"

    "You can see not just the present but also the future and the past."

    "Can you make me sleep better? I don't want to have those dreams anymore."

    She put my hand on her chest. "Can you feel my heart?"

"A little bit." After a few minutes I removed it, feeling disturbed.

She smiled and took my hand again. "Do not be afraid. You saw my loved ones. Some died in a good way, some bad, but they're not going to hurt us. They're just telling us either how they suffered or experienced joy." She placed my hand on her chest again. "I'm going to show you, my prince, sometimes these things are good, sometimes bad; but they are just warning us about life. I'm going to show you how to stop it when you want to.

She took my hand away. "You see, I've disconnected you from me and you don't see anymore. It's like a radio that you can turn on and off."

I smiled. "Yes, I understand."

"I'm going to teach you how to control your nightmares so you can look into the future without fear. OK?"

"Yes."

"You are a white prince and will be for the rest of your life." We got up and went back to the parlor where Mima and Majito waited. Gollita said, "We had a very strong meeting today. He can read me even when we break the connection."

Mima clapped her hand over her mouth in shock. "Oh, my God!"

Majito smiled. "I knew it! I knew I could see that in him."

They came over and hugged me as Mima said, "You see? Gollita is going to help you."

Gollita said, "I need to give him something to drink to put him to sleep, but I'm going to need to see him twice a week."

"When do you need him next?" Mima asked.

"If you're not in a rush," Gollita answered, "right now."

Majito said, "We don't have time to lose."

Mima nodded. "OK, we're not in a rush."

Gollita gave me something to drink, and within minutes I was sleeping—but it was the strangest sleep I ever had. I was told later how she had undressed me and prayed to the Trinity over my naked body. I thought in my dream I heard bells ringing and smelled cigar smoke. I saw the various people again, suffering the agonies, and Gollita appeared in my dream; I started to convulse, so they had to hold me down; the scratches appeared and so Gollita sprinkled me with holy water as (so I was told) she seemed to be speaking with other people in the room. Finally, my convulsions ceased, the visions disappeared, and I woke up to see Gollita taking her hand away from my chest.

"How did you enter my dreams and make them go away?"

"You truly want to know?" she asked.

"Of course, I want to know."

"There are three: one is your great-great-great-grandfather; one is your great-grandfather and his son; and a cousin a few generations removed."

"Well," I said, "if they are all members of my family, I don't think they want to do any harm to me."

"Of course, they don't want to harm you. They just want to protect you, because you are a descendant of theirs. You are a warrior."

"A warrior?"

"Yes, because their lives were all cut short, and they want you to help." She handed me a bucket of water and some soap. "Take a bath, get cleaned up, and then get dressed." I did as I was told but was able to hear their conversation from the next room.

"How long has he been having these dreams?" Gollita asked.

Mima answered, "A couple of years ago, I think."

"It's very important we know," Gollita prodded.

Majito said, "I think it's been longer than a couple of years. Maybe three or four, but because Mr. Leonardo doesn't believe in these things, we never brought him anywhere."

"Three or four years?" Gollita asked.

"I believe three years," Majito replied. "Maybe more. That's when we stopped cutting his hair. Verena promised the Virgen de la Caridad del Cobre to not cut his hair for five years if these nightmares stopped. But when people came to visit the family and saw him with long hair, they would assume he was a girl. That would prompt him to pull down his pants to show he's a boy." Gollilta laughed warmly as Majito continued. "I believe that is why they cut his hair. Verena's been feeling responsible for the nightmares because she broke her promise."

"No, not at all. But these nightmares—do they always come around September?"

Majito sounded surprised. "Yes. Oh, my God! My birthday is this month, and he always seems to have the nightmares around now."

"Did anything extraordinary happen in his family around this time?"

Mima said, "Yes, Leonardo lent his car to his employees. They were going to take my eldest son to a big party, but at the last minute I had a bad feeling and didn't let him go. It turns out they crashed because they had been drinking too much. One died, and another could never walk again."

"Anything else?"

"Yes," Mima said. "Last September one of those heavy wooden machines they use to stretch out mattresses fell on top of him, but because of a cinder block it didn't crush him. It was a miracle!"

"Has anything good happened after these dreams?"

"Well," Mima said, "a couple of days ago I asked Julio Antonio for a number to play in the lottery. He thought I should play 86 because it signifies fire. I won first prize."

"Congratulations, but I'm going to tell you something else: your son is being guarded by three spirits of his ancestors. He will live a long and healthy life. He will also prosper and take you away from here. Unfortunately, it was his great cousin who was beheaded by soldiers, and his great-great-great grandfather who was burned alive. A tyrant tries to conquer the hearts of many people with promises. They try to take power like a false prophet. Your son's destiny is to take away the cloud concealing these false promises, but it will also cause your son a lot of sadness. He will likely have to leave Cuba in an extraordinary way. Not in a plane or a ship, but water will be involved. He will try to stop this tyrant because, like his ancestors, he is a warrior. Don't worry about those scratches—they just mean something is about to happen, sometimes good, sometimes bad. It's like an omen. They happen in September because that is not only when his grand cousin was decapitated and his third great grandfather was burned alive, but also when his great-grandfather was killed by Spanish soldiers. Doctors call this a genetic connection; I call it a spiritual connection. I will teach him how to use it and control it."

I had by now dressed and come down the stairs in time for me to see Mima hugging Gollita in thanks, tears coming down her cheeks. Gollita said, "You don't have to cry. You should be grateful for having such a gifted child."

I came over to Gollita to give her a hug as well. "Goodbye."

"I'll see you tomorrow, my prince," she said.

We got up to leave, and as I sat in the front seat between Mima and Majito I fell asleep. I had another nightmare and woke up just as we arrived home. Mima had noticed and asked, "Were you having another nightmare, my son?"

"Yes, Mima. I saw my little brother Nando nearly get killed."

"Oh, my God!" She patted my head comfortingly. "Maybe it's nothing."

As we started to pull up to the house, we could see Nando playing on his tricycle in the driveway. A salesman was leaving the house and got into the car that Nando was playing behind. It was clear he didn't see the boy and the reverse lights came on as he got ready to back up.

This was exactly what had happened in my dream. From inside our car I yelled, "STOP! STOP!!"

Mima honked the horn to try to alert the salesman, but the car backed over Nando and the tricycle. Nando screamed, but apparently the man didn't hear him. Papi was still heading into the house and had turned at the honking and Nando's screams. He started to yell at the man who, still not comprehending what was going on, put the car into drive to head back into our driveway and running over Nando yet again. Seeing now several people screaming, he stopped his car as Mima put our car in park and, accompanied by Majito ran towards the scene, even as Papi also ran towards Nando.

I remained in the car and closed my eyes. "No." I said softly. I opened my eyes to see them pull the mangled tricycle out from under the salesman's car. I feared the worst, but then saw them pull Nando out. He was scratched up, but OK. Mima took Nando in her arms, crying. I got out of the car and slowly walked towards the scene. I went up to Nando and hugged him. "Nothing bad is going to happen," I said to myself.

Everyone smiled in relief and started to walk towards the house. It started to rain, and puddles began to form. I smiled, and as I looked up at the sky a beautiful, multicolored rainbow appeared beneath the sun.

Pinar del Rio, Cuba
1956

A few years later, the family had moved to the city of Pinar del Rio. I had gotten a spot playing baseball for the city, and we were playing at home in Theodore Roosevelt Park against our rivals from Havana. The score was 6-4 in Havana's favor. They were in red and white striped uniforms, while our team wore blue and white. I was the smallest on the team and due to go up to bat next. My family were all there, cheering us on.

Nando, still a little young to play, was yelling wildly at me. "Hit the ball, Julio Antonio! Hit it hard! Hit it!!"

My sisters, seventeen and eighteen, were also there. Disa, the younger, yelled, "Kick their butts, Pinareños!"

In the meantime, one of the taller kids on the team went up to the coach. "Why don't we have Daniel hit next?" he asked. Daniel was clearly the largest of us, and he smiled a little uncomfortably.

I took my cap off in protest. "Why, when it's my turn to go up to bat?" I was irritated, but it was undeniable that I was tiny in comparison to Daniel. My face took on a look of determination. "I'm going to hit that ball and make them eat dust, because we're going to win!"

I looked around at everyone and saw their lack of faith in me. I threw my cap down. The coach said, "This decision needs to be whatever is best for the team."

I said in resignation, "It would probably be best if you had Daniel go to bat. I believe in him."

The coach shook his head. "It's very good of you, but I think you should go take your turn. But you have to do *exactly* what I say." The team murmurs disappointment with his decision. "Calm down," he said to them. He turned back to me. "Because you're so small, their pitcher will assume you can't hit the ball. All you need to do is touch it. Listen to me!"

I nodded. "Yes."

"They think it will be easy for them to strike you out. Just touch the ball; the two on base will run, and we might be able to tie the game up. If you get on, we could even get the point we need to win this game, so just do as I say."

I smiled. "Don't worry, coach. I know we're going to win."

The other kids still didn't believe in me, but one of them, my friend Alfredo, walked up to me. "I believe in you, Julio Antonio."

I smiled. The other team was getting impatient, and their catcher had removed some gear to reveal that it was my friend Sandra playing in that position for Havana. I winked at her as I walked up to the batter's box, and she put her mask back on. My family cheered as I walked up to the plate, as did Daniel. The other team was all smiles, showing to me that they didn't think I had a chance. I swung at the first to pitches, failing to connect, and the coach called a time out.

He came over to me and said quietly, "Do what I told you to do, or I won't let you play ever again. I'll kick you off the team."

I looked at him apologetically. "OK, coach. I'm sorry."

"Go back to your position."

"But maybe I can't—"

"No buts," the coach interrupted. "Do what I tell you to do."

"OK."

I returned to the plate and gripped my bat tightly as I saw the pitcher smile. He made his pitch, and the impact of the ball hitting the bat jarred up my arm as I hit it as hard as I could. The ball sailed through the air, deep into the outfield, deeper, and right over the fence: a homerun. I stood there in unbelieving paralysis until I heard the coach yell, "Run! What are you doing? Run!!"

I ran all the way around, touching each base as I passed it. With the two runners on plus my home run, we won the game, 7-6. The pitcher for the other team looked very upset, but as I came in to touch home plate, Sandra said quietly, "Congratulations, Julio Antonio."

I had barely time to say, "Thank you, Sandra" before my teammates swarmed out of our dugout and hoisted me on their shoulders.

A little while later we were having a party to celebrate the victory in the backyard of my house. I saw Sandra come from inside the house, accepting some cookies Mima offered her on a plate before coming over to me. "Congratulations," she said. "You guys won for the first time today."

"Are you guys returning to the capitol?" I asked.

"Yes, our bus leaves in half an hour. I just wanted to say goodbye."

"Oh, I'm sorry. I didn't really want to win. I don't care, actually."

She smiled. "No, it's good, because now we can have a rematch. By the way, my parents are talking about moving here. Maybe you can put in a good word for me, and I can join your team."

"Oh, sure!" I exclaimed. "They'll probably want you on the team. You're very good."

"I have to go. I'm happy to see you win."

"Well, you're a special girl," I said. We hugged, and the other kids at the party good-naturedly made fun of us as she left.

Chapter 5: Breakfast in Caibarien

We hadn't slept all night, only dozing in snatches of a few minutes at a time. The noise of the storm was enough to keep us awake, but the sound of pieces of lumber and branches hitting our structure would wake anyone up. This storm was one of the strongest to hit the island for a while. I thought to myself that this was a gift from God, and that He couldn't send me a more beautiful, wonderful present. Due to our situation, even though it might seem a little morbid, the more destruction the storm caused in that town the better it would be for us, as it would distract the repressive forces of the communist government in their search for us.

Atacia said, "I want to show you something, a very great place to be in case we ever get discovered here. It's a really good hideout."

She took me to a small metal elevator with a rusty metal gate in poor condition, though the entire apparatus was still functional—barely. She put it in motion, and it shook like a leaf. I asked, "Do you think this will hold both of us?"

"Don't worry. We use it all the time and so far, no one's gotten hurt."

"This is not a comfort. There's a first time for everything, and I don't want to be the first one to die in this sardine can."

After we reached the top. She managed to slide the accordion gate with great difficulty. She had to use both hands near the top and force the bottom wheel with her foot to open it. Once we finally got out of that rat trap, we walked out onto the roof. There we could see the branches and debris left by the wind. It was a royal mess, but we took great comfort in the now-blue sky, a beautiful rainbow stretching across the horizon, giving a very tropical and picturesque look to that lovely morning.

I helped Atacia to clean off the roof, dropping the branches, boards, and other debris down onto the ground below. She took a little broom and cleaned off a concrete table attached to the roof by screws. She went into the shelter for an air conditioner and pulled out some filthy, rusted metal folding chairs. She cleaned it off with the broom and opened one folding chair with difficulty due to all the rust on the hinges. We managed to open four of them and left the rest. She looked at me with a pleasant, beautiful smile. "What do you think of having breakfast up here? Look at the view!"

I looked at the view, but all I could see what desolation. I didn't want to hurt her feelings, and said, "Oh, the garden looks much better. The winds must have cleaned it up."

She said with a great deal of optimism, "Yeah, the garden was a little abandoned, but those strong winds served us well to clean everything up a little bit."

I smiled and looked at her quizzically. She saw my expression as I said, "Yeah, I see the winds took all the trash and dead leaves and blew them to accumulate along the wall. That reminds me of something my Mima would say when I was a little boy and the maids swept the dust and stuff under the beds: 'bread for today and hunger for tomorrow.' It was a Mickey Mouse job, but I guess it's better to keep it this way so that anyone passing by wouldn't think this was habitable. They won't even dare to trespass. And you're right, it's cleaner than when we came in yesterday. It also helps to get perspective from the height we have above the ground."

She smiled as she opened some more folding chairs, trying to dust them off with her hands. "I don't want you to be a pessimist or get grumpy, OK? Sit down, be comfortable, and be happy."

"I'm going to ruin my beautiful designer jogging suit you gave me on these rusty chairs."

She took her blouse off and laid it on the chair. "There you go, my prince. You won't get your butt dirty."

"You don't have to do that, I'm just joking."

"No, you're not. I saw your hesitation in sitting down."

"Honey, if you only knew what I've been through. I've been in places that are far filthier than these rusty chairs."

"Well, why don't you try to get comfortable and let me go and get some breakfast for us?"

"You're sure you don't want me to help you? My mother taught me to cook, and I could make some beautiful things down there."

"No, no—you stay here and let me do this for you."

"OK, my princess."

She looked at me ironically. "Princess? Or slave driver?"

"I offered," I said with a shrug.

"I would like this to be our first romantic breakfast in this beautiful sunshine which is God's present today. This couldn't be any better for someone's honeymoon."

I smiled and shook my head. "If you continue talking about honeymoon and marriage, you're going to scare the hell out of me to the point that when you come back with breakfast I'll be gone."

She looked down. "It's too high to jump from here, and the only ways out are the elevator or over that edge. The last one who tried that broke both his legs and is still in a wheelchair."

"You know, this is a fire hazard. You shouldn't have brought me up here. An old, decrepit elevator and now you tell me there aren't any stairs? This is worse than a rat trap—it's a death wish."

She smiled mischievously. "Love, I don't think I've treated you so badly that you would prefer to break your legs jumping off this building than being in my company. And I don't see you as a man who gets scared easily, of marriage or anything else."

"No, you haven't treated me badly at all. Your treatment has been first class. It's just that the idea of being married is something I don't take very lightly. Even though it doesn't scare me, like it scares a lot of members of my own sex, this is something I believe everyone should take very seriously and not lightly at all. Marriage should be a sacred union. Some people like it, some people don't, some are born to be married, others aren't, but it should be treated as a commitment and so very seriously. Any commitment between two human beings should be honored properly and taken seriously."

Atacia pouted. She drew very near to me and put both her arms over my shoulders. She said in a very sweet voice that was nearly a whisper, "I'm sorry. I don't want my jokes to scare you in any way, shape, or form. I don't want you to ever believe that I don't take marriage seriously. I promise you that I won't use the word marriage again, even as a joke, not on our honeymoon. OK?" She opened her eyes in feigned innocence as she said this last, accenting the "our" in her phrase. She leaned up and gave me a small kiss and patted me on the right shoulder. "I have a question for you—if you had a choice as to which island in the Caribbean you would go to for a honeymoon, which would you pick?"

I smiled, because in spite of her promise she was continuing. I shook my head. "You have no remedy. You are a lost cause." And I positively grinned.

She laughed and walked towards the elevator. "Sit down, be comfortable. I'll have a couple of little surprises and probably a big surprise for you."

"OK, love. Whatever you say."

She got in the elevator and spoke louder to cover the distance. "You be careful—I don't want you to break your legs, OK? That will be the only thing which would prevent me marrying you."

I shook my head with a small smile. "If that is the case, you will be a very lousy wife. The moment I have no legs you abandon me?"

She laughed loudly. "But you without legs would be a worse husband." She shook her left finger at me scoldingly. She tried to close the rusty, flimsy door for that elevator as she laughed at her own joke.

The elevator descended and she slowly disappeared. I shook my head and stood up to walk over to the edge of the terrace and looked down. I shook my head again—it was easily five story building. I drew near to the edge of the terrace, which had only a flimsy half-torn down railing for safety. As I did, a large piece of concrete, corroded by the lack of maintenance and the tropical climate, came loose under my feet. I jumped back quickly and gasped slightly. I turned my neck to see where it went and saw that it had landed down on the driveway before the main entrance of this once-majestic mansion.

I breathed a sigh and said to myself, "This is even more dangerous than I thought!" I decided to stay away from the edge.

I sat down at the table to wait for Atacia and the promised breakfast. A little while later, I saw the elevator moving, and though this was a little too quick for even a mediocre breakfast.

I saw her walk out of the elevator with a small rolling cart and a big box on it. As she rolled it over to me, I asked if she needed help.

"No, don't worry, stay there. I told you, you're my guest. Remain comfortable."

She began to empty the box of its contents, starting with a loaf of bread, plates, knives, and forks. She pulled out a tablecloth and spread it on top of the concrete table and then distributed napkins and began to remove more contents from the box.

"My God, you've brought a buffet!"

She pulled out a cold meats like Spanish ham, prosciutto, salami, anchovies, sardines, olives, and different cheeses. Finally, she pulled out a bottle of Spanish wine from Bodegas la Rioja, Blanco Brillante, which was my favorite wine. I was so surprised that I could not remain on the seat and grabbed the bottle of wine.

I said, "I can't believe it. You must have psychic powers, or someone debriefed you on my personal tastes and favorites. Did someone give you a psychological profile of me? One thing I know for certain is that you're not a card reader, gypsy, or fortune teller. I cannot believe you have my favorite wine in the entire world. I have to order it directly from Spain because they don't have it in the States. Believe it or not, I would rather have all this food than any other kind in the world."

"Honey, this is not my choice. This is what these people in the government eat, and they bring it in from different countries around the world, and we steal it from them. Even bread—the bread they make here in Cuba is worse than a ball in baseball: chewy, hard, and without flavor. This bread is the best you'll ever eat. They bring it from other countries, freeze it, and then heat it in the oven. When you take it out it tastes fresh-baked. That's what these Marxists do." She winked at me with her right eye with a mischievous smile. "This is really what you like, love? I figured you would like what I do because we have a lot in common. One thing puzzles me—how do you know I don't have gypsy blood? You don't have a DNA sample of my blood.

I smiled mischievously as I tried to open the bottle of wine before she snatched it from me. "You sit down. You are my guest. You do nothing, I do all the work." She opened the bottle and poured two glasses out on the table. She handed one glass to me and raised it up. *"Salud, amor, pesetas y tiempo para disfrutarlas[1]."*

    We continued our exquisite meal, our first breakfast together in Caibarien, and our exuberance made it a pleasant experience. That day was very calm in the aftermath of the storm. Everything looked peaceful to anyone who didn't know what life was really like on that island. They would not even dream at that time that eventually a tremendous terrorist act would be change the destiny of international politics and shake the roots of the modern world. It is hard to imagine cruelty, and it's even harder to imagine the extremes of cruelty our enemies possess. When it comes to imposing their political ideological ways of thinking, our enemies won't stop for anything or anyone, with zero remorse for how many innocent lives their perverse agenda causes in the process. Just to fulfill their plans they are willing to exterminate half if not the entire world's population. That shortsightedness doesn't allow them to see the danger to themselves, how it could possibly cost them *their* lives as well. When you start a fire, it could get out of control and though you're planning to burn a small house you wind up burning the entire town.

    After we finished our breakfast, Atacia pulled out of the box she had brought the food in a small metallic container which looked like the ones used by businesses for petty cash. She opened it and removed something that looked very important by the way it was wrapped up and double sealed in a manila envelope with a cord tied around it. She unwrapped the folders and produced first an envelope which looked like it contained pictures. She retrieved two 8x10 pictures and put them on top of the

---

[1] Health, love, wealth, and time to enjoy them.

table before me, one in profile and the other one front on. He looked like he was an Arab. After I looked at it, she turned them around to show what was written on their backs.

"Be extremely careful with these individuals," she said. "They are the global financiers for the international terrorists. As you know, without finances nothing can be done; with finances you can move the world. Sometimes that can be for the best, and at others for the worse. Behind all this is not millions, billions, but trillions of dollars that are circulating around the world.

Without saying anything, I shook my head. She continued reading the back of one of the photos and pointed specific features out with her index finger. "The code and numbers for this particular individual indicate that he is the one who will serve as our contact as the infiltrator of this fanatic terrorist group. As you can see, in the small print is the amount of money this mercenary expects to receive in exchange for his giving us all the descriptions, actual as well as fictitious names used on the passports that they will use in the next terrorist attack they are planning and for which they have been training here in Cuba for several months now. It is possible they might execute their plan at the beginning of the next year. Our information is that they have accelerated their training, which means they may have advanced the day they are going to hit us, which is why it is imperative and urgent that we obtain all this data from this individual, no matter the price we have to pay. We also have to take into consideration that this man, though willing to give us this information, could be a double-edged knife, perhaps just not a double agent or simply because he's associated with them; I've made absolutely sure he would be under the loupe. Remember that they are trained by foreigners and could be simple mercenaries hired by the Russians or Chinese or even agents for those countries, members of the international communist conspiracy, the Tri-Continental. As you recall, that originated here in Cuba, and one of their organizing leaders was the foul-smelling Che Guevara."

I smiled. "You might be joking, but you don't even know. You never had to walk behind him. He smelled of sulfur and had a stench you wouldn't believe."

"I'm not surprised since he was a son of Lucifer. Like father, like son."

I smiled and shook my head. My expression changed as we continued speaking. I could not help but remember and related some of the times I had spent with Che, like the time he shot his best friend in the head in the middle of a highway with no basis for suspicion at all.

Atacia looked revulsed and raised her eyebrows as she shrugged her shoulders. She said sadly, "I can only imagine the stress and the revulsion you must have felt when you had to walk so close and sometimes behind that sadistic assassin who brought so much misery and mourning to so many Cuban families."

I shook my head without replying. I flashed back to all the times I had to pretend nearly twenty-four hours a day, since these people scarcely ate or slept, continually forcing me to be on my guard to avoid being caught.

Atacia brought out what appeared to be a diary and handed it to me. "If you want to show anyone who the leader of this revolution, Fidel Castro, really is, you have undeniable proof in his own handwriting. He was writing his secret memories for those closest to him as a blueprint for anywhere they send the seed of hatred and international terrorism, from the American continent, to Africa, Europe, and Asia. He scarcely imagines that it could be published all over the world. You have the proof in his own hand that he has partaken in every macabre, conniving assassination to take over peaceful, democratic societies."

I took the book in my hand. "Is this really Fidel's personal diary?"

She nodded and smiled mischievously as she raised her eyebrows again. "Yes, my lovely friend, Dr. Valentine. My cousin, Gladys, has been the mistress of Castro for many years. She took this from beneath the mattress of Castro's bed."

I immediately asked, "Do you know what happened to her? I've not heard from her for years and lost my contact after our last job together in Africa. No one in our group ever heard from her and doesn't know what happened to her."

Atacia shook her head. She looked at me sadly. "None of us has ever seen her again. That doesn't surprise me at all. That's what the Castro brothers are famous for here in Cuba—making people conveniently disappear. They must have a personal crematory in which they reduce the bodies to ash to be flushed down the toilet. The best scenario is that they killed her because she knew too much about them, all the dirty laundry of the entire family and the corruption of the Castro brothers, sons, and nephews, who have been living for decades like kings and queens as parasites on the Cuban people. After the diary disappeared, the logical conclusion must have been for Fidel to arrive at would be her because of how close she was to him."

She spoke with conviction. "I can assure you no matter how hard they pushed her, she would never have admitted to anything because she was a true warrior. I have proof of that. If she had started to sing, someone from the communist party of the G-2 would have knocked on my door a long time ago. The only thing we can think of is that after they tortured her without getting any information, they decided to get rid of her." She spoke with pained sorrow as she spoke now. Tears rolled out of her eyes. "Poor Gladys. Heaven knows what these horrible people did to her body. I hope she didn't suffer and died quickly. As the people of Cuba know, the G-2 are masters of making people suffer, from cutting off fingers to castration to mutilation of a woman's clitoris to the most horrible things one human being can do to another. One thing I must tell you: be careful with this diary."

"This is for me?"

"Yes, that is the original. I have copies in different secure places. If anything happens to you or me, someone else will be able to eventually bring it to the eyes of the public. It's a complete confession of the monkey business from drugs to extortion to assassination, any vile crime that a head of state could commit against his or her own people. The most interesting and revealing aspect of this diary is that the people we thought were on our side have been supporting and receiving enormous payments and benefits from the transactions of drugs and even child prostitution around the world, organ harvesting, all with the purpose of poisoning the entire world, destroying all democratic societies and their youth—this is all part of the plan to dominate the world. They don't care about the consequences."

I leaned over the table and took her right hand to hold between my two hands. I kissed her on the cheek. I understood her emotional state. In a reassuring voice and in a tone of conviction, I said, "Atacia, I can assure you that this will never happen on my watch. At least for as long as I am alive. If necessary, I will stop these people one way or another with the last drop of my blood."

She looked at me this time trying to force a smile, which only managed to form as a pained smirk. With tears in her eyes, she replied, "What can you do? They are many, you are only one."

I smiled and spoke with conviction. "What about you? Your father? Your brother? What about the hundreds, thousands, or even millions of women mutilated by the G-2? The orphaned kids who lost their parents to the firing squad? I'm not alone—I can assure you of that. You're not alone. We aren't alone. Behind the dream of power and global control that they have, you just have to recall that this is just a repetition of history. Look back at the German Nazis and Hitler. We are the modern Jews that have been dispersed around the world, forced by these tyrants to leave our homes, families, and everything we've worked for our entire lives. My father worked for thirty years of his life to have a comfortable lifestyle, but that's no longer a future for anyone in Cuba. How did the Nazis end? Like every murderer in history, because there's a Supreme Being watching all of us. All the Nazis that partook in these atrocities, how did they end up? Accused and tried for crimes against humanity, over 500 of them hung or shot. Those that managed to escape spent the rest of their lives being chased by their former victims. Those families clamoring for justice, for them to be returned to pay for their crimes, oblige these fugitives to live like rats, hiding in fear of being recognized for their crimes, living under false identities. In the end, they wound up in the same or worse situations their victims' families had to live in. You have to remember that history flips like a tortilla omelet, and the persecutors become the persecuted."

She looked at me in frustration. "When will this happen? We've had nearly forty years now of persecution and abuse. The Nazis were only in power a little over a decade, from 1934 to 1945."

I smiled ironically and nodded. "You cannot compare Cuba to the Nazis because it's like comparing apples to avocados. As we say in Cuba, there's no disease that lasts one hundred years and even if it happens, no one can resist it for that long." I shook my head. "Believe me, I ask myself the question you just asked many times, and I perfectly understand your frustration. I ask myself how long these despised Marxist-Leninist communists will be in power, with Stalin in his Soviet paradise killing more people than Hitler and his Nazis killed in Germany and elsewhere in the world. A hundred years is a lot of time. We might need to change that saying. Let's hope that this never reaches that mark. Russia was communist for seventy-four years before the collapse of the Soviet Union. If this happens in Cuba, neither you nor I will ever see Cuba free again. That is why we need to be optimistic and continue fighting for our freedom until the last day of our lives."

She looked at me teary-eyed. She wiped her eyes with a napkin from the table and recovered her composure. "Let's take all this left-over food and go back inside. I want to give you a tour in case we have a serious emergency of a secret tunnel we have beneath the room we were in before. It connects this old mansion with the ocean. In case we get caught and have no other exit, I want you to know all the exits in this place. Instead of making this a honeymoon, it would turn into a rat trap with no exit and cost you your life. Just in case I'm not around with you."

I smiled at her reference to the honeymoon but otherwise ignored the comment. Instead, I asked, "What about it? Have you been thinking of abandoning me in case we get into a fight and get a quick divorce?"

She genuinely smiled. We put the remaining food back in the box and returned to the elevator. A few minutes later, and she showed me how to remove the Egyptian rug and move the sofa, revealing a trapdoor in the floor. She took two kerosene lamps and lit them, handing one to me, and we descended some metal stairs beneath the trapdoor. The walls were of cut rock, making it look like a wine cellar which must have dated back to the Spanish Colonial period. It looked like a natural cave with a small stream of water trickling down the middle. The rocks looked very sharp, which she reaffirmed. "Be careful—you can cut your arm open if you fall on one of them."

We continued through the humid, wet environment, carefully picking our way along the sharp, rough rocks which made up the floor, lit by the kerosene lamps. Slowly we continued until at the end of this tunnel we saw a spot of light ahead which grew larger and brighter as we moved beneath the ground of the old mansion.

Chapter 6: Divine Justice

The cave had a giant mouth, but all covered by mangroves, but the late afternoon sunlight pierced through the overgrowth. As the tide went out, this made the cave accessible because regularly the water completely filled the cave, leaving a small lagoon tide pools when it went out. This erosion left small pockets along the cave wall. Atacia put both of her hands into one of the cracks in the wall and pulled a thick plastic bag out. She unwrapped it to reveal several sets of underwater diving gear: fins, snorkel, mask, and underwater knife as well as several belts with pieces of lead attached to act as underwater weights. She handed me one complete set and took another for herself. She wrapped the rest into the bag and replaced it inside the hidden fissure.

She said, "Maybe we can have fun doing a little diving, but it's very important to bring this with us when we leave the cave. If we come right back, it's not a problem, but if the tide gets in it will fill the cave, and the only way to get back inside is to snorkel."

I smiled. "Excellent natural hideout and unbelievable security door to this cave. No one would ever imagine that this exists."

She smiled mischievously. "Maybe our ancestors who had been warriors had hunted like we do and learned to protect themselves by becoming professional spies, not because they chose it but by necessity. Of course, it's easy for human beings to think the worst; that's why they used this natural hideout and made that cellar under the house with this secret passage as an emergency exit. The ocean is the door in and out to anywhere in the world. It makes no difference which country you want to go to, there's a way in and out most of the time to that country through the ocean. It's also an enormous fountain of nutrition to survive on for anyone persecuted by social injustice and corrupted governments, especially these days, when they grow like weeds in every single corner of the world."

    I smiled again as we went through the brush to the beautiful beach of transparent blue water and sand like pure white sugar cane. "OK, let's forget about all these troubles and the craziness we go through each day, forget the rest of the world, and explore this beautiful sunny day and take a few hours of relaxation under the ocean. We could never be safer than down in the ocean. Let's spoil ourselves and be selfish for one single day."

    As I put my underwater equipment on and tied the belt around my waist with a large shark knife, I took a couple of the lead weights and put them in a sand dune with some bushes around it. As we prepared to go diving, we had to remove our clothes, leaving only our underwear to put on the wet suits. As we were getting undressed, we checked each other out, as was natural in our situation. We leaned into each other to exchange a kiss.

    She said, "We should save this for later, or we won't have enough energy to be in the ocean for very many hours. Believe me, this is my favorite sport, ever since I was a little girl. I used to go with my parents on my father's fishing boat. It's been many years since I've been able to go diving myself." She looked at me. "If you remember, we met the first time underwater."

    "Yes, I remember very clearly how I met you underwater off the Yucatan Peninsula."

"I remember that day as if it were yesterday. I was with all my family, my parents, my brother, and a few members of the crew. Everybody saw a small plane approaching the boat in between lightning and thunder, but coming so dangerously straight towards us because it looked like the lightning had damaged the fuselage of the plane. I saw clearly the lightning strike. I was still in the water in my scuba equipment, floating back up. I removed my mask and saw how my mother, father, and the rest of the crew, jumped overboard because it looked like that plane would crash into the boat. Thank God, the plane missed us, crossing instead about four or five feet above our boat and crashing into the ocean. I remember my mother and father yelling at me to get out of the water because the plane could explode as they swam to get back on board themselves. But that day I had a strange feeling that something extraordinary would happen, and I'm always thinking about helping others. I wondered if anyone in that plane could still be alive, and ignoring the yells of everyone else I put my mask on and went down to look for survivors. Thank God I did that.

She came close to me with a mischievous smile on her face and kissed me tenderly on the lips as she caressed my face with the back of one of her hands. She added softly, "I had the feeling that my prince who I would someday give my virginity to was there and that this was the day we would meet. I don't know if I ever told you this before, but with scarcely any air in my lungs, I dove down to where you were at the bottom of the ocean and managed to grab your jacket and gave you the air left in my lungs into your mouth. I don't know where I got the strength, but God provided it to me, and I managed to bring you up out of the rough waters of the ocean. You remember the rest, how you stayed with us for a while until you recovered and got to know us. I was only a teenager at that time, and you were so much older than me, and I never thought that you would make my dream a reality." She gave me another tender kiss. "Thank you for literally coming to me from the heavens and converting a daughter of a humble fisherman, Bonifacio Bonaparte, in the happiest princess of the port of Caibarien."

I embraced her and kissed her passionately. "You are extremely important to me, and the most precious gift God ever provided, not only for saving my life but because you returned to my heart something I never thought I would have again: love. After I had a tremendous deception and treason from a woman who was supposed to be my love at the time, I never thought I would find that again in my life. You brought to me the happiness I've been wishing for all these years."

Atacia stepped back a little, holding my hand and looking deeply into my eyes. She looked at me with sincerity in her eyes and voice. "Really? Really, love? You mean that?"

"Why? Do you doubt that?"

"I'm sorry. I don't want to upset you, but many times I've felt that you're more grateful than feeling the same kind of love I feel for you."

We embraced and I put both my hands on her shoulders. "Yes, I won't deny to you that I have an immense gratitude toward you, but that's just one more compliment to add to the respect, admiration for your character and the dedication you have to the freedom of our country, willing to give your life, if necessary to bring freedom to our people. That's called integrity and moral commitment. This is the biggest and most wonderful formula that anyone could expect from their other half. This is what is the perfect soil to grow a great love and romance that no one can ever break.

"That is why when I think of you, sometimes I pinch myself thinking that you're not real and that you're just a beautiful dream that I converted myself in my mind into reality. I know I have a great imagination. Later, however, when I'm by your side and you prove with your natural attributes and produce the greatest, most beautiful satisfaction and conduct yourself in the most beautiful, unselfish manner. You could have run in my direction instead of away, but you thought of my safety before your own and ran in the opposite direction." I bit my bottom lip to contain my emotion. "You're not a beautiful woman physically, but you possess the greatest kind of beauty anyone can have, which is never changed by time, and that is your spirit. That continues for all eternity."

She took my face between her hands, tears of happiness in her eyes. "Those beautiful words I will save in my heart for as long as I live." She gave me a tender kiss which then grew more passionate.

"I thought we were going to save this energy," I said teasingly.

"We're young, we have enough," was her only reply.

We had not yet completely dressed, so we ignored what she had said initially, removing what we had put on behind the bushes and let our bodies settle onto the beautiful white, sugar-like sand to make love beneath those beautiful blue skies as tropical sun dipped towards the horizon.

Afterwards, completely satisfied, we began to finally go into the water. I cut a stick from a mangrove which had the perfect angle to make a spear and attached a cord at one end to hold onto it in case we might catch any fish during our adventure. Like two teenagers in love, we finally started to explore the bottom of the ocean, not swimming too far from the shore. We found several lobsters and a couple of small fish that I was able to snare with my improvised spear. After several hours, we got out of the water, dried as best we could in the twilight.

The tide was making, so she said, "We'd better hurry, or our way in won't be as smooth as our exit was."

As we prepared to leave the bushes where we had left our clothes, we heard loud voices and yelling followed by gunshots. We ducked down behind the dunes to hide and observe. A very authoritative voice yelled at a man running along the beach, "Stop, or you will die here today!"

They were getting very close to where we lay hidden. I signaled for her to stay down. The light had nearly disappeared, leaving the beach in shadow. We hadn't noticed the passage of time underwater. In life, when we do what we enjoy and have a great companion, time flies. Since the underwater diving was the favorite sport of both of us, we didn't notice how fast it had flown by; not counting only the fishing, we probably made love at least twice that I remember. Being young, physically fit, and having a strong attraction to each other, combined with being practically naked, was a strong combination to arouse one so many times.

We were both exhausted and looking forward to returning to the old mansion, showering in fresh water, and eating all the delicacies that were waiting for us there; we were both very hungry as well. But as we heard the yells and shots, I prayed to God and His Son, Jesus Christ, "Please don't complicate this night and allow us to return safely to our own hiding place, especially after such a wonderful day."

The sun was nearly below the horizon, leaving only a thin line of flame and deepening shadows while the distant shots continued to ring out. I saw Atacia getting pale, fear in her eyes. Her voice broke as she whispered, "That voice I just heard was my father's." She put her index finger on her lips for silence.

I was slightly confused. I had no idea what was going on there. I started to explore to see what was going on. I could see clearly now two men with powerful military flashlights. They were very young, wearing military pants with T-shirts, like typical G-2 Cuban intelligence. They were kicking a man on the sand perhaps twenty feet from us. The one who looked like the leader said very loudly, "You are a spy! We've been looking for you for a long time." He pointed his submachine gun at the man. "You are a worm and a traitor. You will die here today. We'll leave your body here, and once the tide reaches its height you will become shark bait."

The man defended himself and spoke—it was indeed Bonifacio. I felt bad, but without any weapons I had no way to help him. He tried to convince them that they had made a mistake. "You are wrong. Yes, I'm a spy, but I work for the revolutionary government! I've infiltrated the counter-revolution."

The leader yelled, "That is a Chinese tale! You can tell this to your colleagues in the communist party where you work, but not to us. We know who you are. We've been on your tail for a long time, and we have enough evidence. You can confess to us now or we can kill you now. You are the leader of the counter-revolution of this entire zone if not the whole country. You've involved your family, and they'll go down with you, including your wife, Aurora. She is your connection with the US base in Guantanamo. Confess, you goddamned traitor, before we kill you!"

He put his submachine gun and pointed it at Bonifacio's chest. Atacia put her hand over her mouth and tried to get up, but I held her down and signaled for her to stay put. I had a plan. I had been thinking about how to get her father out of this situation, but after Aurora's name had been mentioned, it was clear that they knew about the entire family. I decided to play a very dangerous game. I took my knife out in my left hand and took Atacia's knife from her waist. I whispered to her with my finger on her face, "Stay put. Don't complicate things; let me handle it."

She nodded. I was very satisfied with her trust in whatever I had in mind.

I jumped out of our hiding place with both knives and clashed them over my head to get their attention. "What is going on here, *compañeros*? This is not the proper way to deal even with our enemies, and I know this man. He is the secretary to the General Secretary of the Communist Pary in this town. What have you got against this man and what are you doing?"

I walked towards them with the two enormous knives held high in a non-threatening manner. They turned their attention towards me, totally distracted and training their weapons away from Bonifacio. The leader yelled at me, "Who the hell are you and what are you doing here at this hour in a military zone?"

I smiled. "Of course. I'm a special agent for the MQ-1 and work directly with a special team in the office of the Prime Minister in Havana. To use your same language, *que coño estan ustedes hacienda aqui? Carajo!*[2] What the hell are you doing here in this zone so far away from civilization beating my comrade Bonifacio Bonaparte, who is my contact with the General Secretary of the Communist Party here as well as a personal friend?"

They stood there silently for several seconds in total surprise. I used that to yell at them, pretending to be angry. "Can both of you explain to me why the hell you're still pointing your weapons at me? Am I an enemy, like my comrade Bonifacio? You'd better have your facts straight, or you're going to be in a lot of trouble! Maybe you'll both be sent by your superiors to a reeducation camp."

Both young men looked at each other and automatically lowered their weapons simultaneously. The one who appeared to be the leader said hesitantly, "Can you please show us some identification?"

"Of course, since you can see I'm half-dressed and you interrupted me. I have it back there." I said over my shoulder, "Atacia, please bring my ID from my shirt." I turned back to them. "In return, I want to see your IDs as G-2 or members of the Interior Ministry. Both of you!"

"Very well," they replied nearly in unison.

As they looked into the front pockets of their pants, they took their eyes off of me, the guns pointed towards the ground. I had studied them while I spoke with them, saw how they held their weapons, and knew where I wanted to target on their bodies to neutralize them

---

[2] What the hell are you doing here? Damn!

without killing them. That was my moment. Still with my arms upraised, I threw the knife in my right hand to the man on my left, while at the same time the knife in my left hand was thrown into the man on my right. Both knives were flung into the right shoulders of each man, against which they had braced their submachine guns. The impact from the knives hitting them knocked them down in their utter surprise.

    Bonifacio, being an old wolf of the ocean, was very fit and understandably angry, he jumped onto the leader before I could act to return the assault and mistreatment. He pulled the knife out of the man's shoulder and before our astonished eyes cut the man's throat. Without wasting a second, he jumped on the other man, now terrified after seeing what had been done to his partner. Bonifacio left the knife in the other man's shoulder and cut his throat.

    As he took the submachine guns from the men, he kicked them in their chests, and the young man rolled in the sand. He looked up at me directly in my eyes, and I saw his tears of frustration and anger. Atacia and I were in shock. He said, "You don't know what these degenerate communist criminals are capable of doing." He pointed at the fly in his pants. There was a large amount of blood. He put his hand in one of his pockets and pulled out something like the neck of a chicken. He dropped the bloody knife and yelled, "This is what they did to me—they've cut off my testicles. They said an eye for an eye, and this was in retribution for the soldier the other night." He looked at us with tears in his eyes and took his left hand to his mouth and let out an extremely long scream of anger and agony. He fell to his knees to the sand as he dropped what he had in his hand. He put both his hands over his head and screamed again that loud, terrifyingly agonized scream which came from his guts.

Atacia had walked up to me, completely frozen at that sound. We looked at each other in the darkness. She started to walk very slowly towards her father. She came to one of the young men and then the other. Then she put her hands on top of her father's head tenderly. She said, "Dad, it's all over now. Calm down. God knows that what you did was simply justice. You're not like them. You have to live with yourself and put this out of your mind. We know the evil these people are capable of doing. If it's any consolation, I'm the one who castrated one of those soldiers because they tried to rape me. Thanks be to God that they didn't get away with it. What you did is divine justice: eye for eye, tooth for tooth."

Chapter 7: The Link to Kenya, 666

I saw Bonifacio's emotional state and approached him. I understood the agony and humiliation he was going through because of that physical act which criminally assaulted his masculinity, so I tried the best I could to minimize his pain with compassion. "I'm really sorry, my friend, with all my heart. I don't know what I would be capable of doing if it were me. I think the worst that could happen to those guys has already been done. What else can you do? Kill them again? Clear your mind and don't have any remorse. What you did is exactly what I would have done if I were in your situation. Now I believe the most important thing that we must focus on is to put your wife Aurora and your son Jimbo in a very secure place. I know these Marxist criminals' techniques, and they will be next on the list for these vindictive criminals. I don't believe either you or Atacia want to see anything bad happening to either one of them."

My words made him feel a little better; only he knew what torment he was going through. I needed him to wake up to reality and stop feeling sorry for himself, and the best way was to get him to concentrate on those he loved the most. He shook his head and looked at me. "You're right. I know these people. I've lived in their guts for too long. It is what the Castro brothers do. To prevent retaliation against their dictatorial regime, they also use it to scare the hell out of the rest of the population as a psychological weapon. It's the only way they can maintain their power. It's worked for them for decades, and they learned it from the German Nazis and the Russian Stalinists."

I realized that my words had entirely woken him up, and he knew the danger that Aurora and Jimbo were in. He managed to stand up but wobbled a little. If it weren't for the rapid aid from Atacia and me, he would have fallen onto the sand like a sack of potatoes. I supported him with one arm around my neck while she took the other around hers. He managed to walk with us towards the cave, leaving the bodies of those two young G-2 agents who, in their blind political ambition and search for brownie points and personal credit, had forgotten basic decency for human life, had committed the vilest act against any man. They did that very likely to many people before; now they had found the wrong man.

I turned to look at the tide, which was perceptibly getting higher. The bodies behind us began to float as the tide reached them. I started to see that the prediction they had threatened Bonifacio with would come true for them: food for the sharks. More and more fins broke the surface as they began their circle around the bodies. Very soon a feeding frenzy broke out.

We were at the mouth of the cave and got through the mangroves. The tide still wasn't high enough to swim, but I imagined the sharks eating those two agents, and thought how fragile the line between life and death was. I felt, if I were honest with myself, a little remorse, for I never enjoyed the thought of taking another human being's life, even though I could perfectly understand the situation. Those men may have had a wife and kids waiting for them at home, and those people would never know what happened to husband and father. Even though these G-2 men were careless with their lack for respect for human life, they themselves came to a violent end. They were human beings, and it still bothered me to see them devoured by the sharks.

With this little remorse in my mind, we reached the metal stairs which led to the upper rooms of the old mansion. The water was up to our necks at this point, and one at a time starting with Atacia, helping Bonifacio up the stairs by holding one of his hands. I followed last, carefully helping him set his feet on each step, as I tried to prevent him from falling, which would be more difficult for the rest of us and would consume too much time with the tide making. We finally managed to get up the metal staircase, utterly exhausted as we entered the room and let ourselves lie on our backs on the thick rock for about fifteen minutes. Nobody moved as we caught our breath during our brief rest.

Suddenly, Bonifacio jumped up as if he had been injected with epinephrine. He sprang to his feet without any aid, his eyes bulging wide open as if he had seen a ghost. He took his wet shirt, leaving his waist exposed with two elastic belts which held what appeared to be a waterproof money belt. He twisted it from his back to his front before his stomach and opened the zipper. He pulled out a plastic sealed bag, removing some pictures and documents. He untied the sash and let it drop to the ground.

With an expression of satisfaction, he checked the documents to ensure they were dry and held them up high. "This is what these sons of devils were looking for to put me in front of the firing squad—they didn't even notice this when they searched me. These unscrupulous idiots were looking for a promotion or a hero's medal from this socialist regime, possibly another from the international proletariat. They don't care that this exposure would cost me my life."

He handed the documents to me and said, "Please, make sure that these documents wind up in the right hands. Protect them with your life if necessary. It cost the life of my contact, who they probably tortured and killed before impersonating him. They tried to make me believe that they were his replacements. Thank God I've been well-trained, and it didn't fool me. I just strung them along for as long as I could, until they realized I wouldn't break and began to torture me any way they could find. It nearly cost the life of Aurora because she was the one who was supposed to deliver this to our contact in the Guantanamo Navy Base. Thank God she hadn't been feeling well. I don't think, had she been caught, that she would have been able to withstand the degradation and torture that they put me through."

He showed me his right hand. All his nails had been torn off. He reached down toward his groin. "I didn't care if they took every nail on my hands and feet but taking my testicles—that was the worst thing anyone could do to an enemy. I still can't believe they would do such a thing." He spoke with tremendous sadness; he tried to hold it in, but a couple of tears escaped his control. He shook his head in resignation. "But in the end, they got a lot worse. Thank God and to both of you guys, the omelet turned in my favor."

Atacia interrupted. "Papa, with all my respect, and I appreciate your including me in that, but I did nothing. Not because I didn't want to, but I entrusted all my hope in Dr. Valentine. He told me that if I did anything I would make it worse, and to let him handle it. He did that very well, and he resolved the problem. Don't you agree?"

He nodded. "Yes, he handled it very well.

Then Atacia said to both of us, "We have to say thanks be to God and Dr. Valentine. Honor to who deserve honor. I did nothing."

I shook my head. "You don't have to thank me for anything. It will always be a pleasure to protect and help you. We all have to thank God and His Son, Jesus Christ, because if there were more than two of them, everything would have been different, and we wouldn't have gotten out of that so easily."

We all sat down comfortably on the sofa. I looked through the documents and pictures Bonifacio had given me. Atacia asked Bonifacio, "Where is Mama? And what happened? How did you get into this situation? Why did they have such suspicions of you? Those men from the G-2 had to have some kind of foundation."

Bonifacio said, "Why don't we refresh ourselves? My stomach is groaning like a volcano. Later, when have time and calm, I'll give you the whole tale." He said with conviction, "You have nothing to worry about with your Mama and brother. They aren't in any kind of danger. I'll tell you later with all the details, so you understand better, but those agents acted for themselves. They weren't under any orders from anyone. Just as a precautionary measure, I will bring your mother and brother to stay with us here tonight, even though these two agents wanted to get the credit for themselves for my capture. They told me they had not told anyone of their suspicions against me. They wanted to get concrete evidence against me to bring their superiors. That's why they desperately needed my confession. But if you don't mind right now, I want to take a shower, clean my wounds, and get my mind in order."

I nodded. "I have no problem. You go ahead and take a shower first."

Atacia added, "By the time you've finished your shower I'll have some food and drink, so at the end of the day we'll have a splendid dinner."

Bonifacio said, "Thank you very much, my angel." He turned to me. "Thank you very much, Dr. Valentine, my savior." He took my right hand in both of his. With a small smile he finished, "Will you excuse me now, please?"

I replied, "Take all the time you need and be comfortable. We're not going anywhere and will await you here." I held the documents up and added with a small smile, "I can assure you that I've been waiting for you with anxiety and curiosity. I'm pretty sure I'll have many questions about these documents and pictures."

He walked towards the bathroom as Atacia got some food ready. I sat on the sofa and took the time to look at the material carefully, one at a time. I was full of curiosity to find out what he considered so valuable that he put his life and that of his family's, literally losing his testicles in the process.

Atacia came over to me with a little plate of crackers, cream cheese, ham, covered in red salmon caviar. She held it in front of my face. "You should eat something. You must be as hungry as I am. We spent all day long without having a single bite of anything. These are extremely delicious."

"I believe you." I took one of the crackers and crammed it all in my mouth. Around my mouthful I said, "I'm not hungry. I could eat a bear alive. That's more than hunger."

"By the time my father finishes his shower, you'll feel a lot better if you eat this and drink a little wine." She put a glass of chianti down next to me and filled another glass for herself. She ate another cracker. I could see she was enjoying it very much as she took a sip. Her expression was one of total satisfaction. "God, these appetizers are better than any food I've had before, even the entrees. Maybe it's because I'm so hungry or because it's the first food I've tasted all day."

"You're right—the first food of the day we eat takes our palate by surprise, and it becomes a heavenly joy because you want it so much. I normally eat so many hors d'oeuvres before dinner that I cannot finish my meal. But I like to fill myself up with something that I like rather than something mediocre like dinner. My mother always criticized me for being impatient; but it's only a question of choice and taste. I prefer the appetizer over regular food."

She smiled as she chewed on another cracker. "It's extraordinary how two people who were born and raised in completely different environments can be so alike in taste and preference."

I grinned broadly. "That is a miraculous coincidence when it's not even close to being a genetic connection. It's more divine energy which puts two beings together who sometimes then spend their lives together forever. Call it divine magic, the Great Architect of the Universe, God, Jehovah, or Yahweh."

Our conversation stopped abruptly as I opened an envelope and looked at a picture. My jaw dropped. "Oh, my God!"

Atacia scooted close to me on the sofa, putting her wine glass down on the small table to see the picture I held in my hand better. I still had an expression of utter incredulity.

I spoke softly, nearly a whisper. "Now I understand more clearly. Who could imagine it?"

She looked at me, unable to contain her curiosity. She impulsively held out her hand gently. "Excuse me, let me see." She snatched it out of my hand without waiting for an answer. "Who the hell is this guy next to Che? His face is familiar, but I cannot place it in my memory."

I smiled. "That is Barack Obama, Senior."

"Oh! This is a communist and a leader in the Kenyan government, a senior economic analyst in the Ministry of Finance?"

Figure 8 Barack Obama, Sr passport photo and Kenyan communist flag

"Yes. It's very possible your father introduced him to the entire family when he visited Cuba, trying to establish Barack Obama, Junior's financial foundation which would support Putin's plans of placing a plant in the White House. This individual is supposed to be the key player who will spread Marxist international ideology around the world, backed up by the Tricontinental, Che, and the Castro brothers with Putin's Utopian dream of returning Russia's power through the reconstruction of the Soviet Empire. This time covering the entire world."

Market Madness: Your Sur

U.S. New & WORLD

Obama Campaign Fined Big Donors, Keeping Illegal Don

The FEC levied one of its largest fines ever against Obama's c new documents show.

Figure 9 Article about Barack Hussain Obama's questionable donations for his Presidential campaign

I hadn't noticed that Bonifacio had already returned from his shower and was about five or six feet away from us in the doorway, wearing a nice brown jogging suit, the tag still around the neck. He was listening to my conversation with his daughter; evidently, he had been there long enough to hear me. He clapped his hand in applause with a smile. "Bravo! Right on, 100%. But a lot of people don't know it because there's only one original and two copies of this envelope of what you hold in your hands right now. Exposure of this could break apart all the grandiose dreams of all these Marxists. It is a copy of the signatures, the bank accounts, and original papers authorizing the only people able to move money out of the Swiss banks with key codes. You hold a photocopy of one copy. Record of the negotiations and stuff the Castro brothers wanted one copy far away from the capitol in this little port town, buried in a high tech safe in an office of the communist party here, where no one would ever find it. Only the General Secretary and I have the codes for that safe. Fidel Castro has the original, and the other copy is in Raul's hands, the only person he trusts. Now let me tell you something that you may know a lot about, but not everything: these documents cost Che Guevara his life when he tried to blackmail Fidel during their falling out and was the reason Castro sent him away and provided none of the promised help, completely abandoning him to his luck—to silence him."

    I shook my head. "That is something I didn't know. We're all learning, every day. Not only Che Guevara in 1967 in Bolivia. Obama Senior was threatening them to expose this thing if they didn't give him what he was demanding. The same evil architects went after him in 1982, after he made Che's same mistake by demanding things from the wrong people. He became an unwanted person by the President of Kenya, Jono Kenyatta, and after two attempts on his life in different car accidents, the third attempt killed him. The same bloc did the same to many others involved in this international conspiracy. Everyone who became a threat of exposing the absurd ambition died. This one man, Putin, stops at nothing, without any scruples, and if he needs to, will kill millions of people. Another reincarnation of Satan on Earth from Hitler's time, Putin is the one manipulating all these things. Putin, in his grandiose ideological dream to bring back the putrefied body of the old Soviet Union, is the real leader of all these nefarious international conspiracies. Che Guevara, Castro, and Putin are the triangle which seeks to enslave the entire world."

      Bonifacio took a sip from the chianti Atacia served him. "Do you think these criminals will accomplish their goal? I start to doubt it myself. Let's suppose that, with all the billions or trillions, of dollars directed by the brilliant, evil mind of Putin and funneling the money through Obama Senior's Marxist foundation that is handled by George Soros and his associates, they manage to achieve their dreams and plant the man they've selected as a puppet in the White House, who would only respond to the mandates and orders of Putin. My question is, after they put all these mountains of power and nuclear weapons in the hands of that man, will they be able to control him and not have a rogue element? He wouldn't be just the same as them, he might be worse: arrogant, without principles, with an obsession of controlling the world." He looked at me seriously in resignation. "I just ask myself, if they manage to put Obama Junior in charge of the most powerful nation in the world, what will he do when he finds out that the men who put him in place are the same ones who assassinated his father? The same people silenced his father because he was no longer trustworthy and because after all they didn't need him anymore since he had already produced for them the perfect plant. They could do the same to him."

I reclined on the sofa and took another sip of wine. I rubbed my fingers across my forehead in concern. "I think the lack of morality, greed, and perversion of all these individuals who are involved in these criminal acts against humanity are completely blinded by their ambition for power and material comfort They have corrupted themselves to such a point that they are no longer rational human beings and have become evil beasts, animals capable of everything and anything, no matter how low and horrible it may look to us, just to maintain their power and not lose the luxurious lifestyle they've been accustomed to for so many years.

I shook my head. "I'm pretty sure Putin must have some kind of chain around Obama Junior's neck to pull when necessary, and that could be these documents which have cost so many lives. They are the only proof that connects Obama, Junior to the money which will give him power to win election. I believe we'll see in the future at that moment, if OB, Jr. gets to be in that place of power and wealth, should he find out that the people took him to this position were the same ones who executed his father in order to save the secret conspiracy which brought him to his place, he will close his eyes and ignore it in order to continue in power. Of course, this is my personal opinion based on my experiences of living for years and years in the guts of espionage and deception around the world. Most people don't believe these things are possible because they cannot even conceive that such evil, even in their wildest and most horrible nightmares, could possibly be true."

Bonifacio replied, "I believe you're 100% right. These individuals in general lack the morals, principles, and scruples, particularly so when we're talking about Obama Junior. He didn't grow up with his parents; he was raised by his grandmother. He lacks the most elemental principles that any boy or girl attaches with their birth mothers and fathers. Without that family nucleus, the kids wind up indifferent to morals or character; this is especially true in boys without their fathers. It's very possible that in this case, his father was a total stranger. I don't believe that he shed a single tear when his father died. At best, he felt the loss as if it were a neighbor that he had no attachment to who had died. Those human feelings are extremely important while we grow up.

He shook his head with a sad expression. He stood up. "OK, kids—I don't want to lose any more time. I should have been out there, looking for my wife and son all this while." He took another appetizer and wrapped it in a napkin. He took another one and popped it into his mouth. He added, "Don't eat it all, OK? This is exquisite. Leave a few for my kid and wife."

Atacia grinned broadly. "Don't worry about it. This will be added to our regular dinner. I've made enough to feed an army so that everyone is satisfied. Knowing how much I like appetizers more than regular food, I made a lot of these. She pointed at the lobsters and fish stuck on the mangrove branch. "I've discovered that Dr. Valentine will help me to prepare a great dinner for you guys before he washes himself. We cannot let the fruit of our submarine excursion go to waste."

Bonifacio smiled and nodded. "Yes, yes. I realized that during the struggle, Dr. Valentine never let go of those lobsters. I believe that he has in mind to do something with them for our dinner tonight."

I smiled. "You must have the ability to read other people's minds. I had been thinking, as we went up the ladder, that I would surprise you guys, since you had no idea that I can cook. I wanted to make you some dish that you might not ever have seen before that my mother taught me when I was a young boy. It's called lobster thermidor a la Cordon Bleu. Even though these appetizers are exquisite, you shouldn't fill yourselves up too much. What I'm going to prepare won't be a regular meal; it will be exceptional, and you'll be my witnesses later if you feel sorry because your belly is too full."

"OK, OK," he said as he grabbed two more crackers and wrapped them in the napkin. "OK, guys—we'll see each other later."

He walked away, and Atacia asked me, "Did you want to take a shower first? Or do you mind if I go before you?"

"Why don't we do it together? That way we'll save time, and we'll have ample time to put something together by the time they get back."

She laughed mischievously. "I think if we shower together, we'll take more time. But I think it's a brilliant idea. Let's go."

We left the room, taking the corridor to walk to its end where the showers and bathrooms were. We took a long shower, as she had predicted, because we ended up making love once more there to the point that we almost collapsed the aluminum and glass structure of the shower in the process, as there were no inhibitions about being interrupted.

We finished and dried ourselves and dressed hurriedly, concerned that the family could show up any minute and take us by surprise. However, a long time later we had nearly finished cooking the dinner, preparing extra dishes such as a seafood cocktail and lobster bisque soup. We also added more appetizers from before. When we finished, it looked more like a buffet than a regular dinner on that table, especially for Cuba, where extra toilet paper is considered more a luxury than a necessity.

I looked at my wristwatch. Bonifacio had left several hours ago. I asked in some concern, "How far is your house from here?"

"It's not far." She shook her head. "But, if you're worried about them not being back yet, it's probably because they didn't want to leave the house until Jimbo got home from work. They wouldn't want to leave anything in writing for him which could wind up in the wrong hands and compromise them as well as this location."

I thought about that. "Yes, it makes sense that your father wouldn't want to leave behind any evidence. They've probably been sitting, twiddling their thumbs and more impatient that we are. I hope that Jimbo shows up in time and they didn't force him to do 'voluntary work' after hours, keeping him up until after midnight and making us worried sick about what's happened to them. I don't think it would be prudent for either of us to leave here, especially after what happened on the beach today."

"Yes, you're right." She tried to decorate the table with artificial flowers. She could not hide her own sense of worry and nearly dropped the dishes a couple of times as she carried them from the kitchen to the table.

I walked along the long corridor that led to the bathroom. When I came back, she had made the final touches. I noticed a large bag against the wall which I had passed by earlier. It looked like a Spinet piano. I shook the dust off the felt green covers over the keys, I dusted off the piano bench and piano, and set down on the bench. I tried the keys and was surprised that all the keys were still in perfect function and still in tune. I smiled and decided to have a little fun.

    I played "Theme from a Sunny Place" by Percy Faith and His Orchestra and some Elvis songs, just playing around to let my hands get back in shape. I then played one of my own compositions, "My Cuba Stolen from Me." As I sang, Atacia came in quietly and sat on one of the boxes against the wall, letting me be. The song was full of pain, as I had put all my frustrations since the day of my birth on that beautiful island, until circumstances had forced me to abandon my homeland and family with only the clothes I had on my back, up right to the assassination of my son, something I will never forgive the Marxist communist regime of the Castro brothers for.

My Cuba Stolen from Me

Music and Lyrics by:
Dr. Julio Antonio del Marmol
&
His Cuban Lightning Orchestra

Figure 10 My Cuba Stolen from Me cover art

Tears ran down my cheeks as I sang, escaping my control, since I had assumed I was by myself, and my memories floated back through time, reliving the sadness and agony. For me, it is not just a musical piece; it is an emotional volcano which blows up every time I touch it, releasing all the pain bottled up in my heart for all those years, as well as the guilt I felt in part for being responsible for my son's death, since I had been unable to pull him out of Cuba before those criminal Marxists executed him in revenge for failing to eliminate me for over 56 times. They had decided to inflict pain on me through the most vulnerable and loving treasure I had in my life, my son Julito.

After I had finished, still assuming I was alone, I stood up suddenly in my emotional reaction, slamming the cover over the keys violently and kicking the bench with my right foot, knocking one of the legs off, screaming my agony and anger out loudly as I dried my tears on the sleeve of the jogging suit which rolled down my cheeks like an opened faucet. I heard a noise behind me. Extremely ashamed of my irrational, emotional reactions, which I was unaccustomed to showing since I knew no one could understand the pain I felt unless he or she had been in my shoes. She got up and tried to reattach the leg back onto the bench nervously.

I looked at her, still ashamed. "I'm sorry. I didn't mean to break that bench. I'm sorry. That's not normally me. I'm very ashamed for my attitude."

I went over to her and tried to gently take the leg of the bench from her, but she calmly took it back from me. To my surprise, she noticed my emotional state and my tear-filled eyes, and threw the leg onto the floor angrily. I remained motionless, but when I saw her take another leg in an emotional state and throw it against the wall behind me, I understood something was wrong but not why she was doing that.

She smiled at me in satisfaction as she removed the remaining legs and tossed them against the wall. "If breaking this piano bench could return to you your happiness and tranquility and put an end to that horrible pain you carry with you that these Marxists inflicted on your heart, I will break millions of these benches and the piano as well." She came over to me and caressed my hands. With her own tears in her eyes she said, "Listening to the lyrics of your song is more than sufficient to make anyone who has any sensitivity of a human being cry. Even though I don't know you that well, either your life in full much less your past, but all we have to do is listen to the lyrics of that song and your emotions as you sing with all the profound pain which come from the deepest corners of your soul is enough to communicate all the pain and weight you have on your shoulders and emotional frustrations you carried all your life.

  She hugged me in pure love to minimize my pain, now aware of the depth of pain I carried veiled, hidden, and concealed from everyone else. After a few minutes of silence, we both recovered our composures. Atacia took both of my hands between hers and looked into my eyes. "I want to give you a son, not to replace the beautiful one that you lost, but as an alleviation for your pain."

  I smiled. "Thank you, love."

  Still holding hands, we walked back to the room and sat down on the sofa. She took a couple of glasses and filled them with more chianti, handing one to me. She gave me a tender kiss on the lips. "I want to confess something to you that I think is horrible. I promised my family this a long time ago not to tell anyone as it could cost not just my life but also those of all my loved ones."

  I shook my head. "You don't have to do this or tell me anything which could jeopardize your security. No one, whoever it might be, deserves that level of trust. No matter how horrible it could be, all you have to tell me is that it's a secret. That's enough for any individual with dignity, morals, and ethics—tell that person something is to be concealed, it will be done unless you say differently. I will never betray a confidence. It's a huge responsibility."

She took both my hands and looked into my eyes. "I want to. I love you, and I want to be completely honest with you. Bonifacio and Aurora are not my real parents. They are my adoptive parents."

"OK. That is very common in many families. There's nothing horrible about that." I felt very tranquil as I thought ahead and assumed that what she wanted to tell me was much worse than what she had just said.

She shook her head. With sadness she continued, "Yes, you're right. That's not the problem. The terrible part is not my adopted father and mother. They've maintained the secret all these years. The horrible truth is who my real father is." She raised both eyebrows so high that they nearly disappeared into her hairline. She stayed silent for a few seconds. If she wanted to stop there, it was too late. But her hesitation stemmed from the fact that she was about to break a promise to her adopted father.

"Remember, Atacia, you don't have to do this. You don't have to tell me anything, especially if it will create problems with your father."

She squeezed my hands and said, "My real father is the dictator, Fidel Castro."

I was in shock, utterly caught by surprise and could only ask, "Who is your mother?"

She replied sadly, "Gladys." I was stunned. She added, "I believe that is one of the reasons why they killed her. She told my mother that the dictator had raped her when she no longer wished to have sex with him anymore and this time, she believed that he got her pregnant. This was a few months before she disappeared."

I put both my hands to my face. "Oh, no, my God! Oh, no!" I thought back to the last time I had seen her; she had been pregnant then, but was it because she had been impregnated by the dictator, or as a result of our adventures together in Africa? Based on Atacia's it was possible that she had been conceived during that operation in which we tried to retrieve the machine which caused what some had named the Havana Syndrome. I looked at her sympathetically, and I could see in her a slight resemblance to Castro in some of her gestures and shape of her eyes; but at the same time, I tried very hard not to see any resemblance to myself. Atacia clearly had no clue about the relationship that Gladys and I had, or else nothing would have happened between us.

The confusion, uncertainty, and despair dominated my heart and brain absolutely. A dark cloud settled on my shoulders, making the weight I had carried all my life even heavier. I said, "Honesty should be repaid with honesty. It is the Golden Rule. I have something extremely important to confess to you, but before I say anything I want to tell you there's nothing horrible in your confession. You cannot control who your father is, but what I have to confess now is remotely close to the truth, it will be horrible for sure."

She looked at me in surprise mingled with fear and worry. "Don't worry about it. I don't think anything you can tell me now, even if the world ends tomorrow could be worse than what I've felt in my heart all these years. Imagine if your father were a disciple of the Antichrist or Antichrist himself."

"I know, but what I have to tell you is as heavy if not heavier." I took a sip of my wine to give myself a few seconds to think carefully how I was going to say this to her. "You will be the only one who can determine the magnitude of this, to what extent you can forgive it, believe it, or not."

She raised both hands high. "Before you tell me anything I want to apologize for lying to you for saying that Gladys is my cousin when she might be my mother."

I shook my head. "You should not worry or apologize because you have no reason at all for either one. You did what you thought was logical and complied with your promise to your father regarding your relationship with the dictator for your security as well as his. On the other hand, this is a lot more horrible than what you imagine, as there exists a very strong possibility of what I think is true. I think there are strong odds that it isn't Castro who is your father; but the likelihood is strong, and it troubles me, that *I* might be your father."

Chapter 8: The Lightning Reveals His Identity

I continued, "That would be a nasty reality. But before we go any deeper, you need to know that Dr. Valentine is not my real name. Even though I had a strong reason to lie to you guys, I'm nevertheless going to apologize to you. If think back to the circumstances of our first meeting, you'll understand why I had to deceive you guys. When I recovered consciousness, you guys made me sick to my stomach when you let me know that you had brought me back to Cuba. Just imagine how I felt when you brought me back to the guts of the monster that I've fought against all my life, the totalitarian communist system in Cuba, my worst enemies. Thank God that when you found me, I was returning from a covert operation. The documentation I had on me for Dr. Valentine was one of the names I've used during my clandestine life as a spy around the world. That is what your father, you, and everyone else found in my pockets—the cover I was using as a spy at that time. You assumed I was either from Costa Rica or some other country, since I don't look like a gringo. When I woke up, I saw myself in a very dangerous predicament, wondering who you guys were—real fishermen, G-2, or MQ-1. If either of those last were the case, my life was going to last less than a sardine in the middle of a school of piranhas. But my real name is Dr. Julio Antonio del Marmol."

Atacia put her right hand to her mouth in shocked surprise. She then smiled slightly as she pointed at me. "Oh, my God—then you are the Cuban Lightning!" She looked at me in a mix of consternation and admiration. "Now I understand why you tried to make us believe when you regained consciousness that you didn't remember your name. You at least tried to convince us that the blow to your head you sustained during the plane crash provoked temporary amnesia in you."

I spread my arms. "*Claro, chica!* Of course—what other thing could I tell you guys at that moment? I couldn't force you to turn the boat around to take me back to Mexico. I had no weapons on me, I had lost everything in the crash, including my briefcase which had some very valuable contents. And then when I opened my eyes the first thing that I saw on the walls of the cabin you brought me to with your father was a big picture of Fidel, Che, and the most notorious Marxist communist in all of Africa, from Kenya, Mr. Barack Obama, Senior. It was on his desk in plain view. I ask you, what would you say to anyone if you were in my shoes?"

Atacia nodded. She added with an ironic smile, "You see? This teaches us that appearances can sometime be very deceiving. My family has been against the totalitarian regime of the Castro brothers since the first day Fidel declared himself to be a Marxist in the Plaza of the Revolution in Havana. And that after he lied repeatedly, telling us that he would never be part of the unscrupulous ideological political system which killed hundreds or even thousands of Hungarians when they protested against the communists. Children, women, old men all died because they didn't want to live under a regime worse than the Nazis. In every country this political system is installed in, never by the will of the people but by force, nothing good comes of it nor does anyone prosper in any part of the world where they get power. The people have any other choice but to pretend to agree and conform. Life becomes a true inferno, a hundred times worse than whatever they had before. The way of life they impose on people each day makes everyone equally miserable—they promise equality, but it always produces only equal misery. They become the new kings, with everyone else becoming deplorables, forced to stand in long lines for a loaf of bread for several hours—and low-quality bread, at that."

    I shared her irony in my smile. "Remember always these painful experiences you're living in today so that in the future you can be a great witness. No one's told you anything; you've suffered it yourself. It makes no difference what country we end up in during our attempt to escape this socialist system, maybe we will manage once and for all to remove its mask. These deceptive communist Marxists promise a paradise to everyone; they just forget to add a macabre diabolical funereal music to the Soviet international anthem. In the end, all we have is blood, mourning, and misery, which no one ever even imagines living in. The poorest people in America are rich by comparison."

    We looked into each other's eyes, nodding in agreement. Atacia took my hand between hers and gave me a small smile. "Whatever the country which the circle of life brings me to, I don't care when or how, my only wish is to be with you, if you accept me and it wouldn't be an inconvenience. I would love to finish my life by your side."

    I smiled and leaned into her a little to give her a small kiss on the cheek. "It's not an inconvenience at all; on the contrary, for me it would be an honor and happiness. But I don't want to finish my life by your side."

She looked at me incredulously. "Rather, I would want to start a new life with you and enjoy it in plenitude for all the time it lasts, whether it is short or long. Our relationship, if it continues as it is now, will be imprinted in my memory as God grants me life."

Her expression transformed into a huge smile. She took my face between her hands to kiss me tenderly on the lips. "Those words I will treasure in my heart for the rest of my life." She this time kissed me on different parts of my face. These tiny kisses of gratitude grew to be more passionate, ending in excitement which concluded with more splendid sex as we melded once more into each other.

Afterwards, Atacia said, "I don't know about you, but I'm very hungry. It's getting very late. My brother probably had to remain for 'voluntary' work on the piers, so who knows when they'll arrive. Let's have some dinner. Can you imagine it, after eight hours of work, you have to provide another three or four hours of work for free? And if you do not give them the work they demand, they classify you as an ungrateful person, putting you on a blacklist so that you can never get a better job because you didn't comply. What a hypocrisy to call that extra work 'voluntary.'"

After we finished dinner, she put away enough food for her family. We cleaned up, and in complete satisfaction she grabbed a fresh bottle of chianti wine, two glasses, and suggested we go up to the terraces on top of the building to watch the beautiful skies that tropical nights normally display after a storm. We went upstairs, and she didn't exaggerate at all. I had forgotten how many stars one could see in that tropical sky. It was like some famous painter would have rendered on a huge canvas. To top it off, the full moon was orange, enormous and beautiful, and shining like diamonds around the moon where white clouds which brought a celestial expression of God in the middle of all this misery that the island had been subjected to. I felt melancholy as I remembered my childhood on my beautiful island of Cuba. This beautiful night view looked like a message of hope, not only for us, but for everyone on that night that watched that magnificent, spectacular scenery. I remembered the abundance, joy, and plenty in the past which looked like by now was far in the distant past.

    We reached the edge of the balcony with great care, recalling my previous experience of how fragile it was. The concrete and steel bars within it had broken one at a time, slowly transforming the mansion into ruins more and more each year. But the scenery from that height was so breathtaking that I could forget the misery that was continually present on that island.

    I looked at my wristwatch and saw it was already past midnight. I got worried about Jimbo. It was unlikely that someone would stay that long in their workplace. My concern grew by the minute, so I asked Atacia, "Where has Jimbo been asked to do voluntary work before? Has he ever stayed so late?" She looked at me in worry and shook her head wordlessly. She took a deep breath and a long sip from her glass of wine trying to calm her nerves. I added, "If you give me the directions of how to get to your residence, I could go check on your family. Don't worry, I'll be very responsible and careful. At least we can be sure that they're OK and nothing odd is going on there."

    She shook her head. "No. I could never forgive myself if you got caught by the soldiers, G-2, or any of these malicious people we have here during the late-night hours. Especially now that you have confessed to me your true identity." She looked at me in open admiration. "You don't even know—you are a symbol of hope and freedom for nearly everyone in this country. Just imagine the fiasco and the joyful triumph of these communists if they manage to grab you. They will parade you on television, torture you, make you confess things you never even did, and in the end, put you before the firing squad for a public execution." She spoke in sincere concern. "Can you imagine how many young kids on this island whose hearts you would break? The hope of the Cuban Lightning returning freedom to them will be gone forever. You are the last hope of freedom, if not for thousands than for millions of them." She shook her head again and raised her eyebrows like she did whenever she was stressed or unhappy. She pointed at the center of my chest. "You should not even be here in Cuba. You should be thousands of miles away; you are the most wanted individual not only Cuba but all across the world by the G-2, MQ-1, and all the hit men in service to the international communists."

    I smiled. "Don't worry at all about me. I do not fear these people. I've had extraordinarily intense training which makes me capable of getting out of the worst situations. It started when my uncle, Emilio del Marmol, recruited me at the age of twelve, right here in Cuba. Then later, the most dedicated and sophisticated instructors with tremendous efficiency multiplied all the training I've had to another, higher level inside the different intelligence agencies. They provided me with very advanced courses in survival, self-defense, and training in the most sophisticated gadgets and technology. Of course, this doesn't make me invincible, but yes—I'm a very hard bone for these communists to chew on. That brings my enemies to be on the border of frenzied frustration after they've failed miserably to assassinate me for decades. I'm not a religious fanatic, but let's also not forget that, I can assure you with extreme conviction, I have at my back the most powerful of the guardian angels a human being can have. You know his name very well, and He is the Son of God, Jesus Christ. He is the most powerful secret weapon I have in my arsenal. He has protected and guided me in the darkest hours around the world, keeping me safe and sound, happy to be able to continue my work."

As we spoke, I saw something moving. It looked like an object—a reflection of light or something. I grabbed her and she said, "What's happening?"

I put my finger to her lips and whispered, "Sh. I saw something moving in the garden."

We hid in the shadows of the nearly collapsed veranda. We saw a silhouette moving by the light of the moon and starlight, trying clearly to move unseen. From the way the form walked, especially around the hips and the way its center of gravity was shown by the way it carried itself, it had to be a woman. I put my glass of wine down near the ruins of the balcony; Atacia set hers next to mine. "The same way we can see her by the moonlight, she can see it reflecting off our glasses." She nodded, and I put my finger to my lips for silence.

We crouched down. She understood the danger even though she didn't know what was going on. She whispered, "What happened? Do you see anything?"

I kept my eyes on where I had seen movement. There was a tiny light, and I pointed it out to her without taking my eyes off the movement. At that moment, a few seconds later, she reacted, crouching down a little more.

She said in agitation, "Yes, you're right. There is a light coming our way."

"Is there anyone else who knows about this place?"

"No, nobody. My father never showed this place to anyone. He's reserved it for extreme emergencies until the family could leave the country in his fishing boat. No one else knows about this place."

The form continued moving towards the ruined mansion. About a hundred feet from us, I could see the woman's form better—she appeared to be a large person, wearing black clothing with a hoody, had a bow hanging from the right shoulder, with a quiver of arrows over the left. She was an Amazon based on her height and body type. She also had a large caliber pistol on her right hip, either a .45 or even a .50. She stopped practically beneath us. The flashlight that I had originally seen got turned off. She took something from her waist that looked like a sack that was wrapped around behind her back and put it on the cement driveway. She pulled something from the pack and walked towards the doors, leaving our line of sight.

We listened carefully. It sounded like the wooden boards were being removed. A few minutes later, she reappeared in our view. It appeared that removing the boards was creating too much noise. She rummaged around in the bag and extracted a grappling hook with a rope attached to it, swinging it in loops before hurling the hook up a couple of times with no luck; but the third try the hook caught against one of the exposed steel bars. She pulled a couple of times to test the hook's ability to bear her weight and to set the hook in the concrete support. Then she began to climb up.

Atacia looked at me, profoundly worried. "What are we going to do? I don't have any weapons."

The huge woman slowly but very professionally wrapped one leg around the rope, using her other leg and arm to propel herself up to the veranda. I said to Atacia, "Don't worry about it—I'll take care of this mercenary." I scooped up a handful of concrete dust in my left hand.

She looked at me curiously. "What are you going to do with that?"

"We have no weapons, so we must improvise. This will be my primary weapon to neutralize this Amazon. If there's anything I really despise its mercenaries, and I despise very few things. This Amazon mercenary stinks of being a communist assassin. We'll give her the medicine and greetings that she deserves." I knelt on the floor and grabbed two steel bars about three feet long, cleaning them of the chunks of concrete still clinging to the bars. I handed one bar to her. "You might not need this but take it for your own defense—just in case. It's always good to have a backup plan, and that might be you. Otherwise, stay back unless I ask you for help."

I figured that I could put our assailant out of operation by myself. We watched by the moonlight as the large woman climbed up onto the balcony. She dislodged the hook and started to coil the rope, turning away from me as she did. I took the opportunity to stealthily run over to her. As I got close, I yelled, "Hey!"

Startled, she turned towards the sound of my voice to receive the combination of sand and dust thrown full into her face, blinding her completely. She dropped both rope and hook while at the same time she angrily pulled off her hoodie, shaking her head to clear her eyes of the debris. I could tell she could not see me as she stared wildly about her, trying to see me as she rubbed her eyes with the knuckles of her hand. I raised my steel bar, ready to strike her as hard as I could in the head. I could tell she was very professional, very well-trained: even blinded, she jumped back a couple of feet like a rabbit. She pulled a couple of knives with serrated edges, moving both hands around in a circle, keeping me at a distance as she danced from one side to the other. The size of the arc she swept showed that she could not see me, so I silently stood out of range, looking for my opportunity to slip under the knives and hit her in the head to put her out of commission. It took me a little while, as her knife pattern was nearly ninety degrees around her.

    Finally, she turned a little away from me, giving me an opening. I raised the steel bar and moved in close. Suddenly, I heard Atacia yell, "No! No, wait!" I froze. "Mama Teca, is that you? What are you doing here?"

Figure 11 Mama Teca

    The large black woman lowered her knives. "Atacia, *mi niña*? Yes, it's me. Bonifacio and Aurora sent me. You and your companion are in extreme danger. They believe that your brother Jimbo has been arrested. It's possible under torture that he might have compromised this location."

I froze when I heard that. I could not believe that Jimbo would, even under torture, ever give his adopted sister away, much less his own parents. But human beings are what we are, and under the right pressure many people crack. I kept my steel bar held high, as I was still unconvinced, as I listened for a few minutes to the conversation of the two women. It appeared the Mama Teca was a very close member of their family. She had called Atacia "Mi niña", a term frequently used by mothers speaking with their daughters. Slowly I lowered the steel bar down and breathed a profound sigh of relief. It was not in my nature to hurt anyone, especially when it was an extraordinarily beautiful woman over six feet in height.

Atacia came over to me and patted me on the shoulder. "You are a great man. You did a fantastic job, thank you, and thanks to God for your tremendous reflexes to freeze at the sound of my voice. I know what kind of damage you could have done to her by hitting her head with that bar. You had no other option to neutralize such a large woman, but think of how much remorse you would have, since with a blow to the head you cannot predict the consequences."

I nodded. "You're right. Your yell stopped my heart and my arm for a fraction of a second, and I will thank God for the rest of my life for that. But I have a question—how did you recognize her at such a distance in the dark?"

Atacia smiled. "You won't believe it, and it probably sounds ironical, but I heard some celestial voice telling me to not let this happen. I heard them when you threw the dust and sand in her eyes. You saved her life because the violent reaction she had after you blinded her forced her to remove that hoodie which covered not just her head but part of her face. That is when I saw her face by the moonlight and recognized the woman who babysat me, became part of my adopted family, and has cared for me all my life, Mama Teca." She bit her upper lip, her eyes filling with sudden tears as she spoke.

Mama Teca was rubbing her eyes with the knuckles of her index fingers as she continued clearing her sight. She said, "What about now? After all the agony I've gone through, am I supposed to be grateful to this gentleman who has left me temporarily blind?"

Atacia chuckled. "We thought you were an enemy coming to get us. We were only trying to defend ourselves." She took a couple of steps forward and hugged the tall woman. As she did, she showed the woman the metal bar she held. "He was going to hit you with the one in his hand. If he didn't react as quickly as he did and instead hit you in the head with that bar, you would be struck down on the ground; the best scenario would be a hemorrhage in your brain, and the worst case would leave you dead."

Mama Teca looked at the three-foot steel bar, a good inch and a half in diameter. "Yes, I believe you." She looked at me and asked, "Do you realize this is not like the movies or in fiction? This is a cruel reality of daily life. If you hit me with that, I would probably not wake up tomorrow." Atacia hugged her again. "Guys, you have to be careful next time and be certain who is your friend and who is your enemy. This is not like fiction or in movies where people jump off of skyscrapers and don't have a scratch in the next scene."

Atacia smiled as she gave Mama Teca a bottle of water to wash her face. Mama Teca continued, "Well, I have to thank you for not hitting me and putting me in a coma or killing me." She washed her face in satisfaction at feeling the last grains of dust and cement out of her eyes. After she recovered, she held her hand out to me in a friendly manner. "I have no hard feelings against you, remember that. It was all a big mistake. Unfortunately, all this system creates is confusion as to who is friend or enemy now. But I must give you a pat on the back for your efficiency and clever approach. You put me out of combat in a very short time, and I must thank you again for not striking me with that bar. Now we need to get out of here as soon as possible. According to Bonifacio and Aurora, Jimbo has never before stayed so late before at work, even when he had to put in several hours of voluntary work. It's very suspicious, like I said before, and we must leave from here immediately."

"Where are we going?" I asked.

"The only place that's safe. The port and Bonifacio's fishing vessel. That is the way they want to do it. Aurora will stay at the house until Jimbo comes back—if he does. She doesn't want him to be unaware of what happened. We'll wait as long as possible, but we need to leave tonight. We don't know what these communists are cooking up, and perhaps your cover has been blown."

"OK, if that is what my father wants, let's get out of here. But let's go down and pick up the most important documents, arm ourselves with everything we can carry plus a few grenades. We must expect the worst. These communists don't move a single finger unless they have the upper hand. Too many strange coincidences have happened lately, which tells me that what you're assuming is right, and our cover is completely blown open. It's very possible they plan to arrest everyone involved in our resistance group to send a strong message of intimidation and terror through our town and the rest of the island."

Mama Teca replied, "That is what Bonifacio has in mind. That's why he wants you on his fishing vessel so that you can get far away as quickly as possible. He's expecting a very huge retaliation from these communists; but later, when we feel safer and not in a rush, I'll give you more details once we're far away from here."

"Very well," I said. "Let's get whatever we need and make sure we don't leave any important documents behind. Let's wrap them up, very well protected from the water, just in case we have to swim out of here as I did many years ago."

A little while later, we left behind that ruin which once was a palace, a faded reflection of the glorious times in Cuba before the revolution took over. This old building was one more witness of the unforgivable reality the Cuban revolution brought to its own people when it converted the most beautiful and prosperous island in the Caribbean into the most miserable one in just a few short decades, a country where the great majority wanted to work and live in peace and democracy.

We left the gardens as it began to sprinkle, which was a surprise. It was typical in tropical Cuba, but even those of us born on that island were not used to rain on a beautiful moonlight and cloudless night; likewise, a sunny, very hot summer day would surprise us with rain in a cloudless sky. I looked up at the star-filled sky, drops of rain splashing on my face, and I smiled and shook my head. I muttered, "Only in my Cuba."

We walked for a while. Mama Teca had left her Toyota Land Cruiser a great distance away. We got into the uncovered vehicle. The soft top roof had been rolled to one side, exposing us to the sprinkles. She started the engine and said to us, "The enemies of democracy always wait for us to make the slightest mistake—that's why I thought ahead and left my car far away from the old mansion. I didn't want to enter that rat trap and have them accusing me of being a counter-revolutionary simply because I drove up to that old ruin."

Mama Teca drove off towards the small town. Everything looked so peaceful and quiet. Not a single car drove along the empty streets devoid even of pedestrians. I thought about the many people slept through these events during the early morning hours. A motorcycle with a side car bearing three soldiers sped along a side street at high speed, heading towards the piers. It looked like they were expecting action. Everything else closed for the night quite early; only in Havana did entertainment establishments remain open, and everything had to be paid for in American dollars. No Cuban person held US currency unless they had family living abroad sending them money to alleviate their misery. And even those with a little money weren't going to burn it up in nightclubs and bars; they saved it for food and necessities such as toothpaste, soap, and deodorant. This is communist living: work eight hours a day and not even have the most basic needs. This is also why they had to keep piers closed—otherwise, there would be a Mariel boatlift every day until the island was empty.

As we came close to the pier, we heard shotguns, pistols, and machine guns being fired. Another motorcycle crossed ahead of us at a high speed. The second motorcycle gave me knots in my stomach, raising the hairs on the back of my neck. I immediately had a vision of our friends in very serious trouble. It wasn't long before we saw how right I was.

Right where Bonifacio had his fishing vessel, the motorcycles had blocked off the pier. It appeared that Bonifacio, Aurora, and Jimbo had been exchanging fire to get past the soldiers. The soldiers had erected a wooden barricade at the juncture of the wooden pier to the cement quay. As we approached the barricade, the soldiers motioned for us to stop. I said to Mama Teca, "Don't stop, run over them!" I readied a nine-millimeter pistol for firing; Atacia did the same.

We slowed down as we approached the barricade as if complying with the soldiers. Seeing our unthreatening approach, they clustered together as they advanced towards us. Mama Teca pulled two grenades out of her bra. She put them on the seat as she slammed the accelerator to the floor. She scooped the grenades up, pulling the pins with her teeth one at a time. The soldiers scattered, firing wildly as they got out of the way, the spray of bullets flying over our heads harmlessly. We rammed through the barricade, bumping and jolting as we ran over first some of the soldiers and then the barricade. There was a loud crash as we smashed through the barricade, pieces of wood rattling and bouncing off the hood of the Land Cruiser. As we flew through, Mama Teca threw a grenade to each side at the feet of the soldiers that had jumped out of the way. Behind us we watched the soldiers fly into the water as the grenades exploded, cutting the pier nearly in half, body parts of some of the soldiers flying through the air. Those who weren't blown up by the grenades had dropped their weapons and jumped into the ocean as well.

Bonifacio, Aurora, and Jimbo grabbed the bars of the Toyota and held on, stepping onto the runners along the side of the vehicle, Jimbo and Bonifacio on one side, Aurora on the other. In the distance we could hear some shots being fired without hearing the sound of the passage of the bullets. We jumped out of the Toyota and onto the boat as Bonifacio started the Mercury V8 Verado engines.

We pulled away from the pier and ran out of the harbor for open water. As we entered the open sea several miles later, we could see a torpedo boat closing at a high speed towards us—quite illegally, as we were now in international waters.

Chapter 9: Mama Teca, the Amazon

Even though we were outside the reach of the Cuban communist government, we also knew of the multiple violations by the Cuban government committed each day in international waters, assassinating hundreds if not thousands of innocent families who tried to escape the island. Regardless of how much Bonifacio pushed the engines to the maximum output, it didn't take long before we saw that our vessel was no match to the powerful Russian military engines on the torpedo boats.

Figure 12 Soviet torpedo boat

Little by little they cut the distance between us. Soon they started to sound loud sirens and yelling over the PA for us to stop and surrender, or they would sink our boat. Mama Teca turned to Bonifacio. "Captain, do we surrender, or shall we give an Alka Seltzer treatment to these communists?"

Bonifacio looked at each of us for a few seconds. "What do you guys think? Give these guys a fight, or give up? I'm all for fighting them since we'll all die anyway. Surrendering is just leading to death, so we may as well die with dignity. The majority decides, however, because we are not communist." He looked at each one of us in turn; each of us nodded in unanimous agreement with him to fight these communists. He looked at Mama Teca. "You have the green light. Give them the Alka Seltzer."

She went down to the cabins, followed by Jimbo. A few seconds later, Bonifacio slowly slowed our speed, making the communist naval forces think that he was going to surrender, as we had done at the pier.

The torpedo boat remained a combat stance, keeping their deadly weapons pointed at us about four hundred feet from our vessel, ready to sink us in a flash. Unexpectedly, Mama Teca came back to the bridge with an FIM-92 Stinger missile launcher on her shoulder, followed by Jimbo stood next to her with another warhead reload for her. She aimed at the torpedo boat from the bow.

The pilot of the torpedo boat had obviously been well trained. As soon as he saw the Stinger being pointed at them, he accelerated the boat and attempted to turn out of the way. The range was too short, and as they turned the rocket hit them amidships, striking the torpedo boat directly. The massive explosion destroyed the boat, but not before two torpedoes were launched into the water. We watched the wake in the surface as the two projectiles streaked towards our craft, and we all jumped into the ocean before they struck.

    We saw both torpedoes go through the ship, leaving entry and exit holes—but neither one detonated. Clearly, neither warhead had been primed. Taken by surprise by this turn of events, none of us had any doubt that God's hand had protected us on that moonlit night. However, we also knew that God helps those who help themselves, and it was possible that our people within the communist government had disabled those torpedoes. There were those who acted for the resistance, fed by the youth in the mandatory military service who did not sympathize with the communists or like the Castro brothers, that took every opportunity to sabotage the Cuban military, not only in the Army, but also the Navy and other departments of the Cuban communist government. Another possibility we thought of was that it might not even be saboteurs: it could also be poor maintenance on the weapons for lack of time and spare parts that could have made those torpedoes malfunction. Any of those possibilities could have been God's hand that night, though we would never know for certain which of them was the truth.

    With a small smile on my face, happy at being still alive, I thought that I should change my name from the Lightning to the Cat with all these spare lives. I had been certain that I was going to be blown out of the water that night. Our vessel was still sinking quickly with the four holes below the water line. The only thing in my mind at that point was to get to the small lifeboat with an outboard engine we had towing behind our vessel for such an emergency. If I didn't get to that boat quickly, the sinking ship would drag it down along with her by the towline. Then the tragedy would be magnified, stuck in the middle of the ocean with nothing to even help us float once we got tired of treading water.

Mama Teca yelled at me, "Where are you going?"

"To save the boat—that's our only chance for life!"

"OK, we'll get on the ship and see what we can save in the way of food, water, and fuel."

"Good," I replied as I continued swimming to the lifeboat. I got there and rushed to untie the rope and free the boat. As soon as that was done, I helped the others to climb into the boat, first Aurora, then Atacia. The last one to climb into the boat was our captain, Bonifacio, who along with Jimbo and Mama Teca had tried to recover the navigation instruments, water containers and containers of gasoline tied to buoys, food, and the other necessaries we would need to survive for however long we would be in the ocean.

As we brought everything into the boat, we began to feel like sardines in a can—too many people in that small boat combined with all the material we had brought on board to make the available space very cramped. By divine intervention, the vessel remained afloat for well over fifteen to twenty minutes before sinking, giving us more time to shift around in that small boat, start the outboard engine, and get a little farther from the vessel before the suction created by her final sinking would pull us back.

Once we were a safe distance from the ship, I crossed my fingers, and finally watched her go under the waves. Bonifacio tried to comfort us by saying, "Don't worry about it, guys. I communicated with my brother, Luis Alberto, over the radio and let him know our navigational coordinates and the desperate situation we were in. He doesn't live many nautical miles from the

Keys. If he doesn't see us show up in the next couple of hours, he'll get in his fishing boat and start to look for us."

Mama Teca sat next to him. She patted him on the shoulder. "My captain, you always think of emergency exits. Thank you for being responsible like that. You don't know how happy you made me. It gives me a great hope; it probably does the others, in this stressful moment."

I frowned without saying anything. I did not know for a fact if that transmission had been made or if he was just trying to give us hope for our survival of this terrible situation. Jimbo sat next to me and gave me a look of sadness and distress. He forced a small smile which looked more like a grimace. He leaned into me to murmur in my ear, "I've never heard my father in any moment talk with anyone on the radio. Did you?" I turned my head a little towards him. Without saying anything I shook my head very slightly. He nodded, still grimacing. "I know. I know."

Atacia asked Jimbo, "Do you mind if we switch seats?"

"Sure. Come on over."

Atacia, helped by the hands of everyone else, crossed over to my side of the boat and sat down next to me, as Jimbo crossed over and took hers. She got settled and asked me, "In all these crazy adventures you've had around the world, have you ever had such a precarious situation like this before?"

I smiled. "Evidently you've forgotten how you and I met."

She shook her head and leaned in. The outboard motor made so much noise that she had to get close to say softly into my ear. "Do you think I could ever forget the salt water I got out of your mouth when I tried to resuscitate you? It was the first time in my adult life that I put my mouth against that of a strange man's mouth. The brush of our lips gave me an incredible sense of tickling in my belly button."

I couldn't help but smile. "I'm glad you enjoyed it. I felt nothing since I had nearly left the living world and was about to enter the next. I'm really happy that you, at such a young age, have been able to control your fear. That is the first step for any human being to not allow ever anyone else to put you on your knees."

Atacia smiled. "How can I have any fear of anything, when I'm here with my family and with the two bravest men I've ever known or that anyone can imagine: my adopted father, Captain Bonifacio, and the master spy feared most by communists throughout the world, the Cuban Lightning?"

"Well, I'm in second position here, not the first one. My stock has gone down."

She smiled. I almost burst out laughing but held it in and reduced it to a chuckle, the only thing I could not control. Aurora sat on my other side, and I didn't want her to think I had gone mad by laughing so much in this tense moment.

Aurora squeezed my arm affectionately. I leaned over to hear what she had to say. "You know I'm Atacia's adopted mother. It's a great pleasure to be with you tonight. It pleases me very much to see how you guys can share such a beautiful affinity for each other. This is the fundamental basis of the beginning of a sincere and durable friendship."

I held out my right hand by way of introduction. Instead of shaking it, she took it in both of her hands and turned it over, taking me by surprise. She looked at the lines of my hand as she traced them with her index finger as she read my future. That made me uncomfortable. She looked into my eyes. "According to the lines of your hand, you'll have a very long life. You've been through hell in your life, many deceptions and violence." I smiled. I could see she was good; I didn't want to know any more and gently withdrew my hand.

I said, "I've had many of those. Let's hope that this one isn't worse and doesn't continue for the rest of my life. Everything has a limit, and my cup is on the border of overflowing."

Aurora shook her head with a smile. "Well, I don't think you have much to complain about. I see that even with all you've gone through in life, it looks like you're happy to be alive and smiling. You haven't lost your sense of humor. It looks like you enjoy the company of my daughter. That tells me that no matter what hell on earth you've been through so many times, you have never lost your savor for the beauty of life."

I smiled once more, this time a grin. I shook my head as I gently squeezed one of her shoulders. "No, no, Aurora, I will never lose my optimism—that would mean that we surrendered our souls to Satan. I was born a Christian warrior and will die as a Christian warrior; I will never stop my fight for my happiness and that of everyone."

This time she was the one who smiled broadly. "I believe that you found here in Caibarien your other half. Atacia is like you—she never surrenders, never stops fighting. She is full of joy and light, but she never stops. Nothing scares her; she never fears the darkness."

"That is one of the things I like most in her," I replied.

Atacia, filled with curiosity, squeezed my arm to get my attention. I leaned over to her. "What has my mom been telling you? What have you been talking about?"

I smiled. "Only good things about you, my love. Only good things. Nothing bad at all."

She looked at me and grinned.

As I got to know later on, quite a disturbance was occurring in the little town of Caibarien while the town sleeping, and we had our life and death struggle to survive. A helicopter landed right on the front of the rotunda before the Cuban Communist Party headquarters. A small caravan from the government in a fleet of Alfa Romeos and two military transport trucks filled with soldiers surrounded the building. It looked like they were protecting a big honcho in the government. Inside the office, the Prime Secretary of the Communist Party in Caibarien was being questioned intensely and tortured by members of the G-2 right in front of a reclining chair in which sat Fidel Castro himself. He was foaming at the mouth in his rage, sometimes interrupting the G-2 interrogator to ask his own questions of the man. Until now, this man, Eriberto Sanchez, was one of Castro's most trusted individuals. He was nothing less than the nephew of Fidel Castro's mistress and official confidante for many years, Celia Sanchez Manduley from 1959 until her death on January 11, 1980. Eyewitness accounts told me that they had had sexual relations even as far back as in the Sierra Maestra together in the jungle, sleeping in the same hammock.

Castro rolled the executive chair over to stop right in front of Eriberto. Surrounded by all his bodyguards and personal escort plus several G-2 interrogators in the same office, Castro had nothing to fear as he slapped Eriberto who had black eyes and bleeding mouth, whose face bore a completely defeated expression. Even though he wasn't tied, he did not dare raise a finger to defend himself; that was the measure of the fear he had of Fidel Castro.

Castro slapped him again and yelled, "If only Celia was still alive to see the magnitude of damage you could inflict on our revolution! How could you be so stupid to allow this man to dupe you? He's been a miserable traitor. We have one of Bonifacio's crew members from his fishing boat that we've been torturing for weeks. Now he's vomited all the truth, how Bonifacio is involved in, planned, and executed many terrorist attacks across the island and is directly in contact with elements within the US Navy base in Guantanamo and the CIA, and they've been committing clandestine activities inside almost every agency in our government. According to the G-2 and Ministry of the Interior, based on the information we got from that crewmember, he was recruited by the most dangerous spy against our revolution and international Marxist-Leninist ideology has ever faced. The codename for that spy is the Lightning, and his name, we now know, is Dr. Julio Antonio del Marmol. You've been so stupid to allow this man Bonifacio to have the combination to the safe containing the most delicate documents we have as highly classified in your trust. I told you *not* to give anyone the combination of that safe. I gave it to you because you're one of the few I can trust on this island. You motherfucking son of a bitch!" He slapped him again.

Eriberto took it with tears of frustration in his eyes, now bleeding from his nose thanks to Castro's blows. He pleaded, "I trusted this man as you trusted me. That is why I gave him the combination, just in case something happened to me, or some emergency came up."

Castro grew more enraged. "Can you imagine it? You gave this man the combination to this safe?" He pointed to the massive safe in one corner. "The combination that only you, me, and my brother Raul had?" He yelled with all the power of his lungs. "Can you imagine the damage you've inflicted on our internationalist proletariat cause? If that man gets that information to the Lightning, it won't be long before copies of those documents get transmitted to enemy intelligence agencies, who will then publish them through the media. Those documents implicate a high, powerful Senator that we're counting on putting into the White House one day, and in that case all our plans to control the most powerful country in the world will fail. Even if we shoot you a hundred times to resuscitate you each time to see you suffer, telling the firing squad to aim for your legs and arms, you will not pay for the damage you've inflicted on our cause. Son of a bitch!" He slapped Eriberto once more. Castro turned to the others. "We cannot under any circumstance allow these documents to leave the island. We have cut the head of this snake off before it can bite us. Turn the island upside down, if necessary, to find these individuals!"

Chapter 10: Castro and His Filthy Games

Castro turned to a man who until now had been silent, observing everything as it went on from a corner of the room. He asked, "Commander Origeo, how much will it cost us to destroy and eliminate once and for all the Lightning who has caused so much damage to our revolution?

Commander Origeo Angulo was an extremely skinny and tall man in his early 30's with milk chocolate skin and a pockmarked face. He put his right hand on his forehead, uncomfortable with the question Castro threw to him. He knew from long and bitter experience that regardless of how he answered the dictator would find a way to contradict and attempt to humiliate him. He had already been blamed for several things, especially for the frustrated attempts to catch the spy Castro always referred to as the Lightning. These repeated attempts with the G-2 had been meticulously planned, but with insufficient funding to operate outside Cuban borders. He had personally supervised several of his men under his command in the MQ-1, a department of the G-2 who acted as highly paid assassins internationally; and even then, they had repeatedly failed with this one mission.

He put all the respect he could into his voice despite his sour disposition and the resentment he felt. "My Commander-in-Chief, from the moment you commanded my division to carry out this very delicate mission to eliminate this man, I told you repeatedly that he is a veteran professional spy with tremendously sophisticated training. I didn't say that because I saw his training, but because in order to survive inside your own office for over a decade and remain undetected tells us a lot. It has been proven that he circulated among the highest level of ministers in the elite circles of this government until he left the country without a single trace. We don't even know how the hell he left; we only have the assumption that he left through the American naval base under the nose of the most sophisticated intelligence agencies in our country. I've been unjustly blamed many times for something no one before me has been capable of doing. My recommendation from the beginning has been that we need to offer such an enormous amount of money to the international crime syndicate to open their appetite so they will not refuse to sit down at our table and finally bring us the head of this spy, the Lightning. With such an enormous amount of money being offered, we might even cause his closest collaborators to feel the temptation to turn him over and serve us his head on a silver platter."

Castro interrupted him, placing his right hand high. "How much? $550,000? You don't think that's sufficient?"

Origeo shook his head with a long face. "No, my Commandante. Unfortunately, that is not enough. Whoever told you to the contrary is lying to you, cheating you, or duping you, exactly as Bonifacio did with Eriberto. I'll put my head on the butcher's block with that. With all my respect, I'll tell you this, not as a criticism, but just as to refresh your memory. If you had followed my recommendations when I suggested it many years ago this sophisticated, well-trained spy would not be in the world of the living anymore."

Fidel Castro looked at him and interrupted furiously, though he kept his tone modulated. He could not deny the truth of what Origeo had said. He said arrogantly, "You suggested too much money at that time. $1,500,000! Do you have any idea? That was ten years ago or more!"

Origeo nodded, a small smile on his face. "You're right, my Commander. But think about the irreparable damage he's done, not even including what could result from today. Is it not possible that the damage done has surpassed a thousand times more than the $1.5 million I had suggested initially? As a comparison, and correct me if I'm wrong, with all my respect, let's start with Ochoa and the Panama operation, which we all know was responsible for the big fiasco and failure in Panama, the loss of the most valuable of our allies, Manuel Noriega, and that's not counting our loss of control of the Panamanian government once Noriega got deposed. We could pass whatever we wanted through the Panama Canal with the authorities keeping their eyes closed because they knew we had friendly hands not just with the President but the entire local government. In Noreiga we lost not only a valuable asset but also a friend and ally to our government in every meaning of those words. We all know that the man responsible for this fiasco is this master spy, the Lightning, who we're dealing with now, a decade later—he and his entire team."

Castro raised both hands high and yelled, "You're right, I should have listened to you at that time and not to those imbeciles who assured me that they could neutralize or eliminate the Lightning for $300,000 or even less. They said that would be more than sufficient."

Origeo smiled in satisfaction at being vindicated. He shook his head. "My Commander-in-Chief, how can you give credit to these, as you call them, imbeciles, who guaranteed you this? You know very well as well as I do that this spy we're dealing with now, who has been recruiting people in the closest, most sensitive and classified locations like here in the Communist Party headquarters, worked directly with the American President Ronald Reagan. He was directly in charge of the whole operation, the Zipper, which caused the economic collapse of the Soviet Union; not only that, but also the collapse of the Berlin Wall. We can't imagine how many millions of dollars, if not billions or trillions, were used in this sophisticated, high-class operation. To this day, it remains classified in the highest intelligence circles within the United States of America. We only know about it through our own spies within the State Department, especially Ana Belen Montes. Only a small group within the intelligence community and within the government know these details." Origeo raised both hands high as he shook his head with an expression of incredulity. "How can we think that these stupid men, as you call them, could assure you that the most sophisticated hit men the Tri-Continental international crime syndicate can recruit could eliminate a spy of this high level of skill with access to this enormous amount of money with just $300,000? And you believed that would be sufficient?"

"OK, OK," Castro replied. "How much do you think will be necessary for us to offer these international assassins to terminate him over here or anywhere he goes and turn off the light on this Lightning nightmare forever?"

Origeo shook his head once more. "Considering that this is the price from over a decade ago, at a minimum I would suggest double of what I proposed back then."

Castro's eyes bulged out of their sockets like an owl with diarrhea. *"Three million dollars?!* Three million dollars to kill a damned miserable spy?" He shook his head and calmed down. "In my time at the university, we only charged for a job like this $1,500 to $2,000. That was when the Cuban peso was as valuable as the dollar."

Origeo was more comfortable and smiled broadly. "Yes, my Commander-in-Chief—those were golden times. Today it's been raining a lot, and we've had multiple hurricanes cross the island which have not always been merciful to us." He spoke with a little sarcasm in his voice. "This is a nightmare, including our glorious revolution."

Fidel looked at him as if he wanted to strangle him. But he needed him and instead shook his right finger furiously in Origeo's face; but he could not hold back a small smile of his own and said in malicious sarcasm, "Be careful. Be careful with your insinuations, Origeo. For a lot less than that, people that don't have the privilege of being as close as you are to me who have said things like that with a double meaning ended up before the firing squad."

Origeo gulped and came back to reality. He knew how paranoid and deceitful Castro was, and hurriedly tried to clarify what he had wanted to say, raising his index fingers and moving his arms from side to side in terror. "No, no, my Commander. Either you misunderstood what I said, or I wasn't clear. I didn't mean for you to interpret it as having a double meaning."

Castro smiled cynically, enjoying the terror revealed in Origeo's face when the firing squad got mentioned. Castro could not be any clearer with his threat, even one disguised under a jocular demeanor. He raised both hands. "Don't worry about it. I was joking just like you were. Payback is hell, eh?"

"Yes, my Commander-in-Chief," he answered.

Castro stood up. "You have the green light on the amount you asked for. If you need more, don't hesitate. This time, I don't want excuses; I want results. I want the Lightning dead. I want the whole team, dead or alive. The sooner the better, and I want those documents retrieved and brought back here. I'll return to Havana, and I expect that you will keep me updated on the progress of the mission. I'll leave you my chopper and pilot here. That way you can get those sons-of-bitches, wherever they go. You dig holes if you have to, but you pull him out and bring him to me."

"Yes, my Commander-in-Chief. You can leave in peace; with your green light you will see the results. All these traitors and counterrevolutionaries will be caught or killed."

They walked out of the office where they had been interrogating Eriberto. Origeo asked Castro, "What are we going to do with this imbecilic traitor?"

Without even blinking, Castro drew his finger across his throat. "Death—what we do to all traitors. I don't swallow for a moment the pill that he's innocent and was trying to protect us. He knows very well that should anything happen in this office everyone has instructions to call my brother Raul immediately. Make sure that before they kill him to castrate him. With that, we will be able to implicate the enemies that we're currently pursuing as the ones who killed him, just as they castrated the soldier in the Crab Plaza. This will be double the crime to justify our actions and rally the people in this town who will be really outraged by these counterrevolutionaries."

Eriberto's screams could be heard outside the office as the G-2 continued their torture of who was once the most prominent man in Caibarien, now out of Castro's favor, the same tortures applied to hundreds if not thousands of Cubans who demonstrated their disaffection for the Marxist-Leninist regime and the Castro brothers.

Castro said goodbye and got into one of the Alfa Romeos. Several others took up escort positions in front and behind his car and they started back to the capital, along with a couple of troop trucks and some Russian Ural motorcycles with sidecars. Origeo began to give orders to his officers regarding what the final disposition of the prisoner was to be. He then got into the helicopter, followed by his personal escort and Castro's pilot, and they lifted off in search of the fugitives.

Back in the lifeboat, the sun was rising, a small sliver just breaking over the horizon. I woke up, extremely tired and sore due to the awkward position I had to sleep in. Atacia had been pressing against my chest; her mother against my legs, both having found a comfortable pillow as we spent our first night in the open sea. I looked at the motor and saw that the engine had been turned off by Bonifacio to allow everyone to sleep. Instead of keeping watch, he, however, lay on his stomach over the motor. The small boat floated over the waves with only the wind to direct it. It appeared that Bonifacio's communication to his brother, as we thought, had never happened. If it had, we should have had some contact during the night. It was possible, to give him the benefit of the doubt, that he came out but could never find us. We had no lights to guide him and in spite of agreeing to set watches, Bonifacio's position showed that all of us were sleeping. His brother could very well have passed by us without seeing us. I later was able to corroborate from the lips of Luis Alberto that his brother did make that call and gave him the navigational coordinates. They had circled us for several miles but saw no sign of our boat. Bonifacio maintained that he had only recently decided to rest for a few minutes, but he had been watching for many hours before. I had relieved Jimbo in the middle of the night for a watch, and then had been relieved by Bonifacio. Regardless of when Bonifacio had fallen asleep, it was definitely true that none of us was always awake to waken the rest of us should any contact with another craft, friend or enemy, was made.

As soon as I saw everyone sleeping so peacefully as if nothing had happened, I couldn't help but think about the happiness of their dream worlds in which all their problems disappeared. This was especially true for those so fortunate to be able to put their heads on their pillow and fall asleep in a few seconds, even during the worst moments of their lives. I was one of those lucky ones in that I could fall asleep right away; but with the discomfort of my position, I was unable to sleep more than a few short intervals all night.

However, the number of troubles and worries I had in my brain could not compare in any way to those of my companions. I had more than one mission to think about, and if not hundreds then thousands of lives depended on its success. As always one cannot predict what will happen in the next minutes, hours, or days, and all these occurrences followed one after another from the moment I arrived on my clandestine trip to the island. Not only was I in immediate danger, but each incident also brought me farther away from the main purpose for my trip to Cuba. I started to worry about that. No matter how many things happen each day that I want to fix, because it's in my nature to protect people from going through miserable experiences, I cannot abandon the principal motives and target of what I initially planned. I noticed that every day I was being dragged away from my real mission. I understood that some things you cannot fight in life, even though you can battle on many fronts. Unfortunately, you cannot control your own destiny.

    I shook my head fondly as I noticed Jimbo sleeping like a little boy, hugging the Stinger like an innocent kid holding his favorite toy. Atacia woke up and saw me smiling. She leaned in and murmured in my ear, "It makes me very happy to see you smiling in the middle of all this chaos. Your attitude and smile are contagious. It's like that old saying here in Cuba that about smiling in the face of calamity." I didn't reply but instead pointed at her brother. She looked and smiled more broadly and shook her head as she took one of my hands to steady herself while she stood up. She didn't want to upset the boat and abruptly wake everyone else. She put one of her arms across my shoulder and said sweetly, "Good morning, Lightning." I smiled. She gave me a small, tender kiss on my lips. "When do you plan to tell the others who you really are?"

    I shook my head. "Only when the circumstance requires it. I believe that every one of us has enough on our minds. Why give them more to worry about?"

    She shook her head in surprise. "I don't believe that telling them who you are will bring them more worry. On the contrary, I believe it will give them tranquility and a sense of security to be in the presence of someone like you. With your experience and capabilities, you manage to get yourself or anyone with you out of the worst situations. I bet my life that this is not the first or worst trouble you've had to resolve before in your life."

    I smiled and shook my head. "That is precisely what I've been trying to avoid. I don't want to give anyone false hopes. I'm just a man, like everyone else, maybe an extremely lucky one up to now. The one thing that I'm so convinced of that I don't think anyone can get me to my mind about is that I have by my side the most powerful angel guarding my back, and His name is Jesus Christ. I want you to remember the old saying that God says He helps those that help themselves, or at least try to."

Atacia shook her head. She grinned again. "Whatever you think is best. I won't argue with you, but I want to let you know that my belief is that you are too modest. I would never have expected that from the Lightning."

At that moment, Aurora, who had practically been sleeping in my lap, stirred. "What? There's lightning? Will there be a storm?"

We both smiled and looked at each other in the eyes, but then something very much out of the ordinary, almost mystical, happened. An enormous and very noisy clap of thunder shook the entire boat, almost as if lightning had indeed struck near us. On the horizon the sliver of rising sun disappeared, swallowed up by black clouds moving fast, lightning flickering back and forth among the clouds. As if in a musical counterpoint, the powerful noise of a helicopter brought chills along the back of my neck as an enormous multicolored bolt of lightning appeared like a magic act right in the front of the helicopter was coming towards us. The helicopter pilot, clearly accustomed to the rapid weather changes of the tropics, turned immediately and moved away from us to avoid the storm. He circled back from where he came, disappearing into the black clouds. Even so, we identified it by the flash of lightning as a military helicopter with red stars on the sides—the markings revealing it as one of Castro's personal helicopters. It was likely that we weren't seen through the mist over the ocean and the attention-distracting lightning. The surface mist where we were turned rapidly into torrential rain, soaking us utterly even though it lasted for a few minutes. It was as if it had happened just to divert our enemy.

The sky rapidly cleared, and the sun reappeared on the horizon. I checked my wristwatch, and it was exactly 10 o'clock in the morning, and promised to be a beautiful day in that Caribbean paradise. Atacia leaned in and murmured in my ear, "Now I understand what you just said. I have no doubts that you have a very powerful angel guarding your back and anyone with you."

She hadn't even finished speaking before a seagull flew over us with his typical melody which sounded like a blend between a pig in distress and a car in the wintertime that didn't want to start. We all looked towards the sky in search of that marvelous signal from God. Where there's a bird there is land nearby. Bonifacio, however, being a practical captain, rushed to get his binoculars to search for that firm ground. Before leaving, the seagull circled a couple of times, leaving us baptized with a dropping on the stern. Most of the rest of the gull's droppings landed next to the outboard motor and on Bonifacio's binoculars. He cried out, "*Los Cayos*[3]*!*", overjoyed more than annoyed by the droppings. He dipped the binoculars into the sea to clean them as he started the engines and sped towards the land he sighted. Joyfully, he pushed the engine to maximum speed.

Before long, we saw large pinnacles of rock extending up from the ocean and bluffs with vegetation hanging from the cliffs, giving us a beautiful view. The rocks looked like they rose up out of the ocean like a splendid entry into a mansion. Together, they formed a beautiful island with coconut trees and beautiful flowers. Bonifacio slowed the speed of our boat as we got close to

---

[3] The Cays!

the land. What looked like a long strand of beach was in fact a reef, the rocks rising out of the ocean more frequently, forming gigantic walls. Mama Teca surprised us by yelling, "Be careful! Rocks! Dog's Teeth in the water!"

Those sharp rocks were enough to rip the bottom out of even a large ship. Bonifacio didn't have a good view of the rocks, and abruptly turned to avoid them. Unfortunately, at that moment, Aurora was lying on her stomach to wash her face and the momentum of the sudden turn made her fly over the side of the boat into the sea. Bonifacio was able to avoid the rocks, but Jimbo yelled, "Woman overboard!"

Bonifacio pulled us to a near stop and began to circle. He gestured to Aurora to come in and said, "Woman—why didn't you hold on tight?"

As he moved towards Aurora, Atacia yelled, "Mama, are you OK?"

Embarrassed, Aurora said, "Yes, only soaked to the bone. I'm still in one piece."

I said to Bonifacio, "You haven't taught me this marine maneuver you just made, Captain. Is it a new communist one? Do you intend to kill your mate?"

Everyone laughed at the comic jest as Aurora swam to the boat to try and get in. Jimbo yelled, "Watch out, Mom! You have a shark following you!"

Bonifacio increased the speed to get to his wife before the shark did. As he did, he tried to cut off the shark's approach with the boat. As a scuba diver all my life, I knew better than to try to run from a shark. I said to Aurora, "No, don't run. Use your hands to push towards the shark." I knew that sharks could smell fear. She was in full panic. Instead of trying to swim away, she should have turned towards it forcefully to make it hesitate. The shark drew closer. I yelled to Bonifacio, "Try to get her back in the boat, OK? Get me close to that shark—turn the boat a little."

I pulled both of my knives out and leaned over the edge of the boat. Bonifacio realized what I was intending to do and nudged me to help me over. I landed on top of the shark like it was a horse. I could see the line of its body and gills from the top of the boat. It felt something on its back, without knowing what it was. It surfaced in an attempt to shake me off. Its mouth gaped open wide as it went into attack mode. I stabbed both knives into its gills as far as I could. I had to act quickly as once it felt those blows it would dive deep, and so pulled them out of the shark, letting it go. It turned over as it submerged and dove at full speed in its retreat.

That extremely unpleasant surprise was now off its back. The wounds I had made in its gills were mortal, and the hunter became the hunted in what was now its final hunt. Aurora was now close to the boat and was helped on board by Atacia and Mama Teca. When I reached the boat, the hands of the two women were waiting to help me aboard in my own turn. Jimbo and Atacia, full of gratitude, praised me for what I had done. I said, "I didn't do anything that you wouldn't have done if the shoe was on the other foot."

Aurora gave me a vast hug and kissed me on the cheek. "Where did you learn to deal with sharks that way?"

"Those sharks aren't as dangerous as they appear. They always follow the same pattern, and when you learn how to counterattack them, they become easy prey. They will always show their teeth to you, unlike men and their terrible ideologies who never follow the same patterns and don't always show you their teeth until it's too late for you to be able to defend yourself."

Aurora smiled and nodded. "You are 100% right, honey. We in Cuba have all gotten to know very well that kind of human species for many decades now. They took us by surprise and have tried to destroy our lives. But as the old Cuban saying goes, the only animal that trips over the same rock twice is a human being." She shook her head sadly. "What an irony for me to nearly end my life in the mouth of that large shark. That is the only form of death that I ever feared in all my life, even though I was born by the sea. I was never able to make the sea my friend or bring her into my heart, because she took the two most beautiful human beings I loved most, my mother and father, when I was very young." Her voice cracked with emotion. "They were fishermen born here in Caibarien. When Bonifacio proposed to me, I told him that my only condition before saying yes was that he could fish all his life but never ask me to go with him on his fishing trips. I didn't want my children to be orphans like I was when my parents disappeared in a tropical storm. At least I expected one of us to be alive and take care of our kids. And if we got married without his agreeing to that, I would never give him a child." She finished with satisfaction in her voice and a more pleasant expression on her face, "Bonifacio, my handsome, gallant man accepted my condition, and so I gave him our boy Jimbo." She took Jimbo's hand in her left. "God gave us Atacia, a little girl, when I didn't think I would be able to have any more pregnancies." She held out her right hand to Atacia, who took it. She nodded. "Until this day, we have had a great and peaceful family with my son and adopted daughter. Thank you very much for saving my life. This gesture of yours says a lot about you and who you are: not only a brave and generous man, full of love in your heart. You will make any woman you choose as your companion very happy. Men like you are rare these days."

"Thank you for your beautiful words," I replied. Atacia looked at me with a beautiful smile.

We were close to the beach now, and Bonifacio intended to beach his boat there. He looked through his binoculars and pointed into the distance. "The helicopter is coming back!" He handed me the binoculars.

I put them to my eyes. It was the same helicopter coming in our direction. I saw the government emblems and red stars on each side. I yelled, "Yes, yes—I believe that is Castro's personal helicopter! Looks like we've touched a nerve to make him either come over here or send someone to find us and put us down." I pointed out a small cave between the bluffs to our right. "Turn around—don't go to the beach. We'll be a perfect target. Go towards those rocks—they'll protect us."

He yelled, "Everyone hold on!" As he made a drastic turn to the right, he increased the speed once more to maximum thrust in a desperate attempt to get out of that situation. We would be gunned down mercilessly by the assassins on that helicopter as they were accustomed to doing with the *balseros*[4] which tried escape the island, looking not just for freedom but also an escape from tyranny of the supposed communist paradise, looking for a better life for their families without any political agenda.

The helicopter flew over our heads, leaving us without any doubts what its intentions were. Only by the grace of God did we reach the cave before the chopper arrived. We entered the cave, forcing it to gain altitude to

---

[4] Literally "boat people", used for those who escaped Cuba by making their own rafts out of whatever materials they could scrounge together.

avoid crashing against the rocks. We were sprayed by automatic weapons fire which ripped through the rocks, dropping small pieces of rock and gravel like confetti which landed on the heads of Jimbo, Mama Teca, and Bonifacio in the rear of the boat. We knew it wouldn't end here, as they would continue their hunt until they saw us dead.

I asked Jimbo, "Do you bring a rocket when you took your toy from the fishing boat?"

Jimbo nodded. He took a rocket from his backpack and held it up. "We only have one. That's all I was able to take from the box when we encountered the torpedo boat."

I nodded with a big smile. "One is all we need. Remember, when the torpedo boat tried to stop us, we only used one."

Jimbo nodded and smiled in satisfaction, remembering how that incident had ended and enjoying the memory. The helicopter was still circling outside and started to try something different. He lowered, practically touching the water in front of the cave. Though they couldn't see into the darkness of the cave, in their desperate search for blood they began to shoot indiscriminately into the mouth of the cave, firing blindly. Two holes appeared in the left side of the boat, which we began to patch at once. Another bullet struck Aurora in the arm, inflicting a flesh wound. We worked on cleaning and bandaging that as well. We knew that more bursts were coming until they knew we were dead, so we prepared an unpleasant welcome.

I discussed my plan with the others, removing the provisions from the boat, stowing our supplies on a natural ledge as well as seating everyone alongside the cave wall. The only people remaining in the boat were Jimbo, Mama Teca, and I. I took control of the boat and told Bonifacio,

"Stay with the others. If we don't make it, see that everyone else gets to safety."

I heard the engine of the helicopter growing loud as they slowly descended in front of the cave as they did before and prepared to shoot inside. I thrust the outboard motor to maximum, and we sped out towards the cave mouth, taking the pilot by surprise as it appeared we were going to ram him. He immediately rose up to gain altitude and began turning to bring his guns to bear on us. Mama Teca and Jimbo were sitting along the centerline of the boat's bottom, covered with a blanket. The pilot in the chopper could only see me piloting the boat as he turned to prepare for the kill shot. I stopped the boat so that my rocket team would have a steady platform for their shot as Mama Teca, using Jimbo's shoulder, rose up from the center of the boat and pointed the Stinger towards the chopper. Completely in shock, the pilot tried to turn around to avoid the rocket. It flew into the air, moving too fast to be avoided. It hit the helicopter in the center near the back, cutting it into two pieces. The bodies of the soldiers inside flew, some burning pieces which landed on the sand of the beach, some in the ocean. We could see the pilot and one of the passengers still inside the front of the chopper, landing like a sack of potatoes on the white sand of the beach. The ones who weren't so lucky flew into space, bodies all over the place in the water and the sand. I directed the boat towards the beach to look for survivors.

Chapter 11: The Six-Fingered Man's Genetic Trail

As we arrived at the beach I jumped out of the boat. I saw that the tide was rising. The closest we could approach was still around ten feet from the disappearing beachline, so we raised the outboard motor so that we could move in closer, but even then, we remained at a distance; the water was up to our knees when we went over the side of the boat to make our way towards the land. I pointed at the water and said to Jimbo, "The tide's coming in pretty fast. There is no way we'll know how quickly that cave will fill up. We should use this change in the tide; go immediately to get your family out of that cave as soon as possible. The same cave which saved our lives could now be a death trap. We could also lose all the provisions which could keep us alive for weeks. The last thing we want is to stay on this island eating only coconut meat for however long we're here. We also don't want your family, especially Aurora with her wounded shoulder, to swim such a long distance. Let's hope to God that we don't have to stay on this small island for long and your Uncle Luis Alberto comes to our rescue, but we have to depend on ourselves until that time comes."

Jimbo replied, "Be very careful if you're going to check for survivors in that wreckage. Remember these communists all have weapons and no scruples. There might be survivors, and even wounded they could still be a danger for us."

"Thank you, but I have Mama Teca with me. I'm not by myself and in case a dangerous situation rises, she'll help me neutralize our enemies. I don't believe anyone could survive your powerful toy, but half the chopper dropped like a sack of potatoes onto the beach. Even if they survived the explosion, the impact from that altitude likely killed anyone still in that cabin."

"OK, OK—I know you know best; I just didn't want you to get caught by surprise."

"Thank you. Go quickly and get your family out of this cave and onto this beach. This will be our improvised headquarters for a while."

"Aye, aye, Captain," Jimbo said with a grin. He put the motor into the water and pushed the engine to full power as he headed towards the cave.

Mama Teca walked ashore with me. The water was now up to our chests. She bent over and pointed at something metallic in the water by her feet shining in the sunlight. She dipped down under water and brought up a beautiful 9mm pistol and showed it to me. I looked down at my feet and also saw something shining. I went underwater and found not just another pistol, but several other weapons scattered around the sandy bottom. Evidently the explosion had blown the weapons out of the hands of the passengers, scattering their armament all over the bottom of the shoal.

We abandoned the initial idea of looking for survivors and instead focused on collecting the weapons and any boxes of ammunition we could find along with any other hardware, knives, and other equipment the soldiers had. After we got done collecting the weapons, we cut some bushes to give the weapons some place to dry out other than simply lying on the sand. By the time we were done, we saw Jimbo coming back up to the beach with the rest of our people and supplies. We waded out to help receive them and tied the boat off to the trunk of a coconut tree. Then we got down to work, building a small shelter and campsite located strategically on top of one of the larger rocks which gave us a full view of the entire beach in case of unwanted visitors. The weapons and munitions we left on the rocks to dry out but concealed from the open beach in our camp. When I looked at my wristwatch it was one pm; about half the day had been taken up building our shelter. The tide was still rising, and the beach was quickly eaten up by the ocean, the shoreline now nearly level to the coconut palms.

We organized the weapons and provisions into shelters against the weather and used some of the helicopter wreckage as a roof. Now that we weren't as focused on getting our camp set up, we heard terrified screams for help. Someone was yelling for aid from the half piece of the chopper which had landed on the other side of the beach. The high tide had covered nearly half of it with water. Only a sliver of sand still was above water at this point, and as the tide continued to rise, the cabin of the wrecked vehicle continued to submerge.

"Help," the voice cried. "Both my legs are broken, and I'm stuck."

Mama Teca looked at me. "That is exactly what every single communist deserves in exchange for all the innocent lives they destroy each day without any mercy. Children, orphans, mothers, widows, recently married couples, men sent to prison for twenty and thirty years—we should let that miserable pig drown over there."

I took a deep breath. "You might be right, Mama Teca. And believe me, I understand—they killed my son. But think about this for a second, putting your emotions to one side and using your best judgment. What if that individual yelling for help is somebody exactly like Bonifacio or Jimbo, who has never been a communist, with no other alternative than to make everyone believe that they sympathize with this government? Some do it to avoid causing problems for their families; others do it because they're working with us. What if this individual is an exception? He's pleading for his life. What about that? He could be one of our allies who work deep within the guts of Castro's organization. They've risked their lives, bringing us very valuable information for decades to stop Castro's invasions all over the world and his communist ideology as well as the terrorist acts that this government finances all over the world, the revolutions and guerillas they sponsor."

Everyone looked at me with guilty expressions. I breathed in deeply again as I raised my arms high as I heard that voice yelling for help in terror and distress. "When the tree is felled by the weather, everyone uses the wood for fire. What if we make an exception sometimes and take one of those branches and plant it close to the dead tree, instead of taking all the wood because it's easy and available? Let's leave something for the future and plant that little branch to grow a tree for later. I, for one, will sleep better tonight if I don't ignore those desperate screams from someone who might once have been my enemy, but now defeated is begging for his life. I at least want to make sure that I am not committing an unjust act that puts me on the same level as my enemies. If any of you guys want to come with me, I will consider it a great help and it's the decent, humanitarian thing to do." As I spoke, I picked up one of the pistols that had dried out. I checked that it was loaded and cocked; to be certain it was working properly, I fired two shots into the trunk of a coconut tree before putting it in my waistband.

As I left our shelter, Atacia said, "I will go with you if you want."

I grinned in satisfaction. "Of course, I will be very happy if not only you but all of you come with me. There is strength in unity. That unity is what has kept us alive through all these ordeals. Besides, we're not communists or Marxists, we love capitalism and democracy. The majority will decide, not me, what we will do with this survivor of the crash who tried to kill all of us. We should not prematurely judge; let's save his life, give him time, and when we find out who he is and what he deserves, we will decide then what to do with him. At this moment, let's respond to the distressed plea for help and not let our anger or any desire for revenge choke off our good nature. We cannot let this man drown without lifting a finger to prevent it, no matter who he is. That is what makes us different from these atheist, murdering, deceitful Marxists."

The others slowly stood up and followed me. Mama Teca grabbed a pistol and some ropes, slinging them over her shoulders, and we all walked towards the wreckage. As we neared it, we heard the voice continuing to yell for help, now banging on something metal with a pipe in desperation to free himself from the tangle of aluminum, wires, and upholstery that ensnared him. We entered what used to be the control cabin; the water was up to our necks. The man strained to keep his face near the roof of the chopper. He was a mulatto with blue eyes; it was Commander Origeo Angulo. I could see the desperation in his eyes; I had seen his face in multiple intelligence briefings and immediately recognized him as the man in charge of the assassins used by Cuba's MQ-1 to eliminate political and religious leaders opposed to Marxism as well as the Cuban exiles in every corner around the world. I recognized those eyes; they belonged to the man who had tortured me in Libya when I was pursuing the man who had killed my son.

Origeo stared at me as if recognizing my face and was trying to place where he had seen me before. Our eyes met and I could see he had finally identified me. Surprise filled his face as his worst nightmares of encountering me once more, much less in a disadvantaged position. His eyes grew wide, and the iron bar slipped out of his hands as he tried to free himself from the knotted seatbelt which entangled his body. With horror in his eyes he yelled, "The Lightning? What the hell are you doing here in Cuba? I thought you were out of commission. And I thought that this wreck was the worst thing that could happen to me today."

I looked at him unpleasantly. "The feeling is mutual, though I unfortunately cannot say 'my friend.' The only difference is that now I'm not your prisoner at your mercy while you rip my nails out. It looks like the omelet has flipped, and now your life is in my hands like mine was in yours before. As I remember, you didn't treat me very well during our last encounter. I can see that you haven't changed a bit—you've continued to be the same assassin that I always knew you were, still licking the boots of Fidel and his brother like a good dog. In the end, you are always at the service of your master for the bones they throw away from the leftovers on the table."

Everyone except Atacia looked at me in tremendous surprise as they heard Origeo reveal my codename. I could see in Jimbo's eyes a massive surprise blended with joy when I looked at him and saw a bright smile of satisfied admiration reflected in his face. He asked, "Is what he said true?"

I nodded in response to his question. "Yes. That is the only truth that has passed the lips of this criminal mercenary possibly for the past several years."

They looked at me in confusion at the confirmation of my identity. A hurricane of emotions broke as all the very sad, terrible memories of my son's death came crashing back into my mind and soul, completely overwhelming me. My vision blurred, and I supported myself from one of the seatbelts dangling along the wall of that wrecked cabin to avoid collapsing into the water from the sudden dizziness I experienced. The guilt I felt about the death of my son I had bottled inside my heart and mind over the intervening years erupted like a volcano all at once. My mind felt like it was ready to explode.

I had never experienced anything like this before. I thought I had already dealt with those emotions and put them behind me. Tears ran unnoticed from my eyes, and I felt the same horrible pain in my heart as the tumultuous day I received this terrible news. Instead, it had been buried very deeply in my heart; I still felt very guilty about my son's death. I should have, with my professional experience and skills, managed the safety of my son better. Unfortunately, the obligations and complications of the life of a spy took me away sometimes from my responsibilities, and I neglected to put in place the necessary measures and precautions to avoid his death in retaliation. I blamed myself because I had such great diplomatic connections and through the intelligence community and not taking seriously the cruelty of the communists in Cuba were capable of. I continually asked myself why I hadn't taken him out of Cuba beforehand. If necessary, I could have come in a submarine and torn him out of the clutches of the communists and removed him to a safe place somewhere else in the world. I had tangible proof that the only motive for his assassination was to get back at me. That had been eating me alive, bottled up inside myself; now it exploded in my contact with this black man with the blue eyes.

Several Years Before
Havana, Cuba
Maria del Carmen Suburb
Central #14

     It was a beautiful residence on the banks of the Rio Cristal. My son, a young, very fit man of around twenty-three was inside the house, removing his clothes in the bathroom in preparation to take a shower. After he was done, he dried his body off and began to dress in jeans, T shirt, and a black leather biker jacket. He left his room and walked towards the kitchen of the house. He gave a kiss to his mother, who was about forty years old, with European features, long, black hair, and a very beautiful figure. Julio Antonio, Junior, Julito as he was known affectionately, stepped back a little and asked, "Mami, what do you think how I look in my father's clothes?"

     She took her left hand to her mouth with a broad grin as she looked her son over from head to toe. She nodded in satisfaction. "My God, whatever you have inherited from your bloodline cannot be stolen. You are, without any doubt, the best gift your father ever could have left behind for me when he departed Cuba. You are the exact copy of his portrait. Now, seeing you in his clothes, your resemblance to him is something unbelievable." Unwanted tears glistened in her eyes and rolled down her cheeks involuntarily. "How proud your father would be to see you if he were here now. You not only physically look like him but you're also like him in personality. You didn't get it from my family, and your personality and character is the most beautiful gift I ever had in my life."

Julito grew emotional, touched by his mother's compliments and seeing her tears. He hugged her tenderly and murmured in her ear, "Thank you very much, Mami, for your beautiful words. But please don't cry. You know that depresses me and brings me a great deal of sadness, like I saw you cry before when my father had to leave. I don't ever want to see you cry again, please."

She rushed to dry her face on her kitchen apron. "OK, OK. Go to your girlfriend Maria, say hello to her from me, but please ride your motorcycle slowly and carefully. As I've told you before, I don't like them because one of those nearly took the life of your father before you were even born when he worked as a medical inspector in the *Niña Bonitas*[5] as a genetic control inspector in those dairy farms."

"Don't worry, Mami. I'll drive slowly and very carefully." The young man bent over once more to kiss his mother before leaving the kitchen.

He walked to the library in the house, where he took his helmet and gloves. Then he walked into the garage and opened the door. He started his motorcycle and left the house at a very moderate speed.

Not very far away, a man dressed entirely in black sat in the backseat of a black Russian Volga automobile, watched the young Julio Antonio, Jr. through small binoculars, not missing a single detail as the youth left the house. He lit a cigarette; his left hand had six fingers. Another two men, the driver and one sitting in the

---

[5] A special dairy program Castro unsuccessfully experimented with in Cuba.

passenger seat in the car. The six-fingered man continued to follow the young man through the binoculars as he passed close to where they had parked. He then tapped the driver with his right hand as a signal to follow the boy. The car started to follow the motorcycle. Julito had no idea that imminent danger was encompassing him. Happily, he rode his motorcycle, a gift from his father that he maintained and was very proud of, towards the city center.

Figure 13 The Six-Fingered Man

The Volga continued to follow at a safe distance. The six-fingered man picked the transmitter of a police radio. In a profoundly deep voice, the six-fingered man said, "A-6 here, calling H-1. Over."

There was a little static interference before another voice similar in deepness. "H-1 receiving, over."

"The bird is flying his nest on the same route as always. Be prepared. Remember the Commander-in-Chief wants to make it look like an accident. Copy. Out."

"OK. Received and understood. Confirmed. Just as everything has been prepared. How much time do we have?"

The six-fingered man looked at his watch. "Depending on the traffic, which is very light, I don't believe it will be more than fifteen minutes. Over."

"Very well. Everything is in order. The sniper is in place. Green light to proceed?"

"Green light, proceed. No more communication, radio off."

"All confirmed. Over and out."

Julio Antonio turned onto Avenue 100 and drove by the *Fuente Luminosa*[6]. He pulled over into a small bicycle access to a small park and stopped next to the sidewalk by the alley. A very old lady in her eighties with two long braids very well done with little bows at the end of each braid which matched exactly the floral dress she wore. Her hair was completely snowy white, and she was behind a small wagon pulled by a large white goat with a black spot around its left eye that looked like it had been painted on and bells attached to its horn. The lady was a vendor who sold fruit and flowers at that intersection. On each side of the wagon were signs which read "Fruit and flowers, at a low price. From my home to your home." The young man secured his bike on the concrete sidewalk and removed his helmet. He went over to the old lady; as he walked, he pulled a wallet out of his pocket, removing a few bills as if

---

[6] Luminous Fountain, a fountain in Havana

he knew exactly what he was going to spend. It was clear he was a repeat customer as the bronze-skinned old lady with her deep blue eyes greeted him familiarly with a large smile. She wrapped one of the bouquets of yellow roses and handed it to the young man approaching her.

She said, "*Hola, Julito.* There you are—the favorite roses for your fiancée, Maria Teresa." Julito smiled and took the roses in his right hand. He handed the bills to her with his left. The old lady grinned broadly. "Thank you very much."

He replied, "*Hola, Doña Carmen. Muchas gracias* for your great memory."

The old lady touched his shoulder, still smiling as she handed him some coins in change. "My son, that is the only good thing that's left in me in my old age." She held his hand and turned it over to look at the lines on his palm. "Be careful. You have a dark cloud right behind you that wants to hurt you badly." She pointed behind him, right at where the Volga had pulled over to await Julito's next move, causing the men inside to start in surprise; but then she continued to point up towards the sky.

Julito declined the coins as he glanced up towards the sky and a little behind him. Not seeing any cloud, he mentally shrugged it off as nonsense while he pushed the coins firmly back into her hand. "You can use that tip to feed more grass to my friend Pancho." As he caressed the neck of the goat on the back of which hung a sign which read "I am Pancho."

Pancho ignored Julito and continued to eat out of the leather feed bag hanging around his neck. The old lady smiled once more. "I assure you that Pancho and I are both grateful for your tip."

Julito looked at her pleasantly and smiled as he said goodbye. He walked over to his motorcycle and opened one of the leather side bags on the back of the vehicle and carefully settled the bouquet inside, tying it carefully so that the flowers didn't lose their petals in the wind. Reassured that the bouquet was steady and raised his right hand high and said, "You have a great day, Doña Carmen. God bless you."

She smiled. "After you stop here you make my day the best in the whole week because every time you stop by my wagon, you bring me tremendous luck. You should come more frequently, because it's like a stampede comes behind you. Everyone is attracted by your good vibe and those are the days I make the most money all week."

Julito replied, "Thank you very much. I'm very happy to bring you luck, Doña Carmen. It's good to know that I will always be welcome if it is as you say."

Doña Carmen replied a little defensively, "You know I don't make up things—if I tell you something you can bet your life that it is what I said."

He smiled. "OK, OK, Doña Carmen—no need to get upset."

"I'm not upset. You'd better say hello Maria Teresa and you'd better ride carefully on that thing, my son. God bless you and thank you for stopping by."

Julito started the motorcycle, smiling broadly as he shook his head and left. He continued traveling along Avenue 100, followed at a discrete distance by the Volga. Julito stopped at a red light. Even though the streets were deserted, the youth obeyed the traffic signal and waited until the light turned green. A short distance away the six-fingered man and his two accomplices also stopped to avoid drawing attention to themselves. As soon as the green light changed, the driver of the Volga put a portable red light on the dashboard to identify them as a government vehicle as he turned sharply in a circle, the tires screeching over the asphalt as it sped up rapidly behind the motorcycle.

They drew close to the bike and struck it, taking Julito by surprise as he skidded off the road while he fought to maintain control. As he got into the center of the road, a bullet from a nearby building hit the front tire of the motorcycle, fired by a sniper to make it look like an accident. The youth lost what little control of the motorcycle as the tire blew, and he flew through the air, falling in the middle of the other lane of the avenue, where a large eight-wheeled military truck, loaded with equipment covered by tarps had no time to stop. Everything was well-prepared, and the massive vehicle ran over both motorcycle and young man at high speed.

Not happy with just running over the vehicle and rider, the driver stopped a hundred feet past and stepped out to look back. He saw the young man attempting to stand—though the bike was a mangled piece of metal, the youth was not dead. He got back in, put the truck in reverse, and slowly backed up. According to eyewitnesses, this criminal, premeditated act took place when they thought no one was around, since the road was deserted and the surrounding area very open. One would think that the driver would reverse to find out and help the wounded man; but instead, when the truck came near to the accident, it accelerated in reverse, running over both body and motorcycle, dragging them under it across the pavement. There was no way he could survive that second impact, not after the first blow.

The six-fingered man said to the driver of the Volga, "Let's go. Stop by the body." To the passenger he said, "Origeo, take his pulse and make certain he's dead." He pulled a handkerchief out of his pocket and handed it to the mulatto. "If he's still alive, you know what you have to do. We cannot make any mistakes. This young man must be dead. The Commander-in-Chief wants to send a message to our worst enemy, the Lightning, wherever he may be in the world, that this is direct retaliation, and has lost today the most precious treasure in his life, his only son. This will be a great victory and a very strong lesson and message to all our enemies, one the Lightning will never be able to forget for as long as he lives."

Origeo turned around. "I believe that we took too long to do this. It should have been done ten years ago. If we had, we might have stopped the Lightning from doing so much damage to our revolution. That's not even counting the millions of dollars he's cost us in our businesses around the world in drug trafficking, organ harvesting, and yes, nuclear weapons." He added sarcastically, "It's past time for the Lightning to pay the debt he owes our revolution."

The six-fingered man nodded in agreement without any emotional display. "We have to eliminate not only our enemies but also every single seed they leave behind."

Origeo nodded, got out of the car, and walked over to the still form and past the blood-covered yellow rose petals scattered across the road.

Back to the Present

I was absolutely convinced that I had suffered what the medical world terms a nervous emotional collapse or a post-traumatic stress disorder flashback. When you are in a moment of complete weakness, even in good mental health, without even closing your eyes, your subconscious that has received a psychological trauma brings back the old memories like a film, memories that it guards deeply in your mind. I had been only held up by the seatbelt attached by a screw to the wall of the chopper, but I had no notion what had happened during the time I was in that emotional mental flashback.

I later was told that Mama Teca had repeatedly asked me if I was OK as I was motionless while I held myself up in complete silence. They told me that when she asked me if I were OK, I simply would nod and say very abruptly, even in irritation, "Yes, I'm OK." The strange part was that I had no recollection of her inquiries or my response during that period of time, however long it lasted.

I opened my eyes as if awakening from sleep or a nightmare, I realized that time had certainly passed. Mama Teca and Jimbo had cut Commander Origeo free of the seatbelts entangling him. Now, with both hands free, he realized that his legs weren't broken like he had thought. I saw, and I didn't understand how at that moment, that he had a pistol in his hand. He managed to put it to the back of my head. I saw it out of the corner of my eye and felt the muzzle on the back of my head. As Jimbo had been distracted in freeing him, Origeo had taken the pistol from Jimbo's waist.

Now that I was fully back and realized what was going on, the cold-blooded assassin was yelling and pushing the pistol into my head as he spoke to the rest of the group, trying to convince them that he would not take any retaliation against them, knowing that he needed them to enable him to leave that place alive. He told them that he would talk to Fidel Castro and say that he had captured me with their help. He yelled, "Do you know how much this son of a bitch is worth? Three million dollars!" They looked at each other. "Fidel gave me his word. This man is to be taken, dead or alive, and we get the money. It will be more difficult to transport him dead, so let's keep him alive. I'll divide that money between you guys. Imagine what you could do with that amount of money!"

He saw no positive response from them, only long, serious faces, so he continued to try and persuade them that he would guarantee that nothing would happen to them. My mind grew clearer, and I waited for the opportunity in silence until he distracted himself for a few seconds to snatch the gun from his hand as I had been trained. But I had to wait my chance if I wanted to avoid any of my friends to accidently getting injured if he managed to fire the gun.

"If any of you even want to leave the country, I will provide you with passports through my contacts in the government to any country you want to go. Fidel Castro will owe you for your assistance in the capture of the Lightning; you'll be able to go to any country you want and enjoy the money I'll share with you." He still saw no favorable response and grew irritated. "What happened to you guys? Do you have any idea have how much money three million is? Enough for us to relax for the rest of our lives and not have to do anything at all! I'll share it with you guys equally."

A sharp sound echoed between the water and nearly filled cabin of the helicopter. The pressure of the pistol against my head disappeared. I had no idea whether he had pulled the weapon away, if he had been shot, or what. Life returned to my body, and I saw Origeo slowly collapsing into the water with a hole in his forehead. I rushed to grab the weapon still held in his right hand very carefully and saw Mama Teca with a pistol in her hand. I realized that she had shot Origeo. She took a deep breath. "With all my respect, especially now that I know who you really are, for the sake of God and His Son Jesus Christ, I ask you to be more careful and not give your enemies so many opportunities. Remember I told you we should let this guy drown here. He nearly killed you. Maybe you considered me heartless, but our enemies must be eliminated. If we allow them to take advantage of your nobility, not only us but many innocent people around the world will die; we need people like you to recover the freedom that these bandits, assassins, and unscrupulous individuals took from them."

I nodded. "You're right. However, should the day come that, in order to destroy the heartless villain, I have to lower myself down to their level, abandoning my principles and decency, I would rather instead die one thousand times. If I allow that to happen, I will be the one who loses my soul to that heartless villain, and he will be the winner since he has converted me into a heartless villain, as filthy or even filthier than he."

Atacia came over, emotional at my words, and gave me a small kiss on the cheek. "When I listen to you and analyze the meaning of your words, you make me feel very proud, not only of you, but because you made me a better person, especially if I had been thinking differently than what you had told me. Your mercy to humanity is extraordinary and your integrity is out of this world. Maybe to some others that don't know you, you can sound strange and difficult to understand. You have a different personality. But I ask you to please never change. I adore the way you are, and I admire your bravery, and though it's a little crazy, I love more than anything your personality."

Mama Teca shook her head and said to me, "OK, let's leave that romance for later. Let's get out of here before this wreck fills completely with water and drown us all here. Besides, I'm very anxious for you to tell me about all the adventures you have had all over the world. It will be extremely interesting to hear some of them."

Bonifacio smiled and said to me as he patted me on the shoulder, "Aside from the point of personal security, I would like very much to know why you let us discover your true identity from the lips of our enemy."

Atacia grinned. "Not everyone. I knew it."

He turned to Atacia and said teasingly, "Ah! You little traitor, you didn't tell us."

"I'm sorry, Dad, but I promised him to never reveal that. You taught me that when you make a promise you never break it."

"There you go!" he said proudly. "You're my girl!"

As we left the wrecked chopper and headed to the beach, Atacia said to me, "I have to say something that may sound funny to you after I found out that your head is worth three million dollars. That could be very tempting, especially among the communists. They would sell you out for a pair of Adidas tennis shoes." Everyone laughed. "Well, those shoes are a high commodity in Cuba. You can't even find it with three million dollars unless you go to a store that accepts dollars."

The sun was setting as we walked along the beach. The multicolored clouds were building up, and Aurora was the one this time who asked, "Can I ask a question?"

"Sure, you can ask more than one. You're the matriarch of this team. Ask whatever you want."

"I wonder—why do they call you the Lightning? If this isn't a secret thing that could hurt you, I would love to know how that name came about."

Chapter 12: Jimbo and the Radio Sent from Heaven

I smiled. "It might be difficult for you to believe, but that codename was not my idea nor even that of my friends within the intelligence community; they gave me a different codename."

Aurora shook her head in disbelief. Her eyes filled with curiosity, she asked again, "If it wasn't your idea or one of your allies, who came up with it, and why that name in particular?"

We were drawing near to our temporary base camp. Everyone started to sit down on the various rocks we had around the area. Though it wasn't very comfortable, it was better than sitting in the sand. Aurora sat close to me, next to Atacia. She asked her daughter, "Do you know, by any chance, the answer to my question?"

Atacia shook her head with a grin. "No, Mami. It never crossed my mind, to be honest with you, to ask that question of Dr. del Marmol." As soon as she spoke, she put her hand over her lips, raising her right hand high and pointing to the sky as she shook her head. She looked at me and said, "I'm sorry. Really sorry, Dr. Valentine."

I smiled. "Don't worry, Atacia. Since everyone here already knows my codename, we might as well let them know my real name. I don't want them to find out what my real name is from the lips of one of my enemies. Besides, by now there's no longer any reason to keep that hidden. I would prefer them to get that information from friendly lips rather than from one of our enemies."

Bonifacio also sat nearby. As he heard my response, he smiled and said in an ironic tone, "Thank you, Mr. Lightning, my great friend. We are in a great progress moving towards a solid and sincere friendship as you deposit a vote of trust in all of us and not only exclusively to Atacia."

I caught the tone and shook my head. "You're welcome. But just remember, always, our best friend today could be our worst enemy tomorrow. Unless it's absolutely necessary, I don't want to know anything which could implicate any of you guys or put your security at risk. We have to be extremely careful with our identities and the information we possess. Only those who need to know should partake of that information in case a traitor infiltrates our group; then the reach of the information he gets will be limited and the damage that could be done to us is minimized."

As we talked, Aurora was twiddling her thumbs, her curiosity making her restless and impatient because the conversation had been interrupted and did not yet have the answer she was looking for. She took advantage of the pause to say, "Will you guys please be quiet for a minute so that Dr. del Marmol can have the opportunity to finally answer my question?"

The rest exchanged glances and out of respect for Aurora kept their mouths shut. Of course, they wanted to know as well, but they perhaps had less eagerness to get the answer. I took the fingers of my left and caressed my forehead. "Aurora, you couldn't imagine that when you asked me that question for the second time, you identified who gave me that codename. You don't even know how close you are to your own answer. Satan himself, Fidel Castro, is the one who came up with that name.

They looked at each other in confusion. "Let me explain it to you guys. Every time I did some kind of major damage to them, it was at night during a storm with the sky lit by flashes of lightning. When I struck, all the witnesses to some of my actions could say was that there was only a ghostly silhouette in the light of those flashes. Let me give you one example. I took Che's briefcase right under his nose after he had returned from a trip to the Soviet Union. We were inside the provincial military headquarters in Pinar del Rio; two armed guards on the door of the building were from his personal security, and all they can say when they were asked how it happened was that they saw a pale shadow that looked like a young man climbing down from an upper floor of the building. They shot at that shadow, and it disappeared. That inspired Castro to create tremendous myth. And then he saw the pictures that the CIA presented to the United Nations of the nuclear missiles the Cuban government had in a Russian base proving to the entire world that Russia had ICBMs in Cuba at San Cristobal. He spotted in those pictures the same pale shadow of a man illuminated by a flash of lightning; only this time the shadow was leaning against a military truck filled with missile warheads. That left no doubts in Fidel's mind that those pictures were taken either by the Lightning himself or one of his accomplices, even though they could not see a face, but only a blurred shadow, backlit by a bolt of lightning in the sky, and yelled as loud as he could, 'That son of a bitch, the Lightning!' Ever since he yelled that, the name stuck like glue in the archives of the G-2 and the Cuban intelligence reports forever my nickname or code as the Lightning."

Aurora grinned as she shook her head. "What an imbecile! Fidel Castro, who believes himself so intelligent, is the one who created that superspy enemy who is now the pale shadow of the resistance and hope for freedom of all the men, women, and children on the island of Cuba." This time, she was the one who caressed her forehead with the fingers of her right hand. "Now I understand why they would put such a high price as three million dollars on your head. To some countries, that's an insignificant amount. But to this country, once one of the richest islands in the 50's to be the poorest in the world country in an economic shambles, where our citizens don't make enough money to buy toilet paper, it's a fortune."

As Aurora spoke, Bonifacio pulled from the lifeboat large waterproof duffle bags they had managed to get out of the fishing boat before she sank. As he emptied one out on the sand, he took from the pile some hammocks made from nylon threads and some blankets. With a big smile on his face, he said, "Talking about daily necessities, Aurora, would you please help me distribute these hammocks and blankets to the rest of the group? However long we are on this island, sleeping comfortably is a necessity to keep our minds and bodies in optimum condition. That is the only way you guys can be prepared for the worst. You can find a corner among the rocks or bushes, whatever you're more comfortable with, before it gets completely dark with the coming nightfall, which is approaching at a rapid pace. Secure your own place where you are comfortable, but not too far from each other so we can defend ourselves against any aggression."

As Aurora distributed the blankets and hammocks, she shook her head unhappily at her conversation with me being interrupted by her husband. She said no word, however, and continued to do as he had asked.

This was the first night we would spend on that island. There was no way to guess how many we might have to spend here. Apparently, Bonifacio's brother Luis Alberto hadn't gotten the location right and was still looking for us; the worst scenario was that Castro's forces had sunk his boat and he was in a worse situation than we were. I wasn't used to depending on anyone, and in my mind, I was trying to find an exit from this situation without abandoning my friends. At that moment, we heard Jimbo yelling on the beach. Whatever he was saying, it was unintelligible. Optimist that I always am, the first thing that crossed my mind was that Luis Alberto had arrived to rescue us in his fishing boat. Jimbo had excused himself earlier, rubbing his belly as he told us that he had to go to relieve his bowels. We had been having such pleasant conversation that we hadn't noticed that he was gone longer than such a necessity would require. At the sound of his yells, everyone stood up and looked around for him, each thinking something different.

We saw him emerge from the shadows with a large smile on his face and something in his arms. It looked metallic with cables hanging down. He set it on a rock in front of us and we could now figure out that he was yelling that it was the radio from the chopper.

I asked him happily, "Where did you find it? Does it work? I had looked for it and saw nothing in the wreckage."

"It was far back along the beach, buried deep in the sand."

"Does it work?" I repeated.

He shrugged. "I don't know. Not yet—we have to let it dry thoroughly before we turn it on and check the function of the emergency battery. We should give it plenty of time to air out so there's no moisture inside the compartment. The only thing we should not do is to turn it on now. The sand I found it in was wet. It's possible the moisture didn't get into the sealed case, but it's very difficult to predict, so we should wait at least overnight so that we don't risk the chance of short circuiting the whole thing, which would burn everything out and possibly destroy our possibilities of being able to use it. Remember also we have no parts for this at all. I know a lot about radios because I fix them in my house, and there's a good chance we can make it work if its internal workings aren't damaged."

Bonifacio jumped up from his rock and danced around a little before embracing his son. "You may have saved our lives, my son. How did you find it?"

"Well, I was digging a little hole like some cat to put my feces, and I saw some wires sticking out. I dug around some more and found this radio. It looks fully intact, completely undamaged."

Bonifacio said, "If this really works, this will be our ticket to get off this island. I will be able to get ahold of Luis Alberto, who will come immediately, and we'll be out of here in no time."

Everyone exchanged hopeful looks. The radio that, thanks to God, Jimbo was able to find before the tide completely covered it as it reached its local maximum, I thought that we all had tremendous luck. This was our first day during that horrible ordeal during which all of us nearly lost our lives. We gave thanks to God that we were all still alive with only one flesh wound in Aurora's shoulder. We might only have to sleep there one night.

Everyone got busy securing their hammocks to trees and bushes. Atacia brought her hammock over close to me with a small, mischievous expression on her face. "Can I ask you a favor?"

"Of course," I replied. "What can I do for you?"

She replied, "Any place you put your hammock, could you please tie mine up next to yours? I'll sleep a lot more securely next to you."

I smiled. "Thank you." I took her hammock in my hands. "I assure you, love, and I will sleep a lot better close to you and smell the fragrance of roses on your skin. I will have very pleasant dreams."

She leaned in and kissed me on the cheek. "Thank you very much. You're always gallant and genteel. I won't take very long. I'll wash myself in some salt water to cleanse my body before I go to sleep. OK?"

"No problem, take as long as you want. I have to figure out what would be the best and most strategic way to tie up our hammocks, or I will be the one who can't close my eyes all night, worrying not just about me but also you as well. Under no circumstance can we allow ourselves to be caught by surprise."

She smiled. "I'm very sure that you will find the most secure place so we can both sleep like angels. But please stay awake for me, because I have a very nice surprise for you."

I raised my eyebrows mischievously. "Yes? If that is what I imagine it is, I'll wait for you all night without closing my eyes."

The others were completely occupied finding their best places for night long comfort. Atacia came over and kissed me on the lips followed by another that it started to become passionate. She gently held me down, her left hand on my chest. "This is a very little foretaste of the great surprise later."

"OK, I'll be waiting for it."

She turned around, wrapped a towel around her neck from her duffel bag, and disappeared into the shadows, now under the light of a giant full moon with a yellow-orange halo which reflected across the ocean and the white sand. It gave me the impression we were no longer on Earth but another planet.

A little while later I finally found under what appeared to be the thick foliage of a mangrove tree which not only gave me a view of the entire beachhead. Behind us there was a huge cliff wall which offered tremendous security. No one could approach from that direction to surprise us from the rear. I looked at my watch—it was already after midnight. I wondered why Atacia was taking so long, but knowing well the opposite sex, I smiled, thinking that she might be naked wherever she was taking her bath and admiring the reflection of her body in the moonlight. I decided to wait for her. The big mistake I made was to lie in the hammock. I forget that this day had not been a typical day; for that matter, it hadn't been a typical week. This day, however, had been filled with both physical and psychological strain for me, and I was extremely exhausted by the emotional episode that brought back the memory of the assassination of my son Julito.

I hadn't even considered that it would take only a few seconds to fall into a deep sleep. The next thing I heard was a tickling in my ear and a whispered soft voice, "Liar, liar—you promised me that you would wait for me awake." I opened my eyes and smiled. More than anything what woke me up were Atacia's wet lips so close to my ear. She whispered, "If you want me to, I'll leave you in peace to continue your beautiful dreams. But I found such a beautiful and unbelievable cave in the mountain, right under our feet, with a beautiful waterfall and plenty of crystal-clear drinkable water. We won't have to worry about water at all anymore for as long as we're here. This is the most fantastic place that even in my wildest dreams I could never imagine existed. If you don't mind, I want you to come with me so I can show you a new adventure, and I will be able to deliver my promised surprise to you, something beautiful, that will stay in our memories for the rest of our lives."

I got out of the hammock. "You don't have to tell my anymore. I only want to say one thing before we go, and that's my most sincere apology for falling asleep. I swear to you that it was involuntary. The stress on my body and the psychological stress I endured today betrayed my good will to wait for you until the first light of dawn."

Atacia replied with a huge smile, "I'm just kidding. I understand perfectly what you're saying and what's going on with you. Sleep is much like our emotions. They both are not very simple and very difficult on many occasions impossible to control."

Now I was the one to smile, in satisfaction this time. "You are 100% correct in your comparison. It's not only eloquent but also extremely intelligent. Our emotions, on many occasions make us say and do without thinking twice which we later have to repent for, even though we know that it will be repeated again and again because it's part of our emotions."

Atacia smiled and gave me an exaggerated nod with her head and folded her hand to her breast in a courtly manner. "Thank you very much for your beautiful compliment. But be very careful; when you praise too much you make me used to that extraordinarily good feeling when we receive it from someone who really got our attention. If later because you got a little more comfortable with me those compliments will be infrequent or stop completely. My ego will be bruised then and sad."

"You don't have anything to worry about. As long as you continue to be the way you are without changing your personality, I'll never stop those beautiful compliments which are like a little compensation that every intelligent person that possesses good, virtuous qualities deserves. That way you remunerate them in celebration of their qualities. My Mima always told me one thing I never forgot: honor to those who deserve honor. Unfortunately, many people don't compliment you for your good manners, intelligence, or other excellent virtues that you possess. Many times, it is solely because of resentment that they don't possess those virtues. They let themselves be so controlled by jealousy and dark sentiments that they convert themselves into beings full of resentment and frustration. They live their lives trying to imitate others that possess those natural virtues, knowing for themselves that they will never be able to even come close to those they try to imitate. They also fail to take into consideration that they've been missing the opportunity to cultivate those virtues that they do possess. They're too busy looking at the grass in others' yards, instead of making their own grass green."

Atacia asked, "Are you speaking from your own personal experience or simply figuratively? I perceive a very deep pain in your soul behind your words."

I looked in her eyes and smiled once more. "Your simple but exquisite emotional sensitivity and your feminine instinct give you the power to penetrate very deeply my words and expressions and then be able to analyze even the pain that sometimes I try to hide in my heart. Especially when I speak of a hurtful memory involving a big stab in my back from either a very close friend or some member of my family."

Atacia looked at me tenderly. "Who inflicted so much pain to your heart that you can remember it so vividly?"

I smiled without replying. We had entered the stunning grotto she had discovered by a crevasse. We crawled inside and saw a beautiful waterfall running over a massive cliff, larger than the one before which we had set up our camp. The water fell into a huge pool of crystal-clear water, surrounded by wildflowers; orchids floating around the edge made it such a magical place, as if someone created that as scenery to make an extraordinary celebration like a wedding. The scenery was indescribably beautiful; all she had told me before did not come even close to reality.

I turned to her and said, "Love, I wouldn't be surprised at all to learn that maybe this was the place in 1492 where Christopher Colombus first arrived in Cuba and knelt in the sand to say those beautiful words recorded in history books: 'This is the most beautiful land that human eyes have ever seen.'"

Atacia looked at me in satisfaction to see my total fascination for that beautiful place she had discovered. She opened a blanket and put it on the edge of the lagoon; at one edge a small cascade allowed the water to escape down to a creek which ran straight to the ocean. We sat down together in silence, admiring this extraordinary masterpiece of nature. She turned around and said with a grimace, "If you want to, and you don't have to answer me, but I would love to know who you were thinking of when you were just talking to me with so much pain and emotion in your soul. Even if you don't want to talk about it, I believe that speaking of our past deceptions and emotional pain make us all feel better with ourselves. It will also weld us together in this new relationship we have.

The past pain will take us to consolidate and bond our relationship emotionally, making the present and future better for us. It will facilitate the road to true happiness that we all look for in our lives."

I smiled and said jokingly, "Are you absolutely sure? It's not just sugarcoating because you also want to satisfy your curiosity?"

She slapped me on the shoulder at being caught. "I swear to you that's not my primary motive. Curiosity is only a small reason, which is only natural, to know who hurt you so badly. It's mostly because I want to know. I was being completely truthful to you."

I smiled. "Don't worry. I was just joking. But I have to tell you that even though I, like everyone else, have had a good portion of deception in my previous romances, this one is not related to a relationship with a woman. This is about one member of my family, my youngest brother, Nando. I loved him very much and cared for and protected him when we were kids like a mother dog protects her puppies. I saved his life when we were kids when a car in front of our home didn't realize that Nando was behind it. The driver put it in reverse while Nando played with his tricycle, and nearly ran over him. I yelled as loud as I could, which my mother always said I had a thunderous voice. My yell caused the driver to freeze and slam on the brakes, just in time to avoid making Nando into a meatball beneath the car. The tricycle could never be used again because, fortunately, when he ran over it, Nando had rolled back, and so the car ran over the tricycle and not over his body. I remembered how I fought even with my friends defending him because he was always smaller and weaker and not very bright, saying things that sometimes were offensive and upset the other kids. None of this did he ever take into consideration. When he always went behind my back, instigating and creating problems for me all the time, gossiping with my sisters and telling my parents lies and things that he invented just with the purpose of hurting me. His only satisfaction was to create trouble for me. In short, I don't even know that I had my worst enemy at my back for all those years we grew up together—my little brother. As we grew up, this became more evident as he would go behind my back to tell negative things to my girlfriends, trying to turn them against me, inventing things about me exactly when we were little kids.

"Later, after I confronted my brother, and I really despise confrontations, I knew that if I didn't hear from his own lips, I would never have believed that anyone could be such a huge idiot as to an intention to separate me from my family. Unfortunately, I had been living all those years keeping myself blind out of my love for my family. I never in my wildest imagination could consider such a tremendous treachery coming from any of them. A very important and unforgettable lesson that I learned on that day. From this enormous deception I became completely convinced that in reality love without doubt was completely blind. That day, the last drop had filled up the glass; I was furious when I found he had betrayed me and could not deny it. With extreme pain in my throat and soul, I asked him what I had ever done to him to deserve this, why he had tried to hurt me so badly. His response to me was to shake his head with an emotionless expression and say, 'Nothing. Absolutely nothing.' That answer took me completely by surprise, as I expected that he might at least invent something or bring as a poor excuse of something I did when we were little kids. He could not come up with anything at all, because all my life I had stuck up for him, excusing his negligence or careless way of conducting himself to others, creating problems for me, sometimes even putting me in the position of fighting my best friend in order to protect him.

"I could not accept the answer he gave me, so I asked once more, 'Can you explain to me, if I never did anything to you, why you are always against me and side with my worst enemies that you know for a fact are looking for ways to hurt me?' This time his answer was even more outrageous and painful, something I will never forget for as long as I live. He didn't even have the guts to look into my eyes, staring at the concrete of the driveway where we were talking, far away from everyone else so we could talk in private. Finally, in a broken voice, he said, 'You never did anything to me. The problem isn't you, it's me. I always wanted to be like you, but I couldn't. The more I tried, the less I accomplished. I never wanted to be your shadow—not even that, and that was the reason I'm furious with myself. I've been trying all my life to compete with you and always ending up as I got frustrated to be destructive to you.' My eyes almost bulged out of their sockets when I heard my own brother say that, and tears grew unwanted. It was the last thing I wanted him to see, but the knot in my throat kept me mute after hearing these disgusting and unbelievable words.

I shook my head and said, 'I've been caring for you, protecting you all my life as we grew up, got myself in trouble because you made it happen, I've been loving you, and will continue to love you because you're my brother, as we grew up and received the same wound. But your disloyalty has broken my heart into pieces, and this is the last time you will have the opportunity to hurt me emotionally. I ask God to forgive you, even though you are agnostic or a very confused individual that doesn't even believe in God. God forgive you for the pain you've inflicted on me. Of course, it's not only your fault; it's also the fault of the Marxist communists that you hung around and associated with while you were in Cuba. Those corrupt villains have filled your heart with hatred, but only you can fill yourself with such diabolic, dark sentiments to the point that you open the doors and allow Satan into your heart to come in and steal your soul. I forgive you, but for this reason I don't ever want to see you again for the rest of my life. You will not have another opportunity to hurt me again, my brother. This is our final goodbye, and this is the last time I ever want to see you, Nando.' That was the last time I saw him." I was growing emotional, so I stopped there. I don't know why, but every time we talk about jealousy, anger, and resentments, I could never avoid a dark shadow filling my heart with pain and sadness whenever I think of my little brother that I had loved so much and had taken care of for so long."

Atacia came over to me and hugged me with a kiss on my cheek. "Thank you for opening up to me and telling me that sad story. I believe that maybe this will finally heal your soul so that you don't feel that pain for much longer. All the things you've told me shows me that you have great trust in me in order to tell me these personal secrets that you hold in your heart."

I tried to smile, but it was only a half smile. "You perhaps don't believe this, but you are the first person in my life that I ever told that story to. I never even told my mother or father so that I wouldn't bring sadness to their lives and hearts. From the time that conversation took place, all I could feel for my little brother was an enormous, profound pity. I put myself in his shoes and I could not imagine how detrimental and sad his life could be, trying to imitate somebody that in reality was not. How absurd and crazy that person could be? How frustrating could it be for him when he saw he couldn't be like me? No one can be like another person, not because that person is better or worse. In the end, during this conversation with my little brother, I had forgotten the reason I was so angry with him and substituted that rage for a beautiful memory that I had of him when we were little boys, and I completely was ignorant of his dark frustrations and what he had been doing behind me."

Atacia and I looked at each other and hugged once more. As we did, something strange happened. We heard a dog howling on the beach. We looked at each other and then towards where the howling was coming from. We took a few steps to see if we could locate the source of it. A powerful light illuminated the sky quite suddenly, like some multicolored flare. We were caught by surprise without the remotest idea as to what was going on or where those howling dogs came from. The howling was getting louder as they came closer to us by the minute.

Chapter 13: The Wild Beast

We climbed down the creek to its mouth in the ocean, where the current was strong enough that the pure water extended well into the sea water before becoming brackish. A small, oared boat was heading towards us, already in the zone of pure water. We came out to see who might be in the boat. The level of the water within the creek was up to our knees, but as we neared the mouth the water rose to our waists. We could see by the light of the full moon a man with a long white beard stood in the middle of the boat, holding a kerosene lamp in his right hand, along with two small children. The kids yelled to us, "Hola, we need help!" They waved their arms about, trying to catch our attention.

The older man held his left hand over the lamp as he tried to direct the weak light in our direction. Atacia yelled back, "Hola! We are here and can help you! What do you need?"

The old man removed his captain hat to see us better and as well as showing us his face as we waded out to them. Soon the water was chest high, nearly to our necks. The old man yelled in desperation, "We've been more than three days at sea with no food or water! We have no idea where we are."

Sitting in the center of the boat between the two kids was a white dog with light grey spots that looked like a mix of a Samoyed and Akita. It had stopped howling as soon as it spotted us and now watched us curiously. It was strange that it didn't bark at us but might have been because both kids had their arms around his neck and were controlling it, protecting it and keeping it calm and relaxed, because we were after all strangers approaching the boat. That huge dog otherwise could be a tremendous threat. The old man turned and murmured advice to them as they held the dog, not wanting to scare the help they had been hope for that was coming to them after so many days.

I approached the boat by the side where the bearded man was as he held the lamp. I said, "Put your lamp on the deck of the boat and use your hat to scoop some water out from overside in the ocean." He looked at me uncomprehendingly. He was unaware that the current of the fresh water we were coming from was still fresh. I told him to take a sip, but he remained motionless, so I scooped some water up in my hands, put my hands to my lips and drank to show him the water was good. I said, "You're in the mouth of a river. It's not salt water; you can drink it." Atacia duplicated my demonstration to reinforce what I said.

The man leaned over the side of his boat and used his hat to scoop up some water as I had instructed. Very hesitatingly, he took a sip of the water, still unconvinced. His face lit up with joy and scooped more water up for the little boy and girl to drink. He picked up a couple of things we couldn't see, but as he dipped it down to gather water it looked to us like a rubber boot and a nylon fishing hat. He scooped water up and gave it to the kids. "Drink slowly," he instructed, "so you don't get sick. Take very small sips, and don't forget to give some to Venus." The dog, on hearing its name, howled.

I smiled and said to the man, "Those howls saved you. They caused us to investigate, which brought us to help you."

The man caressed the dog. "Good dog. As always, you are our guardian angel." He looked at me. "Her name is Venus; my name is Captain DeAngelo Gaytan." He pointed at the kids. "Those are my grandchildren, Rolando and Jamina."

I replied, "Nice to meet you guys. I am Dr. del Marmol, and this young lady is Atacia."

Both kids clearly had been educated properly. They stood up and gave her a little bow with smiles as they continued to drink that exquisite water joyfully and gratefully that they had been without for several days.

Captain DeAngelo asked, "What are you two doing on this desert island?" He might have been a little worried for the kids' security, since he had no idea whether we were communist sympathizers or fellow castaways. A shadow of worry crossed his face.

Atacia replied cautiously with a small smile on her lips, "A torpedo boat, believing we were trying to escape Cuba, sank my father's fishing boat. We've survived by a miracle of God. Our lifeboat brought us to this desert island."

Captain DeAngelo replied, "You are luckier than we were. My entire family died, including my son and daughter-in-law, when a MiG attacked us with machine guns without any warning in the middle of the ocean. They might have assumed for the same reason you were torpedoed, that we were leaving the country illegally to look for a better life, something that doesn't sit well with them as it makes them look really bad internationally. The only thing we have left from that attack is this small rowboat to save our lives."

I shook my head as I listened to his horrible story. It was nothing new to me, knowing very well, like the vast majority of Cubans, that attempting to leave the island in any way, forced to leave by the Cuban government, risking death in their desperate need for basic necessities. This is the false paradise the Marxist system in Cuba has sold to all the inhabitants of the island but also to the entire world, and no one was allowed to leave it. Not happy with making millions of people live in misery, they want to export that misery to the rest of the world which is nothing less than a hell on Earth. Desperate to convince the world that the Cuban people support that totalitarian system, they commit the most horrendous crimes against those who dare to leave the country illegally. Only a small number of hired assassins that sympathize with the regime enjoy the privileges that no one else has. These supporters of this horrendous, corrupt political system that has completely destroyed the nation not only economically but also all aspects of the society are the same type of people who destroyed Russia in the time of the Bolsheviks and Stalin, where millions of inhabitants died from disease and starvation.

I saw DeAngelo trying to put his rubber boots on in preparation to get into the water. "No, you don't have to go overboard," I said. "Toss me a rope and we'll pull you to the beach. No need for you to get wet when we're already in the water."

He picked up a mooring line and tossed it to us. "Thank you very much."

"You're welcome. Get ready and we'll pull." I took the rope in my hands and took the lead. Atacia took hold right behind me, and we started to walk towards the beach, towing them behind us. We took them to the same spot where we had initially tied our lifeboat when we arrived at the island. As we neared it, I saw the water had come in through the bullet holes left by the helicopter, and it was now half sunk.

As we got near the beach, Venus jumped out of the boat joyfully at the sight of the land. She ran back and forth around the beach, getting her exercise after so many days in that cramped boat. Rolando and Jamina imitated the dog's actions, not waiting until we had run the boat up along the sand. They jumped out after the dog, full of energy, happy now and more relaxed after the horrible experience of seeing their mother and father killed before their eyes by the MiG. They released those black emotions and followed the dog along the wet sand, trying to forget the ordeal they had just endured. They knew now they were in a safe place, no longer in the water.

DeAngelo jumped out of the boat. He looked at our half-sunk boat for a few seconds. "Is this the lifeboat you used to get here?" I nodded as I finished tying his boat off on the same coconut tree ours was moored to.

I said, "Yes. It hasn't even been twenty-four hours since we got here. Even so, it feels like an eternity; until now I hadn't seen any sign of life, no animals, only marine seagulls."

He furrowed his eyebrows. "Well, you should be very happy of that because the government is accustomed to placing on this isolated island soldiers to observe who comes in and out of these remote locations. They call them observation points—they build towers and put soldiers in them with very powerful radios. Whatever they see they are instructed not to confront anyone but instead call the coast guard and aviation to take care of business, just as they did to you as well as us." He shook his head. "I wonder sometimes how much longer this corrupt and disgraceful system in our country will last."

I understood his frustration and pain as well as the loss of his family. I put my arm around his shoulder and looked on as Atacia began to play with the children and

Venus, who looked like they enjoyed it even though it was very late beneath that multicolored full moon. They threw a wooden stick for the dog, who grabbed it and brought it back to whoever had thrown it. They each took turns throwing the stick and began to separate as they did. The dog was so smart that every time she returned, she would drop the stick at the feet of the thrower. This particular dog breed was known for its high intelligence.

As the captain and I walked towards them, I asked, "Captain, how long have you owned Venus? Have you had her for a long time?"

"Yes, yes, for a long, long time. She belonged to a great friend of mine, Chicho, someone that I loved like the brother I never had. He was rendered blind, unfortunately, when one of Castro's soldiers hit him in the head with the rifle butt during the protest that took place in the Peruvian embassy in Havana which provoked the exile of hundreds of thousands of Cubans through the Port of Mariel." He fell silent.

I asked, "What happened to him?"

"He left Venus with me because he was supposed to leave Cuba as a political prisoner. His brother in Miami was supposed to come and pick him up, which he did. Believe it or not, for weeks and weeks Venus cried and howled, missing him as if she had lost a very great love in her life."

"Dogs can be extremely sensitive, especially the ones with a great genetic cross that results in even more intelligence. I believe Venus is probably a combination between Akita and Samoyed. What happened to your friend Chicho? He should be very happy in Miami now. With the advances in technology and medicine we have today, trauma-induced blindness can be reversed. I wouldn't be surprised if Chicho got his vision back in

Miami. We have the best medicine and technology in the world in the USA."

DeAngelo shook his head. "No, no. He died from the blow to his head. It created a malignant tumor in the brain."

"Oh, no! I'm sorry."

"Me, too. I miss him very much. Poor Chicho didn't last three months in Miami after he arrived there. But at least he died in freedom, surrounded by his loved ones." He spoke with resignation and sadness. "Destiny is something no one can change, unfortunately. We had discussed many times how I would reunite with him in Miami, but in his last letter he begged me to leave with my family. The only thing he wanted in exchange is that if I decided to do it was to bring Venus with me. That's why we now decided a few days ago to leave the island. I wanted to fulfill that wish from my best friend, and so we brought Venus along." He added resentfully, "It looks like destiny doesn't want me to fulfill the last will of my friend Chicho, since we have been returned to this damned island where we might now all die at the hands of this horrible criminals."

I put my hand on his shoulder again. "Remember this, my friend, which I learned from my mother. It's never over until finally we stop breathing." I put my other hand right under his nose. "You're still breathing; I can feel it against the hairs on my hand. That means it's still not over for you. As long as there's life there will exist hope and that the next day will be better."

He gave me a small half smile. "You are a strong optimist, eh?"

"Yes, with no remedy at all, all the way to my grave. But remember, God says that He helps those who make an effort to help themselves. I need your help now."

'What can I do for you?"

"I need to cover this boat as soon as possible. After what you told me during your tragic story, the danger that they've been looking for us might have just multiplied. The plane that attacked you guys a few days before will probably report to their superiors and believe it or not this place where we are now as well as every single island around us is now a hot spot where these communists will concentrate their search to find me and everyone that is with me. I cannot tell you anymore since I don't know you enough, but I'm a very, very valuable jewel that this government would give an eye to get their hands on. That doesn't even count the torpedo boat which attacked us, the crew of which will never return to their place of origin. We sent them to the other world with no return ticket. We have two alternatives to assure our survival. The most intelligent option and desirable for me is to camouflage these two boats, since the engine of our boat could be used on yours, which is still sound and useable and would allow us to leave this place alive, especially if the rescue we've been hoping and waiting for has not been destroyed by our enemies. This small boat with an outboard engine will allow us to transport ourselves to the fishing vessel we're waiting for to rescue us. It cannot get close to the beach due to the shallowness of the water. We could use this boat to take us out to the fishing boat whenever it arrives."

DeAngelo asked, "What is the other alternative?" He looked at the boats, realizing how much work the camouflaging would be.

I shook my head and frowned. "The other one is the most desperate and last alternative that we would ever want to face. It would be to burn both boats, so we don't leave any trace for anyone looking for us to know that we ever arrived on this island. That is the only way to erase all evidence of our existence. That is our last resort; obviously, it's not my first choice of preference, but it's the only way to survive if it comes to that particular moment."

He said, "I agree with you. We only burn the bridges behind us when there is no hope of going back." He put his fingers to his lips and whistled loudly, which caused Venus to stop playing and raise her head. She ran towards him. "OK, we cannot waste time. The night is ending, and the day will be here soon." He gestured for the children and Atacia to come over to us.

This was not the first time in my life that I had a premonition which saved not just my life but those around me as well. Like a clairvoyant, I could see with extreme clarity a small plane flying over the beach; the sun high overhead, indicating it was the middle of the day. I sprang into urgent action; with the help of the children and DeAngelo, Atacia and I started to pull the small boat under cover first, out of view beneath the mangrove roots and other vegetation. We covered it with dead leaves from the coconut palms. It wasn't very difficult as it was a small boat. The one that I knew would be difficult was our boat, which was twice as large. We would also have to remove the outboard motor, which was quite heavy. The half-sunken boat was even heavier than before due to all the water that had leaked inside. We had plugged the holes with strips torn from one of Aurora's dresses as best we could, but it wasn't sufficient to keep the water completely out. We had no buckets or bailers, which was going to make that job more difficult. But using the rubber boots and fishing hat, we were able to get about ninety percent of the water baled out after a couple of hours.

Once we removed the outboard motor, we found out that there wasn't enough manpower among us to bring the larger boat to where we wanted to hide it. Fortunately, the noise of the dog barking and the kids yelling on the beach, playing while we were emptying the boat woke everyone else up in our base camp. They climbed down the cliff and came to provide some very welcome help which hastened things along. A short time later the other boat was dragged under the bushes, and we camouflaged both craft from any airplane or helicopter that might fly over.

After we were done, I explained why we had to get all of this in a rush so urgently before the sun rose. I related the story of Captain DeAngelo and my concern that the danger of being discovered had multiplied with another incident in the same area taking place roughly the same time our own boat had been sunk. The greatest worry was that when the pilot of the MiG reported the incident when he returned to base he might, in order to get merit, that he had found counterrevolutionary activity in that area. The zone would be considered a red one where they should concentrate their patrols over the next weeks or months. I left out my premonition in relating these events to my friends. I shared it only with Atacia as we walked back to the camp. I was completely assured that what I saw would eventually happen, if not the next day, then the day after.

I looked at my wristwatch when we finished and saw it was around five thirty in the morning. I was totally exhausted and only wanted rest, even though my mind was filled with worry about what would happen in the next couple of days. My extreme optimism continued to keep my spirits up, in spite of my worries; I was trusting to my faith in God and hoped for a better day when the sun rose which would allow us to manage the evil and darkness with our divine light which would protect us. I put my head and immediately down dropped into a profound sleep.

A hand shook my shoulder. A woman's voice said, "Wake up, Dr. Marmol. I need to tell you something extremely important."

I shook my head and drew a pistol from my waist as I strongly grabbed that person by the throat. She had no way of knowing that she had interrupted a furious fight I was having in the nightmare I was having. Fidel Castro, dressed in black clothing, was trying to suffocate me with a pillow, helped by his brother Raul and Che Guevara. In that nightmare they had penetrated the island; even in my dream state I wondered how they did that without our hearing the engine of any plane or helicopter. I discovered they had arrived by submarine. I had Castro by the throat, as we fought and wrestled.

This is what was happening in my mind as I woke up; I realized I was on the sand and had that good black woman, Mama Teca, her eyes bulging out of the sockets as she said hoarsely in desperation and distress, "Dr. Marmol, please wake up! It's me, let go of my neck, I can't breathe. It's Mama Teca, Atacia's friend."

Now fully awake, I jumped back and released her neck, lifting my knee from her chest and taking my pistol away from her head. She coughed several times as she tried to regain her breath and clean with her right hand the blood from a tiny cut she had over her right eyebrow that was going into her eyes. I studied her and understood as I looked around to see no Castro brothers or Che Guevara. I said, "I'm sorry. You have no idea how sorry I am. You woke me from a nightmare about the Castros and Che Guevara coming to assassinate all of us. After cutting all your throats with sharp knives, they came to strangle me because they wanted my body in one piece for public display."

Mama Teca was still coughing and recovering from the blows I gave her. I had applied to her the dragon twist garrot, which few people can survive if it's held for too long. She tried to smile, but it was lopsided and instead looked like she was about to cry. After she recovered, she said, "This is a good lesson I will never forget. Never touch the Lightning, even if it looks like he's asleep and looks harmless. He will still burn you and you will have horrible surprise."

I shook my head. "I repeat—I give you my most sincere apologies. It would never cross my mind to hurt anyone, especially you. I hope you understand my frustration. Over the past twenty-four hours, while trying to find the solution to get us out of this precarious situation of being stranded on an isolated island, this situation has diverted me from my mission here in Cuba. It could cost the lives of hundreds of thousands of people in my second mother, the USA. Unfortunately, I cannot give many details of what this is about, and even if I could it would be difficult for you to understand why I do what I do for a country that isn't even mine. For your tranquility, however, I'll tell you that you guys are my priority. I guarantee that I won't abandon you or leave you behind, even if it means I have to put my life on the line to do it. No matter how urgent mission that brought me here is, I won't abandon you guys in this predicament until I know for a fact that you are secure and out of all danger."

Mama Teca replied, "Thank you very much for your dedication and good will, not just to us but to every nation and human being. That was the reason I made the mistake of putting my hands on you. I wanted to wake you up and talk to you." She started to get up from the sand and I held out mine to help her up. She said with a pained expression and a cracked voice from her intense feelings, "My friend, I have a deep admiration for you and respect. But I have to tell you that you have to stop feeling obligated to be responsible for all of us and everyone who comes around you. You cannot save the entire world, and that is a tremendous weight on your shoulders, too huge a responsibility for a single person to be able to handle. I don't know if you've been gifted by God or Nature or very well-trained by those who care for and love you, but now, for the second time, you leave me with no doubts that you have had excellent teachers. You are not a tall man. I'm over six feet tall, you couldn't weigh more than 175 lbs, and I'm over 280 pounds, yet you put me down out of combat in a matter of seconds.

She added emphatically, "I want to learn that hold you put on my neck before we part ways, whether it's judo or jujitsu. You not only immobilized me, but it was impossible for me to get you off of my neck like a cat on top of your chest. Even though a cat is small, it digs its claws under your skin and so is even more painful to tear off of you. I tried to get you off of my neck, and for a few minutes I thought that unless you woke up, I would lose my life right there. I started to get dizzy from lack of oxygen and was rapidly losing strength from my arms and legs.

She shook her head and raised both arms high as she coughed several times, "I think that if you are capable of doing this half or completely asleep, I don't want to see what you could do when completely awake and in fully in control of your faculties and sense."

I shook my head with a small smile. "I think you give me a lot more credit than I deserve. I just did it out of self-preservation, something you yourself have done in the same spot, moving by the preservation instinct. At that moment I perceived you as an aggressor who attacked me to try and take me down. It was only a self-defense reaction."

She shook both hands negatively as she shook her head. She said with irony, "OK, let's assume what you say is right, and it's just self-preservation. If we ever have a confrontation with any of our adversaries, I want you to be in my corner, not in the opposing corner, OK?"

I smiled and put my arm around her shoulder as I examined the cut over her right eyebrow. "You should just disinfect this. It's not deep, but like any wound it could get infected." I wet my finger with saliva and worked on cleaning up the dried blood near the wound. "How did you get that cut?"

Mama Teca jerked her head back and raised her neck as she rolled her eyes. "That was the first blow you gave me when I tried to wake you up. By the way, did you think carefully before you get these new refugees into our camp? I trust you and your judgment, but I want you to remember you're not the savior of the world, and the cans of soup and other food that we saved from Bonifacio's ship, if we're lucky, will last for a few days. These are three more mouths to feed, not counting the dog." Her worry was reflected in her face as she shook her head. "Imagine how much that enormous dog will eat—probably more than three of us, and we can't let her starve. It would be inhumane to do to that beautiful dog."

"What do you suggest I do with those people, who are worse off than use because they lost all their loved ones to that MiG?"

"Don't take me as a heartless or harsh person. I'm thinking of the survival of all of us."

I smiled. "Listen, don't worry so much about tomorrow. We have food enough for everyone, including them, today. Tomorrow, God will provide. With faith and hope, and I have plenty, we'll only be here a few days more. When we finish all this canned food, we have plenty of food with those coconuts. And water is no longer a concern; Atacia and I found a beautiful lagoon with plenty of pure water for the rest of our lives here. Think positively, and don't worry so much about tomorrow. God will provide enough until we get off this island. Faith can move mountains."

I touched a nerve. She squeezed her shoulders, shook, and crossed herself as a really bad memory flashed through her mind. "Let's hope there hasn't been any shaking in these mountains. If God moves them, there will be a massive earthquake which will send all of us headfirst into the ocean where we came from." She repeated that as she crossed herself again. "I'll tell you something you reminded me of when you spoke about faith and God moving mountains. As a kid I saw one of those earthquakes take away a bigger island than we are on right now. It was swallowed and removed from the map and went down to the bottom of the ocean." She shook violently and began to grow pale and grey. "I saw my entire family die on the north Atlantic coast here in Cuba when I was only six years old."

I took the fingers of my left hand to my mouth. "I'm sorry, Mama Teca. I didn't mean to bring you any bad memories for you. It appears that I tried to comfort you with peace, tranquility, and hope, and instead I brought back dark, hidden, tortuous memories."

Suddenly, a terrified squealing came out of the bushes, like a pig that was being slaughtered. Seconds later, an enormous beast with eyes shining yellow in the moonlight erupted from the bushes at high speed. That squeal which woke everyone up was followed by another scream from Mama Teca as the enormous animal ran towards her and struck her as it tried to run between her legs, its tusks tangled in her mesh dress. It dragged her along with it while she continued screaming at the top of her lungs as if she were held by the Devil himself. She was tossed up and down by the huge wild boar, his tusks so sharp that it looked like he could slice tree trunks like a lumber mill. Behind the boar came Venus, who had her powerful jaws locked like a shark on one of its rear legs in an attempt to trip and hold it. She didn't let go, and so she was being dragged behind the boar.

    I drew my pistol, my training keeping me calm in the midst of that confusion while everyone else screamed in tremendous distress at what they were seeing and uncertain what could be done. I pointed my pistol at the beast, waiting for the moment for him to turn his head so that I could have a clean shot and avoid harming either Mama Teca or Venus when I pulled the trigger. Finally, the wild pig slowed down, turned towards me as he tried to get rid of the powerful jaws of Venus, encumbered by the tangled Mama Teca. I had that clear shot; my pistol was braced over my left arm, and I fired one shot in the dark, hitting the boar between the eyes. Silence fell as the boar abruptly stopped squealing and dropped onto his front legs. Mama Teca rolled free to the right as the rest of the beast's body dropped, her net dress still tangled in its tusks.

    We ran towards Mama Teca, thinking she might be badly hurt. As I drew near, I asked, "Are you OK? Are you hurt?"

    "No, no—I'm not hurt. Only my ego is a little bruised. This pig dragged me like I was a toy in a dog's mouth. For a few minutes, I was riding him like a wild horse." She kicked the body. A little more relaxed, she said, "I thought the Devil was come to take me and steal my soul like they did with my mother and father when they were swallowed a long time ago. Thank you very much," she added to me. "I'm starting to believe, instead of the Devil, as you say we have to be positive and it's God who wants to provide us with sufficient food for the rest of our stay on this island."

I smiled. "That's my girl. I like it like that, with a lot of faith in your heart. What do you think? Like I said to you that God will provide tomorrow, but He didn't wait too long. He even provided for the dog. Do you like that? And you were so worried not too long ago." Venus finally released her grip on the pig's leg, since it was no longer moving. "What do you think about our new warrior?"

"No doubt in my mind now that we have a good warrior added to our team," she replied. She went over to Venus and patted her. "Good dog, good dog, Venus."

Atacia came over to me and asked discreetly, "Who is going to clean this huge animal and butcher it? I've lived by the ocean all my life, not in the jungle."

I replied, "I'll do it, don't worry. I know how to do it. With everyone's help, we can preserve some of the meat in salt water. We won't need refrigeration. First, I need a couple of hours of sleep, since I haven't closed my eyes all night. Only for a little while before Mama Teca woke me up."

"I'm sorry, and I'm sorrier than you for doing it," Mama Teca replied.

Atacia said, "You know what? I think the best thing for you is to go to our cave so you won't be bothered by anyone so you can get some good sleep time and recover your strength."

"Sweetie, I think that's a great idea," I answered.

The sun was rising on the horizon. The kids had woken up a little, but the ordeal that they had survived exhausted them, and they dropped back into a deep sleep. Aurora started to open some cans beans, lentils, and sardines, and then started to get a fire going so she could prepare a good breakfast for everyone that new day. She warmed the cans over the fire, and everything smelled exquisite.

As she looked at her mother's preparations, Atacia came over to me with a smile. "The way you're looking at the food my mother is preparing, I think it will be a good idea for you to eat something before going to bed."

I raised my eyebrow in surprise. "Did I make it so obvious that my stomach needs maintenance?"

She smiled. "You and your phrasing. Yes, it needs maintenance, and you hardly ate last night. It is probably completely empty."

"Yes, I'm so hungry I might cut off a piece of that beast and eat it raw."

At that moment, Jimbo ran excitedly into the camp. He said, "Dr. Marmol, I turned the radio on, and it's functional. Come with me; I have a very nice surprise that I believe will be delightful for everyone, but especially for you. I know if we are anxious to leave this island, you are even more eager than we are to continue your mission."

Chapter 14: One Way Out

Atacia said, "I don't mind you going with Jimbo, but you should eat something first. You had nothing yesterday and on top of that you haven't slept. I don't want to interfere with your *vida loca*[7], but I want you to just remember that when we don't give the body and brain the rest and fuel they need to keep going, they both start to malfunction. That is the last thing we want to happen to you, especially now, at a moment so critical to everyone here. We need you with a fresh mind to be able to find a way out. If it hadn't been for your equanimity and calm, combined with your fast reactions and our new angel Venus, we would have lost the most loving of us, Mama Teca, to that huge wild boar—which was a surprise, considering until now we thought this island was utterly deserted. Without eating or sleeping properly, maybe next time you won't react as you did at that moment."

I smiled. "You're 100% right. We should all be completely alert, no matter what happens next, but I think the radio takes priority. Don't you think the food and my sleep can wait a little bit in light of that? This radio could be our only salvation for getting out of this place. If we manage to establish contact with your uncle, that will be a blessing. Then we can come back here, I'll eat something, and then I'll follow your advice and go to our new hiding place in that cave where I'll find complete tranquility, not be bothered by anyone, and recover my energy through

---
[7] Crazy life

sleep." She nodded her understanding. "Why don't you come with me and Jimbo, and find out what his new discovery is that he wants to surprise me with? At the same time, we can try that radio to see if we can establish contact. We're sitting ducks on this island. The sooner we manage to get out of here, the less danger we will put everyone in."

    The children had woken up from all the commotion, but exhausted as they were, they had fallen back into a deep sleep after they ate the food Aurora had prepared for us. As soon as they heard us leaving, however, they woke back up and came looking for Atacia, because she had shown them love and care by playing with them that night. Her tenderness and joyful attitude with them had earned the trust of these kids who were so eager for the affection of anybody, as they had lost the principal fountain of love in their lives and the most wonderful care, their parents.

    As they approached us, Rolando brought something in his hands that Venus jumped around to try and take away from him as they walked in the sand. I looked more closely at the object the boy held, it appeared to be a water sport ball that people play water sports with—but it looked professional, not a cheap one. I asked him if I could see it. He politely handed it to me. "Of course, sir. My sister Jamina found it right behind those bushes over there." He pointed to several young coconut trees growing together near where we were. It was multicolored like a beach ball.

    I looked at Jamina, who looked at me timidly, as if she were in trouble. I understood and said to put her mind at ease soothingly, "Jamina, don't worry. You're very lucky to find this beautiful ball on this desert island. I just need something from you."

A little nervously, she replied, "Sure, what do you need?"

I caressed her hair and returned the ball. "I just want to know where exactly you found this ball. Can you tell me? Do you remember, honey?"

She nodded, a little more relaxed. She took my left hand and guided me to where the young trees grew in a grove, forming a very compact bush. Everyone followed me, not understanding my concern over the ball. The trees weren't even five feet tall yet, growing together in a clump. I saw a perfect place to hide something. I understood that wherever the ball came from could lead to something else. I bent over and began to peer between the bushes while everyone else looked on curiously.

Atacia saw me come out empty-handed. "Did you think you were going to find another wild pig in there?" she asked jocularly. She was also very curious about my intentions.

I didn't stop and continued searching, using my boots to dig in the sand around the bushes. To the surprise of everyone watching, I pulled up a wire with my shoe. I took it in my hand and pulled. A large antenna with a microphone, both wrapped in plastic, were tied to the other end of the rope. I knelt in the sand and began to dig with both hands. Jamina and Rolando came over to help me. Atacia continued staring at me, as did Jimbo. They noticed near the end of the rope tied to the plastic bag that I was pulling out a canvas duffle bag. They were all surprised, especially Atacia, at how I was able to divine that there was more buried here. It was like I had found some buried treasure.

The duffel bag was very heavy. I opened it up and began pulling the contents out: condensed milk, beans, soup, forks, knives, spoons—everything very well wrapped in rags and paper, as if someone had tried to preserve it quite well. Many other things in the way of survival gear and even two carafes of chianti wine, a huge bucket with covers for cooking with water and an ax. This was a massive treasure find for us. I looked at Atacia and said, "It's not another wild pig, but something a lot better. These are not just the tools we need to cut up that pig but also the necessary tools to cook and preserve it properly. That pig will give us food for months; let's hope we only need it for a few days. We can save it for someone else by putting it in pots with oil to preserve the meat for a long time. Apparently, someone left this behind after encountering other pigs, and they were prepared for survival. My only worry is that whoever left them behind buried here will come back. According to Captain DeAngelo, the communist government of Cuba has established small platoons of soldiers on this island to man observation posts, reporting the movements of everyone who come in and out of this island. That tells us that every day, hour, or minute that we stay here could cost us our lives if they come back."

Jamina asked, "Can we go down by our boat to play on the beach?"

"Yes, honey. But always look to the sky with your ears and eyes open. The moment you hear any motor from a plane, chopper, or boat that comes close to the beach, don't let them see you. Run and hide. These men are the same assassins that killed your mother and father." Both kids looked at me in fear, their eyes wide open. "I'm sorry that I have to be so harsh and tell you such horrible things that should not be shared with you at such a young age, but I need you to remember what I'm telling you now. I know it's hard for you to remember this, having the experience you have with your mom and dad, but the only reason I have to do this and tell you this against my principles and will is because your lives are not the only ones which will be lost if anyone sees you on the beach. It will be all of our lives, including your grandfather and Venus. Do you understand?" They both nodded with long, scared faces. "We'll take care of you, even if something happens to your grandfather, but we need you to grow up a little too soon because we need you to be our eyes when you're on the beach and let us know immediately if you see anything. You don't want us all to die, do you?"

"No, we don't want that to happen," they replied almost in unison.

"Do you understand what I'm saying?" They both nodded. "OK, then I need you guys to help me bring all this stuff to Aurora. Then, after that, we'll go to the beach where you guys and Venus can play with your ball until we come back." A little happier, they smiled at me, probably forgetting everything else I had said.

We took the duffel bag and its contents to Aurora and Mama Teca, who received it with smiles. "This is a gift from God," Aurora said. "How did you find it?"

I held up the ball. "I didn't find it; Jamina did."

Atacia said, "Jamina found the ball. You found the rest of it, though I didn't know how you did it."

"I knew that the people who left the ball must have had other stuff to leave."

"No doubt about it that you have an extraordinary brain. I would never have discovered the rest of this stuff from just finding the ball."

"It's not an extraordinary brain. It's my training. I have to thank those who taught me to notice the little things in life. Life is like a ball of twine that you unroll to find the end."

Mama Teca said, "OK, this will make my life a lot easier. I'll help you with that pig. With these butchering instruments, anyone can do anything, especially someone like me that was born on one of these islands."

Finally, we went down to the beach, where Jimbo had the opportunity to show me his surprise. He had found another metal box from the helicopter with missile projectiles which would fit in the Stinger he had. To make sure they functioned properly, we took one, loaded it, and walked along the beach to what was left of the helicopter. The tide was now going down, and the wreck would now be clearly visible from the air. We were able to do two things now—test the weapon and get rid of any evidence that anyone was there to searchers who might fly over or land on the island.

After we were finished, we put the Stinger away. Atacia and I walked with Jimbo to where he had the radio set up on some rocks. He turned it on. There was static and a short-wave whine and crackle of interference. We were very happy to hear that, as it proved the radio was working. All we had to do now was to figure out the best way to transmit a message to a fishing boat or Luis Alberto. We tried different channels on the radio, but there was no response from anyone.

"I have an idea," I said. "Remember, there was a portable antenna in that duffel bag. We could bring it back, and perhaps it and that microphone will be compatible with the radio." I had no doubts now that this place had been used before as an observation point for Castro's military. The more corroboration I had of this, the more concerned I grew. It would be the worst thing to happen to us if these communists returned while we were still on the island.

I suggested that Jimbo take the radio high up the cliff to try not just with the antenna but also with the higher altitude so we might get a better signal. At the same time, keeping the radio far from the beach might prevent our only source of communication from landing in the hands of our enemies.

Atacia looked at the kids enjoying themselves so immensely with Venus. "We're going to go up there—do you think we can leave the kids here for a few hours more?"

I furrowed my eyebrows in thought and checked my wristwatch. It was only nine in the morning and the sun was still low above the horizon. I didn't like the idea of leaving the kids alone, but I didn't want to ruin their happiness by interrupting the game they were enjoying so much. I said to her, "OK, let them stay here, but remind them please that anything they see or hear that's out of the ordinary to immediately run to join us. Refresh their memories—it's not just their lives. If anyone sees them or their ball, they will be killed along with us and their dog. Also let them know that if they hear their grandfather's whistle, that means danger. If they don't have time to run up the cliff, run to where we have the boats camouflaged and hide. They'll be safe there, especially tell them not to leave the ball under any circumstance."

"Very good thinking; the same way you're thinking, the communists might think as well—if they see a ball, there's someone here." I smiled and nodded my agreement.

We waited for Atacia to come back after leaving instructions with the kids. The news was happy for them, and they waved at me with both hands. I returned the waves, and we left for our camp. I said optimistically to Atacia, "I've got a good feeling about this radio. I believe strongly in my heart we will get out of this rat trap if we can manage to get it to function. We'll be out of here sooner than you could believe. I'm just dying to see if our antenna and microphone are compatible with that radio. I believe they are and if not, we can adapt them. It will take a while, but I believe it can be done."

She looked at me and grinned. "I adore your optimism. It's like an injection for my soul of hope and my spirit rejuvenates and dances to hear you with such conviction as you can read the future."

I smiled. "The only thing you never will be having to worry about is not having the same optimism that I've shown you since the moment I met you so many years ago. I always prefer to be an irredeemable optimist and dreamer. I believe I can accomplish what anyone else can; even the most impossible things can be in the reach of your hand with that optimism and faith in your heart. On the contrary, pessimists are always frustrated and drown in their absurd negativity. They give up on their hopes before they even make the most miniscule effort to conquer and achieve their dreams, only because they are in such a terrible panic of failure. That panic and negativity pessimists drag around is a very thick chain on their spirits that prevents them from the opportunity and beautiful possibility of ever enjoying the sweet flavor of triumph."

Atacia said, "Wow! That is the most beautiful words I ever heard from anyone; but not only beautiful but profoundly and absolutely real that in my opinion should be written down for everyone who has a pessimistic personality as a universal message, and so change from pessimism into optimism by your words. I don't know of any pessimist in the history of the world not only in science, art, or any other field, that ever accomplished anything."

"Not even getting off this island alive, eh?"

She smiled and slapped my shoulder as she kissed my cheek. "I don't have any doubts in my mind that you will get us all safe and sound off of this island."

Jimbo protested, "Hey!" He pointed at his cheek. "What about my kiss? I'm the one who found the radio."

She smiled and gave him two kisses. "You found the radio—but have you figured out how to make it work? But you got two kisses, so you don't get jealous. Everything is like a pie—you need the strawberries, sugar, and flour together. And with a leader like Dr. del Marmol we have accomplished what we have so far."

I smiled. "But you do a great job, Jimbo. We all are grateful to you for finding that radio." He smiled proudly.

As we approached the camp, the smell was beautiful and exquisite. If I was hungry before, I was starving now and would eat a rock. For a moment I worried that the exquisite odor would travel to another island, bringing unwanted visitors. Our surprise on return to the camp was great when we found Mama Teca, dressed like she was attending Carnival, only in her underwear and a flowery apron taken from the duffel bag, her hair wrapped in a floral head scarf. Her clothing hung nearby on a bush, removed to protect them from the blood splattered all over the ground. She had skinned the boar, hung the carcass from a coconut tree branch, and cut the pig nearly in half. They were frying up ribs and pieces of meat in big pots. Aurora was eating one of the ribs and handed one to me. It was still hot, and I nearly burned myself on the hot grease as I bit into it. She handed a rib to Atacia and Jimbo as well.

Captain DeAngelo and Bonifacio were sitting with big bowls of fried pork. Another surprise lay on banana leaves on rocks: two huge bunches of bananas.

Apparently, she had been busy while we were down on the beach and found several plantain trees and brought bunches to the camp, using the leaves as cutting surfaces for Aurora to fry up. They were having a ball together, like some assembly line. As Mama Teca had said, she was born on one of these small islands, so I wasn't surprised that she was used to this kind of butchery of animals. She did this with great pleasure as a kind of revenge against the beast which had scared her so badly.

I said to Atacia, "I could not hold back my hunger anymore. It makes my stomach crawl with more strain than the wild pig gave us earlier. I believe it would be a good idea for you to prepare a plate with those delicious-looking pork ribs and some fried plantains. Bring them to us as an appetizer so that Jimbo and I will not interrupt our work. We need to figure out where we're going to put the radio antenna as soon as possible. OK?"

"OK, go ahead and continue to work. I'll join you in a short time."

Jimbo looked at me with a big smile. As we looked for the best location to set up our radio, he said, "That's a great idea. I'm extremely hungry, too. All I have in my stomach was my breakfast, which was just condensed mile and water that my mother gave me early this morning, long before the commotion surrounding that wild pig's invasion of our camp."

I smiled. "Well, at least you had some milk or something to digest in your stomach. I haven't even had a tiny crumb of bread since yesterday morning."

Jimbo jerked his head up in surprise. "Really?"

I nodded. "Yes. Nothing at all."

"Don't you have any headaches or dizziness from not eating for so many hours?"

I looked at him with a smile. We set up the radio on top of an enormous rock with a very smooth top much like a table. To steady the set, I put several small rocks around it to make sure that when we worked with the buttons and tuning dial, the unit wouldn't move around or jiggle too much. I twirled the tuning dial a few times and saw the radio remained steady. Satisfied, I said, "My friend Jimbo, hunger and thirst are physiological needs of our bodies. Our bodies send those signals of need to us are right here." I pointed to my temple. "If you learn to control your thoughts, even if you can't get rid of those needs or cravings, you can still learn to suffer less from your body's demands when you cannot control that fulfillment like we're in the middle of nowhere. You can't snap your fingers and get an apple; but you might just get a coconut by climbing one of the coconut palm trees. Of course, like everything in life, you learn how to control it, as I have in survival courses and the special training I received. Training helps us control our bodies and nature's call when we lack the ability to meet those needs or to put it off as long as possible until we can provide the body with those needs. The people who don't prepare for it and aren't trained suffer the most."

Jimbo looked at me in admiration and nodded his head in conviction. "I would like to learn from you all these things, if you have the time, while you're still around."

I smiled. "It will be a pleasure to teach you everything I know. As proof of that, here's the first lesson." I pointed to my temple with my right hand once more. "Remember, everything is in your mind. If you think of bad memories like remembering the smell of rotten animals lying dead in the street, you will lose your appetite and lose your craving for food. That way you don't suffer as much from a lack of food. The same thing you do when you're thirsty—think of any time you went to the ocean and by some chance swallowed some salt water. Your thirst will go away at once at the memory that water isn't always sweet. Of course, it's not a permanent remedy to physical necessities, but for sure it will extend your craving until you can be able to provide food and water along with any other necessities you might require. That makes your agony less intense."

Jimbo nodded. We heard voices on the radio at that moment as I switched it on. The lights were all functional. The voices were the captains of different fishing vessels talking to each other. We could not get onto their frequency for transmission, however. At that moment, Atacia arrived with two plates full of fried plantains and ribs. She grinned from ear to ear, her eyes shining with joy.

She said, "Oh, my God! I think we're close to getting off this island."

I said, "I love your optimism very much. There's a very big difference between hearing them and getting them to hear us. But there's no doubt in my mind that we've made major progress, and with the equipment we have we should be able to make it work. But now we should follow your advice to maintain our energies by eating something. A little later, Jimbo can climb to the highest point of this cliff and find the ideal location to set our antenna."

Jimbo said, "Absolutely. You guys can guide me, and I'll move the antenna around until we get a clear signal. Let's start to eat." Without waiting for us, he sat down and began to eat.

I said to Atacia, "I think you should get Bonifacio and Captain DeAngelo. They have more experience with these kinds of radios on their boats. I'm a little afraid to begin communicating with anyone because your father might have some kind of codes to communicate with his brother and others without interception by government vessels. Since they've been doing this for many years, they might even have some kind of secret codes between them for use when they catch some kind of fish protected during those periods to avoid getting fined by the government. Let's hope that is the case and they can speak to each other in code and your father transmits the correct location for your uncle to pick us up without being intercepted by the communist government. The last thing we need is for us to establish communication, and instead of being visited by Luis Alberto we instead receive unwanted visitors in the form of torpedo boats coming to get us. After all that's happened recently, I don't have any doubts that they're searching for us everywhere."

Atacia smiled sarcastically. "Let's hope that they continue their search for a very long time and never find us. That is a visit that I would not enjoy receiving."

Jimbo said with a mouth full of food as he shook his head, "Me, either. That will be a worse commotion than that wild pig last night."

Atacia noticed that Jimbo was inarticulate because of the mouthful. "Jimbo, will you never learn that it's very bad manners to talk with your mouth full while you're eating?"

Jimbo gestured negatively. "Ahhh, we're in the middle of the jungle and you're talking about manners!"

"Yes, Jimbo—manners are what makes us different from the wild pig, even in the jungle."

Jimbo answered, "Why don't you go and get Dad, tell him to hurry up and come over, since we need him here badly? The radio is working, and we need his expertise to contact our uncle."

"Oh, now you want to get rid of me. Before you were hungry, but now you're full you want to send me away!" She shook her head unhappily. She turned and left. "Thank you, and enjoy your meal, Jimbo."

"Thank you very much, Atacia!"

A little while later, as we finished up our food, Bonifacio and Captain DeAngelo arrived. Both of them had broad smiles; it appeared that Atacia had let them know of our progress with the radio. They had full stomachs and the news combined to put them in an excellent mood. I got up from my seat by the radio and allowed them to take my place. Bonifacio turned the dial listening to the frequency sounds, the lights changed color as some turned off while others lit up as he searched for a signal to tune into.

Jimbo stood up with the antenna in his hand. "Where do you want me to put this?"

"Go up to the top and keep moving it until we tell you it's OK. Once we give you that signal, that antenna doesn't move, even if you have to sit down on top of it."

"Sit down on it? Do you want to poke holes in my butt?"

"You might not find a place where you can wedge the base of the antenna, so you may have to support it and weight it down with rocks."

Bonifacio turned the radio around to look for a slot to plug in the portable microphone I had given him. I leaned back and said, "I'll tell you what I found and perhaps you can pick it up from there. The clearest conversations were between 100, 150, 175, and 200 kilohertz." Captain DeAngelo was looking at the diagram on the radio to determine its range and other specifics. I added, "This isn't a marine radio—it's a helicopter radio, so keep that in mind. There's a big difference in the frequencies used between broadcasting over the ocean and air."

Atacia returned with Mama Teca and Aurora. Everyone was happy with their full stomachs and filled with curiosity about the voices they had heard on the radio. They listened for themselves as we tuned in on the frequencies I had related to Bonifacio and Captain DeAngelo. Bonifacio had just tuned to a frequency with voices talking about temperature, position, and the nautical miles in which they were fishing close to the Gulf of Mexico.

I said, "If this reaches as far as the Gulf, we could call my friends in the USA to come help us." Now that my appetite was satisfied, I started to yawn frequently.

Atacia noticed it. "Why don't you go and lay down for a few hours? Jimbo, my father, and Captain DeAngelo can handle it; it's all in their hands."

"Yes, yes," Bonifacio said. "Go rest before you collapse. You haven't slept for two days."

DeAngelo agreed, "Yes, Dr. Marmol. You must be exhausted. We'll need you at full capacity soon. Those yawns are calls from your body asking desperately for help."

I smiled and nodded. I got up from my rock slowly because I was feeling lazy. Atacia offered her arm to me when she saw the difficulty I had getting up. I said, "I'm sore because I'm doing too many things at once."

As I moved slowly, groggy from the food, I heard in the distance the engine of either a plane or chopper. No one else heard it because it was very far away. Like I received an electric shock, I jumped away from Atacia, checking my wristwatch and then looking at the sky. "Oh, my God, we've been sleeping. The kids are on the beach and a plane is coming!"

"No, there's no plane! You're hearing things, it's in your mind."

"It's twelve o'clock. The sun is up. Do you remember what I told you?"

Her head jerked up. "Oh, my God, the children! We've been so distracted by the radio that we've forgotten about your premonition. Get the children, Mama Teca—we have to get them out of danger, there's a plane coming!"

Even though she didn't hear it, she was in motion at once, following my warning. Everyone else went into high alert. Captain DeAngelo whistled as loud as he could. I looked at the wristwatch again sadly. I hoped that perhaps I was overreacting, but the sun was in the middle of the sky and my watch read what I saw before—twelve noon. I hoped I was wrong but with the distractions of food and radio, time had flown out of our hands unnoticed. DeAngelo continued to whistle to his grandchildren.

We could hear Venus barking in response to the whistle, running up the cliff towards us. Fortunately, the children down below could hear clearly the engine of the plane clearly. It looked like a small Cessna from the Cuban Navy that was scouting the area. The children ran in panic towards where we had the boats in camouflage, knowing they wouldn't make it to the cliff. Both realized in the middle of the beach they had forgotten the ball on the beach. Both of them turned and ran back. Rolando remembered what I said to him about the ball he yelled "The ball!" He turned around, while at the same time Jamina remembered what Atacia had said about her grandfather and dog dying. The plane had descended to around one thousand feet; they wouldn't have enough time to get the ball and make it back.

Atacia and Mama Teca came down the cliff, covering themselves with dark grey blankets, each of them jumping on a child, covering themselves together, trying to look like a rock on the beach from that altitude, whispering for the children not to move.

The plane flew overhead as it searched the beach. They could hear the engine of the plane as it passed by. Those of us on the cliff crossed ourselves, expecting the worst. The plane continued on, however, without opening fire. We hoped that that the pilot had not seen anyone running, just two large rocks on the beach. But something must have caught his attention as we watched the plane circle to come back around on another pass.

I yelled, "Get off that beach! This time they'll confirm what they thought they saw."

Captain DeAngelo whistled shrilling once again to send the additional signal to Mama Teca and Atacia. The plane started to circle as Mama Teca and Atacia sent the kids running like wild rabbits towards the boats. As we watched, we didn't think they would make it, that the plane would catch them before reaching the boats. Mama Teca and Atacia scooped together with their hands all the seaweed nearby on the beach to make it as large as possible and covered it with the blankets before running to the boats. What was left behind looked like a large mass of sargasso lying on the beach. The children jumped into the boat covered by the palm leaves, and close behind them Mama Teca and Atacia dove inside. As they entered the refuge, the plane dove down and opened fire with a spray of bullets at the blankets and seaweed on the beach. Pieces of blanket and seaweed flew into the air mixed together. The pilot and copilot must have thought that what they had just shot up was exactly that from that altitude: a large growth of sargasso deposited on the beach from the ocean.

We prayed to omnipotent God, at any rate, that this is what He put in their brains, and that they would go away. The pilot showed some persistence, perhaps unconvinced that what we wanted him to believe was real and made a very long circle as if he were leaving. But far out, he turned around for a last pass. I yelled down, "Don't move!! This guy will come back, either for the kill or to convince himself that there's nothing there!!" I turned to Jimbo. "Come with me. Let's go get the Stinger and be ready in case we have no other choice. If we have to, we'll burn them out of the sky, but only if it's absolutely necessary and there's no other option. I don't want any other vessel to disappear in this particular area. They would probably mobilize an entire army around all these islands, and it will be very difficult for us to get out of here alive. We have to take into consideration that this zone is probably already declared by them a very hot and dangerous one. The last thing we want to do is blow up this plane or have another aircraft or vessel disappear in this area."

We went down and took up a position behind a rock, the loaded weapon on his shoulder. We patiently waited, having already cautioned everyone to stay down. The plane came in; I pointed it out to Jimbo. This time, however, it made only a small circle twice right on top of the beach. Then it took off, convinced that there was nothing to worry about there.

We breathed deep sighs of relief as we watched the plane disappear. We regrouped at the top of the cliff, this time with the children in tow, who hadn't moved a single muscle as they waited for the aircraft to disappear.

I was exhausted not only from the nervous tension but all the disrupted rest we had over the previous days. I decided to retreat to the hiding place with Atacia, where I finally hoped to be able to rest for a few hours without any further disturbance.

Chapter 15: Abomination in the Island

Those few hours I had planned to rest became without my knowing it many hours as my completely exhausted body demanded more rest than I had in mind to give to it. I woke up at last, and looked at my wristwatch to see it was five pm on the dot. I looked around and saw Atacia sitting near the water's edge on a rock close to me. She had a plate of food nearby and looked at me as I stood up from the improvised bed of blankets and sand very close to the edge of the lagoon at the foot of the cascade. I looked at her with a small smile. "Isn't it incredible how our bodies respond gratefully to a few hours of sleep and rest?"

Atacia grinned broadly. "Well, everything depends on what you call 'a few hours.' To my mind, I consider twenty-four hours to be many, not a few."

I didn't follow her. I looked at my watch once more in confusion and saw that it still showed five in the afternoon. "I don't know what you're talking about. I've checked my watch twice to make sure it hasn't stopped running. I know I went to bed at one pm; I looked at my watch, and now it reads five."

Atacia smiled ironically. "You are right, one hundred percent. That was yesterday. Today is a day later. You went to bed at one pm *yesterday.* You slept all day yesterday, all night, and most of the day today. The total of consecutive hours of sleep you've had is twenty-nine hours." She stood up and brought the plate of food over to me: some pork loins, a can of black beans, and some fried bananas, with one of the bottles of chianti we had found in the treasure discovered the day before. She put the plate down next to me on the blanket. "You have no idea how many times I've brought this plate back and forth yesterday for my mother to reheat it again. I imagined that your stomach would need maintenance again after so many hours without food."

I touched my belly with my right hand. "Now I understand why my stomach continues to make those strange noises it made yesterday while you guys hassled with the radio. Now I know. How could I sleep for so many hours without noticing it?"

"You didn't even know how exhausted you were, probably, but your body knew better."

I sat down to eat. "By the way, what happened with your father and the radio? Did he finally establish contact with your uncle? Or is everything still in limbo?"

"Yes, he established communication at last. He managed to talk to my uncle."

I smiled. "That's great! That tells me that we might get off this island very soon. But you don't look very happy—what's wrong?"

She made a sour expression. "Well, not very soon, as you say."

I paused eating. I asked in surprise, "What do you mean by that?"

"Let's forget about it. Finish eating your food, and you just woke up. Eat in peace, and I'll explain it to you as soon as you finish your meal. Enjoy it before it gets cold. I don't want to spoil your appetite."

"Too late—you already did." I pushed the plate away from me. "I cannot continue eating with my curiosity unsatisfied and with that sour tone in your voice and sorrowful look on your face. It tells me that nothing good or pleasant happened during my sleeping journey in the dream world. From the beginning your voice and face have revealed that you're not happy at all. What's up? I won't be able to eat now until you tell me what's going on."

She looked at me and sat down next to me on the blankets. She put a hand on my shoulder. "OK, it's nothing to be depressed about. My uncle and father had been in touch several times during the day, and my uncle's the last message said that it would be not just a crazy idea but also an assured death for all of us as well as whoever intends to get us out of this place. The communists have multiplied their surveillance around all these keys and islands. My uncle believes that we should be patient until they get tired and pull out all of the forces they've deployed out of this area." She tried to smile as she attempted cheer me up with something positive and hopeful. "According to my uncle, there will be a lunar eclipse soon. When that happens during a dark night, it changes the climate and brings in a heavy fog. We should wait until then because under those conditions we should escape unnoticed. Uncle Luis Alberto knows these things well and is a very experienced navigator. He repeatedly urged my father to wait and not waste our lives unnecessarily, especially since we have plenty of food and water to hold out for months."

"For *months*?! Oh, my God."

Atacia squeezed my shoulder. "It's that or put all of us in danger of losing our lives, including those who try to get us out of here. He could see the torpedo boats constantly passing by his ship, checking everything around, like sardines in a small fishing boat."

I took a deep breath and squeezed my chin in worried concern at what she had just related all that had occurred while I was having sweet dreams. It was a sour reality. Like I always say dreaming is beautiful, reality sucks. "How long do we have to wait?"

She shook her head with a long face, raising her eyebrows. "I don't know. This is very difficult to predict. Everything depends on how long these communists decide to maintain their tight security cordon in this area." She put a little optimism into her voice as she continued, "It could be only a few days."

I shook my head, understanding she was trying to make me feel better. I also understood that through a strange game of destiny we all were now at the mercy of our enemies and whatever they decided to do. The days she was talking about could be weeks, months, or God only knew how long we would be condemned to wait there patiently. I realized that being irrational and impatient would not bring any good consequences to us. Instead of being angry or depressed, I decided to thank God once more for still being alive. We were, after all, in an ideal place which had ample water for the rest of our lives but also enough food for a long time, probably longer than I planned to remain there.

I smiled. "Well, reality sucks, but *que sera sera*." I pulled the plate of food back to me and continued to eat.

Atacia looked at me in surprise. She raised both arms and said, "That's it? You always react to bad news this way?"

I smiled again. "What can I do? Cry like a little boy and say I don't want to eat anymore and be hungry for the rest of the day and then beg your mother for the food later? The only truly bad news that you could give me would be that one of our friends, including Venus, has been killed. Everything else has a solution which could knock on our door at any moment. It will be with your uncle or some other person—I will find a way of getting off this island eventually with the help of all of you. We must remain positive. Let's hope that the exit from this island won't be in wooden boxes or body bags."

She smiled, this time joyfully from my dark joke. "Ha, ha, ha. I see you haven't lost your sense of humor yet."

"Never. I would rather die a hundred times than be a sour puss."

She smiled this time in satisfaction. She leaned over to me and gave me a tender kiss on the cheek and then my lips. Smiling one more time, she took my face between both hands and said with mischief twinkling in her eyes, "Mm, mm—I want more of the exquisite flavor of plantains on your lips." She kissed me again, more passionately and longer. She repeated it many times, the sound of the water falling over the cascade into the lagoon providing a beautiful background music. In the midst of that extraordinary natural beauty, we forgot about the troubles of the world and allowed the sexual attraction we had for each other to take prominence that grew little by little, through this ordeal, like a wildflower in a savage environment. An extraordinary, beautiful love that neither of us had expected took hold of us by surprise.

That danger and uncertainty from the past few days we had been through together bonded us in an extraordinary way. Right there, we took our clothes off and made love over the blankets on top of the white sand to the music of the national bird of Cuba, the Cuban trogon. That little bird sounded like every other bird, imitating them in perfect tune in such a refined manner that when it sang all the other birds would gather near to sing along with it. Like the distinguished conductor of an orchestra, very well coordinated, it directed other birds to sing sometimes in unison with it. The nightingale, always the second in the orchestra, would come and sit next to the trogon, in a different tonality yet in tune, they made a romantic moment a lot more beautiful than anyone could imagine. I have never forgotten that moment, and I will recall it clearly for the rest of my life.

Atacia took my face once more between her hands after we were both totally satisfied and exhausted, our bodies soaked in sweat. She looked into my eyes, love filling her eyes, and said, "I have to thank God first for practically dropping you into my arms out of the sky. Then I have to thank you for your love and gentle and humor that conquered my heart. You've made me laugh in the most precarious situations. That is something anyone has ever been able to do. I only ask one single favor—never change your character or personality. These are the best qualities you possess. Though we can never predict our destinies, never let the disappointments and sadness in your life in the future steal those beautiful qualities."

I smiled and kissed her tenderly on the lips. "Love, I'm the one who has to give you many thanks. First for your beautiful words that I know come from your heart. But I can tell you with tremendous conviction, knowing that I know for a fact that your feelings and mine are identical. What you feel in your heart is exactly what I feel for you right here." I pointed at my breast with a very resplendent smile on my face. "Be try to be thankful not only to God but also to you, I'm the one most indicated for that. You not only are the most extraordinary woman I have in my life but also with your magnificent qualities you've saved my life when I was semi-conscious after our plane was struck by lightning and crashed during that tropical storm on the Yucatan Peninsula." I shook my head, now with a small smile. "You risked your life to save mine. At that moment, I was only a stranger to you. I was incapable of appreciating that altruistic act, and that makes you a dignified exemplary woman that I have to respect until I die."

She leaned over and took my face yet again in her hands to kiss me tenderly on the lips. She said with a smile, "To tell you the truth, when I saw the twenty-foot-tall rough waves, I had to think twice before jumping to get you. But when I saw your body taken up into the air like a seagull's feather by those furious waters, I could not let you die. And that's when I didn't know you." She raised her eyebrows and pointed to the blankets where we had just made love. "Now that I know you I will not even think for a fraction of a second before jumping into such rough waters to save you."

I smiled. "Really? You wouldn't think twice anymore? It was that good for you?"

She looked at me mischievously. "You don't even know, honey." She dramatically raised her eyebrows as she spread her arms high over her head. She pulled them down over her breasts and the rest of her body. She said sensually as she closed her eyes and shook as if she was having a spasm, "Now I say to the ocean, take me, cruel ocean! But I don't want to live if I don't have him by my side." She laughed and jumped over me, making me lose my balance, and we rolled naked out of the blankets over the sand. She continued to laugh and giggle, continuing to yell, "Yes, cruel ocean! If you take us, please make sure it's far away from this island and the communists! Please, please!"

She began to laugh contagiously, and we both rolled into the water of the lagoon, looking to cleanse our bodies of the sweat and sand. We spent some time in the cold, refreshing water, and walked over to the cascade, hugging each other, and enjoyed the natural shower until we decided to go back to where we had left our clothes on the rocks. We shook the blankets out to get rid of the sand and used them as towels. Then we got dressed, and I opened the bottle of chianti, handing the bottle over to her to take the first sip.

She refused, "No, no—I'm fine."

"OK." She watched as I took the first and second sip.

As I was about to take a third sip, she held out her right hand and said, "It's not fair that you should have all the fun. I believe we are partners in the same misery, so we should share both misery and happiness together. Don't you think so?"

"Of course. I offered it to you first, not only because of courtesy but also because you're a woman."

She smiled and said, "You're better than anybody, being a man of the world, should know that for good or ill, we women are very timid and indecisive."

"Well, you're not either one."

"Well, not in everything. But in the end, remember, I'm a woman. Once in a while we get caught in our indecisiveness."

I took the bottle and smirked. "Have it your way. You women are always right. I've been thinking very carefully and I believe that we should go to the other side of the island and explore it."

She looked at me seriously. "You mean to tell me you've been thinking while we've been having sex?"

"Remember, my brain has two sides like everyone else. One side is awake, the other sleeps. One thinks while the other does. Most people use only half or even a quarter of their brains. I had a great time with you, but I also have to figure out a way to get you, me, and the rest away from this island. Then I'll be at peace with myself and then I can continue to do the work I came here to do in the first place that I've unfortunately been detoured from. Let me tell you what I think: I believe that there's a very strong possibility that the other side of this island is not being watched as closely. There's even a possibility that it's not even being watched at all. This particular coast borders the Caribbean Ocean. If the other side is on the Atlantic Ocean where the waves sometimes are so high that the best captains in the navy sometimes lose their vessels, there's a great possibility that they won't have anyone watching that side."

"If that is true, how will that help us?"

"Think about it. You told me not too long ago that your uncle is a very experienced captain. If that's as you say, and we go to that side of the island to find out there are no patrols because of the rough waters, we might be able to get out or at least make the attempt where they least expect it. If we're on this island and we go to the roughest, most difficult ocean to escape from here, that will be for them a huge surprise, which we can use to catch our enemies with their guard down."

Atacia raised her eyebrows. "That's not a bad idea. Of course, that's assuming everything is the way you think it is. But the one thing I don't understand is how you will manage to get all of us through that rough water; we will have to leave our boats here. We can't carry them to the other side of the island."

"That's the least of our problems. First, we don't need that boat, because that engine will catch the attention of anyone who might be there watching. Your question of how we get to your uncle's ship is very simple. With the tools we found, all we have to do is lash together some coconut trunks into a raft. We have the tools, we have everything we need in that beautiful bag from our treasure trove. Guided by one or two of us in the water on that raft, we could all reach your uncle's ship during the silence of the night, right under any patrols of the government that might be watching. We won't have to wait for months until a lunar eclipse or until Heaven knows when these guys decide to leave."

She smiled. "Your idea is brilliant. The notion of staying here for months is not attractive to me."

"You're being optimistic in thinking it could be months. To my way of thinking, communists are unpredictable. If they decide to leave a permanent post to guard this area because of the danger it represents to the government, we could be stuck here for years."

"Oh, no!" She shook her head.

"Everything is possible when you're dealing with evil people like our enemies. I'm not a man to sit down and wait until the mangos are ripe and fall from the tree. I am a man who climbs the tree, takes the mangos while they're still green, bring them down to cover them with a blanket in the humidity, and get ready to eat them before anyone else."

Atacia nodded. "That is one of the things I'm most proud of about you. I fully support you. Let's go. When will we explore the other side of this island?"

"Tomorrow morning. Let's go to the camp, tell your mother to prepare several rations of food, because we'll need to take food and water for at least a week for contingencies as we search and have enough of both to not make it harder than it will already be our path. We have to be prepared and bring a couple of very sharp machetes in case we encounter dense, heavy vegetation we need to cut away. This will make it easier and faster for us. Our journey has to be fast, efficient, and precise. One of us will come back and bring the rest of the group if we discover a place where it will all be OK. You never know—we might find better fruits and many other things to eat in that part of the island, and we won't have to bring anything else. We don't know that yet, but when we do, we can tell the others what to bring and what to leave. We have to prepare and figure out the time it will take for us to put together a raft. Your father has to coordinate that with your uncle and be sure to bring the radio with him, that way he'll be there the day we take off, ready for us."

"Don't worry—I'll cover all the details with him. You make sure you bring with you the weapons and whatever you think is necessary in case we encounter our enemies. I'll make sure that I find the way to bring enough water and food with us and some blankets and hammocks, so we won't have to worry about where we sleep."

"OK," I replied with a nod. "Let's go back to the camp and get ready, because the sooner we do this the better. This place is the most dangerous spot on the whole island because we know someone has been here before, and that someone must have been from the government to have left all these treasures behind. Let's get out of here before night comes on. We should prepare everything tonight and coordinate our plans with the others. We'll need their help if we want to leave this island safe and sound."

A little bit later, after we got back to the camp, we discussed our plans with the group. I was very satisfied to see that everyone embraced my suggestion with joy. Nobody wanted to sit down and wait for the communists in Cuba to decide for us how long we were going to be stranded on the island. We exchanged several ideas, and in the middle of the discussion, Mama Teca said, "I don't want to contradict you with all my respect, and I agree that this is the best way to proceed, even if the circumstances don't come the way you plan, I think it's the best choice we have. I like it very much. Even when someone wants to hurt you, or in this case kill you, and they've been waiting for you on your doorstep, the most sensible and smart thing to do is get out by the back door, especially when they have to their advantage not only in power and numbers but also the weapons which we don't possess." She looked at me ingenuously. "I believe that I could be a great help, because you guys alone in that jungle will take a lot of time to complete your plans, especially if you plan to build a crude raft. But if I go with you, not only will we divide the workload between us, which will make things easier and expedited."

I nodded. "I have no objection at all to your proposal. I think it's a great idea. The only reason I didn't include any of you with this expedition, which I had planned to do by myself until Atacia volunteered to come along, was because it would be the first trip of exploration to find exactly what risks exist out there. We have no idea what we'll find on the other side of this island. We assumed that there were no animals here and look what happened the other night." I smiled. "I always say that volunteers are welcome—but not the kind the communists call 'voluntaries', with a gun to their heads."

Mama Teca didn't wait for a second and stood right up. "You can count on me, and I will be your second volunteer, since Atacia is the first one. I think it will be good for you guys on the trip. I'll prepare myself for the trip and am ready to join you on this new venture."

She didn't think for a moment about what might be on the other side waiting for us. Now Jimbo asked, "With all my respect and if it's not an inconvenience, I'd like to go, too."

"Of course it's not an inconvenience. I want to bring all of you, but I don't think it would be smart. Let me say this to you—this expedition could be a very dangerous one. We have no idea of what we'll find on the other side. In the middle of the night, like that wild pig, we could have a big surprise in our faces. Let's hope that we don't find any government crews set up as an observation post, like the one they had here at some point. We could even discover a secret biolab constructed here by the Chinese with Heaven knows what." I shook my head. "This is precisely what we're trying to determine on this particular trip. It's not fair to put everyone at risk. That's why a small group of us should scout and prepare the way to bring the others finally off this island safe and sound."

Jimbo said, 'You don't have to worry about me. I'll come prepared, because I'll bring my Stinger to sting them with. I have a lot of spare missiles, remember, that I found on the beach."

"OK, Jimbo—if your mother and father and sister have no objections, for me it will be a pleasure. You could be a great help on this trip. Remember, though, that each of us will be responsible for bringing the rations of water and food, at least until we are on the other side and can discover whether the resources exist to resupply ourselves with food and water. We'll only be walking during daylight with our eyes wide open in case the communists have left behind natural traps on the ground, like the Vietcong would do in Vietnam. Those traps can be deadly, and I and my team have found them in these keys and islands around Cuba. They copy these methods, they say, to prevent the Americans from invading, but it really is nothing more than an excuse to scare the hell out of people trying to escape Cuba and its miseries. That is why every step we take, even during the daylight, must be very careful. I don't want to lose any of you in this jungle to one of those deadly traps. I don't want to scare you but to prepare you. Keep it in your mind: communists, like Nazis, have no scruples, and I don't think they even have mothers because they're not born of women but of Satan. That's why they have no remorse; they have no human conscience."

Atacia asked, "What time tomorrow morning do you want to leave?"

I checked my watch. "At first light. In this season, that should be around five thirty in the morning. I just want you guys to prepare to leave now. In the morning, I don't want to wait for anyone. We need to put the time to good use to advance as far as possible each day. Say your goodbyes tonight, because I don't want anyone to waste time in the morning doing that." I turned to Bonifacio. "Start to mark the passage of days on one of the tree trunks starting tomorrow morning. If we're not back in seven days, move this camp immediately to the most secure location you can find. That will mean something went wrong and something unfortunate happens to us, the first thing the communists will do will be to thoroughly comb this island. The cave we showed you guys is the best place to hide. Nobody knows it exists because it's so hard to find. I don't want us to get caught and have you suffering the same misfortune of being taken by surprise."

Bonifacio replied sadly, "Let's hope things don't go that way, and we'll see you guys very soon as you've planned. You find the other way out from this island, a more secure and speedier one than the option my brother suggested." He took the other bottle of chianti he had been saving in his hammock and held it up. "We should open this to celebrate your exit, like they do in the navy when they christen a new vessel. Let's open it and drink to your great success, luck, and the hope for all of us."

"Why don't you do something better? Save that wine until we're all on the other side, safe and sound and ready to leave this island. We can use it to give us energy and calories in case we need to swim. Don't you think that would be more practical? Let's leave this trip in the hands of God and hope for the best."

"OK," Bonifacio replied with a little smile, not completely in agreement. He crossed himself reverently. "Let's hope to God." He wrapped the bottle back up and put it back in his hammock. The others crossed themselves and murmured agreement not just in their voices but also in their hearts, praying to God that all would go well.

We went to sleep, and the next day as the first light of dawn broke, we left the camp. Even at such an early hour, Rolando and Jamina were awakened by the barking of Venus, who noticed that we were leaving. We walked for a long time. The sun was very high in the sky; I checked my watch to see it was two pm. We felt a breeze that was much cooler, even after all the exercise we had over the previous hours. The vegetation started to grow sparse, and the trees were much taller. It was still a tropical environment, but it was more arid, and the variety of flowers became different. We walked further, and we began to hear a new sound, monkey-like screams and deeper, more guttural noises that we couldn't identify. The monkeys sounded like they were distressed. It gave us chills because we hadn't been used to hearing any such sounds. The only sound we had been accustomed to were beautiful tropical birds and their harmonic noises with no disturbance.

The first shadows of the day lengthened as afternoon wore on, warning that night would soon come. We scouted around for a good place to camp and stopped for the night for some food and rest. We started a fire to warm up some of the food we brought, made some small talk discussing the difference in temperature and the noises we had been hearing. We extinguished the fire to avoid an animal scattering the flames and went to sleep.

A few hours passed, and everyone woke up to a chilling screech of pain. It sounded like monkeys fighting amongst themselves, possibly over territory or position. There was more growling from a different animal. From the throaty sound, it might have been a gorilla having a similar dispute that the monkeys were having. We looked at each other, wondering what animals these were. Our hammocks were slung close to the ground, near each other. We had no idea that such animals existed on the other side of the island and after the encounter with the wild pig, we knew that all things were possible and so were all fully armed with plenty of ammunition. Small monkeys, similar to the green monkeys of Barbados, might be what we were hearing. Nobody knew for sure how they got to these little areas, but some theorized that they would find these islands on floating trunks or some other means to end up in different places. Most of them weren't anything to worry about. They ran from humans and were no danger to anyone. Most of the rural folk that lived on these islands paid hunters to kill these monkeys, which would eat not only the bananas and other fruit they cultivated but even the trees themselves, which was the livelihood for these people who now had no other option but to sell their produce to the Cuban communist government.

The screaming, irritating noises continued off and on all night. They finally stopped; but the noise had kept us awake turned out to be a good alarm and warning. Even though we all had weapons and had come prepared, especially Mama Teca, who had enough with her one bad experience, we all started to raise our hammocks up higher in the middle of the night. She did it first, getting up and slinging it from branches that were higher up on the surrounding trees, and the rest of us followed suit. Everyone began to go to sleep; still half asleep, my mind was worried about some of the monkey-like screams, but more about the other sounds I still had no explanation for. It puzzled me excessively, being unable to identify the source, and so none of us rested well. The mystery surrounding those noises made me think that sometimes when we're not happy with what we have and desire something else. I thought of the beautiful musical cascade in that cave where the birds sang so beautifully, and that what we were leaving behind was a Paradise compared to what God only knew waited for us where we were going now. That northern piece of land in the island was like the dark side of the moon and brought depressed feelings to my mind which forced me to get out of bed several times throughout the night. Eventually I just got up while it was still dark with my eyes constantly scanning the bushes, ready for action. I thought I saw small yellow eyes in the bushes watching me.

I didn't know what was in the bushes, but I kept my eyes on them. Suddenly, a squealing erupted behind the bush I was looking at. I pointed at my pistol at the source and clearly saw the bushes move. I fired twice, and a guttural scream of pain erupted, waking the others up. Everyone saw a body suddenly flung out of the bushes towards me. Thanks to God and my paranoia, I twisted to one side and avoided it, the body missed my shoulder by a fraction of an inch and smashed against the tree behind me where my hammock was tied, tangling itself in the hammock and leaves. I jumped and took the pistol in both hands and approached the creature. The bushes around us moved, but nothing else came out. It appeared that whatever was hidden from us was spooked by the gunfire and was running away.

The first light of the sun broke over the horizon. I saw what looked like a monkey the size of a chimpanzee, motionless in the tangled mess of my hammock and the tree branches. I went closer to examine it, my friends with me in complete shock, realizing that this monkey's body was headless. It appeared that it had been torn off, pieces of flesh hanging from the neck and shoulders, it was also missing an arm, which had likewise been chewed off. It appeared that a larger animal had been eating it while it was still alive. Chills broke out over my body as the hairs of my neck rose up. Helped by my friends, we disentangled the body of the monkey. Based on my profound knowledge of animal genetics I guessed from the red color of its fur with white over its chest, it appeared to be a monkey that was a genetic experiment in crossing of diverse other Caribbean mammals, albeit phylogenetically carnivorous. My greatest doubt was who would have created this abomination and for what purpose. The most important and dangerous part was what the other abomination might be waiting for us out there was. It might be of monstrous proportions and was running around this jungle. It was capable of flinging an animal that weighed over 180 pounds through the air like a feather, even after I shot at it.

    After we had separated the half-eaten body from my hammock, I walked to the bushes and now with the sun completely risen and, followed by my friends, we could see blood from where the bullets had hit the beast which had caused it to retreat, leaving behind the missing arm from the monkey's body. It appeared that it had been sitting there, eating the monkey as it watched me sitting up in the hammock. Pieces of skin and chewed meat from the monkey were scattered on the ground. That concerned me and changed our plans completely. Now, even if we found a secure exit from that island on this side, we had to eliminate that genetic abomination before we brought the rest of our group, especially the kids, which would be very easy prey for one of these beasts. It would only take our being distracted for the briefest moment for them to be taken in the blink of an eye, and I would never forgive myself for that.

    We packed up our stuff and left the camp site. As we walked further, we started to smell the salt air of the ocean and the odor of seaweed, and we knew we were only a few miles from the sea. The vegetation started to be thinner with a kind of prickly pear cactus with fan-like leaves and long thorns, indicating the climate was getting even more arid. It was definitely the northern side of the island. I had been following the blood trail left behind by that strange beast and thought to myself that we had to be very careful, because predator animals became more dangerous when wounded. We had no idea how badly wounded it was, so I said to the others, "Be careful. The strength of that creature which could easily take the arm of that monkey would take one of ours off in a single swipe. We have no idea how many of those things are out there."

We had no idea what it looked like, what it was, and what kind of danger it actually represented. It was all left to our imagination, though our tension and fear of the unknown caused the worst images to form in our minds, each of us enhancing the image of this predator, making it worse than we were even imagining. None of us, no matter how wild an imagination we possessed, came close to the magnitude of repulsiveness and grotesquery of the beast we would soon encounter.

We started to listen to the seagulls flying high over our heads as well as other marine birds. I checked my watch to see it was noon. The sun was at its height, brilliant as always in the Caribbean, but the temperature was certainly more moderate and pleasant than where we had been before. As we forced our way further into the jungle, we came to a clearing. As we descended to the lower elevations approaching the coast, we saw stone structures which looked manmade from thousands of years ago. It looked either Mayan or Aztec, with male and female human faces sculpted in enormous dimensions into the rocks. The ruins appeared to have once been a city or village. In the center was a small pyramid of animal skulls and bones, artistically put together, some with weeds and ivy growing amongst them.

    We drew our pistols, ready to fight, as we saw small flat constructions with mushroom shaped roofs, built of rocks and adobe. There was a massive one in the center that looked like some kind of altar with the sculpture of some kind of goddess, wearing a tiara with green and purple stones, emeralds, and pearls. As the sun moved, the reflections from the stones moved with it until they pointed like tiny flashlights to a large rock at the base which looked like a humongous cooking pot that had a pole in the center for looked like what ritual sacrifices of animals or human beings. As we got closer to the large image, I noticed the reflection of the stones changed position. We could now see her eyes were a beautiful emerald green, something extremely strange and hard to believe without seeing it for oneself. We could clearly see in the eyes of the image streams of red liquid like tears coming down over the rocks around the pot at the bottom. It was blood.

    We looked at each other, lacking any logical explanation for this phenomenon. We all knew rocks didn't cry. We were silent in absolute respect at what we saw but some also terrified about this source of confusion. Only the seagulls high above that flew in circles broke the silence as they gradually got lower to where we were. I remembered while traveling in fishing boats how the seagulls, knowing they would feed on the innards of the fish we caught, followed the same ritual.

    Suddenly, the flow of the fluid stopped. The seagulls, however, grew more agitated as they waited for food. I said to the others, "Stay together and be alert.

Let's make a circle so that each of us sees a different point and not get surprised from behind."

We formed a circle, looking towards the sky. Even as I finished my suggestions, a flock of crows descended from the sky, landing on the arms of the statue. Several monkeys the size of a chimpanzee with yellow eyes came from the various small structures. It looked like they were preparing a coordinated attack. They had red fur with white chests—just as the same coloration as the one that had been thrown at us in the camp by the mysterious beast. Now that we could see the heads, we saw they had snouts which came to a point, more like Doberman pincers than anything like an orangutan; they had very sharp fangs, which told us they weren't exactly accustomed to eating bananas—these were carnivorous guard dogs of some kind. Luckily for us, there were only eight of them—twice our number, but we had more than twice their strength in weapons and ammunitions to oppose their claws and teeth. We watched them carefully, noticing they could destroy a human body in no time.

What appeared to be the dominant leader began to scream. I said, "Everyone stay silent." It looked like they were about to attack, and I said, "Scream as loud as you can!" We all yelled and banged our chests like apes, and they froze immediately. I didn't want to kill even these creatures, and I wasn't ready to waste any bullets.

They rushed towards us, and we opened fire. Six fell down dead a few feet from us, but two of them were merely wounded, and one jumped on top of Jimbo while the other jumped on me. It bit my forearm, locking his jaw on my arm as it began to shake me. What he didn't expect was what I did next. I bent my leg and kneed him directly in the groin with all my strength, even as I prayed that I wasn't attacking a female and instead was hitting a male in the testicles. It was a male, and his eyes went blank as he screamed into my face. Since I couldn't shoot him, I reached over my back with my left hand and pulled my Commando knife. As he licked the blood streaming from my right arm, I grabbed the fur of his shoulder with my right hand. I sliced under his jaw with the knife in my left hand, cleaving him clear to the skull. He realized the hard way that I was a hard bone to chew on, that I was not simply another easy prey. He couldn't know that I had been dealing with worse beasts, the disciples of Satan, Che Guevara and the Castro brothers. He certainly wasn't expecting me to knee him in the groin as I had. He only made a single sound as my blade sliced into his skull which echoed around as he collapsed. I pulled my knife free and pushed the body into the sacrificial pot. The body convulsed as the last of his life left him.

    At the same time, the monkey on Jimbo had found a big surprise as well. He had locked his mouth on one of Jimbo's legs, but Mama Teca had grabbed him from behind and with her knife cut his head off. The bites of these monkeys were so unnatural that even with the head cut off she had to pry the mouth open slowly to avoid further damage by causing punctures to turn into slashes. Upset as we all were, she picked up the monkey's body and threw it onto the sacrificial platform. The hunters had filled their quota for the day with their own bodies. The seagulls circled and descended upon the body of the decapitated monkey and began to gorge themselves. Once a few seagulls flew off, the crows came in to get their fill, starting with the eyes.

Our arrival searching for an escape unintentionally started a chain reaction which would disrupt something that had been going on there for years as well as disturb the future plans of a genetic breeding program designed to take over the world. That sinister place looked more and more diabolical by the minute. I had never seen that species of monkey anywhere. It looked more like a cross of a monkey with the features and ferocity of a Doberman pincer. Atacia touched my shoulder. "You're wounded. We need to attend to it."

Figure 14 The Weird Monkey Devil

"Don't worry, handle Jimbo first. It's not that bad." I wrapped some tape as a tourniquet around the bite wound to stop the flow of blood. Helped by Atacia, as we did this, a small monkey which looked like a young one about a third the size of the others, came out of nowhere, screaming and running as it went into the main structure. "Let's try and grab that one—it's a young one. We can find out how they were created. Maybe it can tell us that."

We divided into teams. Atacia and I went into the main entrance while Mama Teca and Jimbo went around to the back. Our surprise was great as we entered this rough structure which appeared to be something out of the Stone Age, to realize it was only a hallway. Huge, widened steps of white marble with black lines descended down to a subterranean palace. Atacia pointed to a stream of blood along the marble floor.

We went down the stairs, lit by torches in sconces along the walls. I stopped and gestured for silence with my right hand to Atacia. I whispered, "Let's not proceed. Go back, get Jimbo and Mama Teca, and I'll wait for you here. Then we'll follow to see where this little monkey went."

Chapter 16: Rock of the Monkey Devils

Atacia went to look for Mama Teca and Jimbo. They returned a few minutes later and had barely gotten down the marble stairs before we heard the desperate screaming of what appeared to be a young woman. "Please, help me! Help me! I need help!" she implored.

We heard movement inside the walls and then the sound of shoes echoing down the long underground corridor as someone ran. As we followed the trail of blood which the beast had left behind as well as the young monkey, we now added to our search the location of the first human voice we had heard on that island who sounded like she was in trouble. We took into consideration that it could all be a trap using a woman's voice, well prepared by our enemies to entice us, so we proceeded with extreme caution, our weapons ready, fingers on the triggers.

We continued down the long corridor and saw along the walls different engraved images of lions, serpents, and enormous triangles and planets. It also looked like meteors falling in the mouth of a giant volcano, as if the meteor was causing the eruption. We came to an enormous door at the end of the corridor which blocked our path. We tried to open it, but it didn't budge. I used the pommel of my knife to rap against it and see if there was any response from the other side. We heard the voice of the woman say, "Pry up the right tile in the floor. In the hole press hard with your feet—that will open the door."

Jimbo did as she had instructed. As he pressed down on the trigger mechanism, the immense stone doors slid into the walls, revealing a room beyond. We saw a very young woman with extremely long, braided hair, stripped naked and tied to a pole. Her hair partially covered her breasts as well as her private parts. She looked like a Greek statue of some goddess of indescribable beauty. Her eyes were large and green, the exact same hue as the emeralds we saw on the sacrificial platform outside. Her skin was olive colored, but her facial features were European. She wore a tiara with emeralds, rubies, pearls, and other precious stones adorning it. She looked like she was the original of the statue we saw outside. She was tied by leather belts, her feet together against the pole in the center of the room, like a trophy mounted in a frame by some hunter to display to the world. The pole was carefully polished with some kind of varnish.

Her terror was plain to see. "I am Vanessa. Please, untie me. I've been here for a long time as a prisoner of a crazy maniac. Hurry! Dr. Chao will come back very soon, even though he ran for his safety when he saw what you guys killing all his experimental, very well-trained fighting monkeys. He'll be back soon, bringing more not just of these small ones but also his large ones who are greater abominations. He will also be back with his personal bodyguards." We rushed to untie the belts which bound her to the pole. Mama Teca took a blanket out of her pack to cover Vanessa's nakedness. As she covered herself, she said, "This crazy maniacal pervert sat in front of me for hours to occasionally masturbate. He's a very sick, crazy man."

Jimbo found some stairs and climbed up. "This is how he saw us and probably released those monkeys on us. It looks like a very sophisticated hoax designed to put fear into any rural people who once lived here." He pulled out a couple of IV lines connected to the eyes of the statue. Using both hands, he held up a suction handpump. One end went to a reservoir with the red liquid, with the other end terminating at the eyes of the statue. He tasted the red liquid and laughed. "Unbelievable! It's the juice of wild berries! It's a very sweet, good juice." He put both hands in the container and scooped some up to drink. He filled his canteen with the juice. "This is great—I'm going to take some of this."

Vanessa became agitated. "We need to leave as soon as possible before this demented man returns from his lab. It's not very far away from here. We need to hide. They have the protection of the Cuban communist government."

"OK," I said. "Let's get out of here, guys. The last thing we need is for this guy to alert the authorities to our presence here—assuming he hasn't already done that after we killed his monkeys."

"Oh, no—you didn't kill *all* his monkeys, and the big ones are the worst, truly an abomination of nature. Don't worry about this, because even though the Cuban government is protecting him, they also charge him a very high rent in dollars for any service he solicits from them. I guarantee that Dr. Chao will not call for help until he exhausts all his resources. Believe me, he has a way through those animals of destroying everyone and keeping his problems under control. Even so, you should have no doubts if you actually give him a big surprise by showing that you're not easy prey, he won't hesitate even though he has to pay a high price to communicate with his elements in Cuban intelligence to come here and kill all of you."

We were now leaving the strange structure, built by ancient hands now used for multiple purposes to scare what few inhabitants of the local islands might happen to venture here. Though it looked ancient, inside the marble and other decorations had been added more recently for the pleasure and comfort of someone, making it look more like a work of art than a building built from coral stone, decorated with black and white marble. We left rapidly. As we got close to the ocean, we looked for a good safe place to not only camp but also prevent anyone from finding us while we hid. The last thing we wanted was any confrontation with that Machiavellian Dr. Chao, who was apparently in Cuba to conduct genetic experiments, whether on behalf of the Chinese government or himself—which we couldn't know. What we had seen so far of them, they were not precisely holy, and I had no doubt in my mind that this man was not attempting some good contribution to humanity, especially with those monkeys with faces and heads like Doberman pincers, the tremendous aggressiveness multiplied by their intelligence and capability of destroying a human body in seconds.

As we came near the ocean, the young monkey we had been trying to find crossed quickly in front of me, screaming as if in distress. When he came near Vanessa, he jumped into her arms to everyone's surprise. He held her neck with one of his arms, but not in an aggressive manner—it was more affectionate. We had even pulled out our weapons in preparation to defend ourselves against an attack. Vanessa smiled and hugged the monkey tenderly. "Cookie, Cookie," she said softly. The small monkey caressed her neck and hair tenderly. Then he put his head close to hers, their foreheads touching in a genuinely affectionate manner.

After a few minutes, he jumped from her arms to the ground. He grabbed her right hand and pulled gently, as if he wanted to guide her someplace. Vanessa looked at us with a smile, gesturing reassuringly with her left hand to show that she had confidence in the creature. There certainly was a bond of friendship between them; perhaps it had been born and cultivated through their mutual captivity. These two, under those strange circumstances under Dr. Chao's dominion, must have bonded. I and my friends had no idea what was behind all of this, but certainly looked like that they both had been in the same circumstance that we were in and wanted to get far away from this place as soon as possible. Dr. Chao, in particular, did not represent any goodness or friendship to either of them, having abused them both in different ways.

When I was a child I had learned from my maternal grandfather which I remembered: "those that are the enemies of my enemies, or even if they have not been my friends, at least deserve my vote of confidence." We continued between the scrub bushes behind Vanessa and her monkey. We were very cautious, prepared for any surprise since we didn't know either of them well. I pulled my pistol out, ready for use, and my friends followed my example. Even though that monkey was small and looked fairly harmless, he came from the same genetic cross and bore the same features as those which had attacked us very aggressively, so we kept our guard up fairly high.

We walked over the rocks a short distance to the water, extremely dangerous because they were slippery with dead marine algae, which grew everywhere and was pushed by the strong waves onto the rocks. Very slowly, carefully, because the rocks were razor sharp, commonly called in Cuba 'dog's fangs.' I smiled as I thought of that while we walked slowly over them. A little slip could create very serious injuries. It crossed my mind that we should change the name to something more appropriate based on our recent experience, and now call them "Teeth of the Abominable Monkey" or "Rock of the Monkey Devils".

As we walked in line, the violent, high waves broke over the rocks, splashing us with the salty, cold water and soaking us completely. As we got down among the high rocks, which presented a little less dangerous area, one of the large waves hit us all but took Atacia by surprise. She lost her balance and slipped, almost landing on those deadly rocks. If it hadn't been for my rapid reaction, she might have been killed by the rocks or the deep ocean.

I turned to the others. "You guys have to be careful where you put your feet with each step. It will be fatal for any of us—landing on these rocks will be like landing on double-edged knives, which will cut you wherever you touch them." After seeing Atacia's near mishap, I started to think twice, and nearly stopped our excursion, because any of us, including Vanessa, had no idea where the monkey was taking us. I raised my hands to signal a halt and began to turn around; but when I started to do this, I could see an enormous cave down the cliff which looked like the one we had used a few days before when we arrived on the other side of the island to save our lives from the helicopter. It was right below us.

Until now, the monkey had seemed to be a question mark, but now I looked at it with a very excited and surprised expression on my face as Cookie jumped on top one of the rude boats that appeared to have been constructed by one of the indigenous people, apparently abandoned there. I wondered where the people were, but my heart was full of joy. If we should eventually find the people, I thought that they would not mind at all if we used one of those boats to get off the island. This particular boat had been built not of coconut tree trunks but of royal palm tree trunks. Royal palms provided tiny little coconuts used by peasants to feed pigs and ground up as feed as well for chickens and other livestock. The trunks of this tree were also used for canoes and multiple domestic utensils. The small smile on my face transformed now to a gigantic smile of happiness as I observed right before my eyes what we actually most desired to get off the island. Eight of these canoes, something we now didn't have to build, were waiting for us there, a great gift from God. I had no doubt of that and praised the Lord now for the monkey.

Cookie looked like he had been reading our minds and brought us to a real treasure which would save us so much time and effort. I never before in my life had I been so joyful to have made a mistake in judgment of somebody like I had with Cookie the monkey. We went down the cliff and entered the dark cave after we inspected the tied-up canoes. It appeared they had been there for a while, but they were moored in a sheltered cove protected by the rocks, completely shielded from the waves. They were tied off to a long trunk of another royal palm.

As we entered the cave we were received by a very huge colony of bats, disturbed in their sleep as we were entering during the daytime. They took us by surprise as they flew out, forcing us to put our heads down. The monkey replied to their squeaks with a large shriek, trying to catch them in his paws. We went further into the cave, which proved to have many different passages leading away from the main entrance. It appeared that our guide knew the place very well and where he wanted to take us.

Whenever Vanessa tried to go down a different passage, he would scream and pull her hand towards where he wanted to go. It was as if he wanted to show us something.

After a while of walking slowly in the darkness, our eyes got accustomed to the dim light. Then we saw light at the end of one of the passages. From high above where we were multiple cascades fell into a pool, like the one Atacia and I had discovered on the opposite side of the island. It was different in that between two of the cascades this one was a huge one, separated by fifteen or twenty feet of distance from the smaller falls. It looked like a huge column or curtain of water falling down. The major difference was that while the other one was filled with multiple varieties of wildflowers with great fragrance, this one had little geysers coming out of the ground, filling the cavern with the stench of sulfur which caused us to put our hands to our noses against that repulsive, ugly odor. Even Cookie covered his nose as we took the last passage. He guided us to climb a stairway carved into the rocks. As we did, we saw once more a trace of blood, recent but still not very fresh.

I stopped and gestured everyone to be cautious, even though everyone was on full alert, expecting any danger. We entered a large cavern with a large hole in the ceiling through which light shone and illuminated the area. We stopped, paralyzed by what we saw. Like a spotlight, the light shone on a stone seat, like a throne, but without fancy and precious decorations. A huge beast in proportions, with horns like a ram and a face like a chimpanzee or similar primate, long haired and having very long nails on its feet. It looked like half gorilla and the other part alpine goat. We froze in astonishment; its eyes were open, and each paw rested on the sides of the throne like some king.

Cookie without any hesitation or fear, walked up to the beast, not even paying attention to Vanessa's call to return to us. He grabbed one of the beast's arms, lifted it up, and let it drop. It fell limply, showing that it was dead. We remained there, still uncertain. Cookie now took the chin of the beast and moved it back and forth. As he did, the beast's neck relaxed, allowing the chin to rest on its chest. We knew now that the beast was either profoundly asleep or had no life left in it. We still weren't fully convinced, so I walked towards the body to examine it, pistol in one hand, ready to shoot it in the head.

I got very close to it, and I could see between its teeth a piece of the monkey's skin to one side. I knew now with certainty that this was the beast which had thrown the monkey's body at me. I checked its body and found several bullet wounds. I wondered what kind of strength the animal had to not just rip off the other monkey's head and arm before throwing the corpse at me. I took my knife and forced the mouth open and removed the skin. Its teeth, to my surprise, were not those of a gorilla or a ram, but that of a tiger shark, a tropical shark that could grow to twenty feet or more, known for its aggressiveness. I had no doubts that Dr. Chao was in Cuba working on something that meant nothing good for humanity.

I stood up and was about to climb back down the stairs from the stone throne where the beast had chosen to die when I noticed a glint of reflected light from the rays of the sun coming through the hole in the ceiling. It looked like something metallic, so I leaned down to examine it more closely. It looked like something made of chrome, perhaps the pull tab of a zipper. Curiously, I took hold of the pull tab and started to unzip it; it took me around the neck of what was supposed to be the beast's neck. I finished the circle around and to everyone's great surprise the head detached from the rest of the body. It was the mask of some costume, a human head revealed beneath it. That human head looked very much like a caveman. We looked at each other in confusion, as the head appearing beneath the mask was no less grotesque and repulsive than the mask which had covered it. We couldn't see any reason for this elaborate hoax, since the reality of the man was frightening enough.

The caveman had very thick eyebrows, deep set, tiny eyes, huge and pronounced cheekbones. Cookie, to our surprise, grabbed the mask I had dropped over the legs of the supposed beast and after he looked at it for a few seconds, poking his fingers through the eyes, made a screeching noise of discontent and threw the mask away with all his might. It looked like whatever this man had done brought bad memories to the monkey, and heaven only knew what that was.

Vanessa reprimanded Cookie, "No, no—you don't do that, little monkey! That is a bad boy!"

Cookie appeared to understand the scolding and put his head down as a sign of submission and shame. This time, Vanessa with her index finger indicating that she wasn't very happy, said "Cookie! Go and bring that mask back over here."

It hadn't gone very far from us, and Vanessa pointed where the mask lay and where she wanted it returned. Cookie looked at her from beneath his eyebrows in his shame and pretended to not hear her. He shook his head like he was having little spasms. He looked up at the hole in the ceiling and pointed with the index finger of his left paw into his left ear.

Vaness repeated, "Cookie! Cookie! Here! Here! Bring it over!" She was sounding more upset now from the tone of her voice, repeating her gestures to direct what she wanted, her eyes clued on Cookie's. Cookie didn't want to get into any more trouble or upset her more than she was, and in a comical gesture, he put his head down trying to avoid her stare, walked very slowly, grabbed the mask on the point of a finger on his left hand. As he did, he shuddered some more, sticking his finger through one of the eyeholes. He walked very slowly towards where Vanessa was pointing—only instead of depositing on the lap of the beast, he put it at her feet. She pointed once more to the beast's lap. "No, not here. There, or from wherever you took it."

Cookie bent over, shuddering once again, but finally put the mask on the beast's lap in obedience, performing the same comic gesture of repulsion as he had before. He left the mask alone and blew air on both of his paws. Then he slapped them together as if he were wiping or dusting them off, making unhappy grunts as he did.

Jimbo had been climbing over the wide steps on the lateral side of the room which had been carved into the rocks like an amphitheater all the way to a long, carved observation window. He turned around and said, "Quiet, guys! I see people coming. There's a pathway leading underneath here through the jungle—they're going to pass right under us." He motioned for us to come up and see what he was looking at. He put his left index finger to his lips.

Anxious to see for ourselves what was going on, we climbed those steps up to the top to join him. They were like stadium steps, very large and wide—very strange in a large cave like this. When we got to the top step, we looked out and saw the jungle on the other side. Vanessa climbed up next to me and murmured, "That is the path to the lab, where Dr. Chao has nearly everyone in my village, including my family, as prisoners, forcing them to work with no pay, giving them only food and clothing. Anyone who tried to escape is killed. They make everybody work, day and night, building different kinds of pills."

"How many people, including your family, is he holding as slaves?" I asked.

"Probably over fifty. Well, that was before they caught me when I was trying to escape several weeks ago."

"Why didn't they kill you?"

She grimaced as she pointed at her temple. "The only reason I'm not dead is because Dr. Chao is a sex maniac and sick in the head. He never put a finger on my body, but from the time they caught me and brought me back, he kept me naked, tied to that pole, only freeing my hands to eat or go to the bathroom. He's spent hours watching me, sitting in front of me, and as I told you before, sometimes masturbating in my presence."

I shook my head in disgust with an expression of revulsion. Vanessa added, "Probably the other reason I'm still alive is because I'm the daughter of the medicine man, and everyone in the village respects my father, which also may be why I haven't been raped and killed by one of his experimental beasts. There's no doubt in my mind he has a sick mind because those experiments come out even worse every time. Talking about the Devil, look at him there!" She pointed at a little man walking along the bottom with one eye only, the other covered by a black patch. "You see this diabolic little disgusting man? He has the darkest, most Satanic heart you can ever imagine. Whoever doesn't know him might feel pity for him."

I watched the group go by. We could see the little man, completely bald when he removed his hat to wipe his head with a handkerchief, riding a black horse with a canvas safari hat, another red handkerchief tied around his neck like a scarf over his shoulder covering his narrow neck. If it hadn't been for that, he would look like he had no neck at all. As I stared at this man, I understood Vanessa's words about how he might inspire pity, because he looked like a half-formed fetus. One of his hands was thrust into his shirt above his waist like Napoleon Bonaparte. He didn't look like a complete human being. Several donkeys loaded with provisions accompanied the procession—it looked like they were planning to hunt for us for a few days. Vanessa let me know that the place with the sacrificial platform used to be the village where all these families had lived in peace and harmony for all of living memory before this man arrived on the island, bringing with him those cavemen or beasts.

    Two of these men wearing the same ram's masks came in front like an escort. Evidently Dr. Chao used this to intimidate into submission those peasants who had been living on the island so far away from civilization using their own religious beliefs. Some of them were imported from Haiti or Africa, and these poor people, some of them illiterate, were very easy to control. Dr. Chao wasn't going to waste this opportunity to use all the tricks he had in his book to terrorize these people into working for him as slaves. Looking at this man and what he had been doing in that island, I could see the reflection of the dark face of the Marxist, communist, and old totalitarian ideologies, as they allowed this to happen in what was supposed to be Cuban territory. Of course, this ugly part of these ideologies is keeping secrets from the rest of the world. I didn't know for certain, but I believed at this moment that was very possible that Dr. Chao was leasing the northern part of the island to do whatever he wanted there, and as long as he shared his profits from his activity with the Cuban government, he would have their complete support and protection.

I asked Vanessa, "How many men or beasts normally does Dr. Chao have guarding the laboratory building?"

"Not many. They use all the locals and right now he's brought a good part of his bodyguards, evidently to catch you guys because you eliminated eight of his most ferocious guardians. I count six as they pass beneath us—that includes the two cavemen with the ram masks."

I nodded with a smile on my lips. After they passed by us, we began to descend the stairs. Atacia asked me, "What are you thinking? What's going on in that head? I hope it's not what I'm thinking."

I nodded. "Evidently you've been learning to read my thoughts through close proximity lately."

Jimbo grinned. "Whatever you're thinking and whatever you have in mind, you can count on me. I'm ready to go." He held up his Stinger.

Mama Teca looked at me with a long face. "I don't know what you have in mind; remember, this is not our fight. We have our own fight and priorities. We have to bring Aurora, Bonifacio, Jamina, Rolando, and DeAngelo from our camp. They are our priority. We should not deviate."

"I think you forgot Venus, the dog that saved your life, and you have a great concern that we wouldn't be able to feed her. You were right, she eats for three of us. But if you remember, in the end exactly as I told you, let's worry about the bread for today—God will provide an abundance tomorrow. If God's been listening to me, He gave me a rein check in advance by providing us a remedy that same night. The dog you worried about feeding provided us with food for at least a month, certainly for as long as we would be on the island."

Having no argument, she put her head down. "Yes, I know. But I don't like to deviate. Why don't you tell us what you have in mind so we can stop assuming what you want to do, and we'll probably be more relaxed knowing that you don't have any crazy ideas so we will sleep better tonight."

"That is precisely what I want to talk about: what I have in mind. If you guys approve my plan and we all agree, because this is not a tyranny but a democracy, then none of us will be sleeping tonight."

"Oh, my God! I knew it!"

"Remember, it's in your character to be a pessimist, and you don't look at the bright side of everything as I do. And when we look after the well-being of others, we get rewarded by Providence, save ourselves, and God makes it easy on us." I grabbed the ram mask from the lap of the beast and raised it high. "What I have in mind is very simple: we will take the lab from Dr. Chao. We will destroy his power which facilitates his totalitarian abuse over these people, while at the same time we will exterminate all his disgusting research into abominations that he might even be doing with human beings. We will return to Vanessa's parents and family the freedom, peace, and dignity that they deserve, along with all the inhabitants of this island, and at the same time, we assure ourselves a safe and efficient exit from this island. We cannot leave this evil, conniving mercenary, Dr. Chao behind; if he's not dead or neutralized, he will be like leaving a double-bladed knife in the hands of our enemies to turn it back against us to slaughter us."

Mama Teca smiled as she listened to me as she nodded. "Up to a point, you're right. We cannot ignore the obvious." She took the ram mask from my hands and smiled mischievously. "I would like to know who you have in mind to replace this caveman in order to be able to cheat and pass for one of them. It has to be somebody very tall like me, and physically fit." She turned around to present her back to us, mask in hand, and then put on the mask. She turned back around and raised both arms high and growled fiercely, very similar these men had been trained to do to scare the village population and had heard the previous night which had prevented that night's worth of sleep, probably according to Dr. Chao's plan to scare us and psychologically terrorize us into leaving at once and so not be a threat to him or his dominion.

Cookie screamed in terror and ran to the arms of Vanessa. I said to Mama Teca, "You've got the role. We don't need any more auditions."

Mama Teca pulled off the mask and smiled. "I knew it! That's what you had in mind that you didn't want to tell me. I'm the only one who fits the role. You see? I'm starting to learn how to read your thoughts, too! Atacia isn't the only one who has that privilege."

I nodded a little ambivalently and patted her on the right shoulder. I whispered in her ear, "You need to make me another demonstration of your mental reading, because this one was too easy and not difficult to figure out."

She looked at me with a small smile. With the mask in her hands, she said, "That's only fair."

Vanessa tried to calm Cookie down, who didn't remove his eyes from Mama Teca with the mask swinging in her hands. I said to Mama Teca, "Put the mask on and take it off several times. We need to make Cookie used to it so that he realizes it's just a mask. We have to make him comfortable enough to not scream every time she puts it on, or we won't be able to bring him with us. We need absolute silence for what I have planned to give us the surprise factor; if we lose that, we'll fail miserably."

While Mama Teca took the mask on and off in front of Cookie, I debriefed them what the plan I had in mind was. A little while later, a little more time than I had expected, Cookie finally mastered his fear and was no longer screaming. We felt now that he wouldn't announce our presence when we got near the lab. While all this transpired, I stared at the dead beast sitting on the stone throne, examining his physiognomy, thinking also that as soon as we finished this new mission, we all had to remove that body from the cave and burn it. Eventually, it would start to decompose if we had to remain there for several days.

As I pondered all these things, I noticed something once more on the right side of the corpse's neck. As Cookie had moved its chin and dropped its head onto its chest, I hadn't seen something which I now saw from a different angle, something that shone and was becoming obvious to my eyes. I stood up and walked over to the body, carefully, examining the neck and said, "Oh, my God!" Separating the long hair, I found another zipper beneath the hair on its neck, which I parted to avoid jamming as I now unzipped it, revealing that the beast's body was only the second part of a costume. The costume was very elaborate; someone had dressed this caveman to look more horrible, fearsome, and disgusting than he already was.

Mama Teca was the first to notice what I was doing. "Oh, my God—the whole thing is a costume?"

"Yes, that's great, because now you won't have to work in the dark. When you dress in this, there will be no difference between you and one of them."

"That will make my job a lot easier!" she agreed.

The others gathered curiously. I said, "OK, guys—let's help everyone to be able to get this costume off in one piece without tearing any of it in the process."

We managed to remove the enormous body from the costume. That caveman, there was no doubt, was an ugly being, and must have been the product of some experimentation. He had the dimensions of a Sumo wrestler with a mawashi[8], but his facial features were by no means Japanese.

Mama Teca removed her clothes as she got into the costume, offering her clothes to Vanessa to offset her nakedness. We left after we once more discussed the details of the plan and followed Vanessa and Cookie towards the lab. When we arrived there a little later, to our surprise we saw a completely modern structure made of metal and glass, something that looked like an interplanetary station out of science fiction with parabolic antennas as well as multiple satellite and radio antennas—it must have cost millions of dollars. There on that tiny island, I knew immediately that though we hadn't planned to be there, God in His Providence intended for us to uncover this evil complex. Everything indicated that this was not financed by a single man, especially not that crazy sexual deviant just to satisfy his fanatic experiments and ideas, whatever they might be. Everything looked, from the magnitude of elaboration and sophistication of the buildings, either many governments and nations were involved in this venture, or possibly be several well-funded private institutions with the objective of performing multimillion-dollar drug manufacturing in a clandestine manner. The reason they had these structures in the

---

[8] The proper name for the loincloth worn by Sumo wrestlers.

middle of nowhere and them hidden from the rest of the world meant only that something morbid was going on there, and that little one-eyed man had a Napoleonic complex to control the world. That qualified him to be the perfect mercenary to act for whatever big hands were behind these projects.

Figure 15 Dr. Chao's laboratory

We studied the entire facility for a little while. Everything was according to Vanessa's intel, and Mama Teca put a rope around Vanessa's neck. I said, "Remember our plan—no shots unless it's absolutely necessary. We don't want to alert the other guards inside the facility. Eliminate the guards outside and then control the rest inside." Vanessa picked Cookie up, and they walked towards the main gate.

Vanessa held the knife behind her back that I had given her, and of course Mama Teca had a pistol and a machete at her waist. As they approached the gate, Atacia went around to get the other guard at the same time that Vanessa reached the gate so that both guards were put down at once without raising an alarm. All we could see was Mama Teca's machete swinging and the guard's head flying off. At the same time, the other guard was put down by Atacia. This guard post was near what looked like a helipad. Everything happened very quickly. The guards were down, and the entry was cleared. The first phase of our plan was completely successful, and I thanked God for the intel we had been given by Vanessa which made this success possible. I reflected at that moment that this is why so many operations fail: they lack inside intelligence.

I moved inside to the labs accompanied by Jimbo, following the two women who acted like vacuum cleaners before us. Room after room we saw guards down or some of those masked men lying incapacitated. In less than half an hour, we were in the center of the lab, where nearly forty or fifty people, as Vanessa had told us, were working naked making opium, amphetamines, and other drugs. The machinery functioned like an assembly line, some with stickers designating the USA as a destination disguised as medication, and others going to various countries around the capitalist world: England, France, New Zealand, Germany, etc. The people cried gratefully as we informed them that they were free.

As we entered Dr. Chao's office, we could corroborate through his papers his ideological plans to control the capitalist world strategically through their own financial resources, to destroy each country's established societies through corruption and bribing of political and religious figures. He wasn't just a maniac mercenary; he was a piece of the political machinery of the global Marxist plan to dominate the world. In my experience as a spy, I saw in Dr. Chao a sexual deviant, a depraved man with no scruples or religion, the perfect disciple of Satan, sent into the world to destroy humanity at large. Tears welled in my eyes as Vanessa's mother and father hugged me and the others, thanking us for what we had done. Mama Teca also had tears in her eyes and had no other choice than to give me a thumbs up.

I said, "This is not complete. This is the beginning. You have to do the rest. We cannot leave behind a double-bladed knife, because then we will be the victims. You have to do your job, take control of your destiny once more, and execute the small group that went over there to try and find us. We will help you, but you have to do your part."

Vanessa's father introduced himself to me. "I'm Juan. I will personally decapitate Dr. Chao and offer his head to our gods in order to redeem all the evil he's done to our people."

Mama Teca removed the head and costume to alleviate their fear. We knew now that it would only be a matter of time before Dr. Chao met his Waterloo. The inhuman slavery these people had been submitted to by these unscrupulous and evil men under Dr. Chao's command and protected by the Cuban Marxist government of the Castro brothers came to an end on this little island today. The eyes of Vanessa, filled with tears, as she embraced her parents, brothers, and sisters. I never will forget that moment for as long as I live.

Chapter 17: The Unexpected Iron Ship

Jimbo came over and asked, "What are we going to do with this place?"

I replied, "First of all, you have to be sure that no one is left inside the building. Even our enemies—anyone that's alive we pull out to safety. The other thing is that we don't waste anything that could be useful in any way for us to leave this island: fuel, food, or anything else that might come to mind. Then, we need to withdraw a very prudent distance because we have to consider that this structure is at least 90% glass, which when it explodes can fly a long way. Then you will give them the same medicine we gave that chopper on the beach when we arrived here."

Jimbo exclaimed happily, "Yeah!" He grinned broadly. "We'll light up the sky with fireworks!" He gave me a high five with his right hand.

I said, "Please be sure you follow my instructions. I don't want anyone getting hurt when you blow that place into a thousand pieces."

"Don't worry, I'll follow your instructions to the letter."

Atacia came over and whispered to me with a long face, "I overheard something that you should investigate."

"What happened?" I asked her curiously.

"I heard Juan having a very private conversation with Vanessa. He told her about the iron ship."

I didn't understand. "What? An iron ship? What do you mean? What's that?"

She shook her head and shrugged her shoulders. She spread her arms and smirked. "I don't know, either. It caught my attention. They spoke in whispers in a private area far from all of us. When I came over by them, they went absolutely silent. Dead silence as if they didn't want me to know what they were talking about. I've learned that when I see something odd to share it right away with you, because even the smallest things can cost us our lives."

"You did great. It was the right thing to tell me this. It's extremely important you keep your eyes open. These are very nice people, very humble, but they are so ignorant that in a way it doesn't matter that we've been helping them. Remember, they are strangers to us. That ignorance could be a very dangerous weapon, a double-edged blade that could, if we don't pay attention, harm us badly. As my paternal grandfather from Spain would say, take the bull by the horns. The only way to find out what's going on between Vanessa and her father is to go and ask Juan about iron ship he discussed with Vanessa."

Atacia smiled. "*Claro, chico. Al pan, pan y al vino, vino*[9], as my own Spanish paternal grandfather used to say."

I nodded and motioned with my head towards Juan, who stood talking quietly with the members of his community as they prepared with their crude but powerful weapons for a safari to get the head of Dr. Chao and his group of mercenaries. We walked over to them.

---

[9] Literally "to the bread, bread and to the wine, wine." Much like the English expression to call a spade a spade.

They both smiled broadly and knowingly as we approached. Juan looked uneasy. He looked me in my eyes and said, "You don't have to worry about Dr. Chao. We will take care of him, and we don't need your help. There's enough of us that, even if he kills some of us, we'll get him on one of our spears. We'll eliminate that Asian monster and his monsters from Hell."

I looked at the crude spears and shook my head, knowing that the machine guns will kill most, if not all of them. "I've been thinking, if you don't mind some advice, that you should take some of the machine guns we took from the guards. You'll minimize your losses because fewer of your people will be hurt or killed. That will give you a tremendous advantage, and you'll take him by surprise since he won't expect you guys to have those weapons."

"We don't know how to use them."

"It's very simple. Smart people don't need to go to the university to shoot a gun. In a very short time, Jimbo could teach you and your men how to use them responsibly." Juan smiled in gratitude and gave me a bear hug. I used that opportunity of his gratitude and humility to ask the one question he didn't want to answer. As I spoke, I pointed to Atacia. "My friend shares everything with me. She didn't mean to pry into your conversation, but she overheard you mention an iron ship to Vanessa. Her interpretation was that you didn't want anyone to know about it, even us. If we're going to be friends, we have to be very truthful to each other. Can you explain to me what that's all about?" I spoke in a persuasive, innocent tone of voice. "I don't want to invade your privacy, but a ship or even a boat of that magnitude could be vital for me and my friends to leave this island and head to Havana, where I have extremely important business to attend to. The sooner, the better. The reason we were in this area to begin with was because we were attacked by a torpedo boat from the Cuban communist government. I don't want to make the story too long, but I believe it's enough for you to understand my extreme curiosity to find out what the iron ship is, where it is, and why you're talking about it. I don't know if it's a fortunately or not, but God brought us to your island."

Juan hurriedly said, "Definitely, fortunately." He smiled and nodded his head repeatedly with emphasis. I patted him on the shoulder.

"Let's hope it is, my friend Juan. Sometimes, our worst enemies are disguised as friends."

He looked at me seriously. "No, we all are your friends. You should be absolutely certain of that." His tone was convincing, and he pointed towards the sky, putting his hands together in gratitude. "Thanks be to the gods for sending you to us. All of you were sent by God, that One I daily to pray to and beg to save the life of my daughter, Vanessa, and all my family and the inhabitants of this island." He put his head down in shame. He took my right arm and said, "Please, I'm going to take you now to the iron ship. I only ask you one thing: please, allow me to clean the bad spirits that this iron ship brought to this island. It is the vessel that Asian monster and his monkeys from Hell arrived in. That is why I had my doubts about whether it would be prudent for me to bring you to those malignant spirits, because they are contagious. The last thing we want is for them to take possession of your souls. But if it is your wish, I will take you to it with pleasure. Follow me to the iron ship."

We followed him in silence for a while. We climbed to the height of the cliff and looked down. In the center there was a clear cove dotted by palm trees with greenish calm waters separated from the high waves on the other side of the natural sea wall formed by the rocks. To my great surprise and joy, I saw a submarine, and I exclaimed, "Oh, my God!" There was a long iron ramp, floated by red buoys which surrounded the submarine and platform. We climbed down and entered the submarine, which had a capacity for twelve passengers, larger than we needed. It was fully equipped as one would expect in any modern vessel.

Juan asked again, "Please let me clean this of the evil spirits before you use it." He went out to the jungle for a while, returning with branches of different trees and bushes. He lit them on fire, blew on the flame, and a white smoke issued from the branches. He passed the burning branches over the ship both inside and out. "With this, we will scare the bad spirits that, should they stay here, they will be bound to their evil masters. Should the crew that brought them here perish, the spirits will become powerless."

The smoke smelled of jasmine incense. After he finished, he said, "Now you can walk around without any more bad experiences, and your good and noble spirits will replace and bring new horizons and glories to this iron ship. We can spread your nobility all over the world."

I bowed to him. "Thank you."

We went back outside, Juan following last, protecting us as he spread that smoke all over the place. Finally, he closed the hatch of the submarine. We walked back to the lab where everyone anxiously awaited us, in ignorance of where we had gone. I said to Jimbo and Mama Teca, "I'll explain to you later."

They had already given excellent training to the men in the use of the machine guns without killing each other or their friends. As Juan returned, Jimbo explained quickly to him how the machine gun worked. Juan refused to take one. "It's OK—you've taught my men. That's good enough."

At that moment, the island men who had previously been slaves under the dominion of Dr. Chao now were changed in a short time into warriors. We knew that they would hunt the evil men down until all were dead; I could read in the eyes of those men something that gave me chills—the thirst for the blood of those who had for so long abused them. And not just the men. I could see the anticipatory pleasure the women also enjoyed of the coming expedition, all save for Livia, Vanessa's mother. Livia and Vanessa were remaining behind in charge of the children. I will never forget the eyes of those men filled with bloodlust and enraged after the discovery of how they had been duped by those masks. I knew at that moment that Dr. Chao didn't have a chance of survival if he came under their hands. I never wanted to see myself in that same situation. Some of the men were armed with machetes and knives; others had spears, and still others had bows and arrows. Only a few had the submachine guns taken from Dr. Chao's guards. Even so, only an act of Satan would save Dr. Chao; like God protects His sons, so also does Satan protect his.

After they left, I told Jimbo and Mama Teca that they should return to our base camp on the other side of the island to bring the rest of our group, since we had an assured exit now. "They don't even need to bring the radio, since we no longer need it. Make the trip as soon as possible, and we'll wait for you in the same cove where the wooden boats are docked." I turned to Atacia and said, "By the time they get back, we'll have that submarine filled with provisions and completely ready to leave the island."

Jimbo said, "OK, I'll leave after I get done with the demolition. You guys get far away, a prudent distance as you suggested before."

I said, "Have fun."

"I will!"

A little while later, we could see the rockets from the Stinger fly through the darkness towards the buildings, one after another. A huge explosion lit up the night as the volatile chemicals stored there caught fire. The children surrounding Vanessa and Livia danced around as the entire structures burst into flames and crumpled in on themselves, finally collapsing to the jungle floor. Vanessa and Livia clapped their hands joyfully at the sight of the place which had held them as slaves for so long be utterly destroyed. As the flames died down, Vanessa, Atacia, Livia, Cookie, and the kids left that place towards the grotto where the canoes were docked where we were to wait for Jimbo, Mama Teca, and the rest of our friends.

We laid down when we got there, making ourselves as comfortable as possible on the rocky ground. We were exhausted from our sleepless night; the first light of dawn was breaking over the horizon. We fell into a deep sleep.

The sun was already very high, and I checked my wristwatch and was surprised to see that it was 2 pm. What had woken me up was the sound of a helicopter outside the cave. The others were still asleep, so carefully I crept past them and out of the cave. I saw a helicopter flying out to sea. I put my right hand over my forehead to shield my eyes from the sun and followed it in the distance.

Vanessa ran out of the cave in panic and over to me. "Can you see it? Can you see it? Is that from the Coast Guard or the Ministry of the Interior? If it's Coast Guard, we don't have anything to worry about—but if it's the G-2, we're in trouble. That's what they do before landing—send a chopper to inspect the area."

"I don't know. I wasn't able to see its markings. When I got out here, it was already far off in the distance."

Vanessa remained agitated and her voice trembled. I could see the panic in her eyes. "I believe Dr. Chao has already given up and is convinced that you guys aren't an easy bone to chew on. He probably called the Cuban government for help, like I told you earlier, to help him remove the stone in his shoe that's too big for him to handle. I knew it! I told you before that this is what he would do if he saw himself lost. It's very possible by this time that he encountered my father and the others from the village, and they killed all his mercenaries. If he's alive then he's retreated into the jungle to call for help. He probably assumed it wasn't the villagers, since they don't have the weapons, and that it's you guys."

I tried to calm her down. "Those are a lot of possibilities you've dropped on me all at once, and all of them are very pessimistic. Coming from you, I understand, because of the suffering and dark times that you spent as a captive of Dr. Chao. In return, I'm going to give you a single possibility, a more optimistic analysis of the situation. Just take into consideration the possibility that your father and his men have already put Dr. Chao in retreat, but not into the jungle as you assume. In my opinion, his retreat is to his place of origin. This could be Havana, the Bahamas, or even China. I have no doubt because I saw with my own eyes, not by assumption or speculation, an emergency helipad in the patio of that lab we just destroyed. This tells me that there is a possibility that he has another of these platforms hidden nearby. Dictators, bullies, and murderers always have some kind of way to escape. They know that one day, eventually, they will have to run to save their heads precisely pursued by their own victims. If I'm not wrong, Dr. Chao used that chopper, since I didn't see one outside the lab. He heard the explosion and saw those flames that must have been seen for miles in the sky. Once he lost most of his men to the machine gun bullets, like a cowardly dictator he ran to save his skin. Even though this diabolic, perverse little midget is definitely a murderer, I don't think he is stupid at all and has the experience to know that he cannot sit on his hands and wait for his friends in Havana, who may not have him as a priority and so arrive too late to help him. He doesn't want to see his head on the tip of one of those spears running around the island in the hands of one of the men he intimidated for so many years. It's logical to me that he ran for his life, probably to someplace close to here, waiting after resting for a bit until daylight, and flying over us to corroborate what he already knows has happened: his beautiful labs have become a pile human bowel.

    I paused and looked at Vanessa. She was much calmer. "Even though these are all assumptions and speculations, my better judgement tells me that all of the villagers should abandon this island and look for another place to live. The only thing this demented man has is his ego. Your father, your people, and my group have bruised his ego, and he will be filled with resentment and a desire to revenge himself on all of you and us. Even though he suffered a defeat last night and ran away scared; once he has the upper hand he'll return and crush you. One of the things all of us, you guys included, have to our advantage is that whoever financed this project and put him as the mercenary head of this multimillion-dollar sinister enterprise, will ever put their trust him very easily again. They've just lost millions—if not billions—of dollars. The puppet masters behind this gigantic project didn't put all of this money up just to see it all burn; they put it in hoping to multiply their investment. Now everything is dust and ashes."

At that moment we were interrupted by the triumphant yells of Juan and his followers, who had returned from their safari with trophies on the tips of their spears: the masks of the costumes, and the heads of the abominable monkeys raised on high which had terrified them. Atacia and Livia joined the group with the children coming out of the cave and received them with hugs and cheers. Four men followed carrying a wild pig on a pole on their shoulders. Juan gave me a big hug. "We are free. We will celebrate this day for many generations ahead. We will remember all of you as our liberators."

I smiled. "Thank you. Yes, you can do that, and that makes me happy and very proud, but you must do this with your friends and families on another island if you don't want to lose your freedom or take the chance that Dr. Chao comes back with reinforcements and not only enslave you again but kill many of you in revenge."

To my surprise, Juan didn't hesitate for a second. He nodded. "If you think this is a good idea, tonight, after we provide all you guys with enough food and water for your trip in the iron ship, we will leave this island in our canoes to the one my great-grandfather brought me from to live and raise me here. We left because there's a volcano there, but there's no volcano more dangerous than Dr. Chao. I would rather live there than be in the proximity of this diabolic man. We don't want to wait and give him the opportunity to come back and try to hunt us."

I gave him a little pat on his shoulder and grinned. "Great idea and clever decision by you. I'm very proud. That is why you should continue to be not only the medicine man but also the chief in charge of this community."

Cookie started to screech, which he did either when he was happy or scared. We lifted our head to see what was provoking his reaction. In the distance we saw Jimbo and Mama Teca returning with the rest of our group, followed by Venus, who howled joyfully when he saw Atacia.

When they got close enough, Jimbo very altruistically and gratefully came over to Juan, removing his Stinger from his shoulder and solemnly offered it to the medicine man. "This is my favorite toy, but I don't think we'll need it any longer. I want you to have it, so if Dr. Chao ever comes back after you, with this magic pipe you will be able to shoot the iron bird down. I'll teach you and your men how to use it."

Juan took the Stinger in his hands, rested it against his leg on the ground, and gave Jimbo a bear hug. "You actually all have been sent by God in our need."

Jimbo grabbed one arm, while I grabbed the other. I said, "You don't have to do that. You're a free man now, the chief of the community. Don't let them see any weakness in you."

"Thank you." He turned and gave me a bear hug as well.

The rest of the day they cooked the pig and brought us fruit and other food. We celebrated with our friends, and when night came, they started a bonfire which they danced around. They wished us farewell on our trip, and we wished them to fare well on their new island. We said our goodbyes late that night, and their tremendous experience knowledge of marine vehicles, those two wolves of the sea, Captains Bonifacio and DeAngelo, didn't take very long to exchanging impressions and inspect meticulously all the equipment to ensure the good function of this modern submarine which had been left behind by Dr. Chao in his hasty rush to save his head. We left the coast in a thick fog, leaving behind that beautiful community of Cuban peasants who followed my advice and made the smart decision to leave that beautiful island in their own canoes where many of them had been born to avoid losing such beautiful freedom. As we left the coast and submerged deep into the ocean, the humongous waves disappeared and a calm, relaxed tranquility invaded the submarine.

  I stood up next to Atacia, watching the kids Rolando and Jamina sleep deeply. I smiled as they practically had both their heads on the belly of Venus, who was also completely exhausted. All day long they had been playing hide and seek with Cookie, bonding immediately as children do in a very beautiful friendship from the moment they set eyes on each other. I looked at them with a little sadness, thinking how short that beautiful friendship could be cut for them as I reflected on my own childhood. As a product of the tumultuous times in which we had grown up in this crazy world, I and my young friends had been robbed of the most precious treasure that any human being possesses. I had observed them all day playing in the sand and understood now the major crime that had been committed against humanity by unscrupulous, ambitious politicians, which was the ripping away from the younger generations the precious treasure and dreams of our infancies.

  As we had already discussed with Captain Bonifacio and Captain DeAngelo, Bonifacio's brother Luis Alberto was waiting for us in international waters to transport them to another fishing vessel which had been helping Cuban exiles to reach the coast of Florida safely, where Captain DeAngelo and his family would finally be transported to Florida along with Venus as he promised before to his late childhood friend Chicho, closing the beautiful circle and fulfilling his promise to bring his dog to his grave for a final farewell.

Chapter 18: The Near Massacre During Transport

The night's darkness was deepened by heavy, dense fog. We said goodbye to our friends and left them in the hands of Captain Luis Alberto to continue into international waters and then eventually bring our friends to their final destination. I felt emotional and enormously satisfied in my heart to be able to obtain safety for another Cuban family whose very brave hearts wouldn't allow them to live any longer under that oppressive tyranny under the Marxist regime that had been responsible for all the miseries in their lives. They looked for nothing more than freedom as a priority at whatever price, even if that price was the highest one they could pay: their own lives.

I reminded of many years in the past to when I had myself had abandoned my beautiful Cuba. It was for different reasons: I had been told that my cover as a spy was in danger of being discovered. The only way to protect my family without implicating them in my clandestine activities and being accused of complicity in the work I had done would be to put a great distance between us. That meant I had to leave. Only in this way would they be considered innocent victims of what I had been doing with no knowledge at all about my activities inside the circle of espionage. For that reason, when I arrived at the US Navy base at Guantanamo and sat in the bunker where they sheltered us, I had a knot in my throat that didn't let me swallow my food. The same feelings of joy for our accomplishment of reaching freedom mixed with the same sadness I felt now of leaving my family behind and every single friend I ever had. The tremendous physical strain from the previous several days of taking us to the base, walking in the jungles, crossing rivers, crawling through the swamps filled with mangroves, Cuban crocodiles, and later swimming for over twelve hours with just snorkels for fear of being discovered by any radar should we carry any metal or SCUBA tanks took its toll on me. I had not been able for days to even have a few hours of sleep. I compared that feeling with what I was feeling now. It had been only on the third day after our escape, completely exhausted, that I finally had been able to sleep for several hours. Those feelings and emotions I had back then were exactly the same as I felt now as I said goodbye to our friends who we had formed in the past few days a sincere bond of affection, thinking I would probably never see them again.

    In the midst of my profoundly sentimental meditations, a very loud siren sounded from a patrol boat of the Cuban navy, which evidently had seen in the foggy night the red and green lights of our submarine. That snapped me back to reality as they turned on a powerful searchlight in the bow towards our vessel. They knew something was there, but with the fog and darkness, they could not make out that we were a submarine. A voice yelled through a bullhorn demanding that we halt.

    We had not yet submerged because we had remained on deck, having transported that precious cargo to Captain Luis Alberto's boat, to watch the boat leave in that mixture of sadness and happiness. Bonifacio, not even consulting with God or the devil, grabbed the shotgun he had armed himself with to guard the transport of our precious cargo and fired several shots at the patrol boat. He managed to shoot out the searchlight, and we heard yells of pain as glass sprayed on the crew manning the light.

Mama Teca and Jimbo were nearest the hatch and dove down inside. Atacia and I were too far away from the hatch, and I grabbed her as we hit the deck as flat as we could. As soon as they saw we responded with weapons fire, they shot at us with high caliber machine gun fire, sparks flying as bullets struck the iron deck in the middle. Bonifacio followed Mama Teca and Jimbo, tossing the shotgun to me, which thanks to God I was able to catch midair.

I was on top of Atacia, holding her down to protect her from getting killed by the automatic weapons fire. Fortunately, Aurora was not feeling well and had never come up on deck. She had said her farewells to our friends inside the submarine. We heard how Bonifacio revved up the motors in preparation for submerging. The enemy fire stopped shooting for a few minutes, but as soon as they heard the engine powering up, they started to fire again, guided by the noise of the engines.

The pitch black of the night was accentuated by the dense fog, but the muzzle flashes of the weapons fire lit up the night, bullets spraying everywhere. Then the firing stopped, either because they ran out of bullets or the weapons had jammed, because the next sound of weapons fire was that of pistols. The shotgun was empty, so I replied with my own pistol fire, helping Atacia up from the deck, moving as quickly as we could in a crouch towards the hatch, as the sub was in the process of submerging.

We finally reached the hatch, allowing her to climb down first. I closed the hatch behind me and sighed deeply with a small smile on my face. I asked Atacia, "Are you OK?"

"Yes, thank you very much. And thanks be to God—that was a very close call, a ticket to the other world with no return."

"We have navigated with extraordinary luck."

Atacia looked at me in consternation with an incredulous expression. She smirked. "Do you call this luck? I don't want to see what you call bad luck!"

"Honey, that boat was a regular navy patrol vessel that discovered us. If it instead had been a torpedo boat like the one that sank your father's ship, you can imagine where we would be now. That is what I would call bad luck."

This time she looked at me with a little smile. "Well, honey, I believe that I should agree with your optimism this time. Looking at it the way you are, you're right—we've navigated with extremely good luck. One of those torpedoes would be enough to send us to eternity, or at least we would be forced to surrender. We don't want to sleep on the bottom of the Atlantic."

I smiled. "I really look with joy to see that, little by little, you've been changed from being irredeemable pessimist; maybe I've communicated a little of my optimism to you. Remember what I've told you several times: with optimism in our lives, we can conquer anything. With pessimism, not only do you accomplish nothing, but you're always full of depression and negativity. Who wants to live like that, surrounded by negativity and depression?"

Atacia came over to me, gave a big bear hug and a kiss on my lips. We separated when Jimbo approached with a mischievous smile. He said jokingly, "I want to be the godfather of your first child."

She blushed in embarrassment. "I believe you should learn to be a little more discreet in order to grow up and be a man. Even if it's obvious to you, try to ignore it—that's called politeness."

Jimbo didn't take her seriously. He grabbed her and gave her a big kiss on the cheek. "You have nothing to be ashamed of. Everyone in our family, even our friends we just said goodbye to, knows what's going on between you two guys. Mom and Dad are really proud of what you guys want to maintain a secret, because love is almost impossible to keep hidden. All we have to do is look at you guys when you're together, and even the looks you exchange with each other is beyond question that you profess a very unique and genuine affection for each other."

Atacia looked at me with a small smile, looking for my approval. I gave her a slight nod. I was expecting her to share with her brother our little secret; with an expression of satisfaction, she turned to face Jimbo with a huge grin. To my surprise, she touched her belly. "Yes, I love him, and he loves me. I'm carrying the seed of our beautiful love in my womb."

I was paralyzed with shock. This was the first even I had heard of this. At that moment, my mind was filled with a series of mixed feelings: first joy, second surprise, third terror. If she was as sure as she seemed to be, I could not leave her behind once I finished my mission in Cuba. My honor demanded it, and the last thing I wanted was for that baby to have the same fate as my son Julito. Very carefully, to avoid hurting her feelings, I came over to her and put my hand over her belly. I asked very softly but curiously, "How long have you known this? Why haven't you told me?"

Jimbo felt a little embarrassed. He was so close to us that he heard me, even though I had spoken in a near whisper. Atacia put her right hand over her belly and replied, looking into my eyes, "Last night, when Jimbo sent those Stingers to blow up the lab, I felt something jumping inside my belly as if I had something there that wanted to get out. It was probably scared nearly to death from the noise of that huge explosion; at first, I was scared too as I felt it jump back and forth. I've never experienced anything like it. As I felt my belly with both of my hands, the commotion calmed down, but I still felt a distinct kick or two. Last night was the first time it occurred to me that I was pregnant since the first time we made love in Caibarien. But this morning, with the helicopter woke me up and you left the cave, trying to avoid making noise to wake everyone else up, I went to one of the corners of the cave to urinate, and I started to feel those same kicks and jumping that I had felt last night. I was completely convinced that I have your baby in my womb because after I caressed it with both my hands, it calmed down and stopped jumping around and kicking. Evidently the same chopper noise that woke you up also woke him up abruptly. As I caressed him with both my hands, he restored his tranquility, and he calmed down to his happy, innocent sleep in my womb."

Jimbo was very close to us, listening to everything we were saying. He grinned broadly. "Congratulations to you guys. I hope your baby is very healthy and you guys can take it far away from all the miseries we have in Cuba." He mimed pulling a zipper across his mouth to indicate his lips were sealed. "Your secret is my secret. My lips are like a closed zipper. Whenever you decide to tell the others, you will. Don't worry about me at all; whenever you find it most appropriate, you will share it with them. I can assure you that they will be very happy and the news that you're going to have a baby will bring joy to our family. My mother and father, like everyone else, has observed you guys together, and see clearly that you have something very beautiful between the two of you, a love that is very difficult if not impossible to find, but it's equally difficult and impossible to hide."

At that moment Atacia interrupted him. "You see? He's doing it again—all the commotion with all the shooting, put your hands on my belly!" She grabbed one of my hands and one of Jimbo's and placed them on her stomach. "You feel it?" We both put our hands on her belly as instructed, and a few seconds later, Jimbo jumped and snatched his hand away like he had been shocked by electricity.

"What is that?" Jimbo exclaimed.

Atacia said, "Don't worry, he won't bite."

He smiled. "Oh, my God—you have a little Lightning in your belly."

I felt the kick as well, but I kept my hand on her belly. Apparently, the baby liked the warmth of my hands, because it calmed down. Slowly, the kicking stopped, but the tiny fetal feet were apparent on her skin. We all three exchanged smiles as there was no doubt that there was a baby cooking in there.

Jimbo asked, "Have you guys been thinking what name you're going to give it, depending on its sex?"

"Didn't you hear me?" Atacia demanded. "I just realized it last night—there's been no time to think about names."

"Well, I thought you might have something in mind."

"I'm just joking. I had a dream last night which gave me the perfect name for him."

"Him? How do you know it's a boy?"

"I absolutely know he's a boy, because I had a premonition like a dream in color. I know for a fact it's a boy."

Jimbo looked doubtful. "How can you guess about the sex?"

"I'm not guessing; this is real. The mother always knows, and yes, I have a name for him. He will be Julton." She looked me in the eyes. "If you have no objections, of course."

I was still a little confused by this unexpected news, thinking of the fate of my first son. I was a little worried as I replied. "You give him the name you want, and think is more suitable. After all, you're the mother. My mother used to say that the father could be anyone, but there is never a doubt about the mother."

"Maybe your mother is old-fashioned, and maybe she didn't have a man like I have. Men like you are unique."

"Thank you," I replied.

She looked at me and knew that I was deeply worried and confused. I was clearly not myself. "Don't worry at all. We're to going to make the same mistake you made with your first son. Nobody is going to know his name by your name. It's the initials of your first and second names combined as a disguise, as is logical for the son of a master spy, nobody can ever hurt him because they won't know he's your son. Nobody will be able to hurt him and only those who love him and protect him will know who he really is."

I smiled. "There's no doubt in my mind that if this baby's chromosomes carry your genetic characteristics as dominant the moral qualities and a little portion of your bravery and intelligence, he has a great possibility of maybe changing the world, which I haven't been able to do. Out of this miserable, corrupt world today, you never know, our baby could make a better world for tomorrow." I grew sad then. "If he manages to survive and grow up to adulthood."

Atacia came over and hugged me around the waist. "Who is the pessimist now?" I took a deep breath in silence. She took my face between her hands. "Nobody and no one will harm our baby. You and I will defend him, if necessary, with our nails."

I took another, deeper breath, compressed my lips in deep concern. "Honey, only God and his Son, Jesus Christ will have the power to protect our son with all the enemies we have around us."

There were lateral benches against the wall of the sub with seatbelts for each individual. We sat next to Aurora, who was really worried when she saw us, asking if we were OK after the sounds of firing outside.

Atacia crossed herself and smiled. "You shouldn't worry about it, Mom. We got out of this one smelling like roses without a scratch on anyone, thanks be to God. We have to say that it was a tremendous miracle that anyone didn't get injured. I think the only ones who got hurt were our enemies. At least that's how it sounded from the screams of pain we could hear between the shots."

Jimbo was still standing nearby, holding the hand bar which ran along the top of the bench. He said, "Yes, it's really a miracle, especially for you guys, who were farthest from the hatch." He shook his head with a small grimace. He looked at his mother and pointed with the index finger of his left hand. "Since I was a little boy, my mother used to tell me not to give or loan my favorite toy even to my dear friends if I didn't want to suffer a great deception." He looked directly at Aurora. "I should have thought twice of your words before I gave my favorite toy to Vanessa's father. I didn't even take into consideration that we might have another unpleasant encounter with the Cuban Marxists. The shower of bullets flying over my head from our enemies made me understand my major mistake of not following to the letter the very savvy and knowledgeable advice of my mother. As we say in Cuba, *el que da lo que tiene; ha pedir se queda.*[10]" He frowned in self-disgust. "If we had my toy with us, I would have sent those evil people to where they belong instead of humiliating ourselves by running like scared chickens because they had bigger toys than ours."

Aurora reached out to take his hand in compassion and loving support with a sad expression on her face as she listened to her son's pain and humiliation. Jimbo, understanding his mother's gesture, let go of the hand bar and took it tenderly and reciprocal gesture of love. She said, "Jimbo, you should not feel guilty because you didn't follow my advice." She gave him a small smile as she shook her head. "I didn't always follow the advice of my parents like I should have. Everyone does that, Jimbo. That's called growing up. We think we know everything until we know

---

[10] Whatever you have, if you give it away you have to beg to get a little piece back.

that we know nothing and discover we still have a lot to learn. But that is the only way everyone, including your sons and grandsons, get experience in life: trial and error. We won't always have the beautiful gift of our mom and dad advising us. This time, we were very lucky. If you think about it, you don't need to punish yourself for the mistake of giving away your toy; we didn't need it to save our lives. I don't think any of us will see those people ever again. At least, that is what I expect." She crossed herself. As she did, an extremely violent explosion shook the entire vessel from bow to stern.

Jimbo, who was only holding on with one hand, was wrenched out of her grasp as he sprawled across the deck while the lights blinked on and off. Shaken like a sardine can, the alert siren started to sound as the lightning changed to red emergency lights. We saw with sorrow as Jimbo rolled across the rubber padding that covered the deck while we remained seated thanks to our seatbelts. Water started to seep across the deck. A second explosion, more powerful, boomed sounding like it was inside. The water started to gush into the compartment.

Bonifacio's voice came across the intercom as the engines ceased. "Silence, everyone! We're under attack."

We remained motionless, not moving a muscle. Bonifacio cut the siren off, but the red lights continued to flash. The sub shook, but otherwise silence descended on us, the red lights creating eerie shadows. Jimbo remained motionless, stunned by hitting his head on something for a moment. He stirred and started to move towards us, but he was prevented by the sea water that was gushing in. We must have ruptured part of the hull. Atacia started to take her seat belt off to help her brother, but I motioned her to remain still. I gestured the same to Aurora, who was also trying to get up, and held my finger to my lips. Clearly there was a vessel out there with sonar, so we needed to remain absolutely still. Our voices would be picked up as clearly as our engine noise.

Another explosion shook us, rolling Jimbo around the deck again. I reached out to grab him, but he rolled back to where he was before. I realized I did the right thing, as both women would likely have injured themselves. I gestured with both arms and hands for everyone to remain in place.

Nothing happened for a few minutes. I gestured to Mama Teca to follow me. We removed our seatbelts as another, more distant explosion shook us. Holding ourselves by the hand bars along the ceiling, we reached Jimbo, who was bleeding profusely from a cut on his forehead. I took my shirt and T shirt off, ripped them in pieces with my knife, and improvised a bandage with a couple of strips I cut, tightening it around his forehead, and stopping the flow of blood. With Mama Teca's help, we seated him next to his mother and sister and strapped him in. Then we went in search of Bonifacio, trying to assess the damage we had sustained.

As we reached Bonifacio at an opportune time. He was trying to stop the flow of water at the flood control valve but was struggling to activate it by himself. We were able to help him place it, stopping the inrush of water, which was now to our knees. He immediately started the manual pump to get rid of the water. After we finally repaired the damage, the water level started to measurably decrease.

Bonifacio put his finger to his lips and whispered, "That son-of-a-bitch we encountered must have called the coast guard with our location. Using their sonar, they managed to get an idea of where we were, even though they didn't know what we were, they followed the engine noise. They made radio contact with me, demanding that I identify myself. I went deeper, pushing the engines to maximum speed to try and get away from them. That might have been my mistake. I should have turned the engines off and ignored their call. Without any engine noise, they might assume it was whales in the water, and eventually give up without trying to blow us out of the water. When I increased the speed, it was instead clear to them that we were a submarine, and that's when they started to bombard us. I assumed the distance was great enough that they wouldn't be able to catch up with us, a small vessel moving at high speed, and that was my miscalculation. Instead of resolving the problem, I made it worse." He shook his head in disgust. "I'm sorry, guys. It was a mistake in calculations. Let's hope the damage isn't too bad so we can continue our trip without any more trouble."

I took a deep breath and whispered back, "Let's hope you don't repeat this mistake in calculations. Instead of taking me to the capital of Havana for that important meeting that I'm now two weeks behind schedule for, one of those explosions could send me to the other side of the island."

Mama Teca smiled. She whispered, "If that happens, I just hope that we get to the other side of the island in one piece, and I hope you give me a good recommendation to your friends in Guantanamo Base."

"Unfortunately, my great friend and intelligence contact at the base, Mr. Atkinson, is no longer there. But let's hope whoever replaced him has the same decency, patriotism, and principles that he had, and not a mercenary in the service of foreign powers who for a handful of dollars has sold himself to the highest bidder."

She replied, "Unfortunately, my friend, I learned as you have as well, that those who receive a paycheck for this kind of work are not always loyal to our cause or ideology. They could receive of a hundred percent bigger payment than their paycheck, which can sometimes corrupt and convert a wonderful and great man into a vulgar mercenary. Sometimes some are moved by economic necessity, others simply by greed and the power of money. They start like a little game, tempted to the venture of being a double spy, and then when they get deeply into the game it slowly destroys their conscience. They have to create more lies and ignore more and more of their principles, and in the end lose their souls. Then they want to get out, feeling horrible about themselves, finding sometimes that they're extorted by the same ones who recruited them so that they can't get out of that deadly trap. It's almost impossible for spies to get out because they risk in the best scenario of being publicly exposed by their own people; or in the worst scenario, being killed."

I smiled. "Sounds like you've been working for the intelligence community for too long. At least, you never let me know that you are involved in this kind of work."

"No, I'm not. I just got a great teacher and great convictions as to how our enemies work and how intelligence and counter-espionage work and function."

I gave her a small smile. "I have had many mentors: my uncle, professors at the University of Havana, and my intelligence friends in other nations. They all taught me to never trust anyone and question without exception even your best friends and family. Love and care for those people who you know are truly friends, but always remember that your best friend today can be your worst enemy tomorrow. Don't absolutely believe in anyone, or anything you hear, and only half or a small portion of what your eyes see. Even when you have a perfect picture before your eyes and you think there's no doubt that this is the truth, you could have the greatest deception of it being a master fake and you wake up to an incredibly painful reality."

Chapter 19: Don Donato del Marmol, the Rebel

September 21, 1868
Nearly 90 years before the victory of the Cuban revolution
Santiago de Cuba

Don Donato del Marmol y Tamayo, a very well-dressed distinguished gentleman with an aristocratic look pulled up in his coach. The coachman, Tomaso, a black man dressed in a tuxedo, stepped down and opened the door for him. Many other coaches were waiting nearby; Tomaso went and joined the group of other coachmen as several other well-dressed men were heading into the club. As Donato climbed out of the coach, he was dressed in a white suit, black shirt, a tie with black and white stripes, and black shoes with white spats. He wore a refined white Panama hat with a black bandana and carried a walking stick in his hand, as was fashionable. He walked to the front door of the building with a sign with engraved Venetian glass which read, "Private Club. Gentlemen Only." The streets were cobblestoned, but the sidewalks were impeccably clean in this not too large city of Santiago de Cuba that they used to call the second capital after Havana.

Bartolo was the butler for the club, very tall, like Abraham Lincoln in stature, dressed elegantly as well with a long beard and big smile on his face, greeted him.

"*Buenas tardes, Don Donato.* Your friends are already waiting for you in the usual place."

Donato smiled back and replied, "That is very good." He checked his pocket watch. "I'm glad everyone is on time." He handed his hat to the butler. "It's nice to see you again, Bartolo."

Bartolo took the hat from Donato and put it on a hat tree where several other hats were already hanging. "Please follow me."

Donato followed him a short distance, past a large room where several businessmen played at various games. As he passed by, they nodded to him in respectful greeting. They continued through the room and went through a door with a large glass window to enter the restaurant of the club, where several people sat at different tables, eating various dishes. It appeared that everyone knew Donato. Even those with food in their mouths stood up to bow in his direction making gestures of respect with their hands.

They crossed the restaurant and into the kitchen. Inside, a heavy-set man, who looked like a Galician, red-faced with a hat which accentuated the ruddiness of his complexion, oversaw others preparing gourmet dishes such as lobster thermidor and rack of lamb, all of which looked delicious. They passed through the kitchen and stopped before a door which Bartolo unlocked with an old skeleton key. He opened the door to reveal the vegetable cellar for the restaurant. The two men crossed to the other side of the pantry where a suit of armor stood on display, attached to the floor by its feet. Bartolo moved the suit in a half circle, revealing behind it a concealed door with a cord hanging from one side on the frame. He pulled the cord three times, causing a small bell on the other side to ring. Almost immediately, as if someone were sitting by the door waiting for the signal, a small, barred window in the door opened. A face looked out to check who was ringing the bell and opened the door. He was a large man, well-muscled and sporting a large mustache.

As soon as he saw Donato, he greeted him with tremendous respect. "Good afternoon, Don Donato. Please some in. Everyone is waiting for you to start the meeting."

"Thank you, Federico," Donato replied. The door was closed behind Donato, who walked towards a long, huge wooden conference table where fifteen men awaited him. Some were smoking pipes, some long Havana cigars, but all of them stood up out of respect for him. Donato del Marmol was clearly the undisputed leader of the group which was meeting in this clandestine manner. It was clear they were planning an armed revolution to liberate themselves from the oppression imposed by the Spanish Crown over the island of Cuba.

Figure 16 Don Donato del Marmol and his fellow patriots

    Donato moved both his arms and hands to signal to everyone to sit down as he began to speak with them as friends. From the way they were dressed, they were all industrialists and businessmen, most of whom were born in Cuba but descended from the Spanish race. "My friends, it is with joy today I bring important news to all of you, and that is why I called this emergency meeting. I've made an agreement a few hours ago in an important meeting with various civil and political organizations, including the Masonic Lodge, that we will all agree to create a joint force to independently elect a provisional

President to lead us. The most important goal is the ending of the Spanish colonial power in Cuba and the creation of an independent republic, uniting all the political and religious factions. This government will be a Cuban government, free of foreign interests, to establish a new, sovereign, and free Cuba. All the wealth in our country won't be stolen and taken away to foreign nations. That wealth will stay in Cuba, in our country, for the benefit of all the Cuban people. We will create the most prosperous country if not in the Caribbean islands, then in the entire American hemisphere with the wealth we possess in minerals, agriculture, and luxury goods, all to the benefit of the Cuban people. With all the wealth we'll generate, we'll not only be free Cubans, but they will never again be able to steal it to take to Spain. It will be a fountain in our island for the future economic and social growth and wellbeing of every citizen to create better schools and universities for our sons and grandsons. I repeat, not only for our economic freedom, but we will be free of tyranny, from politicians who never have the best at heart for our country. We will be a free nation and free Cubans once and for all."

  Everyone stood up and gave Don Donato del Marmol a standing ovation, genuinely from the hearts of these patriots who had tears in their eyes and hearts filled with joy at these words. The celebratory mood did not last for long. The cheering and applause were not done before the bell on the door started to ring furiously—the signal for danger or emergency. It continually rang without stop. Federico ran to the little window and opened it to see what was going on. Everyone around the table looked at each other. Everyone who was supposed to be there was already present. They looked at the man at the door.

Bartolo was whispering to the guard at the window, relaying whatever news he had to convey.

Very tense seconds passed. No one moved a muscle. The man nodded to what he was being told. He turned abruptly and his hands held high, he signaled for danger, holding both hands up, closing one hand into the other, switching one hand to the other. Everyone at the table moved towards the far end of the room. The man with the mustache ran to the group, put his right hand on one side of his mouth and whispered, "We must have an informant within our group. The carabineers from the Count of Balmaceda are raiding the place." He went to the far end of the room, took a little pedestal that had a marble bust of Napoleon Bonaparte secured to the top of a flagstone, which he moved to reveal an iron trapdoor in the floor. He pulled the door up which revealed a set of metal stairs leading down. Everyone in line hesitated to descend them. He said, "Don't worry about it. Even if they find this place, which is nearly impossible, they'll never find that escape door. I'll stay here, but only as a security measure because it is my duty to get all of you to safety. In this kind of emergency, you never know exactly what will happen, and I need to put you out of danger. You are the future of our free republic." In a very formal and organized order, the men prepared to go down the iron stairs, waiting for Don Donato, but he refused to go before anyone else. "It's not time to be gentlemen here. You have to move. If they break through that door, everyone will be killed."

To provide an example to the others, Donato reluctantly went down the stairs. It was apparent the exit had not been used in centuries due to all the dust and cobwebs. The lime plaster which covered the walls was sagging in decay from the humidity. One after the other, all his compatriots descended. The immaculately dressed men got filthy as they walked through that tunnel beneath the foundations of that colonial building. A short distance later they came out of the tunnel, and emerged out behind the back of the building, to the tune of the squeal of an occasional rat which got trodden on unintentionally. They left the area one at a time, so they wouldn't attract attention in the street by coming out in a group.

    After Donato got out, he tried the best he could to clean his filthy clothes with his hands. He tried to likewise clean and adjust his hair, since his hat was back inside the building. As he came out into the street, he had to shield his eyes from the bright light after the darkness of the tunnel, taking care not to be seen by anyone in his condition of disarray. He didn't abandon his class and style, and with his cane in hand, he walked to the cobblestoned street along the side of the building. He spotted his coachman, Tomaso, who waited impatiently as he observed the commotion of the Spanish royal guards breaking into the club from his vantage in the driver's box of the coach. He saw Donato emerge from the back of the building towards the coach. Unfortunately, a squad of four soldiers came towards the coach from the opposite direction at the same moment. Donato quickened his pace to try and reach the coach before them so they couldn't see the state of his clothing.

    Tomaso, realizing the danger Donato was in, jumped down from the box onto the ground to open the door, blocking the view of the soldiers with his body. Donato hurriedly got into the coach at a virtual sprint, jumping headfirst into the coach like lightning before the soldiers got too close. It was imperative to keep them from getting suspicious at the disarray of his clothing. The soldiers started to look curiously at the coach after Tomaso hurriedly closed the door. He jumped up into the coach box, not giving them a chance to think about it, and whipped the horses into motion. The carriage rattled away, forcing all four soldiers to one side, their eyes glued to the carriage. Tomaso nervously looked at the guards and waved with a smile. Donato untied and shut the curtains on the side of the guards so that even though they looked intently to see who was inside the coach, nothing could be seen. Fortunately for Donato, none of them attempted to stop the coach.

    The sun was setting as night came on, a full moon rising in the east. As the carriage traveled along the dusty road to his hacienda, Donato opened the curtains and looked out at the moonlit night. He caressed his chin in profound thought. The road could easily be seen by the bright light of the full moon, further aided by two kerosene lamps on each side of the coach. He wondered about who the traitor within his circle might be. He could not figure it out because only a very small group of very distinguished gentlemen, friends he had known for years, had any knowledge not only of the place where they met but also the time of when they gathered. It had to be one of the men in that group who knew of their clandestine meetings.

    In the midst of this deep contemplation a tremendous impact, as if they passed over a large hole in the road, jarred him out of his thoughts. The coach rolled over on its side. Tomaso hung to one of the sides by the railing as it nearly rolled upside down. Inside the coach, Donato was flung violently from right to left, sent by the impact sliding over the seat and hitting his right shoulder against the wooden door so hard that he grunted in pain, clapping his left hand to it in reaction. He continued to groan in pain, but almost immediately afterwards the coach stopped abruptly, propelling him against the front seat. He hit his head against the wooden back before finding himself catapulted back, landing on the floor of the coach despite his best attempts to hang by grabbing the leather straps used to balance oneself when entering or leaving the coach. Because he was still dizzy from the impact, he could not manage to get up off the floor. He decided to stay there, motionless, to recover from his dizziness. He put his left hand to his head and saw when he pulled it away that it was full of blood and could feel a bump on his head. He touched it again and grimaced in pain.

    He didn't know what had just happened, closed his eyes in pain, took a deep breath, and tried to put his head back against the seat to recover. As he did so, a man opened the coach door next to him. Donato kept his eyes mostly closed and watched from beneath his eyelids to see who was there. In the shadows he saw a man get into the coach half-way and put his ear over his chest to listen for a heartbeat. Donato identified the man by the odor of cheap cologne the man wore. It was Federico.

    Federico yelled to someone outside. "Donato is unconscious, but it looks like he's still alive."

    A voice outside asked, "What do I do with the black coachman?"

    Federico did not reply as he was too busy checking Donato's pockets for valuables, an occupation far more important than answering the question. He took Donato's wallet, opened it, and saw it filled with large bills. The man's eyes gleamed in the darkness in avarice. There was a golden emblem attached to the wallet which read "Donato del Marmol y Tomayo." The man put it away and pulled a gold chain out of Donato's suit. It was attached to the pocket watch, a very expensive minute repeater. He put the golden watch and chain in his pockets.

The man outside asked again, "What do I do with this black coachman? Remember, the Count of Balmaceda has only paid us to eliminate Donato and make believe it's a robbery gone wrong."

Federico said irritably, "Don't waste bullets on that stupid black coachman. Cut his head off with a machete. He's just a worthless slave and could identify us."

The other man sounded irritated in return. "You're crazy. I don't kill black men with Santeria images and colors hanging around his neck. That will bring bad luck. I certainly won't kill him for free. You want to cut off his head? Come here and do it yourself. That's not a part of the deal."

Federico was trying to strip the two-toned shoes off Donato's feet when he heard the insubordination in his partner-in-crime. He already had his pistol in hand and pointed at the head of Donato, who thought his last moment had come. Federico fired, but the gun jammed. Irritated by the malfunction, Federico left the supposedly unconscious Donato, to clear the jammed weapon. He climbed out of the coach to deal with both his weapon and his co-conspirator; this was what Donato was waiting for.

Donato slid his right hand under the cushion of the seat where he had a secret compartment containing a Sharps derringer pistol. Donato whispered, "Federico." Federico turned. Donato yelled, "Federico Gaitan! Traitor! God forgive you for your sins!" He shot Federico, two holes appearing in his forehead as blood ran down his cheeks.

Unfortunately, Federico managed to pull the trigger on his own pistol, managing to hit Donato's already injured right shoulder. As Donato climbed out of the coach, he realized that these bandits had opened two large channels in the road to ensure the coach would flip over. This well-prepared assassination plan had been financed by the Count of Balmaceda, the vindictive man representing the Spanish Crown on the island, to suffocate any type of rebellion which could endanger their interests in Cuba.

The Sharps was a four barreled pistol, so with two shots left Donato took a long sword which hung to one side of the coach door inside the coach. Pistol in his right hand and sword in his left, he looked for the other man in the darkness. He saw not a soul—everything was silent save for the chirping of the crickets in the bushes. Hoping for the best though fearing the worst, said in a low voice, "Tomaso! Where are you? Are you OK? It's me, Donato."

Finally, a timid voice replied, "Master, master—I'm here, on the other side of the road. This bandit tied me to the flamboyant tree."

Donato looked and saw Tomaso, illuminated by the light of the moon and one of the coach lamps. It looked like Federico's associate had run for his life when he saw his partner fall down dead in the road. Donato grinned from ear to ear when he saw his good servant safe and sound. He crossed himself. "Thank God that they didn't harm you."

He untied Tomaso, who realized that his master was bleeding profusely from his right shoulder. Not wasting any time, Tomaso took his suit jacket off, pulled off his white cotton shirt, nicely tailored to him, and ripped it into strips for bandages to tie and secure Donato's shoulder. After he was finished, he tied a couple of pieces of the fabric together to create a makeshift sling. Then, between the two of them, they managed to right the coach and maneuver it back onto the road. One of the horses had broken its front leg and lay there screaming in pain in the middle of the road. Donato shot it to put it out of its misery, and they replaced the horse with Federico's mount. Finally, Tomaso, with Donato's help, managed to put the coach in place to continue their trip.

Donato searched Federico's pockets, recovering his personal effects that the would-be murderer had taken. Then the two men took Federico's body and put it over the dead horse on one side of the road. They poured the kerosene from one of the lamps over the bodies and lit it. They stood there for a few minutes to make certain the bodies of both beasts fully caught fire and were burning. Tomaso collected dead branches and wood to keep the fire going until the fire was fully caught.

After a little while, driven away by horrible stench of burning bodies, Donato, helped by Tomaso, climbed inside the coach, and then Tomaso jumped up into the driver's box and whipped the two horses into motion, leaving behind the macabre scene where they had nearly lost both their lives. It was in the middle of nowhere, the perfect location for a murder or double murder.

Donato, knowing now for certain who was behind this attempt on his life, swore revenge as he said to Tomaso, "This man Balmaceda has crossed the line. He has declared war before we even proclaimed our independence."

Don Donato's Hacienda

A while later, they arrived at the hacienda and drove along the circular cobblestoned drive before front of the house. Tomaso yelled for help as he stopped before the front door of the house in front of a huge circular water fountain in the garden. Several servants emerged from the house immediately. The housekeeper, Camila, was a very heavy-set black slave woman normally with a pleasant face. She put her right hand to her mouth and cried in sorrow as she saw Donato's blood-soaked bandages. "What happened? How did this occur?"

Tomaso said, "We'll explain later. Donato needs attention at once. Some bandits ambushed us on the road." Donato, pale and weak from the blood loss, remained silent. Tomaso said, "Help me, Camila." They managed to get Donato out of the coach and walked to the front door of varnished wood with well-maintained black iron exquisite decorations and hinges, typical colonial houses of that era.

As they entered the house they heard a woman's scream of pain, which jolted Donato out of his semi-conscious state. "What happened? Why is Guadalupe screaming that way?"

Taking Donato's weak condition into account, Camila replied with a comforting smile, "It's nothing, my master. You should not worry about it at all. She is delivering another beautiful present for your family."

"Oh, my God—it had to happen now?"

"Yes, don't worry about it. Dr. Muñoz is attending her."

"Why Dr. Muñoz? Why not you, Camila? You've delivered all our babies."

"Don't worry. He was here on his regular weekly visit when my lady broke the fountain and started to have contractions. He decided to stay just in case we needed him. Remember, he is living in town, far away from us. He's a very good man and has been here for hours. The baby evidently is oversized, and he might have to make an incision to help it come out without any problem." She smiled again and added, "I thank God that he decided to stay here, because I've never had to deliver a baby like that before. Now we'll need him not just to take care of our lady, but he'll also be able to take care of you. You look like you're in bad shape; you've lost a lot of blood."

Another scream of pain echoed through the house, this time more acute and filled with agony. Donato jumped abruptly at the sound. Not thinking clearly, he pulled his left arm from Camila's hands and ripped away from Tomaso. Taken by surprise, they were unable to hold him. He turned to try and head for his wife, but his legs, weakened from blood loss, wouldn't support his body. He took a few steps into the huge living room of the house and collapsed onto the floor, hitting his head against a bookshelf along the edge of one of its legs. Several massive books fell off the shelving and hit him on the head and shoulder, rendering him completely unconscious.

The good, loyal servants rushed to lift him off the floor. Camila saw he was fully unconscious with a new cut on his forehead that bled profusely and scared her. Full of panic the servants rushed to bring him into the closest room they could find. She ran to the bathroom to fill a bucket with water and fetch several towels. She tried to clean Donato's forehead, putting a towel on the wound. She said to one of the servants, "Put pressure on that wound. I need to go get Dr. Muñoz to sew up that wound."

She ran out of the room towards the master bedroom where Dr. Muñoz was helping Guadalupe in her delivery. After she ran along the corridor towards the master bedroom, the screaming grew more acute, and the agony of that loyal black slave grew proportionately

Chapter 20: Don Donato's Revenge

As Camila reached the master bedroom, she could clearly see an enormous bloodstain on the white satin sheets under Guadalupe's partially naked body. Dr. Muñoz's forehead was drenched with sweat as he tried to comfort Guadalupe, motivating her and saying, "Guadalupe, you have to help me, and you have to help yourself. You've already had experience. This is nothing new for you. You've told me that the other deliveries were not as difficult." He smiled. "Just remember that though this one is a little more difficult, I have a lot of experience and will be helped here today by Camila. Unfortunately, your baby is a little oversized. But that won't stop you, because you are a woman with great courage, and I don't think you want to lose this baby just because he's a little larger than the others. Isn't that true?"

Guadalupe shook her head. She was a beautiful woman descended from Galician Spaniards from Andalusia, with the deep blue ocean eyes, extremely pale white skin, and red hair the color of the blood on the beautiful satin sheet covering the bed. Her look was a combination of fear and uncertainty, wondering if she would be able to deliver the baby after so many hours of labor. The tender words of courage gave her a boost of confidence.

Camila stood in the doorway, paralyzed while she listened to Dr. Muñoz's words, looking at Guadalupe's vagina. In spite of the previous hours of labor, only the baby's crown could be seen. It didn't matter how dilated the tissue was, it looked like it would be impossible without rupturing the mother for that baby to emerge in one piece. Camila clapped her hands to her mouth, an unusual gesture for her, as she noticed the amount of blood on the bed. She began to doubt, as Guadalupe had, that this would end in a good way. She moved over by Dr. Muñoz's medical bag and took something out. She asked, "Is the baby OK?"

He turned his head abruptly. "Yes, of course, but we need to get it out quickly. We need Guadalupe's help. If we don't get it out as soon as possible, we could lose it."

Camila looked sorrowful and pursed her lips. She almost felt the pains her lady was enduring. With the fingers of her right hand, she caressed her forehead a few times. "I will try to do whatever I can. But you have another patient you have to attend to here in the house. I will take over and do what I can until you return." She put her arm around the shoulder of Dr. Muñoz and guided him out of the room where Tomaso was waiting to speak out of earshot.

She closed the door behind her and said in a whisper, "Don Donato is in really bad shape. He has a bullet in his right shoulder, and he's lost a lot of blood. As they came back from the city of Santiago, he and Tomaso were ambushed by bandits." Tomaso waited impatiently as Camila filled Dr. Muñoz in. She added, "Tomaso will give you all the details, but I don't think there's any time to waste. The most important thing is for you to go immediately and stop the bleeding in Donato's shoulder and in another wound that he has on his head. I will do my best with my Lady Guadalupe and see that she doesn't lose her baby, but I beg you, the minute you're done with Don Donato, come back here immediately. I've never in my life had such a complicated delivery. This baby is enormous, as you've seen yourself; the size of its head seems to be like a one-year-old child, not a creature that's only just beginning to enter this world."

Dr. Muñoz nodded. "I agree. I'm starting to worry that she won't be able to deliver this baby and we will have to sacrifice it by cutting it up to save the mother. I hope it doesn't come to choosing between her and her baby. I've never in my long career seen a baby of such large proportions." He crossed himself. "God help all of us in this difficult case." He put his right hand on Camila's shoulder and squeezed it affectionately. "Try to be your most persuasive but be firm. If she doesn't keep pushing, we may lose them both. That is the most important thing until I get back. Don't let her give up, at least not until you get the baby's head out. That's the only way to save both their lives. I'll come back as soon as I finish with Donato." He opened his medical bag to check its contents and make sure he had what he needed. He went into the room, took Guadalupe's blood pressure and pulse, nodding in approval at how strong both vitals were. He wetted a small towel in a small basin next window, squeezed the excess water out, and wiped the sweat away from Guadalupe's forehead, who tried to smile in gratitude, but only managed a half smile.

Camila came over to her and took her hand. "My lady, rest for a little longer. I want you to recover your energy. We have to finish this work—we already have had nine months of hard work inside your body building this baby. We can't afford to lose that. I believe he will be a great blessing to this family, because everything good and beautiful is only achieved with bravery, persistence, and love and with great sacrifice."

Guadalupe smiled a little as she looked at the good and lovely black woman who had been in the family ever since she was born, beloved by the entire family. She asked weakly, "Who taught you those beautiful words, Camila?"

She replied as she bent over to kiss Guadalupe's forehead with a big smile, "You, my good and beautiful lady."

By this time everyone had left the master bedroom, leaving the two women alone. Camila took both of Guadalupe's hands between hers and looked into her eyes. "My lady, I have an idea that might work and resolve the problem of this complicated delivery. But it's something I've never done before, and I need your approval. I believe I could not just save your life but also that of the baby, but it's risky. Do you give me your authorization? I repeat—this is something I've never done before."

Guadalupe looked at Camila and squeezed her hand. "What do you have in mind, Camila? Don't even tell me. Whatever you have in mind is going to be good, noble, and beautiful. You have my OK and my blessing. I'm already exhausted—it's been over six hours and I've lost a lot of blood. These horrible contractions are so painful. It's been weakening my willpower to the point of closing my eyes, stop pushing, and let myself go in the Hands of God, whatever it is will happen. If He decides to take me to the other world, at least I won't leave by myself—I'll be leaving with my baby. That may sound selfish, but if it's His will, I accept it."

Camila looked at her, weeping. She squeezed those hand harder. "No, no, my lady—remember your own words that you taught me. Everything good and beautiful in this world is only achieved in great sacrifice, bravery, persistence, and love."

Guadalupe, hearing those words, managed to fully smile this time. "What do you have in mind, Camila? I have the greatest confidence and trust in you."

Camila let go of Guadalupe's hands and removed from her dress pocket a small wash towel. She put it on top of the nightstand and unrolled it, revealing a small metallic instrument with a slender point, sharp as a razor. Guadalupe had never seen such a thing. "What is that?"

Camila smiled. "My lady, this is the key which will open the door of salvation for your baby. But also, it will put an end to your suffering and these horrible, agonizing spasms. Like a dam full of water, we open the sluice the water flows out with tremendous pressure. In the same way your baby will float out of your womb. There won't be any more pressure on your muscles, and you will finally release the cargo in your womb, saving yourself and the baby."

Guadalupe asked, "Where did you get that medical instrument?"

Camila answered, "I took it out of Dr. Muñoz's bag. After so many hours and you still can't get that baby out, my guts told me that the only way to save your baby is to use this scalpel. I looked in a medical book. All I need is a few moments to sterilize it, make a small incision below your vagina, and then with the grace of God all your suffering will be over. Hopefully, I won't cut any major blood vessels. This is why I needed your consent, my lady."

With the blessing of her lady, Camila left and ran to the kitchen to put the scalpel in a pan of boiling water for a few minutes. She emptied the pan, put the scalpel on a silver plate, grabbed a long-handled wooden spoon, and returned to the master bedroom, where Guadalupe was again screaming in agony from her contractions, now repeating more frequently. Camila took a bottle of rum and poured the alcohol on the little towel to clean the area that was to be cut. She gave Guadalupe the spoon. "Bite on that if the pain is too unbearable. That way you don't bite your tongue."

"No pain could be worse than what I'm going through."

When everything looked ready, Camila made an incision of approximately one and a half inches, opening the cavity into the body. The baby's head popped out, but the opening was still too small for the baby's shoulders to pass through. Camila, not liking this at all, made a face as she cut in to enlarge the opening. To her complete surprise, the baby completely popped out, and the cry of the newborn filled the room. Camila cut the umbilical cord and washed the amniotic fluid off the baby. She checked the baby and inserted her finger into its mouth to wipe out any remaining phlegm that might have built up as a result of the long delivery. Finally, once cleaned and wrapped up, she brought the baby to Guadalupe with a big smile on her face.

Guadalupe received the baby, which immediately went to one of her breasts and began to suck, quieting down. The door opened, and Dr. Muñoz entered, beaming in glee. He had heard the cry and looked at the suckling baby, disbelieving how it had happened. "How did you do it?"

With a big smile on her face, Camila showed him the scalpel. "You have to do the rest and sew her up."

"Congratulations for a job very well done," he said. He bent over and began to suture the wound Camila had been forced to create.

Camila said, "Thank you for your compliment, but I think the full merit doesn't belong to me but my gods. When you left this room, I think my soul went with you. When I took the scalpel to the kitchen to sterilize it, I got on my knees to pray to Yemaya, Chango, and Elegua. I made a promise to them which I now must fulfil. I prayed and asked all three of them to not let my lady or the baby abandon this world. They aren't ready for that trip yet. It looks like they listened to me and accepted my promise."

Guadalupe smiled in gratitude and held her right hand out to the good and noble woman. Camila took it in satisfaction and squeezed it devotedly between hers in token of the love she bore to the entire family who had raised her since she was herself a baby.

Dr. Muñoz finished his work and walked to the master bedroom to wash his hands and instruments in the beautiful white and black marble sink. Camila followed him inside with all the bloody towels and sheets which needed to be washed after she changed them for clean ones. She got close to him and whispered, "How is Don Donato doing?"

"Very well. Just a little weak but sleeping. I gave him a sedative. When he wakes up it will be a good idea to give him some chicken soup. This will be good for him and help him recover his energy."

Camila smiled from ear to ear, showing the one gold tooth she had in her mouth. "You don't have to worry about it, doctor. I will make sure that this is done immediately. Don Donato has a new puppy to feed, so he needs to recover quickly. As the leader of this family, his business needs his experience and wisdom. You should not leave this house before you have a good breakfast with us. I'll prepare a feast to celebrate the birth of this beautiful baby boy who will bring good fortune to this family and the Marmol house. But now, if you'll excuse me, I will give the great news to my master before anyone else gets to him."

Dr. Muñoz smiled as Camila left the bathroom. He went into the room and faced the dilemma of telling Guadalupe anything regarding Don Donato or remaining silent until Donato himself shared it with her. Guadalupe asked, "Where is Donato? Is he already back from the city?"

Camila replied, "Precisely, my lady, as if you are reading my thoughts. I've decided to go to find Tomaso because he should be already back now from his political meetings. It's still a little early, and you know he never returns until close to lunch midday the following day."

Guadalupe smiled, happy with her baby. "OK, go anyway and find out, but please don't tell him that the baby is born or what sex the baby is. I want to give that surprise to him myself."

Camila made a disappointed face. She replied humbly, "Don't worry. I will do that." She left the bedroom, closing the door behind her. She put her back against the door and crossed herself. She leaned against it, rolling her eyes as she didn't feel very good. She took a deep breath. "God forgive me." She didn't like to tell lies, especially not to her lady, for whom she felt tremendous respect and love. But the circumstances required absolute discretion, and she had done what she felt was necessary. She shook her head and walked away from the door straight to the room where she had left Donato earlier with Tomaso and the other servants.

As she arrived in the room, she found Tomaso sitting in a chair leaning against the wall to one side of the door with the derringer in his right hand at his waist, and

Donato's sword hanging from the left shoulder. "What are you doing with the master's weapons?"

Tomaso hissed for silence as he rolled his eyes in clear displeasure at her loud tone. He said in strong conviction, "Do you not have even the remotest idea of who tried to assassinate our master?" He opened his eyes even wider and added aggressively as he nodded. "Do you know?" Camila looked at him and shook her head wordlessly. Tomaso used her confusion to try and show a superior position even though she was above him and his superiority due to the information he had that she had not as to what had transpired during their ordeal. He leaned back in his chair while Camila remained standing next to him. His eyes seemed to bug out as he gestured imperiously with his index finger to lead down to his level. He lowered his voice to a whisper, "The man who gave the order to kill our master was the Count of Balmaceda."

Camila turned grey, then livid. She opened her eyes wide and could not control herself and said loudly, "My God, the Count of Balmaceda?"

Tomaso hissed urgently again, nearly falling off his chair in the violence of his putting his finger to his lips for silence. The good black woman, understanding her indiscretion but unable to contain her shock, lowered her voice to a whisper as well. "Why?" she asked sadly. "Why?"

Tomaso opened his arms in an exaggerated gesture of ignorance. "I don't know. You'll have to ask Don Donato."

Donato woke up, possibly because of Camila's loud voice. He called out from inside the room, "Camila, is that you? How is Guadalupe? Is the baby OK?"

Tomaso, now quite irritated and looked at her. "I told you! You'll wake up the master with that stupid screaming!" He pointed to the door of the room. "Go, go—go on in and tell me if you need any help."

Camila hesitated uncertainly. She knocked on the door twice. "Come in," Donato's voice said. "Is that you, Camila?"

She opened the door with a big smile and walked in. Donato was sitting up in bed, one bandage on his forehead and another bandage over his right shoulder, with a sling to brace the injured limb. He was completely awake now. "Is everything OK? Is Guadalupe OK?"

Not sure what to say, she said, "Everything is OK." She came over to him and grabbed him with one arm across her chest to fix the pillow behind him and gently eased him back onto the bed. "But you're not OK, you lost too much blood from those wounds."

Donato had no will to resist. She put another pillow behind his neck to make him more comfortable. She took a glass of orange and carrot juice mixed together and brought it to his lips. In a caressing voice, she urged him, "Drink it all. This will give you back your energy." He became quiet as he drank the juice. She picked up a metal bowl of broth left by one of the other servants. "Drink this a sip at a time. Your body needs all the strength to recover from all the stress you've endured these past several hours."

Obediently, Donato drank as if it were coming from the hands of his mother. Once he finished, he wiped his lips with a very nice linen cloth. He burped slightly and smiled as he apologized. He handed the bowl back to Camila. Then he took the blanket which partially covered his body and pulled it up over his body, feeling much better and threw up his hands in joy. He turned to Camila. "Thank you very much, Camila. That juice and broth are injections of life. Please call Tomaso because I want both of you to help me to get into the master bedroom without inflicting any more injuries on my weak body."

"My master, I don't think you should make that effort. Wait for a few hours before you move around. You're very weak and remember how you fell before. We don't want a repeat of that."

Donato replied in a firm, determined voice, "No. I don't want to wait any longer. I'm OK now, and that's why you and Tomaso are going to help me—so that I don't fall if my legs fail me. I want to be Guadalupe's side when she delivers that baby."

She rolled her eyes and smiled at him. She was a loyal woman and smart, determined to keep her promise to Guadalupe. Without saying a word, she went over to the door and called Tomaso in. With their aid Donato got up from his chair at once and went into the master bedroom, where he received the fantastic news that Guadalupe had wanted to impart directly. The baby was clearly a true Marmol, the original black lion, with skin white as a coconut, red hair like the blood shed by his ancestors fighting for freedom, and deep blue eyes like the ocean or the sky, like his ancestors.

Donato took one of Guadalupe's hands in his. "Thank you, my lady." He grinned at her broadly. "You are my queen, and you bless this house once more with your bravery. We will call him Julio Antonio del Marmol—Julio for Julius Caesar, Antonio for Caesar's best friend, Mark Antony, who never betrayed him and was loyal to him unto death, as any man with honor always is. That trait will continue in the bloodline for generations. His name will leave a mark in history as an example, brave and altruistic in the defense of freedom and independence from the cruel slavery of men who enslave their brother man. There should never be any importance about the color of skin or any impediment. That will be the contribution or symbol of the past of the weakness of the present for the better future for the entire world, a world that should be as all good men dream, filled with love, harmony, and happiness for everyone for centuries to come." He spoke emotionally and misty eyes as he felt touched by nature with tremendous pride and happiness for that little creature who so resembled the bloodline of his ancestors, unlike the other children.

    Dr. Muñoz, Donato's best friend and a faithful patriot devoted to the freedom of Cuba, stood up and emotionally applauded this beautiful speech, followed by the good and loyal Camila. She also had tears in her eyes and let go of the baby clothes she had been folding over the side of the bed to applaud. Better than anyone else, she knew that no one under the del Marmol roof had ever been mistreated or harmed; on the contrary, every single one was treated as a member of the family where all of them learned to read and write because Guadalupe felt it important. In so doing, she went against the laws of the time from the Spanish Crown which prohibited the teaching of literacy to any slave. This was done to keep the slaves obedient and ignorant so that they didn't rebel against the Crown. Even though this had serious consequences if the authorities found out, Donato didn't mind for his wife to teach their slaves equally as she taught their sons and daughters. For this reason, among others, all the slaves in the del Marmol mansion were ready to give their lives to protect any member of the family. That was the magnitude of their gratitude because they genuinely felt a part of the family.

August 21, 1868

Amid a furious hurricane which completely devastated the island of Cuba.

    By this time, Donato had completely recovered from his wounds. He was sitting in the dining room of the mansion with the family during the torrential rain and violent winds and harsh weather. The wind whistled loudly; even with all the noise they could hear the bell at the main door of the mansion ring wildly. Camila, always alert to such sounds, said, "There's someone at the door." She got up and hurriedly went to admit the new arrival.
    Everyone at the table exchanged questioning glances, wondering who could possibly be out in the middle of this wild storm to visit. Tomaso had already opened the door, acting as the butler for the family when the full-time servant was away. He welcomed Dr. Muñoz as he took the soaked outer garments and umbrella. The good man offered the doctor a very nice towel emblazoned with the family monogram to wipe his face off. Dr. Muñoz thanked Tomaso gratefully and followed Camila who met him in the entryway.
    He said to her, "This is the worst hurricane we've had in the past ten years."
    Camila smiled. "Thanks be to God that this mansion was built precisely to deal with this kind of weather. Any of kind of hurricane cannot touch the strong construction because Don Donato always was overly safe not just for his family but all of the rest of us and maintains a provisions room behind the kitchen completely full of the basic non-perishable food necessities for just this kind of situation, expecting at any time any of these storms. It's extremely dangerous to walk out in this kind of storm unless it's an extreme emergency. We never know what these strong winds will bring with them. My mother told

me when I was a little girl that one of her cousins lost his head completely from a metal sign propelled from a bodega when he tried to return home during a hurricane like this."

Dr. Muñoz gulped, his eyes going wide as his fingers caressed his throat. He smiled wanly and said, "Thank God, Camila, that I arrived here with my head still on my shoulder." He nodded. "Yes, only in an absolute emergency should we walk out in a hurricane."

Camila smiled at his taking her indirect hint. They walked together into the vast dining room where Donato politely gestured for Dr. Muñoz to take a seat at the table in spite of his surprise at the visit and the extremely serious news it might bring. "No, no," he politely declined. "I'm sorry to interrupt your family dinner."

"Don't worry about it." He turned to the servants. "Bring a plate of food for him."

The food was immediately brought, and the appearance and delicious dished placed before him utterly overrode his polite refusals. "OK, I'll join you," he said with a smile. He began to eat nervously, saying, "I'm here because something gravely urgent has come up that I need to communicate to you."

Donato opened his arms in his usual optimistic character, "In this hurricane that's so dangerous? If you made it to my house, everything urgent can wait, no matter how bad it is. Eat first, share with us a great moment, you're a member of our family, and afterward we will go to my private study and discuss your grave news which brought you to my residence in such a hurricane. There we will have a glass of our favorite cognac and smoke one of my delicious Havana cigars. But only after dinner."

Dr. Muñoz had no other choice but to eat, which he did with pleasure, enjoying fully the delicious food brought to him. After the dessert, Donato made his excuses to the family and the pair walked away and entered the study. Donato shut the door and sat down in one of the elegant, overstuffed leather chairs. He picked up a box of Havana cigars, offering one to Muñoz, who accepted, and selected one for himself. He then took two glasses and filled them both with cognac. They toasted each other and took a sip. They lit their cigars and continued their conversation.

Donato asked, "OK, my friend—what information do you have to convey to me? It must be extremely important to get you out at the mercy of these high winds and torrential rain."

Now a little more relaxed, Muñoz's face was still anxious. He took a deep breath as he removed from his coat a small piece of paper. He unfolded it and handed it to Donato, who looked at it seriously. Donato's face became grim. "Where did you get this?"

Dr. Muñoz said, "You should abandon this island immediately, before this hurricane clears up completely, before the winds and rain stop. All the names on this note, without exception, will be arrested on charges of sedition and conspiracy against the Spanish Crown. You'll note that the first name on that list is yours.

Donato shook his head as he read the list and saw his name. The second on the list was a great patriot friend of his, Maximo Gomes. The third on the list was Jose Marti, the great poet and patriot. Muñoz said, "Everyone on the list is a patriot. If they haven't' abandoned the country already, are in preparations to leave. Even though the ocean is dangerous, they're taking the chance to leave. Any others are in hiding. As you know, everyone that is accused by the Count of Balmaceda with these charges before were all executed by firing squad. There will be no trials—these are your death warrants. They will manipulate the law as they wish. These criminals just pretend for the sake of public opinion. Trials, as you know, are composed by the judge—the representative of the Crown—and the defense and the prosecution—all members of the Crown government. The purpose is simply to strangle anything which resembles a rebellion or revolution that can jeopardize their interest in the island. The Count had a taste of power during his term as acting governor and wants to show the Crown he's worthy of permanent power."

Donato took a long draught from the cigar and leaned back in his chair. "Thanks to you and your good work, the last thing which could cross the mind of the Count is that you work with us. This valuable information you've just provided will save us from certain death as well as the future of our *Manbises* [11]revolution. I will leave the hacienda tonight. I will wait in the city of Santiago until the hurricane subsides after it crosses the island. I will leave for Guatemala, where I'm going to take refuge in our safe house with Maximo Gomez and Jose Marti, along with our other compatriots. I will suggest to them in our exile to visit New York, where we with our contacts in the USA can put together sufficient financial resources to organize an armed expedition to come back to Cuba to destroy not only the Count's reign of terror but also ending the subjugation by the Spanish crown."

Dr. Muñoz replied, "Donato, that is a brilliant idea. I believe our compatriots will receive this with joy."

---

[11] A term originally used by Spanish soldiers as a derogatory term for Cuban guerilla independence soldiers which the Cubans accepted and started using with pride.

Donato smiled as he tapped the ash into the black and white marble ashtray on the table between them. He stood up and shook Muñoz's hand as they embraced. "Thank you very much, my great patriotic friend. I only ask that you please keep your eyes on my family. Knowing that they are looked after will allow me to sleep much better, secure, and confident that I've left my family in good hands, especially my three-month-old baby. You know how to communicate with me wherever I am. Don't hesitate if any unexpected emergency comes up."

They exchanged a sincere embrace of friendship and confraternity in patriotism as they walked to the door of the study. Dr. Muñoz said, "You can go in peace, my brother. Not just me, but all our brothers in the Masonic Lodge will watch over your family's security day and night."

Donato's voice cracked slightly. "This is the most difficult moment of my life, to leave my family behind. My mind still is trying to figure out how I'm going to break this news to my beautiful Guadalupe. I don't know how she'll react. She's a great woman and will understand." Though he smiled, his face was sorrowful. "I hope that she'll understand because our homeland and our future freedom for ourselves as well as our sons depends on what we do today, and every sacrifice we make, however little, will be worth it to our future generations. As the old saying here goes, show a smiling face to the bad weather."

This time Donato was extremely worried. He walked his friend to the front door and put his right arm around his friend's shoulder. "You must be extremely careful. After we all disappear from the island before the eyes of the Count, he might start to doubt who provided us that valuable information you just brought." Donato squeezed Muñoz's shoulder. "I don't want to scare you; just be prepared. The Count is an old fox, and he could lay a trap for you. For example, he could give you wrong information that could make it clear to him the cover who ever provided the information to the rest of us. Be careful—that could cost you your life if he can prove that you are the leaker. Remember, the circle of this individual is very small, and the people who possess this information is few, because the Count doesn't have the luxury of having many friends. His character is so abusive, and his controlling nature converts him into a very anti-social and obnoxious person. I've observed very much his personality for a long time now. I became very close to him, to the point where he invited me and Guadalupe to his palace not too long ago where you assisted us on New Year's Eve. I've visited him for a while, going to all his parties at Christmas as well as other events. My reading of him is that he's an extremely dangerous individual. That is why I caution you again—be careful."

Dr. Muñoz looked into Donato's eyes and saw the sincere worry there. In genuine affection, as he still had an arm over his shoulder, he grabbed Donato's hand across his shoulder in both hands and said, "Thank you, my friend. Don't worry. I know the beast, and I know how to deal with it."

"I don't remember if I've ever said this before, when you were here tending my wounds after the ambush, but before one of the mercenary bandits died, I heard him say that the Count was the dark hand which had sent him to assassinate me. That told me that he possessed enough information about our clandestine activities from his own spies to try to eliminate me and every one of us, one at a time. That is why I formulated the plan that I will now put in motion as soon as you leave of sending a message to intimidate with the same weapon that he used against us to put fear into his brain and not let him sleep in peace, filling his heart with horror. This will make him think twice after I've left for my exile about starting a personal vendetta against not only my family but also those of my other compatriots that he's included in that list." Donato stroked his long mustache and thought for a few seconds. "You know better than anyone his habits and his character. What can you tell me that could help me to help hurt him the most? What are his most precious or spiritual toys which will affect him the most if I take them away from him.?

    Dr. Muñoz stroked his chin as he stood near the door for a few seconds as he thought. "I've got it. There are three things that he adores. In order, his rooster named Napoleon, the champion of all the tournaments around Cuba and his prize that he shows every visitor to his palace. Second, his black Paso Fino horse named Achilles. Another prized trophy of his. The third is a most beautiful and exquisite slave with bottle green eyes named Claudia. They brought her as a present in Egypt from one of those Pashas. That woman is his mistress with whom he devotes all of his free time. He cares for her more than he does his own wife." He smiled mischievously and shook his head. "I don't blame him. She's a gorgeous woman. But I don't think you want to hurt her. You can pick any of those three things, and believe me, you'll get his attention. Whatever your preference is, if you want to send him a message of horror, you can take one of these three treasures."

    Donato stroked his mustache again. "Why not take all three?"

    Dr. Muñoz smiled and raised his eyebrows in surprise. He shook his head. "I don't think that you possess the luxury of that much time to develop a plan that would be successful to do all that. Remember, you only have hours, if you're lucky." He looked at Donato with a little worry. "Take into consideration that these three possessions of his are extremely well guarded. Because of that, they will be if not impossible then extraordinarily dangerous targets. To take on a venture of this magnitude and succeed will be almost impossible."

Donato had a small smile of satisfaction. "The more difficult the venture is, the greater the scare it will produce in our enemy. This is precisely what I'm looking for: intimidate him in a way that he won't even dare to move a finger to harm our families."

"My friend Donato del Marmol, I know you are a man of great principles and incalculable bravery, but this is not a venture for a single man. It will require an army, and a very well-trained one. The castle of the Count is not just a palace—it's a fortress, prepared for any attack, with the security practically impenetrable. My friend, you have to remember that you have a new baby in your house. I believe, because I know the kind of man you are, that you want to see this baby grow up to be a man."

"Dr. Muñoz, precisely because of him and the rest of my family, as well as the families of my compatriots, I have to take this venture to the end before I leave for my exile and be able to be peace in my mind. Otherwise, when we all return from our exile, each of us will find not one of our loved ones alive. This is what normally cowards and murderers do: they use the opportunity and circumstances, when they think we are on the run, considering flight a sign of weakness, to try and destroy their adversaries. Because they have no decency, they don't even consider that the families are innocent and have nothing to do with anything else."

Muñoz furrowed his eyebrows and shook his head. "I don't think, Donato, that nothing I can say will make you desist in your ideas; but only an act of Providence will allow you to not only take on this venture but also allow you to get out alive from Balmaceda's palace."

Donato looked at him quite seriously. "Of course, I need all the angels in Heaven by my side. Without them I will never accomplish my plans." He crossed himself and added, "I believe I have the most powerful angel behind my back, who is Jesus Christ. With His favor, I will send this devil to where he belongs. Let me tell you one thing: the impossibility of what I intend to do is precisely what will take our enemy by surprise. As you said yourself before, the palace is not an easy target, very difficult because it is protected against attacks by multiple forces from many directions. They expect a well-trained army; but what they haven't even imagined or prepared for is penetration by one, two, or three individuals who can go in the dark and climb their walls, unseen within the shadows. The element of surprise which is the most essential factor to win the most difficult battles."

Muñoz proudly and moved by the courage and assurance of Donato and answered with a cracking voice, "If there's anything I can do to minimize the risk, you can count of me, my very great friend."

Donato put his right arm across his friend's shoulder again. "No, no—you've already given me the most powerful weapon that I can have to neutralize our enemy, the Count of Balmaceda, and that is your information. Without that fountain of intelligence that you just provided, I cannot make my plan to inflict the most effective and vital wound to our common enemy. And for that I have to give you my most sincere thanks. Now you should return to your home and family with extreme care in these violent winds and rain. This hurricane will be my best ally, and you will inform me in the next days, weeks, or months what kind of effect, positive or negative, that we obtained with my venture will inflict on the soul and mind of this evil man."

Donato and Dr. Muñoz embraced once more, this time in a most symbolic manner as the doctor tried to hold his emotions in check and hide them from Donato. But now, with tears in his eyes, he thought that he would never see this great friend, Donato del Marmol, alive ever again. After they said their farewell, Dr. Muñoz tried to hide his face to avoid Donato seeing his emotion, Donato opened the enormous door with difficulty, as the winds were still quite strong. He then closed the door and walked towards his study.

This time, he went behind the desk and sat down on the comfortable chair, pulled open a drawer in his desk, pulled out some paper monogramed in multicolor with the family crest and its lions on either side, and dipped the point of his pen into an ink bottle. He began to write:

To the Count of Balmaceda:

You tried to kill me. My message to you will be short and clear. By now, it is clear that you know your attempt to assassinate me has failed. Let me inform you that your mercenary spy paid a very high price—his life— for this failed attempt. A much higher price that whatever you promised to pay him; another death on your conscience, Count of Balmaceda, since your mercenary spy is dead, as you will eventually be. By the time you receive this letter, I will be far away in exile, but my eyes will be very close to you. You will find them in the shadows of the night, observing all your movements and your family. Even in the light of the sun, in plain daylight, in the shadows of the bushes or a large, healthy tree next to you, my eyes will be watching you, waiting for the precise moment to repay you in the same coin, only now that coin is growing as time passes. The screaming voices that ask for justice for all the lives that you cut short, like a villain that you took with no scruples, only for the ambition of power. Your fall starts tonight on this darkened night of a hurricane. Your days are numbered, and I will observe you closely day and night, ready to cut the thread of your life and everyone or things that you love in your life, one at a time. How do you feel? There is nothing you can do to stop this. It is unavoidable. To give you a little prelude, I will start by giving you a little example on this very stormy night. I want you to see patiently my first three gifts of initiation which will be the beginning of your future. Welcome to the Inferno that you have created in your surroundings. I hope you enjoy, Count of Balmaceda. I will be in your blind side for the rest of your life.

> *Good luck,*
> *Donato del Marmol.*

Figure 17 The del Marmol family crest

After Donato sealed the envelope and pressed his signet ring into the soft wax, he left the study and went further into the mansion to give instructions to his multi-function servant Tomaso. "Get the coach ready to leave immediately."

Then he went in search of Camila, finding her in the kitchen. He brought her out into the hallway out of earshot of the others. "Pack my bags for a long journey. I'll be gone a long while. Bring this sealed letter to the hands of the Count of Balmaceda." He then told her how he wanted it to be done, and explained in detail what was to be done on the way to the Count's palace, how he wanted to do everything, each step at a time. That visit would be a surprise to his worst enemy.

Camila limited herself to nodding at each point Donato instructed her, asking no questions. As soon as Donato left to join his family in the living room, Camila crossed herself, bit her lower lip in distress, and mumbled to herself a brief prayer.

Donato went into the vast living room where Guadalupe and the children were. One at a time, he embraced each child and told them that he would be leaving for a very long trip, that it would be longer than any other he had before. None of the kids were surprised by this, as Donato was continually traveling around in his business, sometimes being absent for months. The only thing which produced any kind of surprise for Guadalupe was when Donato said to his eldest son, Donato, Jr., something he had never done before. In an emotional voice and wetted eyes, he said, "Remember, you are the one who represents our family. While I'm absent on this venture, you are the master. I make you responsible to represent our family, if necessary, you can give your life for it. Take care of your mother, your younger brother, and your sisters, and I deposit in you all my trust."

Donato Jr. was still quite young to receive such a humongous responsibility, but with pride and extreme confidence from his father's words he hugged his father. "You can go in peace, Father. I will not only defend and protect my family with my life, but I will also not let any harm come to anyone in this house."

Very proud of that response, Donato caressed his eldest son's face with a smile. "I know. I know that you will like the great and good del Marmol that you are. Please, now take your sisters Siboney, Clotilde, Teresa, and Lupita to your rooms for a little while. I want to have an adult talk with your mother, something intimate and confidential, before I leave."

His son respectfully replied, "Yes, sir." He said to his sisters, "Let's go for a little while." They followed him out.

Donato came close to Guadalupe, where she stood with tears in her eyes, not just from the sad news but also for his departure into exile as he explained the situation. He gave her an overview, showing her the list of all the men who were to be arrested soon; she could see his at the top of it. He took the infant Julio Antonio in his arms and said, "Don't worry—I assure you that he will not grow up fatherless or an orphan."

Guadalupe embraced him, and all three stood there in silence for a few minutes in that long embrace. She broke the silence at last with tears in her eyes. "You should already be out of here. The hurricane is starting to weaken, and you need to be far away from here as soon as possible before the carabineers come searching for you."

Donato left the living room followed by Guadalupe with the baby in her arms. She followed him all the way to the front door. As Donato climbed into the coach, she broke down and began to weep as she watched him leave. Donato, now inside the coach waved at her while she took the baby's tiny hand in hers to wave back.

Camila sat next to him as they disappeared into a night made darker by the strong winds and rain, the carriage wildly rocking from the storm. She looked at Donato with the envelope in her hands that she was to personally deliver to the Count. She asked submissively, "Master, are you sure you want to do this?"

Chapter 21: The Defeat of Evil

Donato looked at Camila and noticed her lips quivering in terror. He took her hands in his and looked straight into her eyes as he searched for the most loving, persuasive words he could find. "No, I don't want to do this, from the bottom of my heart. But I'm convinced if I don't do this, and I didn't want to tell you the details, so you didn't become frightened. Fear is the worst enemy we can have, and I need you to be calm and together in order to execute my plans properly. I know for a fact otherwise that none of you will be alive when I and my friends return from exile. There's one thing I know about this man: he's a real coward, but he's also a cold-blooded, conniving assassin. In our absence, he will try to destroy everyone in our families, with impunity he will confiscate all our properties and wealth, stealing the fruits of our work for the past several decades and that of our ancestors because he will think that no one will be able to stop him." He squeezed her hands in his.

He added with conviction, "Remember: as we say here in Cuba, always take the bull by the horns until he eats the dust of the arena. Otherwise, the bull will nail his horns in your back or butt if you try to run and escape from him." Camila tried to smile at the offered joke but only managed to give a smirk. Her face was contorted in worry as she listened to the last words of Donato. Understanding her anxiety and fear, he continued to calm her as best he could. "Remember, Camila, the Count of Balmaceda is not a man like other men; he's a man who has sold his soul to Lucifer."

Camila crossed herself as her eyes opened in a disorderly manner, her breathing became very agitated as she replied, "Don't take me wrong, my master; I'm not worried about what he will do to me. I'm worried about the damage he'll inflict on our family."

Donato said with conviction as he pointed at the letter she held in her trembling hands, "I assure you that after he reads that letter, and digests it, and after I've finished with him, he won't dare to raise a little finger against any of you or my friends. Especially with the tremendous surprise that I will send him in company with the message you are delivering today." He leaned back in his seat, letting go of her hands. "Just remember my instructions: as soon as you deliver this letter into his hands, retreat. Don't stay one second longer than you need to be in his company. I don't want any of you to get hurt." Her eyes opened wide. "You're going to pick me up at the same place you'll drop me off at, several miles before you reach the palace."

"Very well, my master Don Donato," Camila replied. Though she wasn't calm, she was resigned to placing her faith in Donato's ability to avoid putting any of them in danger.

He reached his right hand out to place it around her shoulder. "Remember, with the favor of God, all will go well, exactly as we planned it." He pulled the cord next to his seat which rang a bell in the coachman's box. As soon as he heard the bell, Tomaso slowed the coach and stopped by a huge mango tree next to a sign pointing along a narrow, muddy road. Under the cover of the heavy rain and strong winds which still howled insanely from the hurricane, Donato took a bag that looked much like a surgical bag. He stepped out of the coach and said to Tomaso, "Remember, I will be waiting off the road behind this tree. If you get back before me, hide there so that anyone on the road won't notice you and get suspicious of you at being out in this weather, so close to the palace. That is if you return before me. I expect to be back before you arrive.

The loyal servant replied, "Very well." He tapped the horses and left towards the main entrance to the palace of the Count of Balmaceda.

As Donato walked, his eyes not completely adjusted to the darkness of the forest, he tripped and nearly landed on his arms in the muddy road. Fortunately, his reactions were quick, and he grabbed a mango tree branch which prevented his fall. He bent over to see what had tripped him. He held the object close to his face and saw that it was a beautiful, large mango, ready to eat, which had been ripped from the tree by the wind. As the lightning flashed and lit up the road, he could see the fruit littering the road, all displaced by the hurricane wind.

Very carefully, he zigzagged to avoid tripping on more of the fruit, picking his way to avoid falling on his face. The darkness grew denser as the rainfall became heavier. He could only see portions of the road lit by the flashes of lightning. Finally, he reached the high stone walls, almost twenty feet in height, which surrounded the palace of the Count, turning it into a real fortress.

Donato was very fit, a man in his prime, and tossed the bag over the wall and climbed it without great difficulty, avoiding being seen by the darkness and protected by the hurricane, as all the guards had apparently retreated into the guard shelters. Some of them used the opportunity to sleep on duty. Once on the other side, he discovered that the guard shelters had been built not very far apart, perhaps only a couple of hundred feet from each other. As he had been told, the place was very well guarded indeed. He passed all of them without problem until he reached nearly the last one. He again tripped in the dark and slid on a palm leaf, which was wet with the rain. He nearly fell on his bottom among the dry branches and rolled onto the wet grass.

The noise caught the attention of the guard inside the shelter, awakening him. The dogs started to bark loudly, and a light appeared inside the shelter. A guard opened the door, a kerosene lamp in his right hand, raised above his eyes to see better at a distance. He moved the lamp around to see where the noise had come from.

Seeing that, Donato covered himself with one of the palm leaves on the ground, watching the guard through the holes and cracks in the leaf, letting go of his bag and holding on with both hands to keep his cover in place which the wind threatened to rip away. After several tense seconds passed, it appeared that the guard didn't want to get more water in his face as he stood in the door. Several branches had broken free of some of the eucalyptus trees, which made plausible explanations for the noise. The trunk of the tree had landed only a few feet from where Donato lay hidden. Some of the leaves, blown by the wind into the guard's face, made him hurriedly close the door. He yelled at the dogs to be quiet as he slammed the door shut.

Donato breathed a sigh of relief as he saw the guard close the door. The last thing he wanted at that moment was a confrontation not only with that guard but any other guard that might be alerted by the commotion, ruining the surprise element which was the guarantor of success in his plans. Being a decent and good man with scruples, the thought of taking the life of that guard who might have family at home did not produce joy for Donato. With a big smile on his face, he crossed himself as he crawled out from his cover behind the trunk and saw the size of the enormous tree which had landed only a few feet from where his head had just lain beneath the palm leaf. He got on his knees and looked towards the sky, feeling the rain on his face. He crossed himself and thanked God for protecting him the entire way on his venture that he felt dutybound to do. "I have to do this no matter what the price to myself personally, to protect my family, my brothers in our cause, and their families." He crossed himself again, picked up the bag, and continued his journey.

      He went deeper past the perimeter, coming to the heart of the fortress, close to the palace where the Count resided with his family along with his most precious possessions: the stable with the Paso Fino and Andalusian horses, close to the slave barracks. Also, not far away, was the building with all the roosters were kept along with their fighting ring. These were the major sources of pride to the Count and his most precious hobby. Donato did a little Eeny-Meeny-Miny-Moe with his fingers and went towards the cock fighting ring.

      He entered without any difficulty and looked at each cage, searching for the name Napoleon, so named because of his numerous victories; perhaps, Donato also thought, because the Count himself had a Napoleonic complex. It was one of the factors which limited his friendships; even those closest to him, like Doctor Muñoz, disliked him profoundly. He thought now that the palace wasn't such a fortress, since he had gotten so close without detection. He realized that his plan was working, because at that moment the hurricane was his best ally. It grew even darker as he walked along the cages. He reached into his pocket and pulled out a box of matches, striking one to see the name plates better with the blue, red, and white ribbons which had been won along with the trophies from various tournament championships.

As he continued to strike matches, some of the roosters began to crow, unused to light at such an unusual time. Just as he had nearly given up, near the end of the line of cages he found what he was looking for. The plumage of this rooster was grey, black, and white, the most famous in all of Cuba, the champion of three hundred and one fights without a single loss. He took one of rattan cages stuck to one side of the place, one on top of the other, which were used as portable cages to transport a rooster to a tournament. Carefully, to avoid the bird flying away, he opened Napoleon's cage and put him in one of the rattan cages. After he locked the cage door, he started to turn around. He noticed to the right of Napoleon's cage was another rooster with the same level of prestige as Napoleon. This one had multicolored feathers, and the name on the cage was Hercules: "future champion, 211 fights with no losses." He took a second rattan cage, deciding to take Hercules as well. He took a cage in each hand with extreme caution, and recrossed the building, heading back out into the storm. Then he made his way toward the stables.

As soon as he entered, he saw a wagon which had several bales of very dry hay. He tied a rattan cage to each side of that wagon. After securing the cages, he went inside the stables themselves, looking for the horse Achilles. He picked up a kerosene lamp which was just outside the stables and lit it. He brought Achilles out of his stall and began to harness him to the wagon with leather blinds over his eyes. He no longer looked like a Paso Fino, but now looked like a standard workhorse. Achilles gave Donato a hard time, being unused to the harness. Donato was prepared and had several sugar cubes in his pockets and used them to induce the horse to remain calm.

Once everything was ready, Donato opened the container of kerosene and spilled it all over the hay in the coach. He kept a little for use, and hung it in front of the wagon, and relit the lamp, guiding Achilles to the opened double doors. He dropped a match on the hay in the back of the wagon and slapped the rump of Achilles hard with a wide leather belt. When Achilles saw the flame behind him, the horse bolted and ran for his life. Donato had pointed the horse towards the palace so that Achilles would run in that direction on the muddy road.

By now the Count of Balmaceda had spoken with Camila as Tomaso waited patiently for her to finish her conversation. She handed the letter to the Count and not taking it lightly, he screamed threats at her. "Tell your master, Donato del Marmol, he had better hide very deep in the forest so that I'll never find him! Tell him to also not to forget to dig a very deep, large grave to hold all the bodies of himself and his friends. They are all dead men!" Camila nodded wordlessly. In a panic, she saw how he crumpled the letter and wrung it in his hands as if he were visualizing Donato's neck there.

She said humbly, "Count, if you are finished, I will go back, if you will allow me."

"Yes, go! Go!"

She rushed into the coach and said to Tomaso, "Go, let's get back to our hacienda as soon as possible. This man is ready to kill both of us."

Tomaso tapped the horse on the rump and rattled out of there by the second arch. Once they were about two hundred yards from the porch of the Count, something caught all three individuals' attention. The rain had stopped for the most part, a mere drizzle now, but the winds were still strong. Balmaceda put his hand to his forehead to try and determine what light was coming towards him from the road, illuminating everything along the path. Not comprehending what it could possibly be, and full of curiosity, Camila and Tomaso, now at a great distance from the porch, could see as the wagon with the burning hay in the bed, ran along the left side of the road towards the palace, making the horse some kind of animal from the other world, with no coachman. Unquestioningly, he was galloping directly towards the porch of the palace. They both crossed themselves, knowing for sure that the flaming wagon with the two cages holding roosters squawking in terror looked like it was being followed by the Devil himself. They knew that this was the message that their master was sending to the Count.

For that reason, Camila thrust her head out of the coach window and yelled, "Faster, faster! We have to get out of the main gate before that wagon reaches the Count."

Tomaso stood up in his box and flogged the horses to get them into a full gallop and get out of there as soon as possible.

The Count summoned his guards, with about twelve men responding, who took up positions in front of the palace, still not sure what was approaching them. The Count yelled, "Form line!" They put their weapons to their shoulders, ready to open fire, still puzzled at what the approaching target might be.

The front line knelt in the mud as the captain of the garrison stood next to them, sword held high as he waited for the object to come within range for his men to open fire at whatever enemy was attacking. No one knew how this wagon could pass the front gate.

Achilles, completely panicked and uncontrolled, continued his run of terror, the flames billowing out behind him and growing larger. Pieces of hay broke away, flaming embers falling onto the road. Neither horse nor roosters had been harmed yet, as the lit hay was in the center of the wagon bed.

Still in a state of confused incomprehension, the captain waited. He finally judged the range short enough and swept his sword downwards. "Fire!"

Unfortunately, at that moment, Napoleon began to crow from his cage. At that moment, the Count understood what kind of gift Donato had just presented him. He yelled, "No, no!" at the same time as the order to fire was given—but just a moment too late, as the soldiers fired.

The captain looked at the Count, not comprehending why he had attempted to halt the orders. The soldiers looked at each other in confusion. It was too late—the beautiful horse Donato had disguised beneath the tack and harness of a workhorse now lay on the ground virtually at the Count's feet, lifeless. The Count walked towards the horse and removed the harness, recognizing his most precious horse. He also looked at both his champion roosters, also now lifeless in their cages—all executed by his own guards.

The guards formed a bucket chain to throw water on the fire. The Count turned, seeing this disaster, made a circle, and returned to the porch. He saw the letter from Donato that he had thrown onto the ground. He picked it up and screamed in agony towards the sky in desperation and fury. A massive roll of thunder followed the scream, as if God was telling him to be quiet and suffocating the echo.

The garrison captain came over to the Count, who was on one knee on the ground, letter in his right hand. He asked timidly, "What do we do with the dead animals, Your Highness?"

The Count only turned his head and then stood up with bloodshot eyes. "Imbecile! If you had been doing your duty, how could anyone penetrate this fortress? It's supposed to be impregnable!"

The captain asked again, "My Count—what do you want to do with the dead animals?"

The Count drew his sword. "What else, burn them with your body for your negligence!"
He raised his sword high and swung with all his might, decapitating the captain. His head rolled in the mud

between the legs of some of the soldiers, who were frozen by this scene while others continued to try and extinguish the flaming wagon, some spilling water as it distracted them. The Count looked at that next officer. "What is your name?"

"Lieutenant Martinez, my Count."

"You will now be the captain of the garrison. You will find the rebel, Donato del Marmol, and I don't want any excuses, or it will be *your* head next. Understand?" The young man gulped and nodded as he looked at the head of his former captain in the mud. He didn't even dare to reply to the Count, who screamed, "Do you understand?!"

He nodded and said weakly, "Yes, sir, my Count."

"Louder!"

"Yes, sir, my Count!"

Not far away from there, still inside the compound near the palace, Donato penetrated the slave barracks in silence. Stealthily to avoid waking anyone else, he stole to the end of the barracks where slaves slept in hammocks on either side secured by a center post and the wall of the building. There was a thin curtain at the end to screen off one hammock, the quarters, such as they were, of the head slave, the strongest and most respected of the slaves. He opened it slowly and went inside. The head slave had small privileges such as screened off quarters, better food, and the ability to go into town. He directed them all, and if any slave had to be punished, he would be the one to hold the whip.

A black man with a thick beard of enormous stature slept there. Donato put his revolver to the man's head, waking him up, and forcing him to get out of his comfortable hammock. Donato felt like he knew him. He leaned into his ear, "Antonio Maceo, if you want to continue to be in the world of living, get out of your hammock and make no noise, please."

The giant, muscular black slave opened his eyes. They bulged out in curious surprise, widening even more as he recognized Donato. He slowly stood up and held his hands high to show he was surrendering. As he stood up, his height was even more impressive. "Master Donato—what are you doing here at this hour of the night?" He spoke with respect and in submission, but his face was worried.

"I need you to take me to the Egyptian slave, Claudia, the preferred woman of your master, the Count of Balmaceda."

Antonio nodded in agreement. "Very well. You didn't need to put a gun to my head to ask me for that. Do you mind if I put some clothes on?"

Donato was not expecting such willing compliance. A little surprised not just by the pleasant response but the rapid agreement of Antonio to do what was asked of him and knowing that such voluntary help would cost him his head if they were discovered. Without hesitation, Donato took his revolver away from Antonio's head and put it away to show his reciprocated trust. This became the beginning of the great and honorable friendship between the two men. Donato del Marmol y Tamayo would pass into history as a major-general, taking with him as a lieutenant Antonio Maceo; the pair remained friends for the rest of their lives. After many battles with Donato, Antonio on his own merits earned a name as one of the greatest generals in the patriotic independence war to free the island of Cuba from the Spanish Crown.

Donato del Marmol silently followed Antonio Maceo in complete, absolute trust. The two men arrived in the slave women's barracks in search of the Egyptian slave, the last possession Donato had in his plans to remove from that malicious murderer, the Count of Balmaceda. As they both arrived in the barracks, Antonio stopped. He said, "You should not come with me inside the barracks. You don't know what Claudia's reaction will be when you tell her whatever you have in mind to do." Antonio continued to try to reason with Donato, explaining that if they were discovered inside the barracks, the head slave there could be given the excuse that the Count had ordered him to take Claudia to him, but only if he were alone. He had done this many times before without causing any suspicion. However, if Donato were inside with him, he would have no excuse to give.

Donato understood the reason as being both prudent and intelligent and agreed. "No problem." He pointed to a Ceiba tree near the barracks. Though these trees were large, sometimes growing well over 200 feet in height, this one was massive, a patriarch of its species. Considered a sacred tree, they were allowed to grow without trimming, landscaping, or being cut down. "I'll wait for you under that tree."

They parted, Donato wishing Antonio luck. Antonio thanked him and went into the barracks. Donato walked to the tree, picked up some dried branches and placed them on the roots of the tree to serve as a cushion. The tree itself served as a massive umbrella, protecting him from the chilly sprinkles which still sporadically sprayed in the night, occasionally light, occasionally heavier, sometimes an actual rain shower. The winds of the hurricane were still increasing in intensity, showing the storm had not yet fully passed. Donato took some more branches and placed them around to make his improvised seat more comfortable. As soon as he sat down, he jumped back up, finding a large thorn which had poked him. Very carefully, he removed the thorn from the branch and tossed it away. A little more carefully, he sat down again. Finally, he found the comfort he was seeking and smiled in satisfaction. He took his gold pocket watch out and checked the time—it was now three am. He smiled once more, because his plan was going very well up to now. Even though the night was still young, he still had some hours of darkness, which was his best ally in his venture next to the storm itself. He had worried as he sat beneath that tree, that he might have to rush to get out of this dangerous and impregnable fortress as soon as possible, before daylight took him by surprise. His life depended on it, and the life of his family as well, for if he perished, they would be exposed to the malice of this unscrupulous assassin. But with plenty of time, his worries lessened.

  A few minutes passed, and there was still no Claudia and Antonio. He pulled out his pocket watch again, and saw it was three fifteen, and wondered what was taking so long. He stood up impatiently, a little anxiety mixed in. He stared at the barracks door. Seven minutes later, his worries multiplied. Perhaps something hadn't gone well. Perhaps the guards would appear at any moment to arrest him. Two things answered his fears: the first one was that Antonio had betrayed him; the second, equally possible, was that the head slave in charge of that barracks, was suspicious of Antonio. Holding him there, someone had been sent to the palace to verify Antonio's story. The curious thing was that he hadn't seen anyone come out of the door of the building; his eyes had been glued to it the entire time.

His impatience grew by the minute, and he reacted by walking towards his right, looking at the back door which led to the latrines. At that moment, Donato's worry turned to joy as he saw Antonio and Claudia leaving by the back door, and not by the front as he had expected. He patted himself on his back, for if he hadn't moved from his previous position, he would have never seen them. Full of satisfaction, something caught his attention a few feet from the Ceiba tree: Claudia was bringing what looked like a small bundle tied up in a shawl. That was strange; he had never mentioned to Antonio what his intentions or plans were with Claudia.

Before he could even ask any of the questions which seethed in his brain, when Claudia came close enough, she parted her long, beautiful hair from one side of her face and revealed a black eye and swollen chin. With tears in her eyes, she embraced Donato, taking him completely by surprise, and said, "God bless you, master Don Donato. You have become my savior on this dark hurricane torn night and saved my soul. I was already thinking of taking my life, and I know that those who do don't go to Heaven." She pulled away from her breast a small floral handkerchief and unwrapped it, showing six seeds to Donato. "One of these seeds is enough to kill an elephant."

Donato shook his head, thinking about the strange joke destiny was playing on him. This entire time he had thought the most difficult part of his plan against the Count would be convincing Claudia to leave her master. He had even thought he might have to use force to accomplish it, and was prepared to do it, even using the revolver. This now turned out to be the easiest part of his venture.

Claudia had tears of joy and gratitude in her eyes. Emotionally, she embraced Donato. "Last night I came to this tree at the start of this hurricane, as is the custom in Egypt. I prayed to Jesus to liberate me from this filthy, malevolent master who is a sexual deviant who never made love with me. He took pleasure in introducing all kinds of vegetables into my vagina because he is impotent and took joy in seeing a woman being hurt. He would do this so violently that he made me bleed down there." She moved her hair away from her face again. "And when I resisted and fought with him, this is what I get. I've seen you, master Donato, at many of the parties in the Count's palace and spoken with your slaves. I know you're a great master, generous and full of love for everyone. I don't care where you want to take me, but I only ask you to take me far away from that monster the Count of Balmaceda."

Donato caressed the bruised face with the back of his hand. He bent down and gave her a chaste kiss on her eye and cheek. He said tenderly and full of care and love, "I promise you that you will never be at the mercy of this unscrupulous, deranged man. He will never be able to lay a finger on your skin for as long as I live."

Antonio stood nearby and heard the conversation. "How is it possible that men with this enormous cowardice? Maybe he doesn't have a mother? Where did he come from?"

Donato smiled. "My friend Antonio, he might have a mother, but that he could be a son of a jackal; and remember, like a demon, they will devour their own sons. What else can you expect from such a man that would do this to a woman?"

Chapter 22: Donato Goes Into Exile

Antonio took a couple of steps toward Donato. He spoke humbly, in a tone of supplication. "Master Don Donato, if you will accept me as one of your slaves, I promise you that I will be loyal to you unto death. I don't want to run away into the jungle and become a *negro cimarron*[12]. I will be your most loyal slave; I only ask one thing in return. After all, I know you're taking a big risk, but I won't cost you anything. I haven't seen my family for many years, and I miss them horribly."

Donato asked in wonder, "Do you know where your family is?"

Antonio nodded. "Yes, yes. The Count of Balmaceda has them on the other side of the island in his other mansion on the extreme Occidental, in his pineapple plantation in the village of Artemisia in the province of Pinar del Rio."

Donato furrowed his eyes in confusion in his countenance. "Why did the Count send your family so far away from you?"

Antonio shook his head with a guilty expression on his face. He stammered, "Everything, unfortunately, is my fault." This took both Donato and Claudia by surprise. Antonio added, "The Count of Balmaceda surprised me in bed with his favorite love, Yamina, and in order to punish

---

[12] Runaway black

me severely he condemned me to never seeing my family again. I was very lucking to keep my head on my shoulders, but he needed me to handle the other slaves." He caressed his neck with his index finger and thumb. His resignation showed on his face. "But I'm very repentant for my sexual weakness, and I miss my family miserably. I want with all my heart to reunite with them one day. I don't want to die without having the opportunity to ask for their forgiveness for what I did. I didn't think twice about it until it provoked the fury of the Count. I know the reason he separated my family and me is because he had to set an example. At the same time, I don't think it's fair to separate me from my family for life." His face grew sorrowful as he bit his lower lip. The sorrow became more apparent in his voice. "Unfortunately, Yamina didn't have the same luck I had, because the Count cut off her head and then hung it over the entryway to the women's barracks for several weeks until it began to stink. That was the punishment he inflicted for her infidelity." He shook his head again. He grimaced. "The Count doesn't take into consideration his own infidelities he's committed daily for years behind his wife's back."

    Donato shook his head in clear disgust as he listened to Antonio's account of the punishment of that poor woman, adding another criminal act to the daily acts committed by the Count toward everyone else, including his slaves. He noticed how sad Antonio was and the tears which welled in his eyes. He put his hand on Antonio's shoulder in compassionate affection. "I hope, Antonio, that one day you will be able to forgive yourself and forget this horrible incident. I see a day not far off where we will put aside our revenge and hatred, and all these perverse injustices being committed today, not just in Cuba but around the world, will at last come to an end. We will all be able to live in a better world, in a humanitarian society where slavery will no longer exist."

Antonio smiled ironically. "My master, your beautiful words sound like music to my ears." He scratched his head with his right hand in confusion. He smiled slightly and asked curiously, "If your dream actually comes true one day, who then will do all the manual work that now us slaves do?"

Donato responded with a small smile of his own. He pointed to Antoino. "Maybe, after all, you guys. Or whoever wants to accept the responsibility to do this kind of work. But this time they will be paid to do it. Black, whites, Chinese, whoever wants to do it. You will do the work as free men and women, not as slaves, sometimes being abused and poorly fed. With a rational limit to the number of hours each day for work, allowing sufficient time for whoever does this kind of intensive work to rest, like a human being, with his wife and children, and not like animals."

Antonio loved what he heard and grinned broadly. Pride and gratitude shown in his face at the beautiful answer he received from the man who was supposed to be his new owner. "Master Donato del Marmol, I can assure you that men like you don't exist any longer these days. If we looked for some more like you, I think we could count them on the fingers of one hand and still have fingers left over. If I doubted before what I have heard from your own slaves, who without exception speak so highly of you, after hearing you, I have none anymore. I can corroborate from your conviction and sincerity that I have chosen a very dignified man to be my master. Maybe my leader, if your dream becomes a reality one day, and I become a free man, for I will follow you to my death, if necessary."

Donato smiled in satisfaction and embraced the large black man, who was now both his slave and friend. Claudia had listened patiently, enjoying the conversation between the two men and impressed by the embrace between the two men. It was the first time she had ever seen a master hug a slave. Completely touched by that affectionate gesture, she asked permission to hug them both. They embraced for a few seconds, but then they heard dogs barking and howling in the distance.

Donato reacted immediately and broke the embrace. He said in a low voice, "Follow me very close. We have to leave here immediately. Something is not right—those dogs should be hunting for me somewhere else, not here inside the castle. It's possible that when we get close to the wall for our exit that we'll have to be extremely careful. The guard shelters there are well-camouflaged to catch anyone by surprise. I have information that they have strict orders to shoot to kill at anything trying to enter or exit the castle perimeter unless it's done at the main entryway. Scaling this wall is considered a high crime by the Count and the penalty for that is death."

The rain and winds began to slacken. It appeared that the hurricane was finally passing away from the island. Donato looked around as they rapidly made their way towards the wall. He glanced at his pocket watch and saw that it was 3:45 am. He said, "We have to pick up the pace. Dawn will be here soon, and darkness is our best ally right now. We'll lose that soon, especially if the hurricane is passing, as it appears. After that storm, the darkness will be replaced with a beautiful tropical sunny day, something I would normally love. But not today—this would be fatal for our plans." He crossed himself. "God, please don't abandon us on our final journey." His mind filled with faith and optimism, he mentally asked God for the hurricane last for a few more hours, something he never asked before. They just needed a little more time to escape from the castle and get far away from the murderous assassin.

    The barking of the dogs got closer, nearer than Donato wished. He signaled to his companions with his right arm to follow him. This time he simply asked them to put the greatest distance possible between them and their pursuers.

    Not far away, the newly promoted Captain Martinez had taken very seriously the command of the Count to bring him the heads of Donato del Marmol and any associates. Martinez mobilized the entire guard of the castle, turning out the barracks. Horses dragged several field cannons and a gatling gun. This took a little extra time for an inexperienced captain, which benefited Donato and his companions. But the captain had received news from the head female slave of that barracks that she had silently witnessed Antonio's entrance and exit from the barracks with Claudia. Instead of sounding the alarm, like she was supposed to do, frightened by a confrontation, she took the option to keep silent without risking herself and later to take the credit for reporting the escape she had witnessed to the captain of the guard. Martinez misunderstood her message and so had turned out the guard initially inside the castle itself, and not on the grounds outside. His inexperience wasted precious time putting together a group of trackers with dogs, using one of the articles of clothing belonging to Claudia that had been forgotten under her pillow in her hammock. Now the dogs followed her scent.

    Antonio, Donato, and Claudia had an advantage in distance, and the young Captain Martinez already very well from recent experience the tenacity and extraordinary military strategic planning possessed by Donato. With the image of his predecessor's head rolling in the mud, he didn't want to pursue Donato until he had overwhelming superiority, not just in men but also artillery to ensure the success of his mission.

The howling of the pack of dogs was getting closer and closer. They reached the rope dangling near the fallen eucalyptus tree which had earlier nearly cost him his life. He gestured for his friends to halt, pointing to his right at the guard shelter. He put his finger to his lips to indicate total silence. Donato crouched down and put his ear to the ground to listen how far away their pursuers were. He motioned for his friends to hide beneath the trunk of the tree and among its branches.

They hid there for several seconds. Donato pulled his small revolver from one pocket, and some bullets from another. Antonio and Claudia watched him in worry, not missing a move he made. He loaded it and slowly pointed the revolver towards the dark sky, as if he were counting. At the same time, he slowly lay back on the branches of the tree. As he had predicted, an enormous alpha dog, a black German shepherd with yellow-green eyes flew through the air towards Claudia, hurdling over them. The eyes of the beast were lit up by the lighting which illuminated the entire scene. Unfortunately, Claudia panicked and screamed. Donato fired, hitting the beast, which, mortally wounded, fell heavily almost on top of them.

In the distance, more gunfire rang out. The rat-a-tat-tat of the gatling gun was heard as well, while the panicked guards fired wildly in all directions. Several holes from the gatling gun ripped into the guard shelter nearby. The yelp of the mortally wounded dog didn't help their mindset any, either.

As Donator reloaded his pistol, he moved forward to put it to the head of the agonized dog, which still was trying to regain its feet as he lay virtually at the feet of Antonio and Claudia. The dog's eyes were open, breathed in agony and then closed its eyes. Donato caressed his fingers over the dog's head. "I'm sorry, my friend, when you return to this world, try to find a better master that you can serve with dignity."

The light in the guard shelter shone out into the darkness as the door opened. The guard juggled awkwardly with kerosene lamp and leash to his dog awkwardly in his left hand as he tied the dog to the door. He held the lamp high as he tried to see what was going on outside with all the commotion and was frightened by the sudden large weapon fire he had been subjected to. He only had a revolver in his hand in his right hand. He yelled in panic, "Who's there? Come out of there, whoever you are! Why are you shooting at me?" The tied-up dog barked furiously.

Revolver in hand, he heard some noise in the direction of the large-scale firing. He began to fire in that direction blindly. A few seconds later, a cannonball hit the shelter, the collateral effect blowing the guard, dog, and kerosene lamp into pieces. Another cannon shot landed near to where Donato and his friends lay in concealment, forcing them to leave their hiding place behind the tree trunk and run in a different direction. A third cannon fired, this time hitting the wall, proving to be the most opportune one of all by blowing a breach in the wall.

Donato looked at his friends and they all shared a smile, since now they didn't have to climb the wall to get out. The young, inexperienced captain had given them a door to facilitate their exit. Quickly, they left the perimeter of the castle as they heard more cannons being fired off in different directions. In the darkness the artillery and gatling gun sounded in the distance like the American Civil War was now in Cuba, and a full battle was raging behind those walls.

Antonio yelled, "*Vive Cuba libre*[13]!"

Donato smiled. "Not yet. We'll be free soon."

They ran, following Donato in the direction towards the huge mango tree. Joyfully, they saw Donato's servants and friends waiting impatiently for them next to the coach. Camila hugged Donato when she saw him.

"We were very worried," she said. "We thought you had been caught by the Count's guards."

"Never," Donato answered. "They will catch me dead, and no other way." He introduced his companions to Camila and Tomaso. He gave instructions to Camila as to how she was supposed to accommodate the new arrivals in the hacienda, far out of view of curious visitors, especially anyone who might possibly be a spy of the Count of Balmaceda. He explained to them that if anyone discovered Claudia in his hacienda that it would be proof enough for the Count to destroy the entire structure and everyone there for being accomplices to the fugitives.

---

[13] Long live a free Cuba!

Camila understood perfectly and replied with a big smile and more relaxed, "My master, we will do exactly as you ask." Both Camila and Tomaso were very happy and proud of their master as they saw that his skills and savvy completely surpassed their expectations. As Donato had assured them both, no one had been hurt in this venture if they had followed his instructions to the letter.

Claudia got into the coach next to Camila, while Antonio climbed up on top of the coach with Tomaso. Tomaso gave Antonio his jacket, scarf, and beret to disguise him to look more like a security guard. Tomaso said, "You will be the coachman and guard of the carriage."

Antonio smiled and saluted him. By now the rain had stopped completely, and the first light of dawn was creeping up over the horizon, illuminating a beautiful tropical morning.

Not far away, in the port of the city of Santiago de Cuba, in one ship a very effeminate and flamboyant character was vomiting all the contents of his stomach into the scuppers. The ship had arrived in the middle of the night and everyone who was not used to sea travel was seasick from the erratic movement of the ship from the winds of the hurricane. This individual was clearly one such person. He was the Duke de Borbón, who had been commissioned by the Spanish Crown to inspect the work of the Count of Balmaceda on the island[14]. The shipping of goods and minerals had diminished considerably, an obvious signal that the Count was not properly administrating the interests of the Crown. This strange character was not really in the best humor after his

---

[14] Having left Spain before the Glorious Revolution of 1868 broke out, he had no knowledge of the chaos he had left behind.

voyage, which had not only been caught by surprise by the furious hurricane but was also unused to being forced into such a trip.

He took a jug and poured some water into the wash basin of his cabin. He began to wash his face with a high-quality soap he unwrapped and meticulously opened. He dried his face with a small towel and put on his feathered hat. He pulled the bellpull several times to ring the bell, which rang agitatedly. The door opened, and a huge black man with a golden turban and large earrings in both ears, entered with a serious expression and submissive attitude. "Yes, my master. What do you need?"

The Duke de Borbón asked, "Simon, is everything ready for us to disembark?"

Simon put his left hand to his abdomen and bowed. "Yes, my master. Everything is ready—your coach and everything else is ready to go."

The Duke said in an irritated tone, "OK, Simon—let's get the hell once and for all off of this ship."

Simon didn't smile and held the door open until the Duke passed. As he left, six carabineers in uniform who had been on guard snapped to attention. After they disembarked, the Duke asked Simon, "Where are my girls?"

Simon said, "They're coming. They're being given a bath. There they are."

In the distance, another black slave, also with a golden turban, was descending the plank onto the pier. In either hand, she held two Afghan hounds. Their long hair was golden and black, with partially black fur over their faces on their aristocratically pointed noses. They walked delicately as if they owned the ground they walked on. They were so well-trained, that even though they were excited to see their master, they maintained their composure. Even as the Duke knelt to receive them with open arms, they walked towards him, their tails wagging furiously as he kissed him. He put his hands in his pocket to give each of them a treat. He said firmly yet kindly, "My queens, let's go to a new adventure into the unknown, following in the steps of that pioneer Christopher Columbus, in our own classified exploration of this now already famous Spanish possession, the beautiful island of Cuba." He smiled broadly. The dogs obviously had a positive effect on his personality, as his demeanor transformed in a matter of seconds from gloomy to cordial.

    The Duke snapped his fingers and pointed with his right hand to signal the two dogs to stand up. Alika, the beautiful Nigerian black woman with the turban, leaned over to disconnect the 24-carat gold chain attached to the dogs' diamond collars around their necks. This time, the Duke clapped with both hands and pointed to the door of the coach, which had been held open all this time by the coachman, who waited patiently and respectfully. It looked like a ritual the Duke was accustomed to doing everywhere he went. He was very proud of both his dogs' excellent training and manners. The first dog leaped into the coach, as he said, "Isabella, go." Isabella sat on the cushioned seat in the back. Then he said, "OK, Alika, go." Alika climbed into the coach and sat next to Isabella. "OK, Cristina." She had been waiting, even though she was unchained, until the Duke told her to get inside.

    The beautiful black Nigerian woman put a hand on the necks of each of the dogs as the Duke applauded the performance of his preferred pets. He pulled out more treats and gave them to his dogs. Both dogs moved their heads down as they bowed along with the slave to the Duke, who now was climbing into the carriage. He sat on the seat before them with a big smile as one of the guards closed the door. The Duke pulled a small cord which rang a bell in the coachman's box, and the carriage took off, leaving the port behind with its precious cargo.

  The coachman had a man next to him with a musket by his shoulder. Standing on either side in the back, to the right and left, two other soldiers held on by a leather belt as they guarded the rear of the coach. Two horses in front of the coach, with two more guards marching in front of the vehicle, and two more horses were tethered to the rear of the carriage, followed by two more soldiers. It was clear that this man was very high up in the hierarchy in the interests of the Spanish Crown. He must have been sent either to replace the Count or bring back a thorough report of what was going on.

  Once they left the city, the roads, the soft, muddy roads slowed the carriage's pace to a crawl. Soon they encountered Donato's coach coming in the opposite direction. Moving slowly to avoid splashing mud onto the coaches, they approached each other, close enough to reach through the windows and shake hands. Donato's carriage had to stop, because part of the road was flooded out by one of the rivers. Donato and his company were petrified the moment they saw the other carriage with all the soldiers. They immediately thought that it belonged to the Count who was looking for them. Everyone held their breath as they watched the carriage pass them very, very slowly. Though it only lasted a few minutes, to them it felt like hours. The sun was up, and they not only had one of Balmaceda's slaves inside the carriage, but Antonio in the open in the coachman's box, and the weapons and artillery fire could still be heard in the distance, which had attracted the Duke's attention as well. Martinez, lacking the military experience, was continuing to fire his cannons erratically in each direction in an attempt to make sure that Donato and his party were killed and in fear for himself of getting ambushed by Donato and have the same fate as the lead dog.

    As they passed each other, Donato could see who was inside the other vehicle and bowed respectfully to the Duke as his soul returned to his body when he received a similar nicety from the Duke. Donato knew him at once because he had been with de Borbón during the New Year's and Christmas parties hosted by the Count of Balmaceda. He could see the perspiration on Camila's face and her trembling lips in a nervous panic. He leaned over to her and gently with his right hand looked into her eyes and squeezed one of her knees with a smile. In a voice of care and love, he said, "It's not what we're thinking, we always assume the worst. I'm guilty of that, too. I know this man. He's one of the representatives of the Spanish Crown, the Duke of Borbón."

    They finally passed each other, and Camila breathed a deep sigh of relief. She took the cross on a gold chain she had around her neck out from beneath her clothing and thanked Jesus as she kissed it and crossed herself while looking Heavenward. She said brokenly, "Thank you, God." She took her right hand to her chest with a small smile. She looked around at everyone. "I think for a second that a small beating of my heart would give us away. That's why I stopped breathing."

Claudia smiled and said respectfully, "You should not be ashamed of yourself because, believe me, I believe everyone without exception did what you did. I beg your pardon, Don Donato, if you didn't stop like we did."

Donato smiled and replied, "I would be lying if I said that I didn't stop breathing as well. For a few seconds as we passed that carriage with all those carabineers, the only thing which crossed my mind was what was in yours—that the Count himself was hunting us. I saw very clearly in my head how all of our heads would roll on this muddy road. Unfortunately, by the force of nature I let loose a tremendous amount of gas induced by all this stress. It felt to me like a gatling gun, but very silent. The extremely horrible stench killed my nose, and I beg your pardons most sincerely for the weakness of my stomach."

Camila exploded in a burst of laughter. "I'm sorry, master Donato—I'm not laughing at you, but I'm laughing with you for your sincerity and honesty. You took away a concern which was weighing on my mind. I could not smell your gas because I could only smell mine! My own bad odor probably overcame yours. I was tempted to check my panties, but with it being so tight in the coach I couldn't find a discreet way to do it. As you made your confession, I carefully slid my hand along the seat to make sure I hadn't soiled myself."

All three burst out in laughter at this point, just as the Duke's carriage left them behind. If he had any suspicions, they were surely laid to rest by the merriment.

Moments later, the Duke arrived at the massive iron gates of the castle of the Count of Balmaceda. The guards at the entry recognized the emblems adorning both sides of the coach with the arms of the Spanish Crown and ran to open the gates. As they tried to open them, a huge cannon hit the guard shelter by the gate, blowing it into pieces, throwing the gate and debris from the wall through the air, killing nearly everyone, including the Duke's horses.
The Duke, in shocked incomprehension about what was going on, opened the door and jumped into the bushes just before another cannon fired, hitting the coach and smashing it into pieces, which flew through the air. The third explosion hit right in the middle of the same area. Debris fell on the Duke as he settled into the bushes. Alika's head rolled almost to his feet, followed by the head of Simon nearly landing in his arms, causing him to scream in panic. He screamed again so loud it might have been heard miles away. He put both hands over his ears and kept silent as he cried like a small child when he saw Cristina's body lying in two pieces. As he started to rise up to find cover among the bougainvillea along the edge of the fortress, he tripped and fell on his face in front of the torso and head of Cristina, muddying his clothes and face. It was too much for this aristocrat, who had never seen such a horrible scene before. Both hands still over his ears, he shook his head. He tried to scream again, but no sound came from his throat. He continued to shake his head and weep, he walked with his shredded clothing, this time looking for someone alive. He managed to ask, "Where in the hell is the Count of Balmaceda?" His voice cracked, and the sepulchral silence of death was his only response.

The cannon fire continued to fall close to him, but he was numbed to it by now. The gatling gun could still be heard firing in the distance, but it suddenly cut off as if someone had ordered it to cease firing. His beautiful coach he had brought from Spain was utterly destroyed. The beautiful Arabian horses were mutilated with pieces of iron from the gate sticking through their bodies. He walked through the debris, trembling, and shook his head in despair. He came over to what had been the roof of the coach and heard a noise. Desperately, he lifted the debris, but half of one of the horse's bodies lay over the corner. He finally raised it completely, and in the midst of this horrible scene his heart leapt in joy as he clapped his right hand to his mouth in surprise. His other dog, Isabella, was by some miracle still alive. Due to the rains a small hole had formed in the soft mud of the road and the roof, instead of smashing her had merely pushed her into the hole and sheltered her from the impact. Muddy but alive and unharmed, the dog jumped out of the hole. He checked her over and saw that nothing was wrong with her at all and opened his arms to embrace his pet with tremendous joy in his voice. "Isabella, God blessed me that I'm not alone on this island with these savage assassins."

  He looked around the devastation of the horrible scene. He knelt down in the mud, no longer caring about his costly clothes, and said a prayer of thanks to God for being alive and having one pet with him. One sleeve of his shirt hung from his arm by a thread which bore the arms of the Spanish Crown. Angrily, he ripped it off and looked at the crest. He shook his head in angry regret. He threw the sleeve onto the muddy road in disgust and ground it under his boot angrily. He said to himself, "I should never have accepted the commission to come to this savage wilderness." He still had no idea what was really going on, but he assumed it was an armed rebellion taking place inside their own forces.

Before what used to be the main gate into the castle, the Duke was undecided which way to go—whether he should return to the port or go inside the castle. He took the easier option to go to the castle. This at least would further his mission, which required him to investigate what was going on in the island and report it to the Crown. He was no longer the fine aristocrat—with one pants leg hanging loose, covered in mud and blood, with his muddy dog, the pair looked more like hobos.

Fortunately, they didn't have to walk far. The distance from the gate to the castle was a long drive as it was, and now he was on foot beneath the tropical sun which was now shining. In the distance, he could see the banners blowing in the breeze from the castle's towers. He walked with his head down in humiliation. When he raised his head again, he saw a coach approaching in the distance. Given the bad experience he had just suffered, the Duke had doubts as to who it might belong to. He looked around for some refuge. There were some bougainvillea bushes in the center between the two drives that he felt he could conceal himself in until he knew who the approaching people were. He embraced Isabella as they hid in the center divider until the coach came close, and he recognized the Count of Balmaceda.

He yelled with all the strength he had left, "Count! It's me! Stop!"

It worked, and the coach stopped a short distance away. He jumped out of the bushes with his dog. The Count did not get out, but several guards approached to identify him, their muskets trained on him. As the Duke saw this, he became infuriated. "I'm the Duke de Borbón, idiots! Put those weapons away!"

The youngest guard, a skinny boy, answered, "Yes, and I'm the Queen of Spain."

Even more infuriated by the mocking comment, replied, "Imbecile! I will send you to the worst dungeons all of Spain!"

The Count heard the strong threat and recognized the effeminate voice of the Duke. He opened the door and jumped out to approach the miserable aristocrat. He looked at him more closely. "Your Highness, the Duke de Borbón?"

The Duke replied indignantly, "No, the Virgin Mary! What in the hell is happening here? What kind of administrator are you? I regret they sent me to this toilet and will regret it for the rest of my life. Are we having an armed rebellion? They blew up my coach, killed my servants, my guards, my horses, and one of my favorite dogs!" His face was red with fury, and as he mentioned the death of Cristina, he broke down and began to sob.

The Count, understanding the gravity of the situation as well as the trouble he was in, put into practice all of his cunning to try and conceal the reality of what happened. He replied firmly, "We don't have any rebels here or any kind of rebellion. It's only a misunderstanding by a very inexperienced young imbecile of an officer hoping to obtain glory by attempting to capture one single rebel. He nearly destroyed the compound by firing cannons within it and has already been beheaded for his stupidity. I personally executed him." He noticed the Duke was still furious and looked at him with murder in his eyes. The Count changed his tone and pulled out his elegant handkerchief from his immaculate clothing and offered it to the Duke. "Why don't you clean yourself up?" The Duke swallowed his anger down and accepted the handkerchief. He wiped his eyes and muddy face, blew his nose, and handed the handkerchief back to the Count, who refused the soiled rage. "You can keep it, don't worry," he said.

    This only infuriated the Duke more as he looked at the handkerchief he held gingerly between two fingers, feeling like he was being treated like a leper. More humiliated, he threw the handkerchief to the ground. "Never have I received such improper treatment anywhere in the world as I have received on this godforsaken island. Please, Count of Balmaceda, take me to the castle where I can bathe, clean myself up, and get decent clothes to wear, since I lost all my luggage. And have someone wash my dog. I will return to Spain as soon as possible."

    The Count replied in surprise, "But Your Highness, you're supposed to be here in Cuba for at least two or three weeks. Give us the opportunity to show you the extraordinary places we have here and what I've achieved for the Crown, not only with the natives but also in agriculture, huge plantations of tobacco, sugar cane, pineapple, mango, and other tropical fruits."

    The effeminate Duke now leaned over and pointed at the Count's face with his muddy fingers. He replied with a cynical smile, "I've already seen enough and more than sufficient disaster which I will never forget for the rest of my life. My two- or three-week trip, right now, in this instant, has been reduced to two or three days—that is assuming I don't find a ship before then to return to Spain and submit my report of this most horrible experience to the Crown."

  The Count gulped as he heard the Duke's indignation. He remembered at that moment the letter from Donato del Marmol. *"Even in the light of the sun, in plain daylight, in the shadows of the bushes or a large, healthy tree next to you, my eyes will be watching you."* Forgetting he was still before the Duke, he said, "Goddamned rebels!"

  The Duke de Borbón said cynically as he raised his right hand with his index up, "Oh, now the truth comes to light. It's not just a young officer with no experience; it's not a misunderstanding. It's the damned rebels that is the real reason for these disasters."

  The Count looked at the Duke as if he wanted to kill him, but kept himself under control.

  Not very far away, Donato and his friends were still traveling in the coach. Tomaso pulled it to a stop near the ocean, where Dr. Muñoz waited near a little boat with two merchant sailors. They helped pile Donato's luggage into the small boat. Donato embraced his friends as well as Antonio and Claudia. He climbed into the boat, and the two sailors began to row out to the ship which hove-to close offshore, waiting for them to take Donato into exile.

  The Spanish Crown put a high price on his head after this incident, and though they had tried to kill him multiple times, all attempts had failed. After he returned to Cuba as a Major-General fighting for Cuban independence, he won many battles, and despite the Crown's best efforts could never lay hands on him.

As Donato looked back at his friends on the beach, they grew smaller as he neared the ship. He also saw in the distance his beautiful palm trees in the country he had been forced to abandon. The future at this point was uncertain, but the memories of stories told to him by his paternal grandfather, handed down from his father. Donato shook his head as he remembered how much suffering they had endured, always trying to defend the principles of freedom and decency for generations now. That suffering not only came from their enemies, but also his own side, as he suffered now, being obliged by ambitious and unscrupulous men in power to leave his family behind and his recently born son, Julio Antonio del Marmol.

He memorized the image of his baby with blue eyes and red hair which had been born with an extraordinary resemblance to his bloodline which had been passed down in each generation. The story of his great-grandfather, Don Francisco del Marmol, as told by his grandfather and father, who was the governor of the important port of Venezuela of La Guaira in the state of Vargas, a noble and decent man who was protector of the humblest. He was unjustly, with many of his cabinet who were equally decent and great men, put in chains, humiliated by a group of rebels under the command of Simon Bolivar, and forced to dig their own graves before the eyes of the whole town. He had been told of the grisly scene when they had been pushed alive into the fire.

Those stories told of his ancestors all flowed through his memory and would remain there forever. Now he grew more resolute because he had experienced in his own flesh the suffering and persecution not just of himself but also of his compatriots and families. "My God, I'm doomed to go through these things, too," he said to himself. Two involuntary tears ran down his cheeks. He tried quickly to discretely hide them. No one had noticed his emotional state, and he didn't want to show any weakness in front of the sailors. As the sailors carried the luggage up into the ship, Donato was received joyfully by his patriotic friends who were joining him in exile. They had a bucket of ice with a bottle of champagne, which they opened and cheered with him, right hands in the air. After the toast, they all drank from the glasses.

After talking with his friends for a while, he walked to the stern to contemplate the scenery as the island of Cuban disappeared slowly over the horizon. His glass still in hand, he murmured, "My Cuba, today I go into exile with a great and horrible pain in my heart for the loved ones I left behind."

Exilio: Sangre, Jasmines, y Rosas
Mi Cuba hoy te dejo detras y ha mi exilio yo hoy me voy
Mi Cuba con mi corazon dañado por el Tirano opresor que mato nuestro amor
Mi Cuba yo te amo con todo mi corazon con tu caña de azucar tu tabaco y tu ron

Mi Cuba contigo yo quise vivir y morir pero al estranjero hoy yo me voy
Yo te ofresco mi sangre mi bella Cuba con mi vida y mi honor en el medio de mi dolor
Mi Cuba yo hoy te pido perdon con lagrimas en mis hojos al ver tu dolor

Mi Cuba tus rosas se marchitaron tus jasmines ya no brillaron y solo quedaron rotas promesas y
    lagrimas de dolor
Por eso hoy mi Cuba viendo tu completa destruccion con mi corazon desgarrado al exilio hoy yo
    me voy

Exile: Blood, Jasmine, and Roses
My Cuba today I leave you behind and to my exile I leave you today.
My Cuba with my heart damaged by the oppressive tyrant who killed our love.
My Cuba I love you with all my heart with your sugar cane, your tobacco and your rum.

My Cuba with you I wanted to live and die but today I'm leaving to the foreign land
I offer you my blood my beautiful Cuba with my life and my honor in the midst of my pain
My Cuba today I ask for your forgiveness with tears in my eyes when I see your pain
My Cuba your roses withered your jasmines no longer shone and only broken promises and
    tears of pain remained.
That's why today, my Cuba, seeing your complete destruction with my heart torn to exile, today
    I am leaving you.

    Dr. Julio Antonio del Marmol

Chapter 23: The Sacrifice of Bonifacio

Cuba, 2000

    A huge explosion shook our small submarine violently, throwing us against the bulkheads like rag dolls. The last explosion from the depth charge that the Cuban naval ship had exploded almost on top of us, doing irreparable damage, far more than any explosion before. The main pumps for the vessel's oxygen ventilation were disabled—not only could we not ventilate with the outside air while on the surface, but our internal oxygen supply while submerged was completely cut off.

    Bonifacio lost his optimism, and he reached under our seats for some scuba gear. His face grew sad as he handed me a wetsuit. He said, "We have to abandon this ship immediately. We're sending too strong a signal, making us visible on sonar. They have our exact location—it's possible they have the latest sonar equipment from Russia. I'll be the last one to leave." He added with a smirk, "Not because I'm the captain, but also for everyone's safety; I have to blow up this vessel on my way out so that our enemies will think that they've destroyed us along with the sub. Otherwise, they will be waiting for us to surface, one way or another, here or miles from here, to finish us off. We are very close to the coast, maybe ten or fifteen miles. Don't surface until you are about to completely run out of air. They will try to track down each of us, even after I blow up the sub, and they won't stop searching for us for several hours. If they don't have bodies, the only way they can prove they were victorious to their superiors is getting some evidence from the sub that we have been reduced to food for marine life and birds. They'll need a piece of the vessel as proof as well. They will even have to prove how and why they used these explosives, or they'll be in a very questionable and embarrassing situation. These days, because everything is in such short supply and the rations from the government are very strictly enforced. Even the toilet paper 'assigned' to these vessels' sailors gets stolen and taken to their homes and families." Bonifacio looked at his wristwatch. "We have very little time—we should leave this vessel one at a time, every five minutes apart, and then swim in separate directions, keeping each other in eyesight. We have to confuse the sonar of our enemies. This is a very rich area for all kinds of fish, and we need to give them the idea that each of us is some kind of fish, so they don't go after us."

    We suited up after several minutes and in a disciplined manner followed Bonifacio's instructions. At five-minute intervals, we left the submarine one at a time. The depth charges the Cuban ship continued to drop ever more dangerously close to our vessel. I swam a short distance away from Atacia, perhaps between six to ten feet, keeping visual contact with her as best I could in the murky, dark water. As we swam away from the sub, an enormous explosion behind us shook us violently. I checked my watch as a strange ominous feeling filled my thoughts. Sudden agonizing sadness nearly overwhelmed me, as Bonifacio didn't have the time to do what he had planned to do. It appeared that one of those depth charges had hit our vessel directly and blown it into pieces before Bonifacio could get out. I looked and saw pieces of the sub shoot past us at a tremendous speed and understood for a certainty that my previous feelings were for a fact true: our friend had died in his great effort to protect us.

Atacia got close to me. Being an intelligent woman, she knew what I already had deduced. I could see her face through her mask and the two tears rolling down her cheeks as she shook her head in despair. She gestured with her thumb up to indicate she was going to the surface to investigate. I held her by one of her arms and shook my head to convey and used underwater signs to say it would be better for her to continue swimming and that I should surface to see if anything could be done. I continued to signal with my right hand for her to continue swimming, pointing towards the coast. She shook her head in disagreement. She still wanted to go to the surface. It was a moment when I needed to be my most persuasive. I touched my temple with the index finger of my right hand and brought it down to my abdomen, to remind her to think of her pregnant condition. The expression on my face and attitude of my head continued to instruct her to swim towards the coast. These final gestures made her accept my logic and she nodded, signaling that she would continue and meet me ahead.

I nodded and gave her a thumbs up and signaled that I would let her know what I found out. We touched our masks together in an affectionate gesture. I let her go and started to swim towards the surface, following the shadow of the large vessel which was anchored not far from where the sub had been.

I grabbed the anchor chain and used it to guide me to the surface in the shadow of the ship. I gave thanks to God that the large explosion had destroyed a multitude of fish, including a couple of sharks, which made the sea bloody, with chunks of meat floating everywhere. A multitude of birds fed frenetically on the area surrounding the wreck. I saw a dinghy with a small crew from the ship exploring the debris field. I could hear a voice on a bullhorn, possibly the captain, ordering the crew back, there were no possible survivors. "We must have scored a direct hit with that last depth charge."

The sailors returned to the ship, and the boat was hoisted up and on board as the captain ordered the anchor to be raised. I had stayed in my position, partially concealed by their own ship, my mask up onto my forehead to see better as I remained near the anchor chain. As soon as I heard that order, I put my mask back on and swam down even deeper, heading for what was left of the wreckage so I could tell Atacia what I had seen with my own eyes.

As I dove down, I saw in the corner of my mask the birds continuing their feeding frenzy. I thought at that moment of something my father had told me when I was a child on several occasions—never give up or surrender. If a tree falls one can be assured that everyone would look for wood for their fires at home. As I swam among the pieces of dead fish and torn-apart sharks, I noticed something in the water that floated partially submerged. I went closer and was shocked to see clearly that it was the head of Bonifacio, still attached to part of his torso. Birds ate the flesh that was above water. His head bobbed down repeatedly from the weight of the birds landing and taking off as they fought each other over what was left of his shoulder, now hanging by a piece of skin to the neck. I knew there was nothing to do, but my instinct was to pull that portion down for burial later. Without thinking twice, I began to swim in that direction, but when I was four or five feet from it, an enormous shark came out of the darkness, jaws wide open, and snatched it away, right in front of me. I didn't even have a chance to touch the head of my friend Bonifacio. I stopped dead in the water at the sight of the gigantic shark. I reached with my right hand to my waist and pulled the large Commando knife, expecting the shark to come after me next.

Satisfied with what it already had, the shark turned around and swam over my head. I followed its motion, knife in hand, I moved sharply and forcefully in the water to show that I was alive and not easy prey. I had learned in my scuba diving courses that anything one does to scare a shark is only beneficial—never swim away from it, or it will take one of your limbs.

I left the wreckage of the submarine, keeping an eye on that shark as it swam away with the head and partial torso of Bonifacio in its mouth. I understood the value of human life more than ever at that moment. Hours before we had been talking and having a good time, and now my friend was blown apart with his head destined for the stomach of a shark.

I swam back for several hours until I surfaced and saw in the distance some coconut palms and breaking surf on a beach with beautiful white sand. I checked my regulator and saw that I had plenty of oxygen for several more hours. I had not seen any of my friends on my way towards the coast. My experience led me to decide to swim slightly towards the right, looking for a sure and secure place to get out of the water. I found a decent place on a rocky portion of the beach which would allow me to get out of the water without leaving any traces. I looked for a crack in the rocks where I could hide my scuba equipment. I found an appropriate place and covered it with debris and seaweed to camouflage it in case elements from the government checked the area or in case they had an observation point in that place, like they did in multiple areas around Cuba to report to the coast patrols any activity they considered suspicious. I started to worry because there was no sign of my friends anywhere. As I had been swimming towards the coast, I used a zig-zag pattern to see if I could pick any of them up.

I prayed that they were all not dead and had managed to reach land safely. I knew I had to be optimistic, and perhaps the reason I missed them was because of the zig-zag pattern, while they had gone in a straight line, reaching the coast quickly by doing this. They could be under the shade of one of the coconut trees, sipping the sweet milk from one of the nuts as they waited for me.

I looked around as I walked on top of the rocks. I had found a large rock to make sure that the tide wouldn't wash it out to sea or expose my hiding place to our enemies. Simply possessing this type of equipment could bring you before the firing squad in Cuba, where it was allowed only by their navy. They considered possession of any long-distance swimming equipment a high crime. I climbed to a higher position to get a clearer view of the beach a short distance away. I put my right hand over my forehead to shade my eyes from the first rays of the sun. I saw movement not very far away. To my joy, I saw three of my friends, Jimbo, Aurora, and Mama Teca leaving the bushes. From my hiding place, I put both my hands to cup my mouth in preparation to yell to them and alert them to my location. Before I could act on that impulse, however, somebody touched my shoulder and put a hand over my mouth suddenly.

I rapidly whirled and pulled the knife from my waist. If my surprise was great at the shoulder touch, it grew even greater as goose bumps broke out over my body to see with joy the smiling face of Atacia. With the index finger of her left hand over her lips, she was telling me to keep quiet. Not understanding, I spread my hands to show my confusion. She removed a tube from her wetsuit pocket that she still wore. She straightened the tube revealing that it was a small, compact telescope. She pointed toward the rocks our friends were walking towards as she handed it to me. I could see one of the Russian made patrol boats from the government on the opposite side of those rocks. We were on a promontory, and across from us another one with a similar configuration of sand and rocks. The terrain rose sharply at frequent intervals, and as they walked from the bushes the elevated terrain shielded their vision to see the boat. Our friends had no idea they were walking directly into a trap. There appeared to be two guards in the boat, with three others walking along the beach, heading in the same direction our friends were heading. They would eventually intercept each other once past the rocks. The wetsuits they still wore would be enough of a red light for any navy patrol.

As I studied the situation, Atacia asked me the question I didn't want to answer: "What did you discover about my father?" She spoke very softly; in an area like that, the wind and open water carries sound a very long way.

I pulled the telescope away from my eyes and looked at her sadly. I replied with equal softness, "I'm sorry; he didn't get out in time."

Atacia crossed herself as she took her telescope back. "God protect him." There was sadness in her voice as she repeated, "God protect him." She held the telescope to her left eye. "And my God protect the others now."

I said softly, "Yes, you're right. We must always count on God's help—without Him we can't accomplish anything. But if we go back to the Bible, it says that God helps those who help themselves and make their own effort to get out of trouble. We can't sit down and wait for Him to help us if we don't do something."

"What can we do?" she asked, the telescope glued to her left eye.

I climbed down the cliff from where I had left my equipment. I put the air tank back on. "I just need a diversion. Don't take any unnecessary risks, just distract those guards on the beach."

She looked at me in surprise as she opened her arms. "What can I do to create a distraction? What do you want me to do?"

Not wasting any time, I continued to prepare to reenter the water. I raised my right hand high. "Improvise, love. Improvise. I don't know what you can do. Dance in front of them, blow kisses at them. As I've told you many times, improvising has saved my life many times. Anything is better than sitting here. I will try to neutralize at least one of the men in the boat. If I can get the lieutenant in command captured, the others might surrender. Not everyone in the uniform of Cuba is a communist; they were conscripted and had no choice. If I can capture that boat, that will be a new ride to the capital, which is my next step in getting to my destination and maybe completing the mission I came here for in the first place."

Atacia looked at me with a small mischievous smile on her face. Seeing my stress, she calmed herself down. "Go with God and don't worry. I've already come up with something I could do to distract these imbeciles. Try to leave that boat in one piece. If you don't do it for yourself, do it for him." She touched her belly with her right hand, caressing it in a circular motion. "He will need you more than I ever could." She shook her head and asked sarcastically, "Blowing kisses at the guard? Is that one of your crazy ideas? I don't know if this will distract them or not, but until now your crazy ideas have always worked. Let's hope that it will continue that way, and then I will follow you to the ends of the world."

"To the ends of the world without any more objections?" I smiled slightly as well. "Believe me, if you have a better idea at all, you need to tell me quickly. Our friends don't have any time for discussions."

She smiled and came close to me. I was already in the water and ready to go. She knelt down and gave me a kiss on the lips with a big smile, her left hand going behind my neck. "Thank you very much for being the way you are and thinking of others, putting your life at risk to save them, especially those you profess loyalty, friendship, and care. That is called altruism. Please don't ever change. That is one reason why I fell in love with you, love you know, and will love you to my death."

I smiled. "I have enough if you love me until I die, which I will try to avoid for many years to come."

She smiled. "I like that much better."

I pulled my mask down, submerged, and started to swim towards the patrol boat. As I approached it, I lifted my mask slightly out of the water. I could hear Cuban music played at a high volume coming from the stern of the boat. It gave me tremendous joy, since the volume of music would cover any noise I might make as I climbed aboard. I had to circle the boat a few times because I could not see anyone. I couldn't leave the water until I found the two men I had seen through the telescope. It took me a while, and I was worried that Atacia might not be able to hold their attention for long in safety. I needed to find the officer in command to use as a bargaining chip. I couldn't see them anywhere. Finally, I grabbed the edge of the deck in the front of the boat, pulled myself up onto the it, and there they were. I understood why I hadn't seen them until now: one of the two guards was a beautiful, olive-skinned mulatta with large green eyes which I noticed as I saw them face to face. They were having sex on the deck beneath the steering wheel of the boat. Both were completely naked with the clothing spread around them. The lieutenant was having the best time of his life. From the strategic position he was in, he could see through the deck level transparent windscreen the only way on or off the boat.

He had apparently sent his sailors ashore on an exploratory mission while he explored the beautiful body of his subordinate, contrary to the code even of the Cuban navy while on duty. If caught by his superiors, he would be severely punished. However, this young lieutenant clearly thought he had everything under control. If his men returned early, he would be able to keep his anchor deeply buried inside his female sailor without any fear of discovery.

He saw my reflection on the surface of the window, Commando knife in hand, right behind him. The woman was on top of him, and he shoved her off. She rolled on the deck as he tried to reach his pants, where his Makarov pistol was. But too late, as my knife was right at his throat while I held him down with my left hand on his chest. "If you don't want to die, stay still. Do not move." I glanced at the young woman. "That goes for you, too."

The lieutenant understood his position and raised his hands in surrender. I moved to my right slightly, allowing him to stand and walk with me. My knife remained at his throat. I reached with my free hand to take the Makarov and hung the holster on the wheel of the boat. The woman, still naked, froze in position as she tried to cover with her arms her breasts. I tossed her shirt over to her. I pulled the pistol out, made sure it was cocked, and said to her, "Grab some rope and tie him up. Then bring some for me to tie you up as well."

At the same time on the beach, Atacia had stripped completely naked and ran in the direction of the guards, screaming frenetically asking for help. The guards had been questioning Aurora, Jimbo, and Mama Teca. They were taken by surprise at the beautiful, naked woman running towards them. What surprised them even more was that she was screaming, "Help! Cannibals! Cannibals!"

Her face and breasts appeared to be coated in blood. In her right hand she held an enormous shark knife. She was crying as she asked the guards for help. Fascinated and wanting to get close to her, the three guards abandoned our friends and went over towards her and presenting their backs to them. Forty or fifty feet away, Atacia fell to her knees and plunged the knife entirely into the sand next to her leg—her lower body was shielded from their view, so all they could see where her head and upper torso. They would see no danger as they approached her. When they got close, they surrounded her, but their PPS submachine guns hung by their neck straps, untouched.

They tried to calm her down as she continued to scream loudly. They knelt down in their assumption that she was the innocent victim of some predator. Once all three were close to her so she could feel their breath against her skin, she pulled the knife out of the sand and grabbed the sergeant by his neck strap and brought him down. With a rapid motion, she sliced his throat. He brought both hands to his neck in utter disbelief as the blood pumped out through his fingers. He tried to stand but fell back onto his head, while the other two tried to stand up in total surprise, fumbling for their weapons without success. Faster than a Bengal tiger, she pushed both of them onto their backs, one with her left hand while jumping on top of the other and stuck the knife into his chest. She pulled her left hand away from the one man and used it to shove the knife as deep as she could with both hands. The blade pierced his heart, killing him instantly, but not before he screamed in pain.

She jumped back as the other sailor began to regain his footing. His eyes were filled with terror and shock as he watched in paralysis, his submachine gun hanging on his chest. His hands didn't even reach for the firearm. Instead, he raised his hands high in surrender. As Atacia brought her knife out of the downed man's chest to a fountain of blood erupted. She jumped to her feet, the knife dripping blood, her eyes fixed on that last man. They looked at each other for a few seconds, and the man began to cry. In a trembling voice, he said, "I'm not a communist!" He took his thumb to his mouth and kissed it. "I swear on my mother's memory—I'm not a communist. I'm here because I didn't have any other choice when they drafted me. I've been married only one year, and my wife will have a baby in a few weeks. Please don't kill me." Atacia lowered her knife. The man put his hands up towards his neck towards the strap. She raised the knife again, holding it now by the blade in preparation for throwing it. "No, I was going to take it off to give to you." He raised his hands again. She nodded to him, and he leaned down, removing the strap from his neck and dropping the weapon at his feet. He then raised his hands and placed them behind his head.

Mama Teca, Jimbo, and Aurora came in and collected the weapons. Aurora took the shirt of one of the dead guards and draped it over her daughter to cover her body. With tears in her eyes, she hugged her daughter. She pointed to the squad's sergeant. "This abuser wanted to take us to the G-2. He didn't believe our story that we were fishers and wound up here after our boat sank. He called us worms who wanted to leave the country illegally." Aurora in her agitation gave his body a small kick.

Mama Teca pulled some creepers from a coconut tree to bind their captive's hands in front of his chest. They all put the submachine guns around their necks and walked towards where the patrol boat was anchored.

After I made sure that the lieutenant and his subordinate were securely tied, I went to the brough of the patrol boat to leave for my search of my friends—but I saw them approaching through the window. With a huge smile of satisfaction on my face, I could see they had one of the guards with them as a prisoner. Atacia had not only distracted them as I had asked but had also neutralized them, saving me the job I had intended to do next. I wondered what had happened, though, since I only saw one guard. For a moment I thought that they had left the other two tied up on the beach.

Full of joy and avoiding speculation, I greeted them and invited them on board. I looked at Atacia then and congratulated her on a great job, "Where are the other two guards?"

Mama Teca said, pointing at Atacia, "She sent them to another world with no help at all from any of us. Let's be clear about that—honor to those who deserve it."

Jimbo and Aurora nodded in support of Mama Teca's statement.

I saw the red substance smeared all over Atacia's body. "Are you injured?"

She smiled. "I had to improvise. Don't worry—it's not blood, only the juice of some wild berries. There were some bushes nearby, and so I used them as a disguise."

Now a little surprised, I said to Atacia, "You were only supposed to distract them. What came over you?"

She shook her head. "Believe me, that is what I had in mind, exactly as you instructed. But, when I saw through my telescope that the sergeant in charge had been questioning my mother very aggressively and hit her in the face with a full fist, sending her rolling in the sand," Atacia raised her left hand, "I saw him after that to reach towards his waist for a portable radio. Of course, you know why he was pulling the radio out. I knew at that moment that I didn't have the time or luxury to follow our plans to the letter." She stepped forward towards her mother. Very gently, she took her mother's chin and turned it towards me slowly where I could clearly see a black eye and a split in her upper lip that was still swelling over the cut along the edge. The blood was still fresh, showing that the blow which Aurora had received was recent.

I stepped forward and caressed Aurora's face with the back of my fingers. I carefully touched the cut on her lip. I hugged her and said, "I most sincerely apologize for not being able to be there before and stop this from happening to you." I looked at the lieutenant and his subordinate, who returned the look with terror in their eyes, not missing a single detail of our conversation. I pointed with my right hand at them and said, "They are the reason for my delay in getting to you guys. I had to swim around this vessel several times because I couldn't see where these two were. Without a positive knowledge of that, I hesitated to climb aboard. Finally, I decided to throw caution away because I was worried about Atacia's ability to be able to hold those guards for long.

"When I got out of the water," I continued, "I interrupted them embracing in an erotic, sexual nature with a high temperature." I looked at Aurora. "If I hadn't been held up here, I not only would have been able to reach you guys as we had planned, and so prevent the humiliation and abuse done to Aurora but also probably the hard time Atacia went through. It gives me great satisfaction to know that the main bully who created that situation has been sent to the other world to pay for his sins and burn in Hell."

Atacia nodded with an expression of extreme anger. "You're right, one hundred percent. I never felt in my life such a temptation to sin, even when I punished those miserable men who raped me in Caibarien. When I saw with my own eyes how that filthy abusive communist pig raised his hand and punched my mother in the face with all his strength, my blood must have filled my eyes because I saw everything in a red haze. I didn't see three human beings in front of me when I looked at those guards. Like in a nightmare, automatically they changed into demons and monsters in the service of the Devil, disciples of Lucifer that should be destroyed before they cause more damage."

She pointed at the captive guard. "This one is alive by a miracle. When I was ready to cut his head off, he screamed at me that he wasn't a communist. Those words, true or not, disconnected me from the flow of blood in my brains, and that that moment I started to believe that I had been detached from God and influenced by the Devil himself." She said to the guard, "God saved your life at the same time he freed my heart, using you as a connector to disconnect me from the revenge and evil the Devil filled my heart and possessed my mind with. Something illuminated my mind and heart at that moment and a voice said that I should forgive this one."

Our other two prisoners, still tied up on the floor, looked up at her in total panic. They continued to listen and observe what we were doing. They looked at each other, wondering what kind of luck they would face because if their lives depended on Atacia, they saw no hope for them.

Atacia stepped forward, drawing her knife. She asked me, "What do you want to do with those two? Feed them to the sharks?"

Before I could answer, the two captives screamed in unison, "We're not communists! We were recruited into the military service. We're not communists!"

The woman pleaded, "Really, we're not saying that just to save our lives. You can find our ID cards which have a SMO[15] label. They're in our clothes, in our wallets."

I said to her, "That won't be necessary. Unless you do something that risks our security, if you cooperate in everything that we tell you to do, I guarantee that neither of you will be harmed."

All three prisoners sighed their relief and breathed more comfortably. My friends looked at each other and then at me as they heard what I said. Each of them had been victimized by someone in the communist system. They knew quite well how that system worked, how it

---

[15] *Servicio Militar Obligatorio*, or the Obligatory Military Service.

would corrupt the morality and principles of all human beings, even those that didn't sympathize with the communists and despise the Marxist system. But because of the tremendous terror and intimidation the government put in the minds of everyone around them, some of the people in order to save themselves would even sell their best friends and families with the fear of being accused of counterrevolutionaries or sympathizers of the capitalist system. Anyone stigmatized with those names could lose their lives in the blink of an eye before the firing squad. Whether or not they had been recruited, my friends all knew perfectly well how the system worked. When these prisoners came before their superiors for questioning, they would each try to save his or her own skin as best they could, and so the best way to handle them in this case for our security would be to eliminate all three of them.

  Since I've been a rebel all my life, I never follow the rules. Some rules were made without any feelings for anyone, and I always followed my feelings. I didn't believe the demagogic philosophy of the Marxists that each of us is exactly equal to the other. My own philosophy was never to consider myself either better or less than anyone. We are all different, for which I thank God every day. Some of us have similar characters and personalities, some others are completely different in every single way. This sometimes is why some people cannot get along and hate each other without even knowing why. In Cuba, we say that such people are oil and vinegar. We are not equally the same and sometimes we find people we are not even compatible with. This philosophy of mine in the past caused some problems for me because of my excessive, extreme compassion for the lives of any being on the Earth, any creature at all. It's even more extreme with human beings.

I assessed the risk to all of us of leaving the three captives alive behind us, and I concluded I had arrived at the right decision. I didn't find, since we were in the middle of nowhere, any need to deprive them of their lives. I said to my friends, "Please, let's do this to fill ourselves spiritually and be better than our enemies. Take them to the beach, remove their clothes save for their underwear. You guys will put on their uniforms, including their hats—just in case we pass any vessel on our way to the capital. Please hurry back—we'll be leaving immediately, since we don't know if that sergeant Atacia took down ever used his radio to call his headquarters and report anything. To give them a chance to live and survive, we should free them of their bonds and hope that they can survive until they see a passing ship or whatever."

As I gave my instructions, Atacia looked into the refrigerator and put some ice cubes into a towel and placed it over Aurora's swollen face. Jimbo and Mama Teca took the three prisoners towards the beach. A little while later, they returned dressed as guards. Aurora, Atacia, and I got dressed, and when we were finished, I started the motor and checked the compass to set our course for Havana. I had the coordinates in mind as to where we would disembark there.

I turned to Jimbo. "You'll be the captain of this vessel. Maintain the same moderate speed so that we don't call attention to ourselves."

Jimbo saluted me with good humor. "Aye, aye, my captain."

"No, you're the captain—I'm just the commander." I returned his salute. We both laughed. We left the beach behind and headed out into the open ocean like we were on regular patrol.

Several hours later, after passing several private vessels and fishing boats, but not a single naval or coast guard vessel, we encountered two large cargo ships, one from Venezuela and the other from Russia, which gave us blasts from their ship's horns under the assumption we were the authorities. As we got close to our disembarkation point outside of Havana, I saw the myth and coercion the Marxists used to intimidate their citizens through television and radio, which constantly mentioned the supreme power of the Navy of Cuba that prevented anyone from leaving the island without being reported to the authorities. We in the intelligence community knew these were lies to keep the Cuban people terrified of trying to abandon the miserable living conditions they endured on the island.

We were about a mile from the coast, when from behind a large rock covered by mangroves, a large raft with nearly twenty-five men, women, children, and extremely elderly people. They huddled together on that wooden raft tied together by cut up inner tubes. As soon as they saw us, they thought they were seeing the Devil. They raised their hands in surrender as they slowed the outboard motor's speed. Their hearts had to be in their mouths and must have been praying. They began to sing the Cuban national anthem with their left hands over their hearts. I could not even imagine their surprise when they saw me gesturing to them to continue going. The man on the engine looked at me in confusion. I gestured more emphatically, and he increased their speed. He grinned broadly and the women began to blow us kisses. Some crossed themselves in spiritual fervor. One girl screamed, "God bless you!"

"You have a happy journey," I yelled back. "God bless you, too."

They were so close that I could see tears in their eyes. Now that they had recovered from their panic, they waved with both hands their thanks and gratitude. Some women lifted up babies to show us. It was a moment of great emotion for all involved; we were as deeply touched as those making their desperate escape. They slowly passed by us, and I could read the hunger, persecution, and suffering in their faces. They might have been persecuted for their religious beliefs, and I remembered what I had read of the French Revolution as a schoolboy. The images of the poverty, privation, and moral destruction and social agonies that was reflected in every one of these people caused a knot in my throat and tingling small pain in my heart as this new Cuban revolution repeated history, destroying in its path everything it touched, forcing its citizens into exile or the firing squad. The lucky ones wound up in reeducation camps, set up in imitation of the gulags of the Soviet Union with the same ideology they implanted in our beautiful island of Cuba; it also brought to my mind the image of the Nazi concentration camps, where millions of Jews were exterminated without reason and to which the world for a long time turned a blind eye to all that suffering. So many miserable memories which history brings to us, and one of them is the French Revolution which brought so much despair, hunger, devastation, and destruction to the major cities like Paris, where people were forced to eat rats, creating epidemics, and the worst malnutrition any country ever had in the modern world which inspired the writer Victor Hugo to compose his novel, *Les Miserables*. All revolutions, without exception, regardless of what extreme ideology engendered them, with their empty, broken promises of equality to the people, all change nations they intend to conquer into misery, with only one thing in common with each revolution: misery for everyone for many years without hope for any dream to recoup and bring back what they left behind from those empty promises. The abundant that they had not considered sufficient for them gets flushed down the toilet by following those extremists in their frustration for society to not be themselves successful enough converting the beautiful prosperous God gave to Earth's nations for the worst nightmares that anyone could ever have in their lives.

Chapter 24: The Dark Horses of the Conspiracy

A little later, we arrived at the coast, and I made sure with my compass that we were at the right destination. We looked for two long colonies of reef that formed a cove with one beautiful sandy beach between the Cojimar and La Chorrera Rivers, overlooked by the Torreon de la Chorrera, an old 18th century coastal fortress. The tower is located between the Miramar and Vedado districts of Havana, made famous as a place where the famous writer Ernest Hemingway greeted visitors, a very short distance from the capital. We had to find a way using only our knives to open a hole in the stern and bows of the torpedo boat in order to make it sink evenly. It took a great deal of effort doing it that way, but we needed to make it disappear from the eyes of our enemies not just for our security, but also for what it represented to the Cuban people as a symbol of oppression and death.

As the boat sank, we removed the uniform hats and blouses, leaving only the pants and white T-shirts. We swam the short distance towards the rocks, looking for dense vegetation where I could leave my friends until I found my contact in that small fishing village. We agreed that my signal when I returned would be a marine bird call; they should not leave that hiding place until they heard it. We practiced until they knew what my call would sound like.

Once everything was settled, I walked carefully over the sharp rocks along the coast towards the white sandy beach. Beyond it, I could see the roofs of the houses of the small village. As I came down the rocks and began to walk along the beautiful beach, I could see in the distance some fishing boats which were tied by ropes to floating buoys, while some closer were attached to blocks of cement-filled plastic buckets buried in the sand.

The village consisted of several little wood houses covered with palm fronds; suspended by poles on the porches were some hammocks. The number I was looking for was number 60 painted red with an enormous picture of Che Guevara on the wall outside. This was supposed to be the president of the CDR[16]; he was reportedly the worst enemy of the Marxists in that place, using his position as a cover. His name was Challo el Bandido. He was also the only mechanic for outboard engines in the entire district.

I could see a large boulder on my way which seemed to mark the end of the street as the houses ended with number 59. I turned around and saw a couple of men on the beach that were pulling a net in from the ocean. As I came near to them, I saw one of them which matched the description I had been given: a long, white beard like Santa Clause, olive skin, and very tall, well over six and a half feet. He looked up and raised his right hand high in greeting me.

I asked, "I'm sorry—do you know the fisherman named Challo el Bandido? I've walked by fifty-nine houses, but I cannot find him. Am I in the wrong town?"

---

[16] Committee for the Defense of the Revolution; a neighborhood watch organization which reported any anti-communist sentiments or activity to the government.

The man was also rather corpulent, and he observed me closely with bottle green eyes, looking me from head to toe. "You're not from around here, are you?" he asked.

I replied using my code. "No, I'm from Pinar del Rio. To be more precises, from the port La Coloma."

When he heard me say that he opened his eyes wide in surprise. He yelled to one of the other men working the nets, "Finish pulling the net out, OK? I'll see you guys later tonight at the meeting of the committee."

One of the men replied with a vague salute. "OK, chief—we'll see each other later."

The man with the white beard turned around. "Follow me, please. I'll take you to the house of Challo el Bandido—he's the one you're looking for, no?"

"Yes, sir." I followed him with no suspicion, since he appeared to recognize me; it was also true that the people in these small towns tended to be very cordial.

I walked close behind him. We passed Number 59, and he continued to walk beyond what appeared to be the end of the row of houses. He gestured to me to follow him as I stopped, because it looked like sharp rocks only beyond. I followed him once more, not understanding why I was being taken to those rocks.

To my surprise, when we reached the end of the rocks, and saw another house: Number 60. It was certainly different from the other houses—it had red glazed tile roofing and was built as if squeezed between the rocks. It was built with cement decorated with red seashells incorporated into the binding substance. As I had been told, a vast mural of Che Guevara was next to the door leading inside. He looked at me from head to toe again as we got onto the porch.

He asked, "Do you want a glass of lemonade?"

"No, no—I don't want to bother you."

"It's no bother at all."

"OK. It's hot, a glass of lemonade sounds good," I replied with a small smile. "By the way, are you Challo el Bandido?"

He smiled as we walked inside. He raised his right hand pointing up. "My friend, patience. You will meet Challo el Bandido soon." That gave me an uncomfortable feeling, and I wondered what was going on with this guy. He corresponded to the description, he had brought me there, but he had still not identified himself to me. Still giving me that small smile, he eyed me once more. But this time the smile looked a little cynical. Before he went inside the house, he said, "Sit down. I'll be right back." The porch was lined with chairs lined with cowhide, and a small center table covered in wood with shelves between them. "Be comfortable, please. You're in your home."

"Thank you." He closed the door behind him, which was also odd; this didn't settle well with me. Even though the chairs looked comfortable, the hides still had fur on them. I raised my hand and called after him, "Thank you very much." I made an appearance of sitting down, but as soon as that door closed, I jumped down off the porch and tried to follow him through the windows without being seen.

I saw him enter his living room, and he took a double-barreled shotgun, opened it to check that it was loaded, and grabbed some boxes of shells. He put them in both pockets and headed to another room, far from where I was supposed to be sitting, which would give him greater privacy. He picked up the receiver of a rotary phone and dialed a number. This was getting stranger by the minute. His description corresponded to every description I had been given, the town was right, why hadn't he given me the counter sign?

I tried not to be paranoid, but there were too many little incidents to let me be completely at ease. I had never met him personally, and I tried to come up with a reason. Perhaps something had happened recently in that village which I had no knowledge of, and Challo might be taking extreme precautions just in case the G-2 had caught the contact he was supposed to meet and instead sent an imposter in order to test him. Suspicion might have fallen upon him, and they might be trying to see how he would react.

In order to make sure, I kept going from window to window, following his movements. When he dialed that number, he patiently waited until someone on the other line picked up. He spoke softly, but I could hear him say, "He is here. Hurry up." He hung up the phone at once and looked around to see if anyone was spying on him, causing me to duck down below the window and cling close to the house's wall to avoid being seen.

Immediately I got a bad feeling that something was wrong, and if I wanted to survive, I had to act fast. Whoever was on the other end of that phone call might not be very long in responding and arriving. Especially with that mysterious whisper—the only person there was me. My brain was filled with doubts about him, worse even than I had from the beginning. That shotgun that he had replaced the lemonade with didn't help ease my doubts in the slightest.

He walked towards the refrigerator in order to get what he had promised, but after he brought out a jar of lemonade with only some traces left in the bottom, he shook his head unhappily. He opened the freezer and put some ice cubes in it, and then filled the glass with water from the kitchen sink. Shotgun in his right hand, he walked towards the door with the glass of ice water in his left hand.

When he reached the door, he put the weapon against the wall. Glass of ice water in his hand, he walked out to where I was supposed to be waiting. I, however, had found an unlocked window, and moving carefully to avoid making any noise upon my entry, I had followed him through the house. This time he had left the inner door open; I picked up the shotgun and checked to make sure he hadn't unloaded it. I remained inside, to the right of the door, watching him through the screen door.

He was looking around in confusion. He put the glass of ice water down on the center table and stepped off the porch to check both sides of the house. I remained inside, not moving. From that position, you could not see any other house in the settlement. The only thing the rocks didn't block was the beach line and in the distance the waves crashing on the sand. The reason people would build houses like that would be to use the practical idea of avoiding the changes of the tide, so a wide strip of beach was left. It also protected from the tidal surge of a hurricane. To the landward side, he was completely invisible from the rest of the village.

He started back towards the house. I immediately took a few steps back, watching him as he walked in, keeping out of his immediate line of sight. He entered the house and looked around to the side of the door, looking for that shotgun. When he saw it was missing, he turned, and terror filled his eyes as he looked right into both barrels as I trained it on him. He raised both hands high and said, "I'm sorry, I promised you lemonade, but I ran out." He pointed towards the center table. "I brought you a glass of ice water instead. Please forgive me."

I replied, "I forgive you for the lemonade, but I don't forgive you for your betrayal." He opened his mouth, and I shoved the barrels into his mouth. In a decisive, firm voice, I continued, "I heard you on the phone. I know I don't have any time to waste with you." I pushed the gun further into his mouth. "I'll make this very clear, so that when I remove these barrels from your mouth you will only have five minutes to tell me the whole truth, and when I say all the truth, I mean if you miss anything, I'll paint that wall behind you with your brains. The first question is why you betrayed me and our cause. The second is who is behind this. Believe me, I don't like to kill people, but you should believe me when I offered to redecorate your house." I pushed the muzzle further inside his mouth some more, forcing him to take a step backward and wince in pain. He knew I was serious, and the slightest move would lead to his losing his life. I looked deeply into his eyes. I said in a very calm voice, "I have never understood why anyone would take pleasure in taking the life of another human being. But when I find in my road mercenaries, hypocrites, and traitors I can understand and appreciate the fundamental origin of that pleasure." I pulled the barrels out of his mouth slowly. At the same time, I reminded him, "My time is limited, and my patience is more so. I'll repeat once more, if you want to live, don't make me repeat my questions."

To my complete surprise, Challo el Bandido, that gigantic man, got on his knees with tears in his eyes. "I know it's difficult for you to believe what I'm about say, but I swear to God and His Son, Jesus Christ, that what I'm about to say is the truth." He pointed with his right hand at the shotgun. "That was not to be used against you, it was to be given to you so you can defend yourself. Will you allow me to reach into my pockets?" I nodded, and he reached into one pocket, removed the shells, and allowed them to spill onto the tile floor, where they rolled around slightly. He reached into his other pocket and angrily dropped those shells on the floor as well. "In order to use that shotgun against you, I only need one shell. It already has two in the chamber, so why did I put all of these into my pockets?" Tears sprung into his eyes as he continued. "I swear to you again, the G-2 have had my two daughters in jail, incommunicado, for the past three months. They showed up here at my house and arrested me and all my family. They only let me go a couple of weeks ago, but my wife and two daughters are still in prison. These people have known you've been coming and have been expecting you for months. Thanks be to God for you and my family that you didn't show up. I assure you if you had that you or even I and my family, would be dead.

  He grew more emotional as he shook his head. "Evidently, your intelligence in the USA has sold you out, or someone there isn't playing straight. They provided this valuable information to the Cuban government. I repeat to you: they have been waiting for you for months. Not just the G-2, but all the other repressive intelligence apparatuses—MQ-1, you name it. All of Cuban intelligence is waiting for you. Supposedly, you would be the Lightning, and the most precious gift they could give to the Prime Minister for his birthday on August 13th. I repeat, thank God you never showed up. They've been sitting in my house, bringing me back and forth from the prison, spending days, weeks, or even months of doing this, and interrogating me and getting my denials. They've started to believe that their information either was compromised or not real. Or there's the possibility that something caused you to change your plans about making this trip to Cuba." His face grew worried, and his voice cracked. "If God allows you to survive this, when you return from Cuba, please blow the whistle to the people behind you. This was a very lucky call that we had this time, and I hope that they will eventually let my family go, since they have no proof of anything. But we have to be prepared; the next time, we won't be so lucky. If we want to continue our fight to destroy this horrible, evil political Marxist system in our country, we have to be ready to act."

I listened to him patiently with extreme attention. Either this guy was the best of the best in covering himself, or what he was telling me was the truth. I still had some small doubts due to what I had heard on the phone call, so I said, "Let's suppose that all you're telling me is true. I have a single question for you: why did you call the G-2 and inform them that I had arrived?"

He shook his head. "I'm sorry to tell you, but you're wrong."

"No, I listened to you on the phone through the window. You told them to hurry up, that I had arrived."

He smiled. "No, no—I was talking to my contact, not the G-2. He will take you to a safe place, you and anyone with you. Your contact is a young man who works in one of the highest places of the government within Urban Reform. Even though he's very young, he's absolutely trustworthy, a patriot and a freedom fighter, with tremendous skills and courage. He'll help you navigate through your mission here and save you a lot of headaches." At that moment, I heard a car in front of his house and jumped. I looked through the window and saw a canary yellow Toyota Land Cruiser jeep pull up outside. He smiled. "Calm down. This is the man who will not only be your contact but will arrange your accommodations for however long your mission in Cuba lasts." He had been sitting all this time on his knees. "Can I get up now, and could you please stop pointing that weapon at my head?"

Still doubting him, but at least more relaxed and almost convinced that Challo might be the best con man I had ever encountered, but at least not the traitor I had imagined, so I lowered the weapon and offered my right hand to help him up from his uncomfortable position. I realized how intelligent he was. He didn't lose his cool and showed that my mistrust had hurt his feelings, but he made no move to provoke me into discharging that weapon. I offered my most sincere apologies while realizing the valuable lesson that even with the most evidence before your eyes, you should be patient and listen to what that person has to say. This will prevent us from committing the most horrible injustice that we will repent for the rest of our lives and bear the tremendous weight on our conscience by executing in our rush some innocent human being.

The contact came up, and Challo introduced me to Arnaldo Valdes. He was the nephew of a terrible man: Ramiro Valdes, chief of the DTI[17], the most repressive political machinery to retain those Cubans who deny serving the revolution, labeling them as social menaces, and sending them to concentration camps.

We said our farewells to Challo and left the beach house. As we got into the Toyota, we noticed that the back had been modified slightly. Instead of seats going from one side to the other, there were two long benches along

---

[17] *Departmento Tecnico de Investigaciones*, Technical Department of Investigations, the organization responsible for investigating and prosecuting what the government deems to be criminal in nature.

the sides, much like a military troop transport truck. Arnaldo drove according to my directions to pick up my friends, who were impatient and worried about me as we pulled up to their hiding place. I put my hands over my mouth and gave the call of the marine bird. At once Atacia and the others rushed to leave their concealment to join us. I introduced them to our new contact, and we drove on the sand searching for the entrance to the main highway which led towards the capital of Havana.

Chapter 25: The Miracles of Necessity

We left the white sand behind us and got onto the paved streets leaving the town; but ahead of us a number of military vehicles and guards were already in the process of blocking that exit from the town. There must have been an informant who had been watching Challo's house and movements and reported to the G-2 that a stranger had arrived in the village, something very unusual for a small fishing town with such a small population. The arrival of strangers was a cause for suspicion.

Seeing the danger, Arnaldo turned aside. He made a U-turn in the middle of the street, which caught the attention of the guards erecting the barricade; an alarm was sounded. He at once reached under the seat and pulled out two pistols, one after the other. He handed one to Atacia and then the other to Jimbo. The shotgun rested close to my leg. He asked, "I hope you have enough shells for that weapon. We will probably need it."

I tapped my campaign pants and replied, "I have enough ammunition; both pockets are full of shells."

"I think you have enough there to give a big headache to these communists."

"I plan to give them more than a headache; I'm going to give them a migraine if they keep persecuting us."

He gave me a smile. "That sounds great to me."

"Let's try to find a place where we can hide so that we don't find ourselves being forced to use these weapons. There are only two ways in or out of this town. If any of them radio the authorities, all they have to do is block both off and we'll be in a mousetrap. Believe me, I have with me a lot more important mission to accomplish than to have a confrontation with the locals in this little town."

"I hate to tell you this, but I don't think these guys are locals. The G-2 and federal authorities have been waiting for you for a while. These are the ones they left behind here to blow the whistle when you're spotted, and that's been done."

At that moment, without warning, they started to shoot at our vehicle. Bullets ripped through the vinyl soft top cover of the Toyota. Our pursuers turned the blue and red lights on the roofs of their vehicles on, indicating to us that we were supposed to stop. I said, "How do they expect us to stop with them firing at us? They must think we're idiots."

The young Arnaldo didn't even try to look for a place to hide. He simply went as fast as he could to get to the other side of town. He pulled a little device on the dashboard. He changed the gear and stomped the accelerator pedal onto the floor. Like he had activated a turbo supercharge, the front of the vehicle raised up like a horse rearing, and we sank into the back of our seats from the sudden increase in velocity as we shot forward.

From the back, Aurora was caught by surprise and screamed. I said, "What on earth?" After everyone adjusted to the abrupt increase in speed, everyone watched joyfully as our enemies diminished far into the distance.

He said, "Watch out—the plane is taking off." While he did give us a warning, it really came too late. We clung to the steel piping that the cover was attached to avoid being flung about. I hit my head against one of those pipes, but fortunately it was covered in foam. It was clear that Arnaldo had put a lot of time into redesigning this Toyota with some custom improvements. I looked with tremendous curiosity at the panel of the interior of the Toyota, which had looked like some kind of elaborate decoration. It didn't look like a Toyota and more like a small airplane prototype. It had several gauges from different manufacturers, adapted electronically, of completely makes from different nationalities. I knew, since I had one back at home, that this was not the dashboard of a 1972 Land Cruiser.

I could not hold back my curiosity in spite of the stress. "What year is this Toyota?"

He looked at me curiously at that question at such a time. Proudly, he said pleasantly, "Nothing in this vehicle is from the Toyota 1972 make. Only the chassis and body's design. I call this a clone of multiple different cars from different years and different nationalities. You would believe it, but it even has parts from a plane, avionic fuel, and components from a Mercury speedboat."

I shook my head. "This is not a car, man—this is a Frankenstein. You created a monster here."

"Well, it's a monster, and it's alive, and everyone wants it. I've even had some ministers and big government honchos begging me and offering me a ton of dollars for it as well as other vehicles I have—but none of them are for sale."

I shook my head. "No doubt in my mind that you guys here in Cuba have the masterwork course in survival. I call you guys true geniuses at turning trash into the admirable and incredible."

He grinned. "Brother, you are one of us. You might remember the old saying that we heard from our ancestors here: necessity forces you always to make miracles happen."

I nodded my head. "I know. I've been a witness to that. I don't know if anyone ever told you, but I lived with you guys here for over a decade. Just a single decade—you've now been living this for four decades, so it's four times worse than what I had to deal with. It's turned each of you into masters of miracles."

He laughed loudly. "I appreciate the compliment and thank you for it, and that you understand the sacrifices we have to make every day to keep these cars running. Challo has also told me of the sacrifices you've made for so many years to bring freedom back to our country. All I ask is that we make together a bigger effort so that we can get out of all this misery we've been forced to endure each day when they converted a beautiful island into the worst toilet of the Americas, these miserable and vicious Marxists...."

He was interrupted by a bullet coming from the soft rear window and hit the rearview mirror. Pieces of the glass spattered across both of our faces, causing him to nearly lose control of the car. I touched my face and felt the blood. I said, "They're just tiny pieces of glass. Don't lose control of the car or we'll be dead. Remember, our lives are in your hands. Thank God that none of that glass hit our eyes. Do you feel anything strange there?"

"No, I'm fine."

I turned back. "Is everyone OK back there?"

Mama Teca said, "We're fine, don't worry about us. We've had our heads on the ground since the first shot was fired."

Jimbo said, "It's not very comfortable back here with these small benches along the sides. If Mama Teca would take her leg off of my head, I will be better."

Arnaldo yelled, "Hold on!" He made another U turn in the middle of the road. The other exit was already blocked off.

This particular entrance was the main one, and there was a Soviet 1.5-ton truck with an M-4 machine gun mounted in the back. A truck filled with soldiers had just arrived.

Arnaldo reached into the center and put the Toyota into four-wheel drive. He went up onto the sidewalk and jumped onto the grass of the park—the only way back to the beach where we had come from. There was a bronze bust of Hemingway atop a cement pedestal and some people walking in the park or sitting and having a little meal. As Arnaldo tried to avoid hitting anyone by zig zagging through the crowd, the situation became complicated. We virtually ran into the side of the monument as he yelled for us to hold on again; we went up onto the lowest block, nearly flipping our vehicle. He managed to get around the pedestal as people ran in all directions, trying to save their lives; but some ran right in the middle of our path, forcing him to swerve to avoid them. It looked like we were going to ram into the podium, but he managed luckily to get up onto the second step, jumping from there and causing the Soviet UAZ, which had in the front bumper guards, to hit the monument head on. The main wall of the pedestal which supported the heavy bronze bust was brick covered by cement. The massive impact of the steel front broke the entire structure, and the heavy bronze bust shook and fell onto the hood of our pursuers' vehicle. The hood had collapsed, the radiator issuing a column of white steam as we looked back. Volcano-like boiling water spewed out, spraying the legs of the soldiers in the front seat, who jumped out to frantically strip off their pants in panic.

We were satisfied to see the UAZ had been disabled. But there was still another coming in from a different direction. They had to slow down because of all the debris in their way, though they still continued to shoot at us. Arnaldo drove onto the grass of the park, taking advantage of our enemies' pause to assess the damage to the UAZ and any injuries their comrades had suffered.

I said to Arnaldo as the pursuit picked up, "Let me see if we can stop them. We now know that the Achilles' heel of those vehicles is the radiator. Let's see if I can put a shell into their radiators and put them out of commission as well."

"OK. Please, be careful."

"I will. Please try to drive straight and don't make any abrupt changes. I want to aim to disable their vehicles, not shoot wildly."

"OK."

I grabbed my seatbelt and wrapped it around my left arm and opened my door. Grabbing the shotgun with my right hand, I kept my left foot on the sideboard and knelt on the seat with my right leg. I leaned nearly all the way out of the vehicle, with my right hand putting the shotgun over my left arm for balance, took aim, and yelled to Arnaldo, "Slow down so they get closer!"

He slowed down a little, understanding what I was trying to do. I could hear the bullets whistling near my ears. Patiently, persistently, I waited until they got as close as possible. I then opened fire on their radiators. First one shot, and then the second one, and I saw white steam rising from the front of the UAZ. Inside the Toyota, my friends had continued firing their pistols to keep their attention away from me. I saw with joy that both of my shots had destroyed the radiator. They continued their fire, even as the vehicle began to overheat, forcing them to slow down.

We were on the sand now. I pulled myself back into the car, put the shotgun back in its place by my leg, unwrapped my arm, and checked in in the visor mirror to see if I had any injuries. That prompted inquiries from the back. "No, I'm fine," I said.

We continued and Arnaldo, thanks to our turbo charged speed, now put a vast distance between us and our enemies. We knew it wouldn't last long, because they would be radioing to their associates, and we would see enemy reinforcements soon. We drove at full speed towards the end of the beach where the two reefs formed the cove. There was no other way to go. I wondered where he was taking us. I trusted the guy because he had been faithful so far, but I thought to myself that there was no way we could cross the rocks. Unless he had a submarine concealed someplace there was no way we could get out that way.

I pulled the shotgun up and rested it against the dashboard. I brushed my fingers across my forehead with my left hand. I could see the short distance we had before we would cross the large rocks. Arnaldo slowed down nearly to a stop. I could not contain my curiosity as I watched him open the glove compartment and take a canvas tool bag out. I asked him, "What is your plan, if you have one? Any idea how we're going to get out of this rat trap we're in right now?"

I looked over my shoulder and could see in the distance some military vehicles with their lights on heading our way, already on the sand. I was getting worried, thinking that the only way out would be to retrieve our swimming equipment and leave by the ocean, but that would leave Arnaldo behind. My friends got out of the vehicle and looked at me in confusion. They looked back and saw our imminent danger approaching.

Arnaldo didn't look worried at all. He removed some tools from the canvas bag, walking around the Toyota doing something with each tire. I could not even tell what he was doing, as he whistled Cuba's famous Benny More's hit song "Santa Isabel de las Lajas." All of us had our eyes glued on who was supposed to be our new friend as he continued whistling and not caring about anything at all while our enemies grew nearer by the second. Those inaccessible rocks blocked our only way out, and if we didn't do something quickly, we would soon be in the hands of our enemies without any hope.

Maybe because of this, Jimbo could not contain himself any longer. In an irritated voice, he yelled as he pointed to the vehicles, "Hey, amigo! I hope that your cloned Toyota with all your innovations has wings. I believe if not, we'll all be very soon *pescados fritos*[18]."

Arnaldo didn't get distracted by any of this. He finished what he was doing on the last rear wheel, whatever it was. With a small smile on his face, he looked Jimbo in the eyes, and then gestured dismissively with his free hand. He went to where the spare tire was held to the frame by screws on a small rear door. The spare was covered in vinyl. He opened the door and when he took it off, revealing a propeller that was attached to the transmission to the jeep. "My Toyota doesn't have wings, but it has an unbelievable tail." He secured the small door with a leather belt on the opposite side of the propellor, giving the blades free motion. "My clone doesn't fly—yet. I'm working on that. It's just an idea. But I can guarantee

---

[18] Fried fish

you that it can swim better than any fish out there." He pointed with his right hand to the ocean.

Jimbo was caught by surprise. Unable to contain his joy, he stepped forward and gave Arnaldo a big hug and kissed him on each cheek. "I love you, brother! You are a genius!"

Arnaldo, this time with a small smile, jokingly asked, "What about it? Do you think we are *pescados fritos*?" Everyone laughed. Now it was Arnaldo the one to say, "It's time to jump onto my boat." He glanced and saw how dangerously close the military were. "Everyone aboard. We're about to take off."

We rushed to get into the Toyota as Arnaldo pushed some buttons on the dashboard as he started to drive along the beach into the water. By the time the soldiers got to the coastline, we were a safe distance from them. Before their very disbelieving eyes, our canary yellow clone floated across the water at an extraordinary speed, escaping from them with no way for them to stop us. In their frustration, they opened fire on us, even though we were far out of range of their bullets.

Jimbo from his position right behind my seat, touched my shoulder and said with a small smile as he tilted his head, "You have no idea how much I miss my Stinger."

I turned my head back towards him and smiled. "If I come across one of them, I promise you that I will give you a Stinger. I think it would be a good birthday present."

He smiled. "How did you know?"

"You didn't figure it out? Your sister and mother both told me that you would have a birthday in three days."

He smiled. "Yes, next week, and we're already in the middle of the week."

Mama Teca touched Jimbo on the shoulder. "Remember, the years don't make you any wiser; just older. But you have to be responsible when you handle firearms. You're not a kid anymore and they aren't toys. They can bring a lot of destruction and death to people, and that's why we have to be responsible and use them only when it's absolutely necessary. I remember you shooting at those people who did no harm to you."

Jimbo didn't take the reprimand lightly. "When will you stop treating me like a kid? You don't have to worry about me anymore. I'm a grown man. I get enough from my mother and sister all the time for you to add to it."

Aurora slapped him on the shoulder and said reprovingly, "You will be a true man when you learn to listen to the advice of your elders, especially those who love you and want the best for you. I don't want you to think because you're a year older next week that you know everything. You have a lot to learn, Jimbo!"

Jimbo protested, "Ouch! That hurt!"

"Oh, come on," Aurora said. "You see? You're still a baby. You can't take a little slap on your shoulder."

Jimbo rubbed his shoulder. "That hurt. That wasn't a little slap. When will you learn that teaching your kids doesn't include beating them up? Is that a lesson Mama Teca gave to you?" He was more unhappy that his mother had bruised his ego in front of all of us that he was at the actual blow. He put on a long face and lapsed into silence.

Aurora perceived his unhappiness and rubbed his shoulder. "*Pobrecito*[19]!" Everyone laughed. "You see? You're still a baby. I'm sorry I hurt you, my baby."

---

[19] Poor thing!

Jimbo sulked in silence. I turned as best I could in my seat, leveraged by my left arm and said, "You don't have to worry about it, Jimbo. You know you are a man, and we do as well. Your family is just joking with you. You showed to us several times during our ordeals what kind of man you are. Even though you're very young, you're very responsible to the extreme of being an altruist and caring more for others than yourself. You proved that to all of us when you gave your most precious toy, that Stinger, to the father of Vanessa when we left the island. You knew they would need it a lot more than you would. I know you knew for sure that the diabolical Dr. Chao would one day return to try and get revenge on what we did to him in shattering his abomination of a genetic lab. You don't have to prove to anyone who you are; you've already demonstrated it to us."

He grinned from ear to ear at my words of support. He gave me a thumbs up. "You really are my best friend."

"Thank you, Jimbo." I returned the thumbs up and turned back to the front. Behind us, everyone remained silent. I felt the need to reaffirm before everyone how I felt about him and not allow him to suffer humiliation, even unintentionally, from members of his family. I saw before us already a beach approaching us. I felt a sense of déjà vu at the sight of that beach, and realized it was the Club Nautico. We drove onto the beach to the astonished gaze of several people, some of whom stood up from their chairs to view the amphibious car leaving the ocean and rolling across the sand towards the street. I recognized even the permanent umbrellas and chairs of the club—old memories came flooding back of my meetings over the years with my uncle, long ago.

We drove towards the street, and I could see my uncle's house. "Oh, my God," I said as the déjà vu flooded me again. An automatic garage door on one of the houses opened, and he pulled inside; I realized it was about half a block from my uncle's house. I remembered all the ordeals I had gone through, how I tried to stop the Castro brothers in their ambitious plans to conquer the world, and all the other numerous adrenaline rushes I endured in and out in that club in Miramar.

    Arnaldo drove into the garage and then closed the door, replacing the door opener in the visor. The doors rolled along aluminum rails like a modern system, and I wondered how he had all this stuff. If my surprise up to now had been great, it grew even more as I saw multiple old and expensive luxury cars, as well as brand new 2000 Hummer H2s of the same canary yellow as the jeep. It brought me back to the large collection of luxury cars Che had in his mansion taken from the wealthy when they left Cuba. Arnaldo had not just cars but all kinds of equipment: welding machines, assembly, a fully equipped mechanical garage with parts hanging from the walls. I revised my opinion—it looked like an assembly factory. This particular mansion, even though we came in through a double door entry, had different garages which all communicated to the interior of the house.

    Understanding our curiosity, Arnaldo tried to explain as he put his hand on my shoulder. "My friend, in this country if you have connections and dollars everything is in the palm of your hand. The blockade and the shortages only exist for blue collar and everyday people and as a cover story. It's just a myth. Anyone inside the governmental families and high ranked military live as I do, especially being the nephew of the worst criminal outside the Castro brothers this government has. The worst scenario is for people of advanced age. They don't have the energy to fight the system, and they also don't have the stamina, living petrified by psychological terror. They know that even though you might have dollars, if you don't have the right connections, you can get arrested and put in prison for over ten years. How unfair, eh? But many people prefer to die of hunger than to finish their old age in the most horrible prison you could have in the entire world. That is what we have here in Cuba."

Chapter 26: Omega Green Scorpions

"I hate this communist system," Arnaldo went on, "including this mansion that I live in. I feel guilty every time I come here, knowing that this belonged to someone who really sweated and sacrificed for many years to give this comfort to their families. It doesn't belong to me at all. This is the remorse and conscience that none of these communists have—how can you enjoy something that was forcefully taken away from someone who worked hard all their lives and even was forced to abandon their own country?" He took a deep breath and shook his head. He opened one of the many doors of an enormous industrial stainless-steel refrigerator. "Oh, well—if I don't enjoy it, someone else will. At least I'm not on their side."

He pulled an enormous leg of ham imported from Spain and two huge balls of Spanish cheeses, one yellow and one white. He put them on the table. "Serve yourself, OK? Eat all you want." He opened a cupboard in the dining room and removed a few boxes of Ritz Crackers and a loaf of sliced white bread. He then pulled out a large bottle of pickles, a bottle of Dijon mustard, a bottle of olives with red pimentos from Italy, some American mayonnaise, Mortadella sausage, and other foods.

"The only thing I cannot provide you with is service," he said regretfully. "I apologize because in my house I don't want any domestics because I don't trust anyone in this country. Unfortunately, that is the little inconvenience we have to endure to keep our security in place. I assure you that it's not just because of my distrust. I don't want to bring anyone here who could not only steal from you but also turn out to be mercenaries employed by my enemy, who could take pictures of the way I live and publish them in the media and on the Internet, which would cause me to be reprimanded very strongly from the high elites in the government for being so careless. I don't want anyone to put their index finger in my face and tell me that they saw me do something or saw something in my house.

"That is the reason I've survived for so many years as a spy inside the highest circles of this government, not because I'm the nephew of the highest official within the first ring of the Castro circle. All these people are your friends and allies as long as you don't get exposed and prosecuted for what no one should know about but everyone else does anyway. I saw with my own eyes how everyone divided up among themselves and their closest ones whatever the industrialists and businessmen left behind when they left the country. Now that they've been running out of the nutrients in our country they've expanded into Venezuela, Nicaragua, and other countries around the world like an octopus. The greed and extravagance of these men have no limit. They won't stop until they destroy the entire world."

As he spoke, he put plates and napkins before us. I sat in one of the comfortable chairs around the huge glass-topped dining room table. The glass was two inches thick and beveled at the borders. I asked curiously, "If it's not too personal, I would like to ask you a question I'm curious about. Do you mind if I ask?"

"Ask me anything. Between us there are no secrets."

"What motivated you to become a spy against not only your country but also your family, since most of them are among the high elite of the government?"

He smiled as he took bottles of Cuban cola from another door of the refrigerator, a large bottle of Italian Chianti, a massive bottle of Dom Perignon, and a pitcher of orange juice. "Do you like mimosas?"

"I love them."

"I have fresh squeezed orange juice they bring every couple of days as well as a gallon of fresh milk from a government farm. Most of the time I pour them down the sink because I'm seldom here and don't eat here but instead at restaurants." He opened the bottle of champagne and offered me a beautiful light blue Baccarat champagne flute. He filled it up and asked everybody if they wanted any. Except for Jimbo, everyone accepted the champagne before the orange juice. Jimbo instead wanted a Cuban cola. He filled up the glasses of the rest of us with the expensive champagne and said to me, "Your question is extremely intelligent because a moment comes in our lives of some extraordinary success that causes us to make this serious decision. We never even contemplate in our wildest dreams of doing them. This is normally an emotional moment, something very specific which either we can feel tremendously proud of later or maybe take us to a very embarrassing and difficult, dark situation for which we could also repent for the rest of our lives."

I asked curiously, "Until today, do you have any of those regrets about what you're doing now? Any moment when you would like to take back the decision you made?"

My questions were designed to search out his motivation and position. In my training, this is the thing to do when you initially begin to work with someone who is highly recommended from other circles as trustworthy to test the ground for yourself and see what his psychological reactions are. Is he completely trustworthy, or someone you need to keep in check? "Have you ever decided to go back to that initial determination you made to be involved in such a dangerous life and the agonies that every spy goes through in his experience in his work?"

Arnaldo grinned at me. Without hesitation, he made me feel better by replying immediately with a shake of his head, "No, no—I never before I made that decision felt so proud of myself. I see how my work can destroy the ambitious and destructive plans of these Marxists to convert the world into unhappy slaves. I felt my best every time I took the mask away from their false promises and brought reality before the faces of people, shredding their hypocrisy even in their national anthem of converting the world into a proletariat paradise on Earth, the greatest fraud that any human being could sell to the poorest of the world. Some of the idiotic intellectuals who have swallowed that sugar-coated pill will get severe indigestion from the economic disasters that the Marxists are masters of creating. They do so intentionally to use them to sow hatred, racial and even family divisions, and destroying our religious institutions in order to take and keep power."

Arnaldo paused and put his right hand to his forehead, clearly disgusted as he spoke. He caressed his forehead with his fingers. He put his head down, and to my surprise I saw two tears roll down his cheeks. He wiped them away quickly in case I saw and said in a broken voice, "Sorry. Can you imagine it? My uncle allowed the Castro brothers to kill my father. He didn't move a single finger to save his own brother. What kind of man can stand by when the government does this to his own family and applauds it?" He tried to compose himself. "I don't know if you know, but my father was on General Ochoa's team. After they sent them with the green light to do what was supposed to be an international mission to help Latin American countries by patriots, those same altruists were converted in the blink of an eye into narcotics smugglers for our own Prime Minister, who washed his hands and let those who believed his idiotic promises die."

    I stood up and stepped over to him, putting my hand on his shoulder, understanding his pain. I was surprised at the information he gave. I didn't have those details before, and they took me completely off guard. I understood clearly why he became a double agent against these Marxist dictators led by the Castro brothers. I thought about how small the world is and how circumstances we didn't expect would return to face us. What Arnaldo didn't know was that my team were the ones who exposed the macabre plan to the international intelligence community. The Cuban government was trafficking drugs to all the embassies around the world, using their diplomatic immunity and supporting with impunity the narcoterrorists in common use between General Ochoa and Pablo Escobar. I kept my silence—I didn't think at that moment that telling him, in his emotional state, would help at all the wound of the loss of his father which had not yet healed completely. Even though it took me by surprise, I didn't want to get into the details to see who his father was on Ochoa's team. I knew now for a fact that one of the guys, not even one of the main ones, was the brother of Ramiro Valdez. Now Ramiro's own nephew had just told me he hadn't done a thing to help his own brother—this was typical in these totalitarian regimes. The same terror the communist system gave to the population was instilled in the leaders as well, and prevented anyone from getting involved for fear of being implicated and losing their government position or maybe even their lives.

Everyone at the table stopped eating, sharing in Arnaldo's pain. Atacia, Aurora, and Mama Teca shook their heads in a blend of frustration, pain, and compassion at his sorrowful story. Jimbo, who had been creating his own elaborate sandwich nodded towards him. "I'm sorry, my friend; I know how deeply painful it is to lose a father, because I recently lost mine at the hands of these miserable Marxists." He grew emotional. "But I guarantee you that I will make every one of them pay for it. As long as I live, I will hunt them like a cat with a mouse. I'll play with them for a while and make them suffer as they've made me suffer by taking my best friend, who was my father, when he had never done any harm to anyone."

Aurora stood up and hugged Jimbo tenderly. "My son, I want you to try and leave your revenge behind. Hate will fill your heart with sadness and not allow you to ever be happy. Even though your father is no longer with us, I know he would never want to see you get lost in your hatred. We both want to have love, happiness, and peace for both you guys, not hatred in your hearts. I don't think your father, wherever he is, will feel any joy looking into your heart full of revenge and hatred. Please try, my son."

Jimbo returned her hug. To put her mind at ease, he said, "OK, Mom. I promise you I will do whatever is possible to forgive the assassins of my father."

Aurora gave him a small smile. "Thank you, my son. God bless you for at least trying to prevent the hatred from taking over your heart. Now finish your sandwich.

You haven't eaten for many hours, and that's not good for your health."

Jimbo returned to his chair and continued to build his sandwich silently out of respect to his mother. He bit his lips as he looked at me and raised his eyebrows in surrender. As everyone ate the exquisite food on the table, Arnaldo sat down next to us with an extra bottle of mayonnaise and cut some slices of ham, cheese, and put some Ritz crackers on his plate. He began to eat as he said, "You are right. You arrived a little later than I expected but thank God for your delay. Otherwise, the lives of Challo el Bandido and his family would be lost by now, not to mention your own lives would be in imminent danger. Now, the most important thing is for you to complete your mission. The information that I will provide you will enable us not only to stop the deaths of hundreds or thousands of innocent people but also inflict a large blow to the stomach of the international Marxists and their accomplices around the world. There will be a big meeting in the private residence of my uncle, Ramiro Valdez Menendez, right here in Miramar.

Arnaldo removed a folded slip of paper from the pocket of his shirt and handed it to me. "This is the combination for the safe which is in his library there, where he puts all the caca that he doesn't want anyone to ever see from the first ring of the Prime Minister's office. All their Machiavellian plans, including assassinations and other crazy things that people cannot ever believe. I will give you all the details necessary later for the alarms and emergency exits from the residence as soon as we get close to enacting this operation, in case something happens we hadn't planned for. You have to be ready to use exactly the exits I tell you to use so you don't lose your life. I will provide you with the clothing that will enable you to impersonate one of the attachés of a leader of the group called Omega Green Scorpions, which is a division of MQ-1. Disguised as diplomats, they are assassins and recruiters. Their only mission is to convince young students in universities and colleges around the world to be used in different manners. Number one, assassins of political and religious leaders who present obstacles for their plans. Number two, recruiting outcasts and young fanatics around them who are easy to convince with the Utopian philosophies they sell, radicalizing them to create disturbances, domestic violence, and destruction of property from burning police cars in cities to sophisticated assassination attempts on senators, including high dignitaries of the opposing parties, all to advance their own candidate for the party of their preference to power, especially in the elections that they have not the smallest possibility of victory in a clean and democratic election."

Aurora put her hand to her mouth to avoid spilling the food she was chewing. She was impatient not to allow the momentum of that conversation to be lost. "My God, these miserable Marxists aren't content to bring their destructive and horrible system to our country but also are looking to export that misery to the entire world!"

I smiled. "That is nothing new, my lovely Aurora. They've been doing this for many decades now. Practically from the very beginning, the Castro brothers promoted the beautiful and noble Cuban revolution that almost everyone supported with the promise of returning democracy, stability, and prosperity to our country. We're still as miserable as under Fulgencio Batista."

Mama Teca nodded. She smiled ironically. "No one knows how valuable what they have is until someone comes and rips it out of their hands." She added emphatically as she jerked her right thumb to her chest, "The Castros never fooled me, even though they did so to millions of people by promising everyone the image they tried to sell of the Messiah. I don't blame people, everyone looks for the golden door to the future and wants to believe in somebody, but I know the genetic roots of the Castro family very well and where they came from— people very close to my family who had worked for them as domestic servants for many years before Ramon, Fidel, and Raul were born. They both come from a dysfunctional family, and all dirty and shady, abusive hypocrites. Not just their mothers but their father as well. What good could come out of the genes of such a sexually degenerate man? That is why nobody wanted to believe what I said before, fascinated by the propaganda of the Kool-Aid they sold to everyone as the new Robin Hood of the Americas; time proved that those born of a twisted tree never have straight trunks. Even if you try to force it straight, all you do is break it."

I nodded. "What you just said is a very cruel reality that millions of Cubans don't want to believe, even after the many political deceptions they've suffered. Everyone looked for that tiny light of hope on the horizon; they want to ignore each new deception. My father believed, who never had exercised the right to vote in any election before, and completely devoted his soul and body to the false promises of the brothers. He eventually discovered that they were nothing but more corrupt politicians."

We looked at each other with sad expressions. Atacia had a small smile of hope on her face. She rubbed her womb which now was growing bigger daily and said emphatically, "If we don't do this for ourselves, we need to get these malignant communists out of our island." She pointed to her belly with her right hand. "Our future generations should not suffer for our mistakes. Let's do it for them, even if we lose our lives in the process. But we have to make it our best effort to destroy this political and immoral system so that our future generations have the elemental principles and morals that should be established in any prosperous society."

Arnaldo grinned broadly and raised his glass of mimosa and said loudly, "I like this very much. Thank you for your little doses of hope, Atacia. Let's toast to that."

We smiled and raised our glasses, clinking them together. "For the freedom of Cuba," we said together.

Arnaldo took us a tour of the residence, which was more like a palace. The second level had ten rooms with their own bathrooms and even jacuzzies. We were able to pick the rooms we liked best, and he came close to me and said, "My message is very clear. This is an extraordinary, humongous opportunity for us to not only prevent a major act which will put the world in turmoil but also a great success would be a setback for the international Marxists and their Omega Green Scorpion organization. They are the principal contact with the financiers and royal leader for the terrorist group that you guys in the intelligence community have been circling around for so many years. This particular contact agrees to provide to us all the information without holding anything back, including bank accounts and names so that our intelligence elite can stop this tremendous act of terrorism which will cause great sadness to the entire world, not just the United States of America.

He took me by the arm with his eyes wide in consternation. "I assure you that this information is completely legit, but you should confirm and verify it. I would not give a single dollar to him until you through the intelligence community communicate to me that everything checks out. I don't have all the details yet about this attack, but I know it will be of enormous proportions and devastating, especially for the USA. It will have international repercussions and cause economic paralysis. It could, according to my contact, destabilize the banking system and the entire international trade. When you finish your interview with him, you should leave the island immediately because if it crosses their minds that this highly delicate and classified information has been compromised, they will not hesitate to kill an entire town. They have invested billions of dollars in this, and if we expose this it will set them back several years."

We said our goodbyes and Arnaldo said, "I have to go to my office. I must verify some things to make sure our movements are secure. Later I will give you more details for the exit plan to get you and your friends out after your principal mission is accomplished with your meeting with one of the elites in the Green Scorpions. You will refer to him by this name and identified to him as the Cuban Lightning, nothing more. I will try to introduce you personally."

"OK," I replied. "That will be great."

He walked to one of the garages. I heard the automatic door open and close as he left. Everyone got accommodated in their rooms; I walked to the garages where I looked through the tool shelves and found several gardening shovels. I took two of the medium sized ones and shook my head. "My God, this guy has so many tools it's unbelievable." Some of the tools he had were still wrapped from the manufacturer—it was clear he was very well connected.

I walked out of the garages with the shovels and went to a bathroom near the dining room. I noticed a stand of towels and took two bath towels, wrapping each shovel in its own towel. Using the back door to the patio which communicated with the back yard, kitchen, and dining room, I put both shovels on a lawn chair. I went back inside and went to the second level in search of Atacia's room.

She had taken one closest to the stairs because of her condition. I knocked on the door and called for her. There was no reply. I opened the door and walked inside. It had its own kitchenette and bar, like a small condo. I heard a motor running in the bathroom and walked inside, where I found Atacia standing naked in the jacuzzi. I realized that the exquisite smell I had detected when I walked in came from here—she had put nearly an entire container of lavender Epsom salt in it. She smiled in satisfaction when she saw me in the doorway and saw my admiring look. She enjoyed rubbing her body with a large sponge, rubbing her belly that she gently used to soap all her body. She raised her left hand high as she used the sponge with her right. She beckoned to me with her index finger as she winked her left eye with a mischievous expression.

She said, "You should come over here close to me. You should not miss this, how, and with what pleasure our baby is enjoying with me what I'm doing. This delicious fragrance, this warm water, and this luxury jacuzzi. There's no doubt in my mind that this baby brings a stamp your bloodline and your genetic connection; also, your preferences and tastes." She rubbed the sponge against her belly gently again. "You have to touch my belly. He's dancing a cha-cha-cha! You can tell for yourself with that touch the tremendously joyful experience that he is having while I sponge my belly."

    I was completely intoxicated with her enthusiasm as she related her experience while at the same time I was aroused by the beauty of her body, even with her advanced stage of pregnancy. Her obviously swollen belly that now made her to me more attractive and beautiful than before. As I looked at her with love and tenderness, knowing that right there in that belly is the seed of our beautiful love that was conceived in the middle of all these tribulations, difficulties and dangers, welding our spirits and bodies into a single body. I slowly approached her, enjoying her beautiful outline as the bubbles for the soap in her motion with the sponge over her body slid slowly as if in slow motion over her precious and firm breasts, floating all over her body and ending back in the jacuzzi.

Chapter 27: My Strategic Treasure

I undressed and entered the jacuzzi, rubbing her belly with my right hand as I sat down next to her to feel the cha-cha-cha the baby was dancing in her womb. A big smile burst across my face, surprising me because I never expected to feel that level of agitation. The baby was moving around within her womb exactly as she had described. I recalled the movie *Saturday Night Fever* and believed the baby was a dancer like John Travolta dancing to the Bee Gees song "Stayin' Alive." It was clear this baby was fully enjoying the hot water in the jacuzzi.

Atacia smiled from ear to ear and put both her hands on my face as she sought my lips to give me a very tender, sweet kiss. Then she moved away and said, "I believe it's been a while with a lot of bad moments in these past months since we've created this baby." She smiled with a little mischief. "Are you prepared to relive that beautiful moment again, even if my body with this swollen belly isn't as attractive as before?"

I smiled and caressed her belly gently, giving her a tender kiss on her lips and then going down to do the same to her belly. "Your body has never before been so beautiful and attractive to me." I sat down in the water as she slowly crawled on top of my legs, her right hand searching between them so she could straddle me comfortably.

An expression of deep pleasure spread across her face as she smiled again mischievously. She whispered in my ear, "Yes, you really are ready. I know you were lying when you said all those beautiful things about my belly, but don't stop lying to me with those beautiful words; they are a tremendous boost to my ego and a huge aphrodisiac to my sexual desires."

She straddled my lap and began to move her body as she put both arms around my shoulders, her hands laced behind my neck. With extreme satisfaction in her face, she whispered in my ear, "I've been missing you very much. We have to forget the craziness of this world a little bit and make love more frequently, so we don't let the time take away this beautiful happiness that you and I possess in the highest degree."

I smiled, leaned against the wall of the jacuzzi, and closed my eyes, filled with pleasure and happiness as well from that beautiful moment that we both enjoyed immensely. I gently rubbed her belly and said, "Whatever you say, my love. I am always at your disposition."

After we finished completely satisfying our sexual desires, Atacia said, "Please let me stay here a little longer and enjoy this moment as if I will never have it again."

I got out and she sat down where I had been, allowing her head to rest against the small cushion along the edge of the jacuzzi, her eyes closed in satisfaction. I gave her a tender kiss on the lips, got out of the water, and said goodbye. I got dressed, and as I closed the door behind me, I saw Jimbo coming down the hallway. He smiled as he saw me, a huge mischievous grin, fully aware of what we had been doing from my wet hair.

He said, "You fulfilled your duty to make my sister happy?"

I replied with a similar smiled, "I did whatever was possible, brother."

He patted my shoulder. "Well, until now I never saw her have any occasion either to cry or not look at you with the same love and admiration from the first moment that I saw you two together in our safe house and refuge in Caibarien."

I shook my head with a little smile of approval. "I didn't know you had that level of psychology and observation, especially in these kinds of details." I returned his pat on the back. "I believe you could be a good spy. This is one of the natural qualities that any spy is supposed to have: to be a good observer of the reactions, emotions, and physical demeanor of everyone around you. This is the most important factor for your survival."

He smiled full of satisfaction at my compliment. "Really? You think I could be a good spy? Or are you just joking with me?"

I shook my head, very seriously. "This is not a joke—it is reality."

We walked down the hallway, and I started to go down the stairs to the garage level. We passed the dining room and kitchen, and I said, "Will you please bring the little beach wagon from the garage? I think we'll need it. I'll meet you on the patio by the pool, near where I left the shovels we were going to use in our treasure hunt. There is a treasure I left behind in a strategically hidden place the last time I visited Miramar during one of my many in and out trips to this island. If my memory hasn't failed me, I will have your birthday present."

His eyes shone like a Christmas tree from joy. He rushed out eagerly to get the wagon. As he left, I opened the enormous refrigerator where I saw Arnaldo had placed the plate with the leftovers, which still included a large amount of sliced ham. I took a couple of slices, put them between a couple of Ritz crackers and took a bite. I had been thinking of this the whole time after I had made love to Atacia. I took a bottle of Löwenbräu beer for me and a Cuban cola for Jimbo and then headed out to the patio and the table by the chair where I had left the shovels. I sat down to finish my snack, taking a few sips of the delicious dark beer as I waited for Jimbo.

I could see in the distance the waves dancing in their usual ritual over the sand of the beach. It was already fairly late, a beautiful night with a full moon. The sky looked like Picasso's "Starry Night" painting. In my home in California in the USA, I had missed the tropical night sky of my beautiful Cuba.

Jimbo arrived pulling the wagon behind him. This particular type of wagon was standard to all the beach houses. It was used to bring things to the beach and bring them home, and the large, inflated tires prevented it from getting stuck in the sand from the weight. He saw that I had brought him a cola. "Thank you very much for remembering me," he said with a smile.

I answered with a smile of my own. "You've got my back, and I've got yours."

He nodded and replied, "Unfortunately, it's not always that way." He pointed to his chest with his left hand. "I can assure you that this one will never let you down, even if they cut off my testicles. I will never betray you."

I smiled and took a sip of my beer. "I absolutely am sure, Jimbo, that this is what's in your heart right now, tonight, at this moment, and you mean it. I have no doubts about it." I pointed upwards with my left hand. "But until you have that moment when those scissors are getting close to your testicles and see that you are about to really lose them, you cannot imagine how you will react. I hope to God that you never need to prove it to yourself. Or how you will be able to control that terror in that critical, desperate moment, when you know that all you have to do to save those testicles is to tell your enemies whatever they want to know. You may have been able to endure all the torture which came before that particular test, but the ultimate one is when you are not only in a disposition to lose your testicles but also your life. Normally your enemies, even after you talk, if they aren't completely satisfied with your information might kill you. In my experience, this occurs at least 99 percent of the time."

Jimbo looked at me with his eyes wide open in surprise. "Have you been in a situation similar to this?"

I smiled. "More than once, Jimbo."

He raised his eyebrows, and his eyes bulged out even wider. He shook his head. "Well, you have to teach me how you do this without losing your testicles, because if you had lost them, you would have been unable impregnate my sister. And you never gave any information that your enemies expected to get or demanded from you. I know," he added with conviction in his voice, "that you're not a man capable of betraying your cause or your friends to save your skin."

I smiled. "It's not a case of not giving them any information at all. You have to be smart in a situation so dangerous and delicate as when your life is in play. You have to use your imagination to find an intelligent exit without compromising your integrity, your life, or the lives of your friends and associates. In intelligence, we call this the magic of improvisation. You have to give something that they believe is valuable but that you know is no longer of any value because the information is either stale or can be controlled once you're out of that situation. Some would call this cunning, but it's something you have to be prepared for before the situation occurs. Then you will know ahead of time what you can say without damaging anyone, including yourself, and whatever you can never say under any circumstance. Do you understand what I'm saying?"

Jimbo was a very clever young man and nodded his head, deep in his thoughts as he digested what I had said. Coming out of his thoughts, he replied firmly, "Yes, of course. I have a lot to learn from you. If you give me the opportunity to continue being by your side, I will not disappoint you."

I smiled again. "For me it will be a pleasure. I only ask one thing: don't try to be too smart. Until you graduate by my side, and I give you the green light to be by yourself, don't proceed solo. You might believe that you already have it under control, but a mistake could not only cost you your life, but it could cost mine as well."

Jimbo nodded in understanding. "I got it. I will consult with you in any situation at all in whatever I get into before I move. No matter whether it's big or small."

"Very well, Jimbo, you got it. This is lesson number one. You will follow me with that wagon and just remember, what you're going to see and we're going to unbury, I left there a long time ago for a night like this so that when I needed it I have it. You always have to be prepared ahead of time and cover your back in case your contacts, even if they are dear friends, don't respond to your call. Especially when you most need weapons, explosives, or anything like that and your contacts have disappeared on you. In the best scenario, it could be a lack of appropriate communication, but in the worst scenario is that your contacts have sold their souls to their enemies for a lot more money than you've been able to pay them. Unfortunately, this happens frequently within the intelligence community when we without knowing it work with mercenaries, who have no scruples, honor, patriotism, or decency. You got it?

"Yes, I do," Jimbo affirmed.

Jimbo was pulling the wagon while I turned on a tiny flashlight on my keychain. I was looking for a particular tile design among the concrete tables with their permanent umbrellas. I opened a compass on my keychain and pointed it towards the ocean until I found north. I stood against the edge of the table and then walked forward, counting five steps.

I said, "Right here." I took one shovel and began to dig. "Jimbo, take the other shovel. You dig on that side; I'll take the other. Don't take long, because if anyone sees us, they'll report us to the authorities, and we'll have unpleasant company very soon." He began to shovel like an excavator, so I said, "Take it easy. You don't have to kill yourself."

A little while later, I heard a click as Jimbo's shovel hit something hard. Jimbo said, "I think I've found something, unless it's a rock. I think I've found what you're looking for."

I came over to him and dug around where he had indicated. It was a clear night with a full moon, it was very late, and everybody in the houses along the beach was asleep. Even so, my eyes were everywhere, because there could always be someone who couldn't sleep and decided to go for a walk on the beach. That was the last thing I wanted to see happen: to call the attention of any neighbor who might wonder why we were digging a hole in the middle of the night. I brushed myself off and helped

Jimbo dig. Finally, we managed to find my large metal ammunition box with handles on either side. Helped by Jimbo, we lifted it up out of the hole and placed it on the wagon. We rushed to fill in the holes to avoid leaving any evidence and then began to pull the wagon back to the house.

We were both drenched in sweat from the amount of physical exercise. Our bodies were coated in sand, in spite of the military attire we had taken from the guards while we pretended to be coast guards. Jimbo pulled the wagon while I pushed from the back to move as quickly to the house as possible.

We were nearly up to the house when we both heard dogs barking in the distance behind us. We simultaneously turned our heads to look back and saw far away flashlights sweeping from one side to the other to signal us to stop. They looked like they were moving slowly over the sand—apparently the dogs weren't used to walking on the sand, and so were slowed down. The dogs looked like they might be German shepherds or possibly Belgian Malinois.

I decided to not allow them to get too close, or they could become curious and open that little gift box for Jimbo, especially if those dogs were trained to detect explosives. When they discovered what we had there, it would be a very serious problem to explain my possession of all of this stuff. I said to Jimbo, "Stop." I opened the metal box and pulled out some hand grenades and put them in the sand. Then I took out a small Stinger and handed it to Jimbo. "Happy Birthday, my friend." He couldn't believe it. With a big smile on his face, he jumped and hugged me. "You're going to have the pleasure of using it before your birthday. Try not to hurt any of those men, but I need you fire it close enough to them to not only intimidate them but also to terrify those dogs. Raise so much sand that you create a dust cloud to prevent them from continuing toward us. That will give me time to reach our patio and bring the wagon into the house. That way we'll disappear before their eyes, and they won't know which house we went into."

"OK," Jimbo replied.

I continued to pull the wagon. We were only about fifty feet from the house. As I left, I said, "Please don't misuse that. We might need it later during our exit from the island."

Jimbo nodded. "OK, don't worry. I will only launch a few and then come in to join you. I just want to get them to slow their approach to us."

The dogs started barking and began to howl like a frightened wolf in the middle of a nighttime forest fire, with the flames endangering the entire pack. I assumed that those guards hadn't come out of the blue. Some curious neighbor must have seen us on the beach and called them. The guards were taken by complete surprise to see those huge explosions so close to them. They had no idea where they were coming from or why they were unexpectedly being attacked, but I felt they must have stuck their heads in the sand for a while in an attempt at self-preservation.

I got onto the patio and passed the pool. Jimbo came behind and shut the wooden double doors which provided access to the beach. We rolled the wagon all the way into the garage and put the Stinger back, together with the rest of the munitions from inside the box. We took the cover for a brand-new Harley Davidson motorcycle which had tires with no wear on the treads and used it to cover the box.

I thought yet again as we removed the cover from the beautiful Harley how in Cuba, now the poorest country in the Americas where people died of starvation and didn't even have toilet paper, the high government officials lived in absolute luxury like any multimillionaire in the capitalist world.

One of the garage doors began to open. We both froze, thinking that the communist guards had managed to open it. But our souls returned to our bodies when we saw Arnaldo returning in one of those luxury cars.

With a big smile on his face, he asked, "Hey, are you having fun admiring my car collection?"

I said, "Yes. You have some beautiful cars. I even discovered a beautiful Harley Davidson motorcycle. That's my favorite brand."

He pointed to a small closet by the side of the garage. "You have all the keys there for every car, jeep, dune buggy, or any other vehicle in this garage, including the jet skis. Anytime you want to take one for a spin, you don't need to ask permission. Either of you guys are free to use it."

"Thank you very much. I will take you at your word one day if it's necessary."

"You have nothing to thank me for. I have to thank you for all the sacrifices you've endured in your fight to restore our freedom. But now I need you to bring everyone to the library. I've brought with me videos, documents, and pictures from the plans we're going to follow in the next few days. I also have the identity of the key individual that you will meet and receive important information that can prevent the worst disaster that ever happened in history and take the lives of thousands of people."

Chapter 28: The Great Love Between Mother and Son

I turned and replied, "OK." I put my right hand on his shoulder. "Go and tell everyone to come down to the library because it looks like Arnaldo brought us good news and he wants to debrief us."

Jimbo nodded and said, "Great. I'll go and get the others." He disappeared through the door leading into the interior of the residence.

Arnaldo came over and smiled with mild sarcasm. "You're not going to believe what my uncle Ramiro just confessed to me in his private office, maybe in an attempt to impress me by the huge trust that Fidel Castro has deposited in him. It could also be another face to cover his insecurity. He wanted to share this with someone, and since I'm so close to him he selected me. He showed me a gem storage case. When he opened it, I couldn't believe it and my jaw dropped. There were at least twenty diamonds, each the size of turkey egg. They were classified as colorless #1 flawless. They had been stolen and, according to the appraiser, they're worth 75 million dollars."

"All together?" I asked.

"No. Each." We walked towards the residence's library, and Arnaldo stopped in the entry door, putting his right hand on my shoulder. He smiled conspiratorially and said, "Where do you think Fidel asked my Uncle Ramiro to put this box and its valuable cargo temporarily?"

I raised my eyebrows and furrowed my forehead as I looked at him. I said dubiously, "In the security box of your uncle's residence?"

He looked at me with a big smile on his face as he shook his head, enjoying my answer. "Exactly."

My eyebrows nearly disappeared into my hairline in my expression of surprise. We walked into the library, and I asked, "Do you know why Fidel asked your uncle Ramiro to keep that enormous amount of money to put in his own safe, when Fidel has multiple safes in the Prime Minister's office?"

Arnaldo smiled with the same sarcastic grin. "You know that Fidel Castro is the most cynical liar that humanity has so far produced. But he is far from stupid—not one single hair on his head is stupid. According to the information I have from Uncle Ramiro's own mouth, these diamonds are a unique collection, nothing like it in the entire world, stolen from a multimillionaire family in South Africa. Castro's mafia had to kill over twenty-eight people, including custodians, women, and children, since they didn't want to leave any witnesses behind. Now Interpol has issued an international warrant in every country around the world with a huge price for the heads for any information about these criminals, wherever these diamonds reappear in any corner of the world." Arnaldo shook his head. "That's why Castro doesn't want them anywhere close to him. Like the cynical criminal that he is, he always thinks the worst of people, like a bandit thinks everyone else is a bandit."

I nodded. "And if anything happens and any of the individuals involved in this operation betrays the Castro brothers over their involvement, Castro won't hesitate for a second and put the head of your uncle in the firing squad after a phony trial to get him to admit that only he was involved in the diamond theft."

Arnaldo smiled and looked deep into my eyes. "You know the monster very well because you lived in his guts."

I nodded seriously. "Maybe you haven't thought about this carefully, but this complicates our plans."

Arnaldo nodded. "Yes, I know. I've been thinking about that." His face was very serious, but his attitude remained positive. "The security in my uncle's residence will now be multiplied. But we have to look at this positively—since you have the connections to get these diamonds into the right hands, can you imagine what we can do with this vast amount of money? And of course, it would mean that our enemies could not use this financial resource. Once everything cools off and Interpol's search for the diamonds gets cold after their non-reappearance, they'll either close the case or put it into the unsolved case pile. Of course, the Castro brothers will, like they always do, find someone in the world interested in buying it, and that money will be used to plant and export more terrorist acts across the globe. Or their giving support to the enemies of freedom and their mission to keep perverting and destroying good and healthy democracies around the world. It's not important to them how many lives this will cost."

As he spoke, he had been moving around the library, taking off the bookshelves a tripod with a projection screen, an 8mm projector, and setting everything up. He set the screen up against the wall on its tripod and pulled out an 8mm reel of film which he loaded onto the projector. At that moment, the door opened to admit Jimbo and the rest of our friends. Arnaldo said to

Jimbo, "Please turn off the lights. The switch is to your left behind the door."

The lights went off and everyone sat down to watch the film Arnaldo had to show us. The first thing we saw were black and white numbers and some letters; finally, images of a very fancy room which appeared to be a banquet played on the screen. Elegantly dressed people and waitresses dress impeccably in tuxedos, served various drinks. Arnaldo started to narrate as the film moved forward.

"This is the inside of my Uncle Ramiro's mansion at one of his great diplomatic parties with envoys from around the world. It is supposed to be a union of non-aligned countries but is only a cover for what is old news now but still functionally the Tri-Continental International Terrorist Union, which you know very well."

I nodded. "Another of what was considered a brilliant idea of Che and Fidel's for exporting terrorism across the world under the cover that they're helping the underdog poor countries against the American capitalists."

Arnaldo smiled with his accustomed sarcastic smile, shaking his head in disgust. We watched a group of women and men walked around. Music played in the background, and Ramiro Valdez, in full uniform as Minister of the Interior, walked around, greeting the guests and chatting with different people.

I said, "Hold it!" He stopped the film. "Please rewind that a little. I believe I recognized some familiar faces among your uncle's guests at this splendid party, some very macabre personalities."

He reversed the film and asked, "What? Did you see any personal relation in the film?"

"Yes, very personal, but it also looked like a professional one, a mixed combination of both aspects."

When he reached the spot which caught my attention, I said, "OK, stop it right there."

He stopped the film where I indicated, and I could see two women dressed to the nines. I stood up and walked to the screen, putting my finger on one of them. "Do you know who these women are?"

He nodded. "I saw them in the Ministry of the Interior. They've been staying very close by, here in the Nautico in Miramar. They are Puerto Rican nationals, and they both received very sophisticated training in radio communications and counterintelligence right here in Cuba. They are considered extremely important and highly valuable for the Cuban communist government. They both have to be extremely valuable to deserve this golden treatment. Every time they come here, I see them escorted as a courtesy by the G-2 and treated like rare diamonds. Do you know them?"

I nodded. "Very well." I pointed to one of them. "This is Ana Belen Montes. She's been working in the US State Department for nearly two decades." I pointed at the other. "This is Marta Rita Velazquez, alias Barbara. According to my research, which I've already passed on to the FBI, Marta Rita Velazquez is the recruiter from Cuban intelligence of people in universities and different high levels of US intelligentsia who have shown any disaffection towards the capitalist system, showing signals of being good recruits for the Interior Ministry in Cuba."

Figure 18 Ana Belin Montes and her recruiter, "Barbara"

Arnaldo smiled sarcastically again. "I believe that in this case, it's more than ideological disaffection for the capitalist system; in this case, I believe that there's a sexual attraction." He pointed at Barbara. "In my opinion, the recruiter didn't use psychological or ideological background on this girl; I think she used sex as a tool to recruit her." He pointed at Barbara. "I had to look twice at this woman because at first she looked like a black man working as a stevedore on the Havana docks."

"What kind of comparison is that? You really don't like this woman—what caused you to make such a derogatory description for her?" I turned it into a joke.

"I'm pretty sure you would spend a summer with her if you had no one else."

Arnaldo pointed towards the fly in his pants. "I have a profound respect for my little friend. I don't think that even if were alone with that woman on a desert island I would be able to sacrifice him to do such an extreme thing." I smiled as he continued to roll the film.

I stopped it again. "Hold it! Back up again!" I saw some new faces I recognized appear on the screen within that group. I walked once more to the screen and pointed at another grotesque face. The arms and hands of the very tall man looked like they had survived third degree burns; he was dressed all in black with a cane; the right hand which held it clearly showed something out of the normal. The hand on the cane handle clearly had six fingers. The cane had a bronze handle shaped like a dragon's head with shark-like teeth and two prominent incisors also made of bronze, and a very long tongue like a short Egyptian dagger. I had clearly memorized the face of this individual, as well as that of his black assistant who always walked next to him: his name was Origeo. The other man had a fiendish aspect, his head completely shaved, looking like a genie out of some diabolical lamp, and he had a very nasty scar on the left side of his face. He had a gold molar which you could see when he laughed morbidly. His blue eyes made him look even more demoniac. He made a perfect complement to the man with six fingers, his face looking like it had been burned in Hell.

These two men usually ran in the highest levels of the communist government of the Castro brothers, and no one ever knew who they were or where they came from. There was, however, no doubt in anyone's mind about the tremendous influence they held over the Maximum Leader and his brother. They came in and out of any maximum-security military or civilian government building without being questioned by anyone.

I had remained silent, looking at these two individuals, my face contorted with rage. Atacia broke the silence. "Do you know these grotesque individuals?"

I nodded. "Yes, unfortunately."

"Are you OK?"

"Yes." I tried to remove from my mind the years of rage I held in there. "These two might not have been the executioners, but I knew for certain that they were part of the planning of the assassination of my son right here in the capital of Havana." Everyone looked at each other in complete surprise. I caressed my chin, thinking of the profound, horrible memories of those years. Even though time had passed, it was still there in my heart which was filled with guilt. All those years I had blamed myself for not being able to bring my son out of Cuba before those assassins had executed their objective. It was nothing more than revenge to punish me, since they couldn't get their hands on me for the work in espionage that I had been for so many years doing around the world, exposing the criminal acts against humanity that they conducted with impunity, exporting genocide and revolutions with the objective of destroying democratic nations and free countries, and converting every citizen in those countries into slaves of their Marxist-Leninist ideology.

Atacia came over to me and put her arm around my shoulder. "Remember, none of us can blame ourselves for what other criminals do. You have to forgive yourself for not acting in time to save your son's life. Until you achieve that, you will never be able to live in peace."

Everyone looked at me. I could feel their compassion, even though everyone remained silent, feeling my pain. After we finished the debriefing, Arnaldo said, "If any of you guys has any question after I explain in detail how we're going to do this at the reception which will take place this weekend, remember every single face because each of these men I will point out are members of MQ-1 Omega Green Scorpions. Each one of them are trained to perfection in committing an assassination with master skill. It could be worth your life to imprint those faces in your mind to avoid them—not confront them—once you get inside the mansion."

We went through the debriefing, memorizing the faces he showed us, one at a time. He said, "When we finish this operation, we will take you guys to the same place you came into Cojimar, where I will have prepared in a key place in between the caves and rocks on the coast something which is a little surprise that you won't have seen before. All I can tell you right now is that its codename is the Bandit. We don't want to take time discussing that and cause you to forget what you've seen in the film. All I'll say now is that it's a gift from O'Brien transported here to Cuba with the sole purpose that your exit and those with you when we finish this very delicate mission to make sure that you get out of here alive.

"Well, if you don't have any other questions, and everything is perfectly clear in your mind, I'm going to go get some sleep for a few hours. I didn't sleep at all last night—my uncle kept me up like these crappy communists do in meetings all night like vampires, planning their macabre schemes to dominate the world until dawn, trying to show to everyone that they're working so hard. Simple fakery and cheap theatricals to show people their high level of sacrifice. In the morning, they go to the mansions they stole from the legitimate owners to sleep in the air conditioners, making everyone assume they're still working during the daytime. That is the philosophy they've been using all their lives." Arnaldo said goodbye to us and went upstairs to his room to rest.

We walked out of the library and went to the kitchen dinette. I asked them, "What if we start the day happy, like my Mima used to say when I was a little boy? Full stomach, happy heart."

Atacia replied with a big smile, "I like that idea. I'll help you with whatever you want to make."

"No, it's not what I want to make; it's what you guys want to eat."

We walked into the kitchen. I opened the refrigerator and suggested "I'll give you two options. We can make a Spanish omelet with shrimp, pimento, pineapple, and mushrooms. It's a recipe Mima taught me when I was a kid. It's delicious, that kind of fricassee with garlic bread. Or we can get pork chops with pineapple and cashews." Almost everyone chose the pork with pineapple. "OK, let's do it," I said.

Atacia came with me. I handed her an apron, taking one for myself, and we got to work to prepare the food, with Mama Teca added to our kitchen team. We made a gourmet dinner with the amount of food we prepared: mashed potatoes with crispy pork skin, scallions, fried plantains, and pork chops with pineapple and cashews.

A little while later, we all sat down around the table as Aurora said, "I believe that calling this a breakfast is an injustice, not just because it's exquisite but also because this is a combination of breakfast, lunch, and dinner. There's so much food here that if I manage to finish my plate, this will be not just my first meal of the day but my last one. I'll be satisfied all day."

Jimbo grinned. "That's what you say now with a full stomach, but I assure you that in three to five hours you'll be sticking your nose in the refrigerator to give yourself a refresher of the meal that you couldn't finish now."

Aurora, a little discontented at Jimbo's comment, replied, "I believe you, Jimbo, will be the first one to return to the refrigerator in less time that you gave me. You, being younger, have a faster digestion than we have."

He smiled and nodded. "It's very possible; but at least I'm not denying that I will be craving this great meal later on. A great meal is like great sex; when we find it, we want to go back for more."

Mama Teca hit Jimbo on the shoulder in reprimand. "Jimbo, you have to remember something: even if what you say is true, you have to be a little more careful to express these things to your mother with more respect. Don't compare food to sex."

Aurora shook her head. "Thank you, Mama Teca, for your constant effort to educate my child. Unfortunately, Jimbo is like what we see in kids today. We cannot expect anything better from this communist society we're living in today, when respect towards our parents is replaced with the respect for the communist government. And if you don't make that change, they put you in front of the firing squad."

Jimbo raised his right hand humbly. "I'm sorry, Mom. What I said was only a spontaneous expression, and I didn't think I was doing anything wrong when I said it. I see you as my best friend, not my mother anymore, after all we've gone through together lately and have suffered together, including the death of my father."

Aurora looked at Jimbo directly in the eyes, listening to his words. She was touched profoundly by them and couldn't control her emotions as tears rolled from her eyes. She stood up and walked towards Jimbo where he sat next to me. She put her arm around the neck of her son and embraced him, kissing the top of his head. "I know that you don't have the slightest intention of offending me. To tell you the truth, from my deepest feelings, I prefer that from now on you continue to consider me and talk to me as your best friend and not like your mother. I will consider myself honored. I find it appropriate, even if the others don't agree with me, but this is very appropriate to your masculinity. You have to show to us that you are already a grown man, and we should treat you as the adult you are, not like the boy Jimbo."

Jimbo stood up with tears of gratitude in his eyes. He crushed Aurora to himself in a fierce hug, which she received joyfully. The rest of us grew very emotional, feeling as I did, the joy and love between mother and son, who welded together in that magnificent moment in that beautiful gesture. We witnessed and would never forget the pure love between mother and son that could only be replaced when a man or woman find in the journey of life the other half of their orange[20].

---

[20] A commonly used phrase in Spanish "to find your half-orange" was found in Plato's "Symposium" in which Aristophanes tells the tale of how humans were originally designed as spherical, but Zeus cut them into two pieces, one male and one female, condemning humanity to find their matching half in order to be whole once more.

Chapter 29: Origeo—the Six-Fingered Man's Adviser

Figure 19 Mansion of Ramiro Valdez

A few days later, everyone was dressed elegantly to attend the major event in the mansion of Ramiro Valdez. Arnaldo had provided each of us great clothing with even copies of Armani designs made in Cuba, so that we were all attired to the standard of international visitors at that gathering. We decided to divide into two teams in separate cars. Mama Teca, Aurora, and Arnaldo were going to use the metallic olive-green Range Rover because of the tremendous similarity this vehicle had to the communist elite G-2, as olive-green was the official color of the government. Jimbo, Atacia, and I were going to use a beautiful Maserati *Quattroporte*, shiny black with light caramel leather seats with the emblem of Maserati on them. By splitting into two groups, we would avoid attracting attention by such a large assembly arriving together at the mansion, but also in case we had to leave in an emergency. It was always better to have two automobiles ready and waiting for us, and either vehicle could carry all of us comfortably and so provide us with a secure exit.

We left the Nautico development and after traveling through Miramar for a while, we crossed Fifth Avenue, and I looked in my rear mirror. Arnaldo was following us at a prudent distance. I kept my eyes continually in the rearview mirror, as we had agreed that if anything went wrong which would force us to abort the plan, he would communicate that fact by turning the headlights on twice as the signal for danger.

As we were about to cross a poorly lit intersection, an unexpected pair of motorcycle policemen came out of the darkness from the side street right in front of us at very high speed. The only signal that we knew they were official vehicles was the red and blue lights they had flashing; but they burst right in front of us even though we had the right of way; typical government individuals, completely ignoring the stop sign without even looking.

Fortunately, my reactions were very quick, and I turned the wheel hard to the left to avoid them, nearly causing us to roll over as we avoided those motorcycles but had to slam on the brakes hard because right behind them was a limousine blindly following the motorcycles. Though I managed to avoid the large concrete light pole on the sidewalk I had to run up on, sparks flew as the side of the limo scraped against the metallic chrome rear bumper of the Maserati, leaving a long scratch on the driver's side of the limo as we glanced off it. It was much better than it could have been; if I hadn't reacting that quickly, the two policemen would have wound up under my car and likely killed, and the only damage to either vehicle was the scratch on the limo.

We pulled over and Arnaldo drove up in the Range Rover from behind, a witness to everything, stopping behind us a couple hundred feet away. As we got out to assess the damage, Arnaldo and our friends in his car got out of the Range Rover. Instead of coming over to us, they went over to the limousine to see if everyone in it was OK.

The limo driver was a tall, skinny black man with a very professional cap. He replied, "Yes, everything is fine. Nothing major, just a little scratch."

Not knowing how Arnaldo wanted to handle this, we remained by our car. We were worried, as this accident could jeopardize and create a definite interruption to our plan and mission. The two policemen took their sweet time in turning around, came back, and stopped close to the Maserati. They took their helmets off and walked towards us, hands on the butts of their pistols, trying to intimidate us in order to hide their own responsibility for the situation. The youngest one said to me, "Are you blind, *compañero*? What the hell were you thinking? Why didn't you stop when you saw the emergency lights as we were stopping the traffic in your direction?"

I was boiling and, unusual for me, I lost my cool. Very indignantly, I replied, "You guys made no signal to stop anyone like regular policemen. I'm not blind. You guys cut into this intersection like bats out of hell at a high speed, not taking into consideration that you even have a stop sign in your direction."

The other policeman was older, a tall, very fit mulatto and appeared to be the one in charge. He listened to my angry reaction, and even though I had made it very clear that I wasn't a happy camper and blaming them, he also tried to intimidate me. He yelled at me, "We're not regular traffic policemen. We are elite escorts with the Ministery of the Interior and officers of the G-2! Who do you think you are, the owner of Havana with your new Maserati and brand-new Armani tuxedo? Here in Cuba, the bourgeoisie don't even have power! Give me your identity card! I think you guys are all going to sleep in one of my cells, the smallest one in Villa Marista! And in this heat, we don't even have air conditioning to offer you in your fancy dress!"

    I watched Arnaldo come towards us and saw his face. He clearly had heard all of this as he approached us. I clenched my jaw and maintained silence to avoid provoking a major incident. The sergeant, believing he had succeeded in intimidating me and asked harshly, "Where the hell are you guys going so fast that you couldn't even slow down?"

    Arnaldo was right behind him now and touched his shoulder. The sergeant jumped in surprise. Arnaldo said, "They are going to the mansion of my uncle, Ramiro Valdez, and are my personal guests. I was driving behind them as escort to make sure they got to their destination safe and sound." As he spoke, he removed his ID from his pocket and showed it to the sergeant, clearly revealing the green and white ID with the Ministry of the Interior, with G-2 in green letters on it. Both officers' jaws dropped.

The sergeant saluted Arnaldo and joined his junior in standing stiffly at attention. Arnaldo very nonchalantly replaced the ID in his jacket pocket. He looked the sergeant in the eyes and said, "You are a big liar. If there's anything Uncle Ramiro and I despise are liars and the negligent within our government. You guys are responsible for all the misery and calamities in our country, making our people suffer." The sergeant's face drained of all color and his lips trembled as he tried to speak. Arnaldo put his finger on the man's lips. "Shh." He used the same finger to point at the stop sign on the corner that they were supposed to yield to which read *Alto*. "Are you illiterate?" The sergeant mutely shook his head fearfully. He pointed to the younger one, who had been more offensive and aggressive. "Are *you* illiterate?" Like his sergeant, he shook his head. "Which of you guys was supposed to stop traffic at this intersection, putting not only your lives at risk but also the passengers of that limousine, who I believe are valuable to the government?"

The sergeant said in a very submissive tone, "Can I speak, *compañero*? You have to understand it's very dark in this area. Many of the streetlights are burned out, and due to the negligence of the people who are supposed to replace them, it takes months for anything to get done. It's like a funeral on this avenue, because everyone avoids it, maybe one car every two or three hours."

"Ah, ha!" Arnaldo said, nodding. "The truth finally comes to light. You shouldn't apologize to me; you should apologize to my friend here, to whom you guys owe your lives tonight. If it weren't for his quick reactions, you would both be dead." He put his right hand on my shoulder. "Thanks to him, and all you did was to bully him and avoid your own responsibility by making him the one guilty of the accident. What happened, if he didn't do what he did at the right time? You would both be dead beneath that Maserati."

The sergeant looked at me again and said, "I'm sorry." I raised my hand to say it was OK.

The interior dome light of the limo lit up as someone opened a door. The passengers appeared to be quite calm and were leaving the vehicle to see what was going on. I heard the familiar voice of Ana Belen Montes, the Cuban spy within the State Department I had been working to expose, ask, "Is everything OK, Armando?"

The driver stood before the front bumper, listening to the conversation. He replied, his hat in his hand, "Yes, yes, *señorita*. Everything is OK, just an unimportant scratch to the limo. I believe in a few minutes we'll continue our journey."

Ana replied, "OK. We don't want to be late to our reception."

Another woman got out of the limo, her face lit by the dome light. I saw that it was Ana's recruiter, Marta Rita Velazquez. Arnaldo realized that these women had also been invited to the party, and their presence meant something really sinister was going to go on at the party, something we had not anticipated.

Arnaldo and I exchanged glances, thinking the same thing. It was a strange coincidence to complete the whole pie as two men got out of the limo by the opposite door, but their faces were blocked by the two women from our angle. But as they walked in front of the headlights of the still-running limo, all four of them curiously bent over to see and touch the scratch. I could now see the grotesque six-fingered man and his assistant,

Origeo. We looked at each other again, not understanding what these people were doing together and what relationship united these four serpents. We communicated only with our eyes and agreed that we would find out eventually, but we understood at that moment that we needed to get out of there before any of these four identified me, even though I was in disguise with thick eyebrows, a prosthetic nose, and a wig. We wanted to take no chances.

Arnaldo said, OK, *compañeros*. There's nothing wrong, you've apologized, and we're all revolutionaries, so we should not hold grudges."

The sergeant was effusive in his thanks. "You've very kind, *compañero*." The two apologized to me once more and we said goodbye.

A little while later, we entered through the huge metal gates with several guards manning them into a massive parking for the mansion. It was like some parking lot for a Las Vegas casino. We parked a prudent distance away from each other, each car facing in opposite directions, north and south. Whatever happened, our cars wouldn't get damaged, and we still had exits and secure transportation to that destination.

Jimbo took his backpack containing detonators, explosives, and his favorite toy out of the Maserati. His Stinger was in two pieces, and he only had to assemble it to bring it into action. We exchanged a last briefing, ready to separate into our two groups, and then we saw the limousine enter the place with its diabolic cargo. We hurried to separate from each other and enter the building so we could avoid them, mingling in with the crowd entering the mansion. We had synchronized our watches beforehand as well as the earbud radios with an emergency code "A fly in the pie, abort" in case something happened.

    We showed our IDs and invitations and were allowed inside the building. Jimbo remained in the parking lot, preparing himself for the midnight fireworks finale. We took all these precautions because we were entering the most secure civilian building featuring the latest technology in the island—devices which easily intercepted radio communications, and there were cameras and various kinds of detectors all over the place. There were even cameras in the restrooms.

    The beautiful entry hall and reception area that we walked into had black and white marble floors, sweeping staircases to the left and right which led up to the upper level, and a huge, expensive chandelier hanging from the ceiling in the middle of the room. The stairs met upstairs in the center, the brass rails supported glass panels with small holes which projected white and blue lights that shone in circles along the ceiling and the floor. It gave the place a very sophisticated, high class modern modeling show. The music came from unseen speakers hidden in the walls, controlled from the main control room of the place, playing a variety of music from Classical to ballads to Cuban music—very select and excellent quality. The entry place of the mansion gave one the impression of being in a theater for a symphonic orchestra performance.

    The service personnel were all dressed in tuxedos, serving Dom Perignon champagne, showing you the bottle as they poured. We pretended to drink, putting the glasses to our lips but not taking a sip. To cover the fact that we weren't actually drinking, we discretely baptized the plants as we moved around with little trickles, being careful as we did so, knowing we were on multiple cameras controlled by the G-2. Fortunately, Arnaldo had told us in our briefing which areas and angles that would keep us out of plain view of the cameras.

Atacia raised her glass to her lips and whispered discretely as she pretended to take a drink, "I see more G-2 agents than any foreign guests." She frowned worriedly. "This is not in our plan. This will be more difficult than what Arnaldo presented to us." She shook her head slightly, unhappy at what she was seeing. "I believe these diamonds have complicated our job tremendously." She put her right hand on one of my shoulders. "I only ask you to not take any unnecessary risks. If you find anything unusual inside the library when you break into there before you open the safe, please abort immediately and find the closest and most secure exit from this place."

I smiled and pulled out my refined handkerchief from the pocket of my tuxedo. I pretended to wipe my lips after taking a sip of champagne and replied, "I actually expected more security than what I've seen so far. I don't think you should worry too much. Our plan is very solid, and we will succeed and very soon we will all be out of Cuba with the fruit of our work in hand." I looked at my wristwatch. "Remember, it's still too early. The night is still young, and at least half of the guests have not yet arrived. This place will be packed in the next few hours with people from all over the world, communists and opportunists. We should not care about them because they will all be drinking nonstop until they get totally intoxicated. Everyone loves to drink, especially when it's for free. It is a tremendous display of a lack of common sense for our enemies, because even some of the security detail will violate the regulations about not drinking on duty. They will take glass cup here and another there, and this will impair their faculties enough to open the opportunity for us because they will make mistakes. Those mistakes are the ones we're going to use to our advantage to achieve our goal and then get out of here safe and sound."

Atacia took the glass her lips again with a big smile on her face this time. 'Thank you for relaxing my mind like listening to Classical music. I have to apologize, because I forgot who I was talking to and what you have been able to achieve in the past, walking through the most intense flames of danger as the Lightning, surviving the most incredible hurricanes, not even slowed or by the most powerful forces of your opposing elements, the water and their intense winds."

I leaned in a little as I put my handkerchief back in my tuxedo pocket. With a small smile I kissed her lightly on the lips. That was not what she was expecting or looking for, because after all these beautiful compliments she had given me. She reached her left hand behind my neck and kissed me passionately, taking me completely by surprise, because it was so public.

When we separated, I said, "You broke the rule. It was unexpected and a beautiful kiss." She put both her hands on my shoulders, her eyes wet with emotion, showing concern in her face. She spoken in a choked voice, "I need to confess something to you of something I did in the past that I'm not very proud of and very repentant about, but you should know. Even though my mother told me never to make the mistake of telling you our secret because this could disrupt crack in our relationship. You might not be able to love me as you've done until now."

    I smiled. This time I was the one to take her face between my hands. I looked her profoundly in the eyes as she had just done moments ago. I said tenderly, "Listen to me carefully, because you must understand clearly, especially if we plan to spend if not a long time, then the rest of our lives together. I only am interested in the present and the future. The past is of no interest at all to me, unless you want to share your beautiful memories as a child or other beautiful memories with me." I added emphatically, "I don't want to know anything ugly or unpleasant about your past. The past is the past, and whatever you did then will never be a motive for me to tear us apart. If you want me to know something in order to produce tranquility to your spirit, then and only then will I listen and I will keep your secret without criticism of any kind. That is what you call the real pure and unconditional love. That is the love I feel for you now. Nothing in your past will ever change my feelings."

    She hugged me with uncontrollable tears in her eyes. She said in my ear, "I will love you until I die. You are the man I've dreamed all my life."

    I took my handkerchief out again and gently wiped the tears out of her eyes, which left two black stains from her mascara on my beautiful white linen handkerchief. We smiled and chuckled as we looked at those stains in the refined handkerchief. She said, "I ask you to forgive me for being so emotional, but maybe that's my pregnancy. I have to go to the restroom to correct my ruined makeup."

"Yes." I looked at my watch. "Don't be long. When we receive the signal from your brother, we have to leave this room, or our lives will be in danger."

"Don't worry, it won't be long. I'll be back right away."

"Remember to check your watch. It's very close for the fireworks to start."

She looked at her watch. "I've got twenty minutes; I'll be back before then."

She walked away to the bathrooms, and from the corner of the room where I had a view of the whole area, I saw Ramiro Valdez surrounded by his entourage and dignitaries. He was enjoying the attention of the sycophants very much. Arnaldo was in the group, greeting his uncle, but then withdrew shortly afterwords to meet Aurora and Mama Teca on the opposite side of the room from where I was. The man with the six fingers had not left Ramiro's side for even a single minute, but Origeo had disappeared. I tried to locate him in the crowd, but he was nowhere to be found. I started to think that he had gone to do something for his boss or to the parking lot to make sure the limousine was secure; that worried me a little. That was the area Jimbo had been working in, and the last thing we wanted was for him to catch Jimbo in the act of doing something he was not supposed to be doing.

I checked my watch again. It was five minutes to midnight. I looked towards the bathroom in concern and saw the smiling face of Atacia on the way out. She raised her arm and pointed at her watch to show she was returning early. She came to my side. As she reached me, we heard Jimbo send the signal over the radio. She immediately left to the right side of the stairs leaving the room, while I headed towards the left and the men's restrooms.

A few seconds after we moved towards our areas, the first explosion lit up the parking lot outside with such tremendous force that glasses and bottles of champagne shattered as they hit the marble floor. We turned our heads to look at each other. That was closer than we expected. As she went up the stairs, I went into the men's room and heard the yelling of people as they dove onto the floor, indicating they thought we were being attacked by terrorists. As I stood in the door, one of the Stinger missiles that Jimbo had sent broke through the Venetian glass, and hit the chandelier, taking down the entire structure, sending pieces of glass flying everywhere as it hit the floor.

A second missile came in and hit the balcony between the two stairs, collapsing the left staircase, concrete flying everywhere, dust choking the air. The panic gained momentum. Ramiro was on the floor with his bodyguards, trying to get him out of the building without a care for anyone else.

Another missile came in from the same place, breaking all of the glass in the front of the mansion and collapsing another portion of the left side of the balcony. I smiled as I walked into the restroom, contemplating as I checked my watch the exactitude of the time of Jimbo's activity, following to the teeth his instructions. By doing so, he made sure than none of us wound up being victims of what was supposed to be a distraction for our enemies.

I looked for a small utility room at the end of the huge bathroom which had. According to Arnaldo's description, a chute from the second level to the utility closet where dirty clothes were dropped form the upper level. I closed myself inside, placing a broom and a vacuum cleaner against the door to barricade it, and began to climb the chute with my elbows and knees. It was very tight in there and fortunately made of concrete, making me thank God once more for my height and light weight, for I would certainly have gotten stuck in there if I were taller or larger.

It took me a while, but I made it up to the second level. It was very dark, with the only light coming through the air vents at the top of the wooden door. I opened the accordion door slowly to make a crack so I could see what was going on in the corridor outside. I could see Atacia had already put both guards out of commission at the door to the library. She was trying to drag a large, heavy man to where I was by herself. I rushed to get out of there. "Wait," I said, "let me help you."

She looked at me with a big smile on her face. I grabbed the guard by the feet and together we dragged him into the closet. She said, "OK, let's drop the body down."

"Wait, wait—this guy is very heavy. If he gets stuck near the top, we can't put the other one in. The other guy is skinnier, let's put him in first."

"Good thinking," she replied

We got the other guard and dropped him headfirst down the chute like a sack of potatoes. He landed on the dirty clothes in the hamper below.

I said, "Let's hope he didn't break his neck."

"I doubt it," she said. "They are numbed. I used my darts."

We dragged the large guard and put him in, headfirst as well. Even though his body slid in perfectly, when he reached the bottom, he was stuck by the shoulders. Apparently, the mouth was smaller than the chute. We closed the door.

Atacia smiled. "When he wakes up in several hours, he's going to have a tremendous migraine." She picked up her large handbag, putting her dart gun inside and then removing a small spray can. She walked into the hallway and sprayed black paint on the security cameras there. I looked at her with an incredulous expression. She said, "I guess you're right—this was not recommended by Arnaldo, but I think it a prudent measure, if you consider the Machiavellian individuals we are dealing with; they must have in place a secondary system for security. I know Jimbo brought down all the power and cameras, what if they have a secondary emergency system? If they do, they'll see us."

I smiled and shook my head, giving her a thumbs up. "You're 100% right, girl. That is something that even didn't cross my mind. This island is so uncivilized and behind other people, but they have the best and latest of everything, including technology for themselves."

We walked into the double door which was supposed to lead into the library. After I entered in the code Arnaldo had given me into the keyboard of the door, I removed a metallic box like was used for Altoids breath mints from my inside tuxedo pocket. I opened it; inside there were small plastic coverings with thumb- and fingerprints. I put these on and pressed my thumbs and fingers on the screen on the door. First a red light appeared, then a yellow, then a green. They moved in sequence back and forth until finally the green light stopped completely unblinking while the other two went out. I turned the handle of the door a little bit and heard the clanking of the double locks releasing inside it. Extremely cautiously, with my hand on my pistol beneath my coat at my waist, I slowly opened the door and entered into the library.

There were two new explosions in the parking lot. Sirens had been growing louder over the screams of panicked people. I walked over to the safe without waiting a single minute. I checked my watch to see what kind of time we had, since the clock was running. This mansion was considered to have the highest level of security from the Cuban government in the entire country. This point had served as a strategic location by the Ministry of the Interior for planning with dignitaries from the multiple countries around the world to plan changes in political and ideological power. These secret plans were done under utmost secrecy to prevent interference form the United States and other democratic countries to stop communist expansion around the world.

It took me less than five minutes to open the safe using the combination Arnaldo had given me. Atacia stood behind me, removing her skirt. Attached to her belly she had a well-folded duffle bag, which made her pregnancy look more advanced and worked for our purposes. She opened the duffle bag on a sofa near the bookshelf. I passed to her the most important documents I took from the safe. I removed the case with those priceless diamonds; our jaws dropped at the size and beauty of those rocks. The room was lit only by a small table lamp next to the safe so that no movement or shadows would betray our presence to the outside.

As we finished, we could hear someone clapping by the door. A hand flashlight switched on and shone directly in my face. "Bravo, bravo. There is no doubt you earned your name the Lightning, but I believe we finally have come to the moment in which you lose the game you've played. Your legend ends right here, tonight. But before I finish with you, I want to know something—who the hell is the traitor inside our circle that gave you the information that allowed you to get this far? Who gave you the combination to the safe which only the Minister possesses? It took you only five minutes to open it. Please don't insult my intelligence by replying to my question that you don't want to reveal the name of the traitor and want to protect him. You will only irritate me more and make your death more painful and slow."

The man moved the flashlight under the chin of his grotesque face in its light. The diabolic image appeared even more grotesque with the light shining up into it. It was Origeo, the assistant of the six-fingered man, or as we called him in our circle, the Six-Six-Six Man or the Antichrist.

Chapter 30: Nothing Is Impossible When You Have God

Origeo looked completely relaxed, his legs crossed as he sat in what looked like a comfortable reclining chair. He glanced at Atacia. "Where have you been? You dropped off the radar and disappeared on us over a year ago." She threw a glance at me before looking at him in disgust. But she said nothing.

I looked at both of them in confusion as very dark doubts started to form in my mind while noticing that the gun he pointed at us was of a very small caliber, as the silencer he had attached to it was larger than the pistol itself. Somehow, he had prior knowledge that we would be here at this hour, sitting behind the door into the library as he waited for our arrival. The first thing which crossed my mind was that the new acquisition in our group, Arnaldo, had betrayed us. It was unfair to him, but because he was Ramiro Valdez' nephew, it was logical to suspect him; his family were muddy waters, and from that water one could pick up a parasite. After all, what could one expect from the genetics of that bloodline? He could have turned us over while we were waiting at his house, or even when we first met. Waiting until now to trap us didn't make sense. The dark suspicions churned like a tornado in my mind.

I scratched my cheek dubiously, trying to order my thoughts. A strong, severe migraine invaded my head, which made concentration more difficult as I tried to come up with a rapid, intelligent exit like I always sought to find in similar situations. None of those previous situations, however, was like the one we had just walked into. I took all the blame for myself—there was much I should have done myself and rather than leaving others to do. I couldn't think straight, and so I kept silent. That could be my best option, since my silence could take Origeo completely by surprise. But not only he but Atacia was surprised as well. She looked at me in silence, not understanding why I didn't do something, so she decided to take the initiative.

She said to Origeo something I had never considered and was more painful than my migraine, like a knife in my back. She said sarcastically, "I had understood that you were a man with ideals, defending a cause, whether good or bad, out of principle. I never imagined that you could be a vulgar, mercenary murderer."

I looked at Atacia in surprise and consternation. She was approaching him as if she had known him for a long time. She had never mentioned this to me at all. Recovering from my surprise, I looked deeply into her eyes and asked, "Do you know this individual?"

Atacia took a deep breath and looked at me guiltily with resignation in her face. She nodded. "Do you remember downstairs that I told you I had something in my past that I don't like at all? This is part of my past which you didn't allow me to finish."

I looked in greater concern. This answer caused Origeo to burst into mocking laughter. He looked at me and shook his head. "Tsk, tsk, tsk. You mean to tell me that you didn't know until now the close and intimate relationship which has existed between Atacia and me?"

I was completely taken by surprise, crushed by that grotesque man confirming it. I could not comprehend how a woman with such a great level of intelligence and physical beauty could have a relationship with a man with such a repugnant, corrupt, diabolical mind and perverse personality, especially a man who associated with one we all considered to be the most sinister character on the entire island, Lucifer's disciple, that mysterious six-fingered man. It didn't take too long for Atacia to remove my doubts as she contorted her face in rage and disgust with a clenched jaw.

She said, "I don't think that anyone with a normal and healthy mind would call a relationship in between one eight-year-old girl and a man of over forty 'intimate.' I believe the correct name is either a child molester or an abusive sodomist, when that little girl is forced to perform oral sex on the adult man that her father had been forced by the government to accept as a custodian and teacher for training not only me but also my brother Jimbo into professional murderers as members of the elite group Omega Green Scorpions. Why don't we call it by its right name and say that I'm one among thousands of other kids who had been recruited into this elite group who were sexually abused, converting many of them into homosexuals and bisexuals." Tears ran down her face as she finished in a cracked voice, remembering the painful, repugnant, and miserable past that formed her early years.

Origeo smiled cynically. He asked sarcastically, "In what of those three sexual categories are you in today?" He didn't deny any of the accusations she had just made, nor protest against them. That convinced me that she was telling the whole truth and reality of what she had gone through at the hands of this man.

I felt a trembling nausea in the pit of my stomach at this individual. Not only was he physically repugnant, but now I also saw that his spirit was in the deepest darkness of the most diabolical kind. As Atacia and he continued their conversation, I felt her left hand touch my back, reaching for her handbag. As soon as I noticed that I reacted in a way to distract Origeo so that she could get whatever she was reaching for.

I crossed my legs on the sofa. "My I get a little more comfortable?"

"Sure, as long as you keep your hands in plain view. Make one false move and you're both dead."

"Thank you. I want to offer you a deal that could be of interest to both of us."

He smiled cynically. "I don't believe you are in a position to negotiate. You have nothing to offer."

"That is your biggest mistake." I was recovering, the headache retreating. I said firmly, "Simply because you have a silenced pistol in your hand pointed at us doesn't mean you have all the cards to win this game tonight. You don't know what measures I took before I entered this library. Those could radically change the ending and determine who will be in the end the winner and who the loser in this interesting game you choose to play with us. I don't believe you have very much to lose in listening to my proposition, because you can accept it or decline it as soon as I finish speaking. Whatever you wish—you're the one with the gun in your hand. Mine is in a holster under my clothes."

He shifted in his chair. I had touched a nerve, and my words had taken him out of the comfort zone which had until now made him feel so certain. "OK. I doubt very much that you have anything to offer, because I will get the information I want, no matter what, even if I have to torture you all night." He forced a smile as he spoke sarcastically. With the index finger of his left hand, he passed it along his left eyebrow, showing me that his nervous state was increasing. I followed his movement and continued to feel Atacia working behind me, her left hand still trying to get something out of her handbag.

    To continue to give Atacia more time, I did as he had done before. With a very nonchalant gesture, I caressed my eyebrow with my finger. Calmly, in a persuasive tone, I said, "It's very simple. You have valuable information that I'm very interested in. Likewise, I also have very valuable information of interest to you. Why don't we exchange our information in a peaceful way, instead of torturing or shooting each other? We're civilized men. Maybe we can come to an agreement."

    He burst out in laughter, returning to his previous aggressive posture in his chair and his bullying attitude. He stood up and yelled, "In a million years! Wake up from your dream. I will take the information I need from your head, even if I have to cut your brain apart and use pliers to put it all together. I'm not walking out of this place without getting the name of that traitor who gave you the combination to the safe and the code for the door so you could get into this place." He pointed his pistol menacingly at us, shaking in rage.

    At that moment, I heard three whistling sounds as the tranquilizer gun fired. Atacia had finally managed to get it out of her bag. Even in the darkness, her aim was precise; the first dart went in between his eyebrows just above the bridge of his nose, a line of blood running down it. The other two darts went into each eye, leaving him blinded. He toppled backward, but as he fell back into his chair, he squeezed the trigger on that small pistol. The bullet passed just beneath my arm, scratching me superficially on the back of my forearm, but continuing through to hit Atacia in her lower abdomen.

She looked down in panic, putting her left hand to the wound which spurted a fountain of yellow fluid mixed with blood. She put the dart pistol down on the sofa and put both of her hands over the wound, trying to contain the fluid. She said in panic, "No! No! My baby! God, take my life, not his, this innocent creature!" She wept, desperation and agony on her face as she looked at me in panic. "I don't want to continue to live if my baby dies."

"Calm down, everything will be OK," I said.

"No, my baby is dead! I don't feel him anymore." She reached her right arm to my waist and pulled my pistol, pointing at her head in preparation to blow her brains out.

I reacted quickly and gave her a sharp slap to the face which made her turn her head to the opposite position from the gun just as she squeezed the trigger. The bullet she intended for her head went across the room, striking a statue of Don Quixote, snapping the head off, which rolled down onto the floor. I rapidly snatched the gun out of her hand and dropped it behind the sofa along with the dart pistol.

I yelled, "Are you going crazy?" I held both her hands at the wrists and shook her strongly. The irrational and emotional attitude she was experiencing wasn't allowing her to think straight. "Your wound doesn't look to be fatal, either to you or the baby. Do you want to kill yourself and your baby at the same time? That will practically be an abortion due to your hysterical and unnecessary loss of your mind."

She shook her head as she forced herself to calm down. If she had completely lost control before to hysteria, now the reason of my words caused her to react apologetically and sobbed, "I thought for a minute that that degenerate had killed my baby." She smiled sadly, both hands on her belly and bloodied from the liquid which still spurted between her fingers. "My baby is still alive—I can feel him moving."

I smiled a little and showed her the wound in my arm. "We've both been protected by the Supreme Architect. If his pistol were of greater caliber, both of our wounds might be more serious. Thank God and you for your precise shots in the dark, which could not be more opportune and effective. Thank you very much, because you saved the situation and my life."

"Thank *you*, because I almost killed myself and my baby."

We embraced emotionally. We took deep breaths, and I said, "We have to get out of here quickly."

"I know."

I took the handkerchief from my tuxedo, folded it, and as she removed her hands, I covered the tiny hole with it. I put both her hands on top of the handkerchief and said, "Put pressure on that." I put my fingers under my nose and then put them beneath her nose. She pulled her head away with a grimace.

She said, "That smells like ammonia."

I smiled. "That is your urine. That means it looks like the bullet ruptured your bladder. That was the best thing to happen. There's no damage to the baby or to any of your major organs. We have to get you medical attention immediately to plug the leak in your bladder, or the good news will turn into bad news, because it can create a very bad internal infection not only to your baby in your womb but also to yourself. Do you think you can walk to the parking lot without losing consciousness?"

She gave me a small smile. "Stop worrying so much about me and think a little about you." She took her underwear off and ripped them with her teeth, improvising a bandage which she tied on my arm. "Don't worry. I took a shower and they're clean."

I smiled. "Thank God you haven't lost your sense of humor. You scared me when you put that pistol to your head."

"After the storm there's always a calm."

"Yes, and I see that your hysteria earlier, thanks be to God, is gone. Now you're in better shape and humor."

We walked towards Origeo's body. I took his arm and checked his pulse. Even though that beast was very tall and massive, all three darts had penetrated to his brain, especially the one above his nose, which entered into the cavity we call in intelligence the Achilles' heel, because this is the most certain and sure way to take the life of any human being with just a simple needle. It doesn't matter how tall someone is or how much that person weighs. I looked at Atacia and shook my head, releasing Origeo's arm, which heavily hit the floor.

"Well," I said, "I think your sexual predator lost his last game. I don't think he will ever molest another child."

Atacia shook her head. "Believe me, it wasn't my intention to deprive him of his life, but maybe the rest of the world will live in greater peace with one less evil mind around."

I leaned over Origeo's body and began to search his pockets. Atacia asked, "What do you expect to find in his pockets?"

"I'm looking for some kind of evidence which connects this man with the traitor in our group. Even though some of us possess the extraordinary gift of seeing ahead a little bit, it's always approximate, and we both saw that Origeo was waiting for us with the complete assurance that tonight and at roughly this time we would be here to open the safe. I'm certain that he had many other more important worries on his mind than sitting behind that door waiting for us, including the assignment that I'm pretty sure his boss with six fingers ordered him to do. I'm completely convinced that someone in our group passed this information to Origeo."

    I continued searching through his tuxedo and pants, pocket by pocket. I found nothing of importance, save that his wallet was full of different national currencies, including almost ten thousand American dollars. Only spies carry multiple currencies in order to bribe people in any country, especially in diplomatic circles. US dollars were like bread and butter in Cuba: if you wanted to have a good dinner or get any key necessity, those who had the privilege of having dollars could use what they called "special stores for special people"—only for tourists and foreigners. Cubans were not allowed unless they had hard US currency in their hands, which opened all doors in Cuba despite the government's hatred of the gringos. Those in Cuba who had families that had abandoned the country to some other nation had the exceptional privilege of receiving from their families a monthly allowance for their survival in the profound economic crisis that Cuba had endured for so many decades. Regardless of the reason these people decided to abandon Cuba, the government classified them as the prodigal worms; even though those "worms" had been supporting the Cuban economy like an IV drip.

    I had almost given up when I noticed something beneath his tuxedo shirt. I unbuttoned the shirt a little and pulled out a necklace made of beads and some multicolored feathers from various birds as well as the teeth of wild animals. I had seen one like this before around someone's neck—but now in my clouded head I could only remember way back, during a Santeria of the African religions longer collar hung in the medicine lady that my mother used to visit, occasionally bringing me along.

That woman lived in Guane, the little town I was born in, in the province of Pinar del Rio. I had been afflicted most of childhood with agonizing, long nights in which I could not sleep in peace. My mother frequently took me with her for card readings; that good black woman helped to get rid of those horrible nightmares in which a sinister man dressed all in black visited me nightly. He had the same characteristics of the six-fingered man and his diabolic disciples. Every night, the same nightmare repeated in which they stripped me naked and put my body on top of a glass table in front of the altar to the African gods Elegua, Yemaya, and Chango. With a very sharp knife, they would open my chest over a white linen cover filled with flowers covering the glass top. After they cut my chest from the throat down, they opened the wound like they were gutting an animal and removed my heart. I would see my heart still attached to my body with the nerves and blood vessels, and it would be handed from one to another as they began to eat it. I would wake up the same time every night, screaming in agonized pain, soaking wet and in tears, sometimes waking my family at two, three, or even four in the morning. This happened for years.

My father was completely exhausted by my mother's pleas to take me to the medicine woman. Medical science couldn't explain it; his eldest brother,

Emilio, was baffled, and he was not only a regular doctor but also a professor at the University of Havana and an obstetrician, gynecologist, and pediatrician. He also didn't believe in these spiritual things but recommended them to my father as a last resort after such an extended period of sleepless nights for my entire family. My father was reluctant to pursue this, as he was a Grand Master Mason in the Lodge in that small town. But the gossip was spreading in that small town, and he was afraid of what people would say if his son was taken to Gollita because of an inexplicable sickness which the doctors could not cure. This beautiful black lady had lost half her teeth and chewed tobacco was able to do what no doctor had been able to do: stop my horrible nightmares and the scratches all over my back, chest, and body which I would wake up with, causing my mother to freak out at the sight of the bloodied sheets of my bed. After all these episodes caused my mother to force me from the ages of three or four to sleep with gloves tied to my hands with my nails cut as close to the quick as possible and polished, just in case I was scratching myself. But in spite of those precautions, I still woke up with those scratches, and my father agreed to let me be taken to her. And it was around *her* neck that I had seen such a necklace.

    I looked at the one I had taken from Origeo and passed it through my fingers for a few seconds as I remembered those days. I looked at Atacia with a small smile of satisfaction. Without saying a word, I leaned over Origeo's body and with both hands behind his neck, I undid the clasp of the necklace. I took his front pocket handkerchief, opened it, and put the necklace in it. I showed it to Atacia and looked at her optimistically. "I believe that in here is the secret which will take us directly to the traitor within us. I don't know for sure yet, but I have a feeling. If I'm not mistaken, it will take us directly to the one who has been responsible for us nearly losing our lives tonight."

Atacia looked at me in confusion, not understanding what the significance of the necklace was. I didn't let her ask any questions. I added, "Don't worry about it now. My supposition has no solid basis; but when I find out, I will let you know. The most important thing now is to take that duffle bag with all these valuable things from here and put a great distance between this place and us. We need to be far away from here to dissociate us from the death of this man. We've given these people enough reasons to put us in front of the firing squad already—let's not add any more to that bucket."

I took another handkerchief from Origeo's inside jacket pocket and proceeded to clean the line of blood from his forehead. I removed the dart and put it in the handkerchief, repeating this for the darts in his eyes, placing the bundle in my pocket along with the collar. I tied them together as if I were securing something valuable. I slung the duffle bag over my left shoulder, barely being able to lift it over the sofa.

I asked Atacia, "Can you walk without difficulty to the parking lot, or do you need help?"

She smirked, "*Claro, chico*[21]." I smiled, and she returned the smile. "I told you before that you should stop worrying so much about me and worry more about yourself." As we walked to the door to the library, she

---

[21] Sure, man.

asked, "Do you think that you will be able with that heavy duffle bag with that wound all the way to the cars?"

I smiled and showed her the bag over my shoulder. "Your strength must be weakness after the attack you had." We were nearly out in the hallway, and she lightly punched me in the right shoulder in protest. "Ouch! That is my wounded wing—or have you forgotten that I'm wounded as well?" She hurriedly apologized and caressed my shoulder soothingly. I smiled. "I'm just joking with you—my wound is on the forearm, not the shoulder."

She smiled and shook her head. "Well, I'm glad you never lose your sense of humor. You got me because you've got a wound on your right forearm, and maybe when I hit you, I struck a nerve. But I know you're a macho man."

We continued to walk around the debris, looking for the remaining staircase down from the balcony, now the only exit from that place, which we had planned to remain intact. Jimbo had been very precise and accurate. I looked around the surroundings in sadness at seeing such an elegant, beautiful, glamorous place now looking like a scene in a war movie after a bomb hit a city.

We got down to the main room. The fire department was already trying to put out fires on the curtains which lined the walls. As we had agreed before, Arnaldo was waiting for us with the Range Rover parked by the front door, the engine running. Jimbo was in the Maserati behind him, and the rest of our friends were also waiting in the back seat. I said to Arnaldo, "Atacia needs urgent medical attention. I have a plan for that, and we need to get to my Uncle Emilio's house as soon as possible. He lives a few blocks away. I haven't been in touch with him to avoid bringing any heat to him, but now we have an emergency, and he is the most suited to taking care of Atacia and her baby."

"OK, no problem. Let's get out of here as soon as possible." He opened the door for us. I sat next to Arnaldo while Aurora helped Atacia get into the back seat.

Aurora started to freak out a little at the sight of all the blood by Atacia's belly and began to cry desperately. "Oh, my God! You're not only losing your baby, but you could lose your life! We have to take her to a hospital!"

"Calm down," I said.

Arnaldo started the Range Rover toward the main gate. I continued, "My uncle is the best surgeon, gynecologist, obstetrician, and pediatrician on the island, and he's only a few blocks away from Arnaldo's house. The most important thing is for you to keep your cool. We don't want to attract the attention of the gate guards by your crying and carrying on—that's the worst thing that could happen." After Atacia had sat down I put the duffle bag on the floor between her feet. "The most important thing is for us to get out of here alive. You have to control yourself—it's OK to be upset, but it could be worse. One of us could be dead. We're all still alive."

Aurora calmed herself down with an effort. "I'm sorry," she apologized.

We reached the main gate. More soldiers were there than before, searching each car. We were several cars down the line, reached a bend, and a young soldier came over without recognizing Arnaldo, who rolled the window down.

"I need to identify everyone leaving this place. I need to see your ID."

Arnaldo wasn't very happy with this. "Don't you know who I am, *compañero*?"

I saw Jimbo coming up behind us in the Maserati in the rear-view mirror. Their faces showed stress and pessimism, and I hoped they wouldn't lose their cool.

The young guard, who had come to the window, even as Arnaldo had been flashed his G-2 ID, he said "These are special guests of the Minister, and the people behind us are our escort."

"I'm sorry, but you have to get out so I can search the cars. I have strict orders to search every single car leaving here so we can document and report to the investigators from the G-2 who will be here any minute." I shook my head. "This zone right now is under the jurisdiction of the highest investigation," the soldier continued, "and this is a crime scene." I slowly reached for my pistol at my waist, ready to defend us. There was no way we could allow him to search the car. The first thing which went through my mind was that Arnaldo had created these theatrics for us to get arrested with the fruit of our work in that duffle bag, which would be a death sentence to each of us. At the same time, it could be a perfect cover for him.

Arnaldo noticed my motion. He gently stopped me with his right hand. While the guard checked his ID, he whispered to me looking straight into my eyes reassuring, "Don't do anything, please. Trust me to handle this."

I could see the sincerity in his eyes, so I left my hand resting on the grip of my pistol, ready to draw it if needed.

Arnaldo yelled to an officer who had just emerged from a car entering the gate. "Lieutenant Calixto!"

The officer turned and recognized Arnaldo. He came over to our vehicle with a huge smile on his face, virtually shoving the young guard out of his way. He shook

Arnaldo's hand. He asked in surprise, "Don't tell me you were inside that place when all this happened?"

Arnaldo made a sad expression. "Yes, you're right, and I have a wounded woman in the back seat who needs immediate attention. I'm OK, but this young diplomat I've been assigned to by my uncle has a bad wound and she's pregnant."

The officer looked in through the window and saw Atacia's bloody wound, Aurora supporting her with distress on her face. Seeing how urgent this was, he turned to the young guard. "Are you stupid or what? This man is the nephew of our Minister, and he has a wounded woman!"

The young guard mumbled in fear, "I didn't know! I didn't know!"

Calixto took the ID and handed it to Arnaldo. Tapping the side of the window he said, "Go! Go!" He turned to the gate guards, "Let these two cars go at once!"

They quickly lifted the gates and moved the wooden barricades to one side. They started to stop the Maserati. "They are together, let them go!"

Calixto pounded his hands together to emphasize the urgency. Arnaldo took the ID. "Thank you, Lt. Calixto."

"No problem, we'll see each other in the Ministry later."

"OK."

"Drive carefully, OK? Don't rush. There's a lot of unusually heavy traffic right now because of all the emergency vehicles coming in and out of this place.

Arnaldo started forward. My window was still slightly open, and coming into the mansion was a limousine. Its window was open, and I saw the six-fingered man with some guards returning. He leaned his head out the window and yelled, "Have you seen my assistant, Origeo, leaving?"

Both guards shook their heads. "The only people who have left so far is Minister Ramiro Valdez, his escort, a few diplomats, and now these people."

The six-fingered man's eyes met mine as we passed by him. I slowly rolled up the window, turning slightly to look at Atacia. We took a deep breath of relief. We both knew she had escaped from the claws of death. If that young guard had opened the door and seen what was in the duffle bag between her legs, especially in sight of the six-fingered man, we would have been summarily executed without any questions asked. The urgency for us to leave the country now increased by the minute. We had been seen in that gathering and evidently the man with the six fingers would soon discover the unconscious guards in the chute. When they searched the place, they would then also find Origeo's body.

I put my hand on Arnaldo's shoulder. "Please, give us some speed. Don't drive crazy, but you have plenty of reason to break the speed limit. We have to get to your house quickly for several reasons. Giving Atacia medical attention is the first priority, but we also left behind eyewitnesses who could identify her, and they will probably be conscious soon. The biggest reason is that we left the body of the man who is supposedly one of the most dangerous men in the island behind in the library, the assistant to that six-fingered man. That same six-fingered man reportedly slept with one of Raul's daughters and so is also supposedly the father of Raul's grandsons, Raul Guillermo Rodriguez Castro, alias *el cangrejo*[22]." I squeezed his shoulder. "The sooner we get to your house

---

[22] The Crab. This gentleman was born with a sixth finger which became deformed due to a botched attempt to amputate it, leaving that had disfigured and slightly resembling a crab's claw.

to finalize and straighten the final wrinkles in our mission and get Atacia her medical attention, we'll be able to take our valuable cargo and leave this country. You and the ones who choose to stay behind will have fewer possibilities of being implicated in anything we did. We don't want under any circumstances to have all the work and sacrifice for our plans to be frustrated at the last minute."

"Don't worry. We will be home very soon, safe and sound, and we'll finish this the same way we started, with smiles of satisfaction on our faces. Thank you, and I have to congratulate all of you because the great sacrifice and effort in enacting the most incredible operation that has ever taken place here in Cuba. You are all extraordinary people. We took the most wanted treasure from these Marxists' hands right beneath their noses in a place that is supposed to be impenetrable: the headquarters and private home of the Minister of the Interior and practical creator of the G-2, the most nefarious organization ever to finance covert international terrorists."

Chapter 31: The Lightning's Greatest Success

After we arrived at Arnaldo's house, Aurora carefully helped her daughter out of the car. I picked up the duffel bag as everyone glanced at it curiously, wondering what was inside. Mama Teca asked, "Did you guys manage to open the safe?"

I looked at her with a sour expression as I carried the heavy bag. "Yes, everything didn't go as planned." I pointed at Atacia's bloody clothing. "The price we paid for this valuable prize is a lot greater than we expected. We both nearly lost our lives in the process."

Arnaldo jumped this time with his own question. "Were you guys surprised by the guards?"

I shook my head as we walked into the dinette and sat down around the table. I said, "The guards were the easiest part of the whole job. It was so easy that Atacia was able to put them both down by herself. It took me longer than expected to climb through the duct to the upper level." The others looked at me in surprise.

Atacia lost her sense of diplomacy and said resentfully, "We have been betrayed. It's obvious. There's no doubt in my mind. Our enemies knew what we were intending to do beforehand. When we walked into the library, one of our worst enemies was sitting comfortably behind the door in a recliner, waiting for us to come in, armed with nothing more than a silenced pistol. You know from that he was there to kill us. The only thing he wanted to know was who had provided the combinations for the door to the library and the safe. He waited until the Lightning opened the safe."

Jimbo asked curiously, "Who is the one who was waiting for you?"

Atacia replied, "The sexual degenerate, Origeo."

Jimbo put both of his hands to his face for a few seconds in disgust. He asked anxiously, "How did you guys escape alive? This man isn't just a professional assassin—he's also the right arm to the one we all call the Emissary of Satan, the advisor to the Castro brothers." He pointed at Atacia. "You know this very well—we both have been his victims when they tried to turn us into professional assassins." He was barely able to contain his rage. Despite his attempt not to break down, two tears escaped his control. In embarrassment, he wiped the tears away on the sleeve of his tuxedo. In a broken voice, he continued, "What a pity it was that I wasn't there with you. I would have enjoyed finishing that degenerate for what he did to us and others."

I understood his pain and gave him a little pat on his shoulder. "You don't have to worry about that anymore, my brother Jimbo. Your sister has already taken care of business; don't worry about Origeo ever again. He will never molest anyone, especially children anymore. She sent him with a one-way ticket to the Inferno, and he'll never be let out of there again."

Jimbo said joyfully, "Oh, that is good! One less enemy for me to worry about on my long list." He clapped his hands together and applauded his sister. "Good job!"

Aurora was sitting near him and said lovingly, "My son, we should never celebrate death of anyone, not even your worst enemy. That is what evil wants in order to steal your spirit." She put one hand on his shoulder. "Remember, my son—we're not like them. We should celebrate only life, never death. Don't allow your spirit to be corrupted by hatred and revenge. This is a weapon Satan uses for evil minds."

Jimbo nodded with profound respect for her, accepting her wisdom without protest. She saw the effort of containing his emotion to please her and kissed him on the cheek. We stood up and left the dinette and went to the living quarters. We got Atacia comfortable on one of the beds until I returned from my uncle's house with help. After we got her settled, I told Aurora not to move her too much but to keep the wound as clean as possible. Arnaldo brought a first aid kit as Aurora started to remove Atacia's clothes in order to treat the wound. We left the room to give them some privacy, Mama Teca remaining to help Aurora with undressing of Atacia and cleaning her wounds.

Arnaldo gave me a jogging suit and baseball cap. I asked him if I could take one of his bottles of wine from the Bodega Riojas winery in Spain, which I thought would give my uncle a smile as well as being a good alibi to anyone who saw me going to his house for my visit. Any of his neighbors might be with the CDR[23], and I didn't want to bring any heat to my uncle for our recent activities. The general population might never know because the government controlled the media, but those with connections inside the government would be hunting us.

I grabbed a garage door opener and put it in my pocket as I left the residence. My uncle's house was a few blocks away, so it only took me a few minutes to reach his

---

[23] Committee for the Defense of the Revolution, a government-sponsored network of people who would, in exchange for extra rations or better living accommodations, spy on their neighbors for any anti-government sentiment or activity.

door and ring the bell. My mind was conflicted—he was my confidant and of my bloodline, but he was also my trainer as a spy. The last thing I wanted was to bring any conflict to him through my unannounced visit. Unfortunately, I kept telling myself, this was an emergency and that he would understand. There was no way I could take Atacia to a hospital, so I had no choice but to go to him for help. That injury complicated everything.

I continued to ring the bell with no answer. I grew distinctly uncomfortable as doubt filled my mind along with a sinking feeling in the pit of my stomach. It might not have been very long, but my anxiety about returning to Atacia made the minutes feel like hours. I didn't want to ring the bell too insistently, but I still looked at the button several times. I couldn't wait any longer and pressed the doorbell again, this time pressing it longer, and I could hear the chimes inside ring loudly. I felt embarrassed, as if I might be overdoing it.

Finally, I heard steps approaching from the other side of the multicolored Venetian glass door with the flamingo designs. I heard the sound of a double lock opening, to my immense relief. To my surprise, the door opened to reveal a tall man with a well-groomed beard that grinned broadly from ear to ear. He was dressed in the clothing of a monsignor of the Catholic Church. He said, "Good evening." He looked at his watch. "Well, good early morning." He spoke with very pleasant manners.

I was shocked and mute, thinking of thousands of possibilities, each one of them worse than the other. I stepped back and checked the house number along the side of the house. I was at the right house, so I asked, "Excuse me, is Dr. Emilio del Marmol still living here?"

This time, the priest looked at his watch once more, which did not diminish my discomfort. I checked mine and saw that it was 2 am. He asked, "Who is looking for him?"

"I'm sorry, father, but my time is very limited and I believe my question is more important than yours. I need a precise, and quick answer to my question—who are you and what are you doing in this residence?" I put the bottle of wine down, opened the zipper of my jogging suit, and pulled my pistol out. Nonchalantly I put it against his belly. His face paled and flushed as different stressors flowed through his body.

He said as pleasantly as possible, "My son, there is no reason for any use of violence."

I picked up the bottle of wine with my left hand and pushed against him gently with my pistol still in his stomach, getting us both inside the house. I closed the door behind me. "Who are you, and where is Dr. Emilio del Marmol?"

The priest remained quiet in his panic. I could have been one of the bandits that ran around these luxury neighborhoods to rob the elderly left alone in these houses by their reluctance to leave their beautiful island of Cuba. These bandits had taken advantage of such people, knowing they have valuable things in their homes.

In an attempt to persuade me, he said with terrified eyes, "My son, there's nothing left of any value in this house. This family has been forced to exchange whatever they had for food to avoid dying of hunger." He pointed at the bottle of wine I held. He gave me a small smile. "If you're looking for money, I can find some if you give me time from some of the tourists which visit my church. I can give it to you in exchange for that bottle of Spanish wine you're holding. You probably don't even like wine." His eyes shone as he spoke, savoring the wine from a vineyard he hadn't seen for decades in Cuba.

"Father, with all my respect, I think your assumptions have led you to two wrong conclusions. First, I'm not a bandit who has come to rob the family of this house. Second, this bottle of wine is not for sale. It has no price because this is a gift for my uncle, Dr. Emilio del Marmol."

At that moment, the door connecting the living room and the dining room opened. The interior looked well-maintained, and my uncle Emilio appeared with a pistol in his hand, a silencer attached. "I recognized your voice at once," he said, "and could identify you even though that fantastic disguise you're wearing. I don't think your own mother would recognize you," he added with a big smile. He unscrewed the silencer from the pistol and put the gun away. "My nephew and best student," he said by way of introduction to the priest, "the best master spy I have ever trained in my entire career. What a pleasure you've brought me to see you again! You don't even know how much I've enjoyed the fake news from this government announcing over fifty times that they have managed at last to kill you. By a miracle, and I thank God every time I see you alive." He stepped forward and gave me a bear hug. "What kind of hurricane crazy winds bring you to our humble home?" Before I could answer, he pointed to the priest, who now was more relaxed, and said, "This is Father Francisco. He's the monsignor here in the capital of Havana."

The Monsignor held out his right hand, and I took it. He took it in a firm grip, putting his left hand over mind in joy, and said, "It's a very great honor to know the man behind the legend in person. You have given every Cuban the hope and desire to fight for their freedom, *el relampago Cubano*[24], and the nephew of my best friend and partner in the fight for freedom, Dr. Emilio del Marmol, a great patriot like all your ancestors." His eyes were watery from all the emotion. He had not released my hand and continued, "Will you allow me to give you a hug of gratitude, my son, and ask your forgiveness for confusing you for a vulgar bandit?"

I smiled. "Of course you can give me a hug, but the one who owes an apology is me, for sticking my pistol in your belly. I was thinking that you were a G-2 agent disguised as a priest who, having discovered my uncle's double identity, had been assigned here as a post to wait for my arrival, in an attempt to trap me." Father Francisco smiled broadly. He shook his finger in embarrassed negative. I returned the smile. "There's no doubt that what I've said all my life is true, most of the time: when you allow your mind the luxury of assumptions, 99% of the time you should be prepared to apologize for being terribly wrong. In this case, we both made the same mistake."

Father Francisco looked at me with admiration on his face. He looked at my uncle and said, "I can tell you with all honesty in my heart that meeting your nephew tonight was divine intervention, because you and I were supposed to meet tomorrow and not today. I now understand perfectly the grand admiration that you have when you talk about him to anyone in our group. Your nephew has exceeded all my expectations. That is why I'm going to ask you a great favor: before he leaves your house, let me introduce him to our team waiting for us in the back." He turned to me. "We're organizing right now a major peaceful protest to paralyze the economy of the entire country. Your providential appearance comes at

---

[24] The Cuban Lightning

such an opportune moment, as it will provide a stimulus to all our group, as you did for me."

Uncle Emilio looked at me to gauge my receptiveness to this suggestion. He raised his right arm high as he saw my continued silence and replied with a shake of his head, "Father Francisco, to me this is not a major problem at all, since everyone in our group has my absolute trust, but I don't even know the urgency or reason for my nephew's visit. I believe that it has to be something of extraordinary importance and urgency. He's never visited without prior notice before." He caressed his chin with the fingers of his right hand. "It's all up to him, not me, based on the time and the urgency he has with whatever mission he's been assigned."

I looked at my wristwatch and looked at them impatiently, caressing my chin in the same way my uncle had silently. I raised the bottle of wine with my right hand and handed it to my uncle. "This is for you." As I handed it to him, I winced slightly in pain.

My uncle noticed that at once. "What's wrong with your right arm?"

I gave him a small smile. "It's just a scratch."

"From what?"

"Just a bullet that missed me."

Uncle Emilio raised the bottle high. "Thank you very much for always remembering your uncle. You know this is my favorite brand, and I won't ask how you got that bottle in Cuba." He put the bottle down on the table. "Raise your hand. I want to see your wound." To make it easier for him, I removed the top of my jogging suit. "Please sit down. This will only take a few minutes. I want to examine your forearm carefully as a second opinion so you can determine whether the wound is of minor or great importance."

I sat down in a chair as he started to unwrap the bandage before the curious eyes of Father Francisco, who asked, "How did you get that wound?"

I replied, "This just happened a few hours ago."

My uncle looked at my wound with a worried expression. "I'm very sorry to disagree with your self-diagnosis, but though this wound isn't deep in the entrance point of the bullet, the exit wound is much deeper. I recommend a very deep cleaning of the dead tissue in that wound and not a regular antiseptic you might have at home but something stronger to kill the bacteria that are starting to grow there. You will need possibly as many as five stitches if you don't want to get a very serious infection in your arm and a nasty scar in the future." He spoke as he looked at my arm. After he concluded his examination, he raised his head. "Where did this happen, and when?"

I passed the index finger of my left hand beneath my nose. "This just happened at the private residence of Ramiro Valdez."

He laughed. "Only you would play with your life like that when someone else could do that."

"You didn't let me finish. Believe me, the last thing I wanted to do was to come here. We're extremely hot right now. They're looking for us throughout the city."

"How many times have I told you to send other people to do this stuff? You're much too valuable to our cause. This was very reckless of you."

"Uncle, I'm sorry, but I cannot give you many details, but the lives of hundreds if not thousands of people are on the line, and I have to bring this information back to the US as soon as possible."

He shook his head. "Only you would be so crazy as to walk into the lion's cage when the lion is hungry for your head." He was growing irritated due to his worry about my safety. He piled the bandages he had unwrapped and put them on the table. "Who else is wounded?"

"How did you know someone else is wounded?"

He looked at me with a grim smile and answered sarcastically, "Have you forgotten, or do I have to remind you that I saw you born and that we both have been playing with fire for all these years? After all this time I know your character. You didn't come here to have this wound treated, you're here for a worse injury than this! You don't care about your own injury." He asked slowly and emphatically, "Who else is injured? Who is it? For you to come here at this very late hour, this has to be very serious and personal to you. You don't come to me unless it's something you cannot do yourself."

I was getting a little angry now at his reproachful tone and said seriously, "Yes, as always you are capable of reading the minds of your enemies as well as your friends." I stood up and pointed with my left hand at my injured forearm. "This wound that's supposed to have killed me, instead leaving an unimportant scratch in my arm ended inside the belly of my partner in that mission, and she is in an advanced stage of pregnancy. In my modest and possibly wrong diagnosis, since I'm not a gynecologist, obstetrician, and pediatrician, that bullet ruptured her bladder, which means she needs urgent treatment and surgery."

My uncle blanched and began to perspire heavily. He wiped his forehead and face with a handkerchief he pulled out of his pocket. "Where is the wounded woman?"

"Only a few blocks from here."

He shook his head, his demeanor changing from one of reproach to one of compassion. He held my hand.

"If my judgement is correct, the fruit of that pregnancy in your friend is the direct genetic connection of the bloodline of the Lightning. Why didn't you tell me the nature of this emergency first? This is extremely urgent, and I know this is the only real reason for this visit at this hour. You didn't disturb me at all, since we were coordinating what Father Francisco was telling you. Congratulations, and we will save your baby." He went to a cabinet in the living room and opened a box of Cojimar cigars. "I know you don't smoke, but this is the tradition in Cuba. Or should I get a bottle of wine for a girl?"

"Thank you," I said. I put the cigar in my pocket. "Everyone in my group is convinced it will be a boy."

He gave me another bear hug. "It has to be a boy to continue your legacy."

"That's not up to me, it's up to God."

He smiled. "That's my nephew." He put together the bandages he had removed from my arm and began to bandage me up. "You can wait until we're done with the other emergency, then I'll take care of you." He looked at Father Francisco. "Please go to the rest of the group and tell them that my nephew is here, who he is, and that we have to leave right now for an emergency call. They should wait for me until I return."

Father Francisco said, "Wait, I want to go with you. I cannot miss the birth of the son of the Cuban Lightning."

I chuckled. "You guys also think it's a boy. Let's hope you're not mistaken, and we get a girl instead of a boy."

Uncle Emilio said, "I'll get my instruments and anesthesia, put them in the car, and get going."

"I need to be there," Father Francisco insisted, "because that boy needs to be baptized immediately. You have too many evil-minded enemies. That little Lightning needs to be baptized at once, and it will be a very great honor for me to do that service for the son of one of the favored Christian warriors of John Paul II. The birth of your child should be kept in absolutely classified silence to the rest of the world so that the disciples of Satan are unaware of his existence and thus be unable to harm him."

As my uncle walked into his consultation room to pack his medical bag with what he thought he needed, Father Francisco walked into the library where the rest of the anti-communist resistance cell waited. I remained in the living room, impatiently looking at my watch. Tremendous thunder broke in the sky, making me jump slightly, breaking me out of my thoughts. I went to the window and looked out as the massive clap echoed in the distance. It sounded like a major storm. As I looked out through the curtain, I could see lightning flickering across the sky, illuminating the street outside. There was a small street in front of the house, with a seawall next to it, some rocks, and then the Atlantic Ocean. The surface was getting very rough, the spray hitting even the windows of the house. A major storm was coming. Another, louder, and longer clap of thunder, very violent. Even watching the storm, I was taken by surprise. It also took me back to the day I was born, as both my nanny, Majito, and my Mima had related to me. As Majito was taking me to the altar for her African gods for protection, she was crossing the hallway to the patio, and one of those powerful lightning strokes hit one of the trees which shattered into pieces, splinters of wood landing close to us. According to Majito, the electrical shock singed her legs. Due to divine intervention, neither of us were reduced to ashes. It appeared that Satan didn't want me fighting him for the souls in this dark, diabolic part of the world.

The rain came pouring down heavily, blown by very strong winds. From the whistling through the cracks of the doors and windows, it sounded like another hurricane. I was extremely uneasy; it seemed like some evil presence was here, like on the day I was born.

My uncle was the first to return. He had a small smile on his face, and in a jocular manner he said, "Satan from his kingdom in Hell evidently wants to sabotage the birth of your successor."

I smiled. "The same way that he did when I was born." I shook my head. "Déjà vu. I know you're a man of science and not very spiritual, from my point of view that what you just said is precisely what I've been thinking."

"Some of us call it historical repetition," my uncle corrected me. "I'm not a fanatic about anything, including religion and politics. But for me to be not spiritual is a very long way, many nautical miles in distance." He smiled again. Clearly his humor was restored at the notion of a new family being added to the Marmol family. "Even though you told me that your wounded friend is only a few blocks away from here, with this change in weather we have to use my car if we don't want to get soaking wet. Besides, I have to bring anesthetic and other things which will be very difficult to carry for even a few blocks."

"Yes, that's a great point and good idea. Also, I think it would be a good idea for you guys to introduce me to your group now, before we leave. That way I won't have to come back here."

At that moment, Father Francisco came back with a group of around ten people. Most were men, only a couple of women. He smiled and said, "I believe we communicated telepathically. I have already arranged for everyone to come and meet you, thinking always that there are complications in whatever we do. I don't want for the rest of the group to be left out of the pleasure of meeting the man behind the legend of the Cuban Lightning. I told them that your time is very tight and due to the gravity of the situation we have to make this introduction and goodbye very short."

    I smiled and shook hands with everyone in the group. A few minutes later we said goodbye and my uncle, Father Francisco, and I left in the old four door black 1951 Buick with a white roof and stripes along the sides. The rain was very heavy, the winds even more violent. The windshield wipers couldn't keep up with the amount of water thrown at the car, forcing my uncle to drive very slowly. More lightning illuminated the sky right before us, striking a transformer on a massive concrete pole. Sparks and fire burst through the air and all the lights along the street went dark. The pole began to sway as if it were about to collapse.

    I sat in the front seat next to my uncle. As we came near the pole, we could all see it falling towards us, looking like it might come through the windshield of the car. My uncle slammed on the brakes. With extreme force and without thinking about it, I slammed my foot onto the accelerator, flooring it. My uncle reacted awkwardly. "What are you doing?" he demanded, his feet still on the brakes. He looked hesitantly at me in wonder and took his foot off the brake. The old Buick responded to the amount of gasoline I was injecting and leaped forward. He had kept that car in excellent condition, using it very little, so even though it was fifty years old, it was still in prime condition. When I gave it more gas we managed to get under and in front of it, smoke rising from the tires even on the wet pavement. The ball of fire that was the transformer on top of the pole landed behind the car in the street, scratching only the bumper. A fiery explosion lit the night sky behind us as it missed hitting us squarely by a fraction of a second. Even many years later, I question if my feet had actually done that on some instinct or if it was Divine Providence. That old car had jumped like a Ferrari when I floored the accelerator.

After we got passed it, Father Francisco leaned back in his seat and crossed himself as he thanked God for getting us through. "Thanks to the Lord that I have the privilege this early morning to witness a real miracle: when evil forces tried to stop the divine grace of our Lord, He won over the demons like He always does."

My uncle silently pulled over to the sidewalk and rested his elbows over the wheel. He turned the engine off. He put his fingers to his temple, trying to digest what had just happened and recover from the tension of the moment. After a few seconds, he leaned back in his seat and shook his head. Finally, he said in a trembling voice, "I've never been scared in my life, and never superstitious, and nothing has managed to impress me. Even though I have quite a few experiences that could be called out of the ordinary, I've always managed to find the way to logically explain them, with the exception of this one just now." He turned to look back at Father Francisco for a few seconds, and then to me. He checked his wristwatch and scratched his neck with the fingers of his left hand in confusion. He tried to find the right words, and then he touched his chin with a sad face as he finally spoke. "For many years I've been very dubious about the story of your birth that almost cost the life of your Mima That I've heard from the lips of Majito as well as those of your own mother. Only now, when I saw my life almost ending, I understood the possibility of some repetition by the malignant diabolical forces that have been trying to prevent the birth of your child, or, if you prefer, your successor." He shook his head. "I never gave complete credit to those stories, but something extraordinary and strange happened when the lightning struck that transformer. It opened my eyes which have been closed for many years. I considered all this stuff ignorance and darkness, but evidently by the light of this lighting has illuminated my heart and my mind, and I come now to understand that maybe the Devil has been playing a trick with me all these years, trying to distract me, using my scientific mind to create a skeptic in me. I have to apologize to you, because I have seen for many years by your side how you've been able to do extraordinary and unusual things which are practically impossible to other human beings.

"Like tonight—what made you cause us to speed up instead of braking, like you're supposed to do when you see danger in front of you? That decision saved our lives. Let me tell you something that you two don't know." He pointed down at Father Francisco's feet. "That cylinder of anesthesia gas is very volatile. If the flame of that transformer had gotten inside this car, the explosion would make us all disappear from this Earth to meet our ancestors." This time he put his right hand on my shoulder. "I have to apologize to you. If some time and someday I make the indiscretion to make you through my actions believe that I have some doubts about the stories of the things you've done, I'm sorry. Father Francisco and I should thank you for saving our lives tonight."

I smiled in total honesty. "My uncle, if I have to tell you the truth, that is exactly what I still question myself: what was the reason or motive which made me react the way I did? I don't even know."

He smiled back. They both said in unison as if they had practiced it, "Ah-ha!"

My uncle started the car. We were approaching Arnaldo's house. I pulled the remote control out and opened one of the many garage doors. He drove into the garage, and we got out of the car. We walked into the dinette where all our friends were still waiting anxiously.

Jimbo said, "Thank God you're here! We've had a very hard time. My sister is having convulsions due to a high fever. My mother is upstairs with her with an ice bag to her head, which seems to be working. All my sister has been doing is asking for you."

Chapter 32: The Bandit Saved My Life

Uncle Emilio looked at Father Francisco and said, "Please, Father, bring me the cylinder of anesthesia from the back seat of my car. There is no time to waste if we want to save the life of both that innocent baby and its mother." He turned to me. "Please, take me to her room."

"Her name is Atacia," I said.

"OK, OK."

"The sleeping quarters are on the second level." I gestured with a nod towards his heavy medical bag and pointed at it with my right hand. "Did you want me to help you with that? It looks heavy; you probably have all the tools you might need for this work." I reached for the bag with my left hand.

He pulled away, which surprised me. He winked at me with his right eye as he shook his head. "Thank you very much, but even though I'm retired from my profession, I'm not so old yet that I cannot carry my own medical bag up one level."

"I'm sorry. I'm just trying to help."

He smiled. As time passed and he grew older, his temper had gotten shorter. As he followed me up the stairs, he said to my back, "Don't take me wrong. I'm grateful for your gentle gesture of help." I nodded. "This shows me that even with all the bad company you've had to keep in your work, both educated and uneducated, you haven't lost the good manners you learned early on in life from all of us in your family."

I gave him a small smile and nodded. "This proves that the integrity and morality which forms the character of any individual is really important without doubt the important examples from one's parents."

"One hundred percent in agreement. Without doubt, you were extraordinarily lucky in that regard. You were born into a good nest with a great family."

I shook my head. "I know you are a man of science, and I don't want to disagree with you, since I see that as we grow older, we don't enjoy being corrected. However, I can assure you that even though I agree with many of the things you've taught me I don't believe that my birth into a great family has anything to do with luck."

Uncle Emilio smiled. "You are always a believer, which I admire. I'm glad you never changed your beliefs to please anyone."

We reached the next floor and went into Atacia's room. She was lying in bed, semi-conscious. Aurora hovered over her anxiously, but smiled as we entered, especially when she saw my uncle with his medical bag in hand. She jumped up from the side of the bed and crossed herself. She looked towards the ceiling and said with profound emotion in her voice, "Thank you, God, for hearing my prayers and my promise to you that I will comply with to the teeth." She crossed herself once more. "I promise with all my heart, Jesus, that my vow will be fulfilled."

Father Francisco entered behind us at that moment and heard with tremendous satisfaction Aurora's expression of gratitude. He put the cylinder down next to the bed and smiled as he went over to Aurora. He removed a beautiful rosary with a gold cross and red and blue stones from around his neck and hung it next to Atacia's head on the headboard. He took Aurora's hands between his and they knelt down together and began to pray in a whisper.

In the meantime, my uncle took Atacia's vitals and temperature. She moaned slightly, but did not acknowledge our presence. He set a portable metal table and placed some instruments in sterilized bags on it. He washed his hands and put on some gloves, removing several syringes from his bag and setting them onto that table next to the bed. He tied a rubber tube around her arm and looked for a vein. When he found one, he took one syringe and injected her with the contents. Keeping the needle in her arm, he removed the syringe and attached another one to it, and then repeated this once more for the third time.

After a few minutes, Atacia opened her eyes in confusion while my uncle cleaned her abdominal wounds. She tried to rise from the bed, but I gently held her down. She apparently didn't recall what had happened. I stood next to her, my left hand over her breast. I said, "No, don't get up or move. My uncle is checking your wounds. Remain still, please."

She looked at me with glassy eyes, confused. A few seconds passed and she recognized me. She took my hand with a tiny smile on her lips. "Oh, my God, it's so good to see you back here."

"How do you feel?"

"A lot better. Before, I had such a horrible migraine that I started to think I was dying and would never see you again."

Uncle Emilio was on the other side of the bed near her feet. "You will live many years, young lady, but this temporary consciousness that you have right now from the stimulants I've given you won't last very long. The fact that you reacted so marvelously to these medications is extremely important and gives me a lot of hope for your prompt recovery. The only thing I will ask of you is to remain calm. That will help you as I now have to start to put you under a general anesthetic for exploratory surgery before the effects of the stimulants wear off. Close your eyes and think of very pleasant, positive things. Your baby is in perfect condition, and it's very probable that I will have to rush his entry into this world a little bit. It will be very rough for the baby at first, being removed prematurely and taken out of the warm bubble he's in right now, but I need to use the same incision so that I don't have to cut you twice in order to repair the damage done to your bladder. It's not just to avoid cutting you twice that I'm going to do this; you are also very close to your delivery, which will cause some severe contractions. After I fix your bladder wound, those contractions which occur during normal deliver could easily reopen the wound I need to close now."

  Atacia took one of his hands and smiled broadly. "You have all my confidence and trust. Do whatever you think is necessary and prudent. I only ask one little favor—please, if for any reason, there is any complication, I want you to remember that if it is between my life and the baby's, I give you with a sound mind the consent to save the baby. Forget about me. All emotions aside, I do not want to live if my baby dies." Two tears ran down her cheeks. "Please, don't disappoint me. I know you're a man of honor based on the conversations I've had with your nephew, who admires and respects you very much from the way you taught him in the past. He's spoken highly of your medical excellence."

My uncle smiled, the mask for the gas in his hand. "OK, OK. Like I said before, relax, and think of positive, pleasant things." He signaled to Father Francisco, who turned on the gas as he crossed himself once more.

Uncle Emilo slid the elastic band over her neck and behind her head. "Remember what I said before: positive, pleasant things. I promise you that when you awaken you will have your baby close to you and nursing at your breast."

Atacia smiled with great satisfaction. She held one of my uncle's hands and said, "With the favor of God."

A few seconds later she passed out. My uncle turned to us. "OK, I'm the leader of this team. This won't be an easy target—I didn't want to say that until she was fully out." I smiled. "This surgery should be done in a hospital with proper instruments, or even in my consulting room, not here. But since I don't have any nurses or other professional help, we have to manage for ourselves. You three will be my assistants in surgery today. Wash your hands with soap and hot water, dry them very well, take those rubber gloves from the box among my medical supplies, and put them on."

Without a word, the three of us followed his instructions to get ourselves ready and started to assist him, Father Francisco crossing himself once more as my uncle began to open the wound further with the scalpel.

A short while later, my uncle pulled the baby through the wound, raised it up, and cut the umbilical cord. Strangely, the baby didn't cry at all. My uncle cleaned him up and passed him to Aurora, who had clean towels ready to finish cleaning him thoroughly. "Make sure you remove the mucus from the nose and ears as well," he instructed.

We were all able to see with surprise how red his hair and white his skin was. He made some slight sounds, still not crying. He opened his eyes, deep blue, the blue of the ocean. Aurora exclaimed, "I'm sorry, but this baby doesn't look like either of you guys."

Uncle Emilio smiled. "It's no surprise, Aurora." He started to close the wound. "I assure you that this baby is the same vivid picture of my nephew when he was born. Of course, babies change over time. I can also assure you that this is the same seed of the bloodline of our ancestor and patriot, Major-General Donato del Marmol y Tamayo." As he spoke, Father Francisco cleaned the perspiration off my uncle's forehead with a small wet towel.

"This baby is destined to do something extraordinary in this world," Father Francisco said. "And not just because of the unusual circumstances in which he entered into this world."

My uncle said, "I don't know what he is destined for, if I had taken even ten or twenty seconds longer to pull him out, he would have been stillborn. He was floating in his mother's urine, and he was about to become septic." He shook his head as he finished stitching up the enormous wound that he had to create in order to save the baby and saturate the wounded bladder.

To all our surprise, the baby did not look premature. It looked fully formed, even slightly larger than a normal newborn child. The door opened a crack as Jimbo opened it timidly. I could see Jimbo and Arnaldo peering in, Mama Teca above them. Jimbo said timidly to me, "I'm very sorry to interrupt, but there is something extremely urgent that we want you to see immediately." His face showed his extreme worry.

I said with a small smile, "I will be with you guys immediately."

Aurora proudly raised the baby high, wrapped in towels still, and said, "Jimbo, you are an uncle! Don't you want to say hello to your nephew?"

Jimbo opened the door fully and came into the room, forgetting for the moment the great emergency. Arnaldo and Mama Teca followed him, all anxious to see the face of the new member of the family.

Atacia started to come out of the anesthesia. Father Francisco asked, "Should we give her more?"

"No, I'm done already. No more."

She mumbled incoherently. Before long, we could understand her more clearly. "My baby—is he OK? I want to see my baby."

Aurora put the baby next to her with a big smile. "Yes, your baby is in perfect condition, and he looks like he's very happy. He hasn't shed a single tear—all he's done is gurgle slightly. Not one single cry."

I came over to Atacia and passed the back of my right hand, forgetting for the moment the wound on my forearm. She noticed the expression of pain on my face as I moved my hand and caressed her cheek. She raised the sleeve of my jogging suit. "Oh, my God! You still have my underwear bandages!"

Everyone looked at us in surprise. Father Francisco and my uncle exchanged smiles. Uncle Emilio said, "I was wondering what strange texture of material you used for that. Now I know!"

She said, "It was all we had at the time. I would rather have gotten rid of my underwear than to have him bleed to death. Would you please check his arm? He's more concerned about others than himself."

My uncle Emilio raised another needle high with a grin. "I was ready to do it at my residence before we came to visit you. But as soon as he told me of the urgency of your situation, I considered your case to have priority. Now that we're finished with you, he will be my new patient." He pointed to me to sit down next to him. "No more delay for this. No matter how urgent your friends' news is, it can wait. Sit down and let's get this done. I have to disinfect your wound and put a proper bandage on it."

I nodded my consent to him. As I started to do as he asked, the little baby held my left pinky so hard I could barely raise it, causing everyone else to laugh. I played with him a little bit until he let go.

Father Francisco grinned at the sight. "I have no doubt at all that we have a little Lightning with us." Atacia smiled proudly.

After my uncle cleaned and disinfected my wound, I left the room, followed by Jimbo, Arnaldo, and Mama Teca. As soon as we left the room, Jimbo closed the door. "I didn't want to say anything in front of Atacia so she can enjoy her baby and not be stressed, but we have to abandon this location immediately."

We climbed the stairs to the veranda on top of the house. Jimbo opened the metal door and said, "Bend over, just in case they're looking in this direction, and keep the rails of the terrace before you."

We went to the edge of the veranda and crouched down. Jimbo handed me some night vision binoculars. "Look at that ruined yacht by that alley."

I looked where he directed. It certainly was the remains of a luxury yacht, only a portion left, but nothing more. I turned in puzzlement. "I don't see anything beyond that wreck. What am I supposed to be looking for?"

"OK, now keep your eye on that boat." He said to Mama Teca. "Go down to the kitchen and turn on the lights of the dinette and the garages. Open the curtains so that the light can be seen outside. After you do that for a while, come back here."

Mama Teca left to do as instructed, and he said to Arnaldo and me, "Someone has betrayed us. A few hours ago, before this storm broke, I went for a walk and noticed something suspicious when I went by that abandoned yacht. When I got near it, I heard voices speaking softly as if they were speaking on portable radios with someone. I looked more closely and saw the movement of small red flashlights. It appears the G-2 has this residence under surveillance. From what I could overhear in that brief moment, they are waiting for corroborating information they have received. They don't want to make any mistakes with the nephew of Minister Valdez and end up in some kind of re-education camp." The lights downstairs turned on. He said, "Look now."

I looked again in the same place, and I could see that what he had said was true. There were two individuals with night goggles in the stern of the yacht, looking at the home as if they were searching for something to complete a report. Whoever was the traitor among us either hadn't provided enough information or they needed to corroborate that information before making a move. I looked Arnaldo in the eyes. "How much time do we have to disappear from your residence before these sicarios sound the alarm and send the communist dogs to hunt us?"

Arnaldo shook his head and looked at me in confusion. He rubbed his forehead with the fingers of his left hand and shrugged. He stroked his right eyebrow with his left index finger in distress. All this was convincing evidence that he was not the traitor among us; that, or his reaction to my question meant he was a master to fake it so realistically. Finally, he said sadly, "It all depends on many factors." He caressed his hair. "For example, my uncle is a very busy man and not easy to locate. I don't think any of these men will dare to enter my residence unless they get the green light personally from him. If they had sufficient evidence against me, my uncle would already have called me in to question me and verify anything at all or hear anything from me that's out of place. He's a very clever man; he's not the Minister of the Interior because he's a moron. Whatever suspicions or information they have, as soon as they pass it to my uncle, he knows very well the bureaucracy with all its personal vendettas and agendas that these communists have against each other, as well as the games they constantly play against anyone they wish to destroy. He himself has been a victim before of these games by someone who wished to gain favor with the Castro brothers."

At that moment the lights downstairs went off. I could see through the binoculars how the two agents retreated back inside the wreckage to get greater comfort and shelter from the rain which was still pouring down. It was certain that they were watching the house.

Arnaldo, as if he had just been shocked, stood up, putting his right hand on my shoulder. "We have to get out of here at once. We can't take any chances; we must be prudent. There will be a greater risk of remaining here any longer than there is in getting ourselves together to take you to where you will leave from. We don't know what amount of information or the kind that they have in their hands. The weather is calming down; the winds are gentler and the rain lighter. I'll go down and prepare the Land Cruiser and take you to where the Bandito is waiting for you to leave the country. If we do this right, we'll be one step ahead of the G-2. If they intend to come in here, they will find nothing and have a tremendous fiasco on their hands, with a lot to explain to Uncle Ramiro, who will then have to tender a great apology to me."

I smiled. "I agree with you one hundred percent. Staying here longer than it takes for us to pack will determine whether we live or die. From now on, any minute these people could break into your house."

Arnaldo nodded. We descended from the rooftop terrace. As we came down, we ran into Mama Teca, who told us that when she turned the lights off, she saw a car typical of the G-2 passing by in the street. I said to Jimbo, "Don't forget to pack your favorite toy and plenty of charges. Maybe we won't need it, but it could be very handy to clear our departure path."

"Don't worry about it," he said. "That's the first thing I'm putting in my backpack."

We reentered Atacia's room, and I found to my surprise a dark stain on the bed with Aurora hurriedly changing the sheets. "What happened in my absence?" I asked in concern.

Atacia was sitting in a chair next to the bed, very pale. Everyone's face showed intense worry as they looked at me silently. My uncle shook his head with an uncomfortable expression on his face. "Unfortunately, patients sometimes don't listen to what the doctor recommends, believing they know better and making fatal mistakes."

Atacia put her head down in shame. "I tried to get up to go to the bathroom, and it appears some of the external stitches came out. Thank God your uncle hadn't left yet, or I would probably have bled to death."

Father Francisco took one of her hands and said gently, "We all make mistakes, my daughter, but you must follow your doctor's recommendations strictly. Your movement must be minimal, you're in a delicate situation, and have had serious surgery. You should be helped into or out of bed. You'll only harm yourself and your recovery will take longer and be more painful. Imagine if the stitches which opened were the internal ones! He would have to cut you open again to repair that damage! God has been with you, or you would not have survived that wound to your abdomen. It's a miracle, as Dr. del Marmol told me. It missed the head of your baby by a hair, and it didn't even cause one scratch." He crossed himself and caressed the baby's head with his right hand. "You must take extreme care of your person for your sake as well as for the health and well-being of your baby, who needs you very much."

I knew at that moment that she could not come with us. I took the fingers of my right hand and caressed my forehead. I said to myself, "God, why do you make things so difficult for me?"

Father Francisco was near me and smiled, putting his right arm around my shoulder. "Trust, my son, in our Lord. He knows better than we do the reasons why He does what He does, even though many times we don't find any logical reason for what He puts in our road."

I shook my head. With a very sad expression I replied, "Yes, Father Francisco. And now what the Lord has put in my road isn't a small, tiny rock. He put a rock the size of a mountain."

My uncle now heard us speaking. "What's going on? What's the problem?"

I said, "Jimbo has discovered that this residence is under G-2 surveillance. We have to leave immediately. I just corroborated it, and Mama Teca saw one of the G-2's cars pass right in front of this house. That means that they've been slowly closing in on us. I know their tactics, and this is what they do like vultures circling over their prey."

Father Francisco crossed himself. "We have to leave immediately before they discover all of us in the same place together!"

At that moment, Arnaldo came in, followed by Jimbo, already with his backpack. Jimbo said, "Is everyone ready?" He looked at his sister sitting in a chair in a bathrobe giving one of her breasts to the baby in her arms. "When are you going to be ready to leave? Why aren't you already dressed?" He looked at me. "Haven't you told them?"

Uncle Emilio said, "Unless you want to kill her and the baby in the process, you cannot take either of them on that very dangerous, rough trip out of Cuba. She won't be ready to travel at least for several weeks if not a few months."

Jimbo looked at me first and then at Mama Teca and Aurora. Seeing our sad faces, he understood that my uncle wasn't joking. As this reality hit him, he asked in confusion, "What are we going to do? We can't leave her here. That would also be a sure death as soon as they arrest her. As soon as those two guards identify her, she's dead, no matter what!"

Uncle Emilio said, "Calm down. I have a better solution. Atacia shall stay with me at my house under my care. The rest of you leave as soon as possible. That is the only solution."

Aurora said firmly, "Yes, I understand and agree. I will stay with her to not only help her but also to help Dr. del Marmol in her recovery."

We looked at her in surprise. I threw the look to Atacia. "Do you want to stay here?" She nodded and held her hand out to me. I went over and took it in mine. "Are you sure of this decision?"

She smiled. "Do you have a better solution than this generous offer from your uncle?"

I compressed my lips sadly and shook my head. "Not now, not at this critical moment with our lives in imminent danger, including my uncle himself." I put all the reassurance I could in my voice. "I never promise anything so that I can never break it, but today I will violate that rule. I promise you that I will return for you and our baby, even if it costs me my life."

Atacia squeezed my hand. "No, never come back to this island, not after what we did today. Please, never come back here. The price on your head will be multiplied, and our son will need you in the future. I only ask one thing of you: give me time, and I will find you. We will reunite and I will bring my baby to you, wherever you are in the world. You can be assured of that, unless I'm dead. OK?" Tears shone in her eyes at the emotional pain of her acceptance that she had to remain behind.

I also had tears in my eyes. My uncle hadn't lost a single second while we spoke, improvising a stretcher with blankets, tied by ropes at each corner, and a doubled blanket tied at the corners with surgical tape to provide hand grips. Very carefully, he helped Atacia to lie down on it. Jimbo in one front corner Mama Teca on the other, while Arnaldo and Father Francisco on the rear, we brought her down the stairs very carefully. I walked next to her in the center holding her head up. We went down the stairs and into the garage, laying her in the back seat of my uncle's car. To avoid being seen from the windows, Aurora lay down on the floor to help support Atacia.

We agreed to have both cars leave at the same time in different directions so the G-2 would have to choose which of us to follow. A few minutes later, two of the four garage doors opened at once. We left in the Land Cruiser, while my uncle, Father Francisco, Aurora, and Atacia departed Arnaldo's home in his Buick.

The rain continued with a little more intensity and the wind blew harder as the storm strengthened again. Jimbo sat on one of the benches along the side of the Toyota, in front of Mama Teca, I in the passenger seat, while Arnaldo drove. Not long after we left the house, Jimbo said, "Well, I believe that we won the lottery without a ticket. It looks like we have a tail. They decided to follow you, Arnaldo."

I breathed a sigh of relief knowing that the others would be safe. Jimbo continued, "Uh, oh—we have another car to make a longer tail. It's a long one, since it's a limousine. Oh, my God—it looks like the one carrying the man with six fingers." Jimbo clucked his tongue. "I should have blown up that evil-minded communist in his limo in Ramiro's parking lot. Unfortunately, when I tried to do that, his assistant Origeo was also there, watching like a hawk. That's why I decided to blow up other cars and leave the limo alone." As he spoke, he pulled the Stinger out and assembled it. He looked like a little kid enjoying his toy.

Arnaldo was watching through the rearview mirror. Jimbo began to roll up the back vinyl cover of the Land Cruiser. "No, Jimbo," he said. "Not here! Let's wait until we get out of the city along the deserted coast road. That will be your opportunity to get them. We cannot leave any witnesses. Remember, Jimbo, any living witnesses will be my death sentence."

Jimbo rolled the vinyl cover back down and put his toy down by his legs. We got onto the highway along the coastline quickly. They dropped back to not be so obvious. Arnaldo spotted a strategic place and pulled over, where we would have a good view of them. The rain was getting heavier again as the storm worked itself up into a frenzy yet again. We parked and got ourselves set. A semi-truck was driving towards Havana, carrying gasoline with the Cuba Oil Union[25] logo.

Jimbo rolled the vinyl cover in the rear back up and prepared to fire. To our surprise, he did something extraordinarily clever. Instead of shooting the limo and the car, he shot his first missile a short distance ahead in the highway, in front of the truck. It was a brilliant improvisation, using the miracle of destiny to provide the perfect moment at the perfect time to destroy our enemies. The truck driver, as he saw the road before him blow up a short distance ahead, slammed on his brakes, causing the truck to skid, jackknife, and roll onto the wet pavement, just as the car and limo appeared in the distance. Seeing the truck, they also slammed on their brakes, sliding out of control on the wet pavement. The truck driver opened the door and jumped out of his truck into the bushes along the side of the highway. The men in the car and limo didn't have that same luxury. As the jackknifed truck swept across the road, it scooped the vehicles between the cab and trailer, hitting them so hard that both truck components flipped on top of them, exploding like a powerful bomb. The only person disappointed was Jimbo, who had no other opportunity to fire any more missiles from his Stinger. Unbelievably, the man with the six fingers, his shattered left arm hanging

---

[25] Cuba Petróleo Union, or CUPET.

limply against his body, managed to climb out through the sunroof of the limo, completely engulfed in flames. His scream was so eerie that it sounded like it came directly from Hell. He walked a few steps and fell onto the asphalt as the fire consumed his body.

Arnaldo started the Toyota; as we neared the water, he activated its amphibious mode. We entered the water, steering towards what looked like a large rock in the middle of the vast sea, disappearing into the rain. I was puzzled, and doubt once more filled my mind as I recalled the traitor in our midst, because he had mentioned a boat or ship that would take us out of the country—but aside from that rock I could see nothing. I grew concerned as it looked like Arnaldo was steering a direct course to collide with the rock, but as we neared it, he slowed down and stopped next to the rock. He clicked a small remote control, and some camouflage disappeared—the "rock" was concealing what Arnaldo had called the Bandit. Before our astonished eyes, we saw the super car of the sea, with a sign on the side which read "Lazzarini Design, Royal Jet Capsule." It looked much like a pod, a little over twenty-five feet long. The interior resembled a sports car in luxury, with leather upholstered seats and large enough to comfortably seat eight plus a pilot. There were even toilet facilities, and Arnaldo told us that it could easily cruise at a little over 30 knots.

Figure 20 The "Bandit"

I said, "What an irony—the Bandit saved my life and has been waiting in the shadows of the night off the coast of Cuba to take us to safety."

Chapter 33: The Thread Finds the Needle

Arnaldo rapidly gave us instructions on operating this fabulous, extraordinary jet boat. It only took a few minutes because the navigation equipment of this vessel was very simplified, practically automatically controlled. All one had to do was to mark the destination on the computer map and it took you where you wanted to go. Once he realized that we had all gotten it, he said goodbye, hugged us all, and got into his amphibious Toyota to head back towards the coast.

The Bandit's powerful engines were already running, ready to leave, which was just as well since we heard powerful sirens behind us. We turned and saw the revolving red emergency lights of a torpedo boat heading towards Arnaldo's craft. A voice on a bullhorn commanded him to stop. "Turn your engine off, or we will have to open fire on you!"

As Jimbo heard this, he jumped up like he had springs in his legs, and I could see the mischievous smile on his face as he knelt on the floor of the vessel and raised the Stinger towards the torpedo boat. Without waiting for any order, he fired the missile, which struck the boat in the stern where the fuel tanks were stored, sending bodies flying into the air. Not far from us we heard Arnaldo use his horns to indicate his thanks for that. We shared smiles and returned the greeting from the Bandit's air horns with greater volume than even the bullhorn from the torpedo boat.

A little while later, we were safely in international waters and out of reach of any of the Cuban government's coastal patrol craft. Mama Teca went to the refrigerator and looked at us with a surprised expression. She said, "My God! Whoever provided you with this fabulous vessel filled this refrigerator as if we were going to spend months at sea. It's completely stocked with delicious things, including something I haven't seen for years except for any tourist friends coming to Cuba—chocolate bars, and my favorite, Almond Joy!"

She grabbed an Almond Joy and began to eat it as she walked towards Jimbo, who was at the wheel of the vessel. With a big smile, he replied, "That is the way I like it—the capitalist mindset. When you head out into the ocean, you can never predict if you'll be navigating for a few days or months. It all depends on the unpredictable weather. In a few hours, we could see beautiful sunshine when the day breaks, or a hurricane could be on the horizon, or even worse, a tsunami—Heaven knows what sometimes. Weather and ocean are both absolutely unpredictable." He looked at the candy bar Mama Teca was eating. "The communists never think about tomorrow. That is why they destroy everything they find in their path as if life were going to end in a few hours." He shook his head. "They are so stupid and fanatic in their absurd philosophy that they act like a gluttonous man sitting at the table, eating until he explodes, not even thinking of saving a little bit for later, when he needs to eat again."

I saw Jimbo put the vessel on autopilot as he spoke to Mama Teca and used the distraction to pull out of my pocket the necklace that I had taken from Origeo. I noticed once more that God worked in mysterious ways as Jimbo without knowing my plans then created the perfect alibi for what I intended to do next. Jimbo jumped quickly in a jocular way to snatch the rest of the Almond Joy from Mama Teca and shoved it into his mouth. In the midst of his laughter, he quickly chewed on it to prevent her from taking it back.

Mama Teca understood the joke, even though she wasn't very happy at the disrespect he was showing her. She wrapped her arm around his neck while using the other hand to stick her fingers into his mouth to remove it. They both laughed while Jimbo struggled to keep his mouth shut.

I knelt down slightly and crept closer to them, pretending like I was picking something up while they wrestled. I stood up and opened my hand to allow the necklace to dangle from my fingers. I said to Mama Teca casually, "It looks like you let this fall onto the ground off your neck."

Caught by surprise as she wrestled with Jimbo, between laughter and joy during that youthful moment, she unconsciously looked at the necklace I held and opened a couple of buttons on her blouse to remove an identical necklace around her neck. Without thinking, she replied, "That's not my necklace. I have mine heeeere...." The last word elongated as she trailed off, realizing the tremendous mistake she had made. She felt trapped and froze in the shock of the moment. She looked at me in the eyes, the guilt and surprise showing in hers. Her voice trembled with fear. "I can explain. It's not what you think."

"What do you think I'm thinking? No one's accused you of anything."

"You're looking at me suspiciously."

The laughter stopped, and Jimbo took a step away. He looked at us in confusion. "What's happened? What's going on?" Neither of us spoke—we looked at each other harshly, and it was clear to him that something was wrong. "Can someone please explain to me what's happened? What's going on?"

I raised the necklace up so he could see it. "Very simple, Jimbo. Mama Teca is the traitor. What don't you ask her how much she was offered from the Cuban communists for each of our heads?"

Jimbo looked at Mama Teca in confused surprise. She had remained silent as if trying to think of an answer that would get her out of the situation and prove that I was falsely accusing her. She removed her necklace and, like a big hypocrite, feigned innocence. She demanded, "What kind of stupidity has come into your mind for you to accuse me of being a traitor? Let me show you how little value I have for this necklace." She meant to throw her necklace overboard past my left shoulder, but she didn't expect my rapid response, as I had expected something like this. My hand was a blur of motion as I reached out and caught the necklace. She grew more upset and agitated. She pulled the Commando knife from her waist and stepped towards me threateningly as she held her left hand out open to me. "Return that necklace to me immediately if you don't want me to cut your throat and drop you overboard to feed the sharks with the lies you've been trying to feed us with."

Jimbo demanded angrily of her, "What the hell has possessed you? Or are you going crazy, Mama Teca?"

She turned to the left and shoved Jimbo with her left hand, pinning him against the dashboard of the boat. Her eyes blazed and threatened him with the knife. "You should not get involved in this! Stay out of it, kid—I don't want to have to do the same thing to you that I will do to him!"

Jimbo's eyes bulged out of their sockets between the tone of voice she used and the massive shove she gave him with all her strength, not understanding even for a second this complete and radical transformation from his old friend, the noble and good black woman, into a grotesque, diabolical creature who threatened to kill both of us without any scruple. It certainly was something which had never crossed either of our minds. In spite of this, the brave Jimbo grew angry and didn't think straight. He yelled at her, "Weren't you trying to throw away this necklace? Why do you want it back? Or is it because you are in reality the traitor within our group, now exposed by the Lightning?"

Mama Teca froze again, realizing her cover was completely blown, her guilt evident to both of us. I used her hesitation to say to Jimbo as I raised the necklace in the air, "This is what Mama Teca doesn't want us to see." I opened the medallion on the necklace, pulled out a tracking device, and held it out. "She has been providing all our movements to our enemies for a very long time, and she is responsible for the death of your father, Bonifacio, and maybe responsible for all the attempts on our lives ever since we left the port of Caibarien. She has been providing our itinerary to our enemies for the sole purpose of assassinating us one after another. Thanks to the grace of God which has protected us, we found a way each time to avoid those traps. I have no doubt that she was the one to call that torpedo boat to finish off Arnaldo as well as us."

She threw her knife towards my head; I ducked and avoided having it plunge into my neck. It flew past my shoulder and hit the wall of the boat behind me. Seeing that she hadn't hit her target, she knelt down, pulled a small revolver from beside her right leg, and pointed it at my head. I raised both arms to cover my face and head. Before she could squeeze the trigger, Jimbo came up behind her and stabbed her in the left clavicle, immobilizing the arm holding the revolver. She turned rapidly through the immense pain of that grave injury he inflicted. He saved my life, but her finger was still on the trigger, and when she turned, she managed to fire off one shot before falling onto the floor, dead.

Jimbo put his left hand over his neck where he was hit to try and stop the flow of blood, but it spurted from between his fingers. With terror, anger, and despair reflecting in his eyes, he tried to smile unsuccessfully. He sank down to the floor. "I'm dizzy. I think I might be dying. Unfortunately, my great friend, I don't think I will be able to be your first mate for the rest of this trip."

I leaned down and tried to help him sit down and give him some positive encouragement. "No, no—don't say that. You have to live to see your nephew grow up. Please, allow me some time to look for the medical kit so I can try to cure you and sew up that wound. It looks only superficial, but don't remove your hand until I have my instruments at hand." As I spoke, I smiled a little.

"You are in luck to have a doctor in the house. Don't remove the pressure on that wound. I'll be back immediately."

Jimbo looked at me with glassy eyes, trying once more to smile. He closed his eyes as if he was trying to rest. I gave him a little tap on his cheek with my fingers. "Jimbo, no—don't try to rest. Remain alert. I need your help. If you don't keep the pressure on that wound, you'll bleed to death. Please, all I need is a few minutes until I can get back with the medical kit. Only a few minutes, please," I begged him.

He opened his eyes and gave me a little nod. I smiled. "Just like that." I patted his cheek. "Stay alert—I'll be back in a minute."

I stood up and went to search for the medical kit, which only took me a few seconds. But when I returned, I found Jimbo with his eyes closed, lying in a pool of blood on the deck. He lost consciousness, and his hand fatally slipped away. I took his pulse and found nothing. I looked at his wound and saw that the bullet had severed the internal carotid artery, which would cause the victim to bleed to death in a few seconds.

I stopped the engine and dropped Mama Teca's body into the ocean. "May God have mercy on your soul for what you've done."

I started the engine again and piloted a few more miles before stopping. I said a prayer over Jimbo's body and carefully lowered him into the dark waters of the night. I'm not a superstitious man, but I didn't feel that putting both bodies in the same place would be appropriate. The body of that hypocritical assassin should be nowhere within several miles of that of the great, decent, and loving friend who had conquered my heart in a short time, earning my affection and love. He became a member of my family by being like a brother-in-law, his nephew sharing the same bloodline with mine. I prayed to God for the repose of his soul and then started up the engine to continue my trip.

      Twenty-four hours later, I had passed the Yucatan Peninsula and then eventually made our way up the Sea of Cortez, arriving at my destination: the small fishing village of San Felipe on the Baja Peninsula of Mexico, where Gervatin Caleneto, my confidant and pilot awaited in a black Suburban to take me to my security house where I was to rest for several hours before flying to my next destination of Los Angeles, California. He was a Brazilian man who had been by my side for over thirty years. I left instructions with him, who in turn passed the instructions on to his most trusted man to take the Bandit out of the water and transport it to my ranch in one of the large garages there and cover it, so that no one would see that luxurious, modern vessel or otherwise attract undue attention.

Figure 21 Dr. del Marmol's safe house

A little while later, I was cooking some food in the house. Gervatin had carefully wrapped in foil paper and plastic the container with all the diamonds. I had decided to bury it in a secure place in the desert to avoid bringing into the U.S. until I could consult with O'Brien what we should do with this valuable treasure. All the other classified documents we had taken from Ramiro Valdes' safe were put in my own vault after taking pictures of them with the camera of my spy pen, which I put in the front pocket of my Navy jacket. No one would have an idea of the valuable classified information I was bringing into the country.

After a good meal of shrimp in garlic sauce and butter, salad with tomato, avocado, and asparagus, mashed potatoes and fried plantains with a couple of glasses of Blanco Brillante wine from Bodegas Riojas, we were both very satisfied. We fed his friends who had remained outside for security, and we decided to rest for a few hours. Gervatin and I got ready several hours later to leave for the airport.

Figure 22 San Felipe International Airport

One of his men, Federico, was to bring the car back to the safe house. It was still very early in the morning. Federico dropped us off at the airport; we said goodbye to him and then took off in a private plane. I pondered in the plane how O'Brien must be worried sick. Our flight took seven hours and thirty-six minutes. We landed at LAX, and I said goodbye to Gervatin, exchanging an embrace. He had not just been my pilot but also my bodyguard for all this time—I owed him my life several times over.

I walked towards the airport parking lot, looking for a public telephone to call O'Brien. He answered, "Thank God you're OK. I was starting to worry about you."

I replied, "Thank you very much for your concern, old man, but you shouldn't worry. Worry gives you extra wrinkles. Remember always that I'm protected by a Supreme Being, a lot more powerful than anything we can imagine. "

"I know, I know. You got it?"

"Yes, all the details from the horse's mouth, the principal financier of the royal leader of the terrorist group we've been circling around. I hope the big guys behind you give this the urgency this requires. Don't let me down like they did before with the normal bureaucracy, or we will have a real massacre on our hands."

"Is it that serious?" he asked in concern.

"More than I can even tell you over the phone. I need to see you immediately. Let's meet at my house in Corona del Mar. How much time do you need?"

"A few hours," he replied.

"OK, very well. We'll see each other there." We said goodbye and hung up.

Epilogue

Three Years Later, French Side of St. Martin's Island
My Birthday.

I sat under a very beautiful umbrella in a beach chair next to my sweetheart Zuyen on the beach during a trip to St. Martin with the blended objectives of business and pleasure. I had enjoyed a few days of rest from my last mission, but I had received a call from O'Brien that he had something of extreme importance he needed to communicate to me in person. It was so delicate that he couldn't even hint at it over the phone. I was already accustomed to these mysterious calls, but the excitement in O'Brien's voice indicated that he had something of great joy in his soul that he wanted to share with me; there wasn't a single tone of worry or stress. I kept looking at each of the watches on my arms.

I held out my hand to Zuyen. We looked at each other. "Is there something wrong?"

"Not wrong, but there's something that happened during this last trip that I want to share with you."

She looked at me in concern, thinking the worst yet again. "Is it something really bad?"

"No, not bad at all. I'm complying with my promise to share with you something we discussed before I left on this last trip. I promised I would share it with you should it ever happen."

She looked at me, her eyes widening in worry. "Did you fall in love with someone else?"

"Not quite, but I had a moment of weakness, and I believe due to this that a child was born."

"Your child?"

"Yes."

"Who is the mother? Where is she?"

"I believe she's dead. The last information I had was that she had been tortured and killed by Cuban intelligence."

"Where is the child?"

"I believe he's with his grandmother; I say 'he' because I believe it is a son."

Zuyen breathed a sigh of relief. "Then it's not bad at all. You have a new child to fill the empty space in your heart for the one you lost. She gave to you the child I could not provide because of my condition."

I grabbed her hand and looked intently into her eyes. "What did I do to be so lucky, my princess, to find you to be so understanding? I don't deserve you at all."

Zuyen smiled and said, "I'm very lucky, too, in having a man of such honesty and integrity by my side. You look like you're having one of those premonitions. Let's hope that this one is a good one and is something which will bring you happiness. You've checked your watches over two hundred times in the past half-hour."

I smiled and replied with candor, "Really?" She nodded and gave me a thumbs up with a big smile. "I have to confess that you're right. I believe O'Brien has a big surprise for me, since today is my birthday. It's not just a premonition; I read from his tone of voice he was full of positive energy."

She sat down on her lounge chair and put her right hand over her forehead to shield her face from the sun. She pointed. "Speak of the king and he shall appear. Hm, hm." She raised the binoculars from where they hung around her neck and looked through them. Surprise showed in her face. "He's not alone. He has a woman with him. And a little kid."

I jumped up as if I had been electrified, looking for my binoculars in my backpack. To my surprise, I saw through the lenses that O'Brien was with a carrot-topped little boy and a middle-aged woman that I couldn't initially identify. I adjusted the focus and saw that it was Aurora Bonaparte, Atacia's mother. A strange sensation of joy ran through my body mixed at once with sadness.

Zuyen said, "You look like you've seen a ghost."

I turned. "Something like that, very close. My contacts inside Cuba have told me that Arnaldo was executed for treason by firing squad, and that Aurora and Atacia had suffered the same fate. But no one ever knew what happened to the boy."

Zuyen put her right hand to her mouth. "Oh, God bless! This is the best present anyone could have on his birthday."

Once they got close to us, two tears rolled down my cheeks as Aurora stepped forward to give me a big bearhug. We separated and she said, "This is Julton, your son. Now I've fulfilled the promise I made to my daughter before she died. I can now finally be at peace."

O'Brien didn't say a word but nodded to verify what she had said. He stepped forward and gave me a hug. "Happy Birthday—this is the great present I prepared for you."

Aurora held her hand out to the little boy. "Julton, this is your papa."

The boy looked at me curiously and turned his little head to her. "The Lightning?" Aurora put her index finger to her lips. He put his little finger against his lips. "Oooh, OK," he said in understanding. "Remember, it's like my mommy always told me, that no one should know my name, since I'm a ghost like my daddy. I'm the Little Lightning, like Casper the Friendly Ghost." He pointed to Zuyen and asked, "Is she my new mom?"

Zuyen had a big smile on her lips as she picked him up. She said tenderly, "If you want it, I will be your new mom. There will be no more changes of moms for the rest of your life."

The boy smiled broadly and nodded his little head. "OK, I like that." He kissed her on the cheek. Tears appeared in Zuyen's eyes as she returned the kiss on his cheek.

A yacht rode to its anchor a short distance away. Three men watched this family reunion; one through a pair of binoculars, another through the scope of a powerful sniper rifle with a massive suppressor attached to it. The third was at the helm of the boat. Both hands on the wheel had six fingers each. The sniper rifle was held by Origeo Angulo, now sporting an eyepatch. The viewer through the binoculars was the short Chinese man, Dr. Chao, who said, "We got him. We knew they would bring the kid to him." Somehow, all three men had survived their respective ordeals.

Origeo replied, "He will finally pay for what he did to us."

As Origeo trained the rifle on me again, he was startled to see that I had a pair of binoculars to my eyes, and I was looking right at him. I raised my middle finger towards him and then pointed towards the sky. I saw him pull away from the scope to look up, where a small helicopter piloted by Gervasin was rapidly approaching. The man sitting next to my faithful friend leaned out, a Stinger on his shoulder pointed directly at the yacht.

Origeo's one eye widened in panic as he yelled at the top of his lungs, "The Lightning! Light and fire! Save yourselves!"

O'Brien was looking at this from the beach through his binoculars, a grin of satisfaction on his face as he watched the yacht explode and three bodies flying through the air. He said to me, "I believe your plan, even though it was very risky to use yourself as bait, has proven to be very effective. You've brought those three flies into our webs."

I raised my binoculars and observed the scene with satisfaction. Zuyen said, "I knew from the beginning because of the confidence I have in you that we wouldn't be in any danger at all. But thank you for eliminating this threat we've had behind us all this time."

I said, "I know it's an extremely small chance of anyone getting hurt. When I returned to Mexico from Cuba at the port of San Felipe, I noticed that they had eyes on me. I let it go in order to prepare this trap which not only gave us the chance to get our boy back but also to eliminate once and for all that danger out of our lives." I touched Julton's head. "I believe this has been the best birthday present that I've ever had."

A Dictator's Evil Mind

Ideas are more powerful than guns. We will not let our enemies have guns, why should we let them have ideas?

Joseph Stalin

===

Political Fanatics

Those men and women that allow their minds to become infected by political fanaticism and give away their guns only open themselves to committing the worst stupidities, barbarities, and unspeakable crimes against their own brothers and sisters and the humanity at large. They destroy their own principles as they choose to follow a false and hypocritical political leader, replacing their own God with his image and allowing this fake leader to control their lives, their country, and everyone's minds. These men and women become only useful fools who eventually condemn themselves to later repentance for having been accomplices to the most tremendous and despicable crimes.

Dr. Julio Antonio del Marmol

About the Author

Dr. Julio Antonio del Marmol is the son of the primary financier behind Fidel Castro's revolution, Leonardo del Marmol. A Grand Master Mason, Leonardo organized his Masonic brothers to provide the funds Castro needed to purchase supplies and weapons. When the revolution won in January, 1959, then-11-year-old Julio Antonio wanted to become part of the revolution. His father arranged to get a letter written by his son detailing a plan to organize the Cuban youth into an army of the future into the hands of Fidel Castro, who flew out to meet the young man. Impressed by the boy's eloquence, he presented Julio Antonio with his own .38 pistol as a gift and appointed him Commander-in-Chief of the Young Commandos of the Rebel Army and the youngest military commander in the revolution. Within six months, Che Guevara showed the youth that the plan was to implement a communist system on the island. In distress, he went to warn his father, who accused Julio Antonio of being brainwashed by an uncle in Havana (who never liked the revolution) and threw his own 12 year old son out of the house. Julio Antonio went to his uncle and revealed everything he had seen, only to discover that his uncle was a master spy going back to World War II, in which he was in charge of the network preventing the Nazis from taking control of the Caribbean and Central/South America. His uncle recruits and trains Julio Antonio, making him the youngest spy in history. He continues in his role, taking secrets from Castro's own office until his cover is blown in 1971. He must leave the island for the US, taking his fight against communism to a global level.

Other Works

Comic Books/Animation Project

Dr. del Marmol has 6 issues of a comic book series based on the Zipper operation, the first five of which have been bound together in a graphic novel. Initially available on Comixology.com, all are now available on Lulu.com, and a meeting is expected soon with the CEO of Lunar Distribution, the largest comic book distributor in North America. We have also a 30 minute motion comic film in the can.

Music

Dr. del Marmol has written and recorded 19 albums of music, each song of which is planned as a soundtrack for some element of the media part of the franchise. These songs are distributed digitally on over 30 platforms, including Apple Music, iMusic, Google, Pandora, and Spotify. To listen to any of Dr. del Marmol's song, simply go to one of those platforms and to an artist search for Dr. Julio Antonio del Marmol & His Cuban Lightning Orchestra.

www.ingramcontent.com/pod-product-compliance
Lightning Source LLC
Chambersburg PA
CBHW060310230426
43663CB00009B/1652